Language and Superdiversity

OXFORD STUDIES IN SOCIOLINGUISTICS

General Editors:
Nikolas Coupland
Copenhagen University, University of Technology, Sydney, and Cardiff University

Adam Jaworski
University of Hong Kong

Recently Published in the Series:

Sociolinguistic Variation: Critical Reflections
Edited by Carmen Fought

Prescribing under Pressure: Parent-Physician Conversations and Antibiotics
Tanya Stivers

Discourse and Practice: New Tools for Critical Discourse Analysis
Theo van Leeuwen

Beyond Yellow English: Toward a Linguistic Anthropology of Asian Pacific America
Edited by Angela Reyes and Adrienne Lo

Stance: Sociolinguistic Perspectives
Edited by Alexandra Jaffe

Investigating Variation: The Effects of Social Organization and Social Setting
Nancy C. Dorian

Television Dramatic Dialogue: A Sociolinguistic Study
Kay Richardson

Language Without Rights
Lionel Wee

Paths to Post-Nationalism
Monica Heller

Language Myths and the History of English
Richard J. Watts

The "War on Terror" Narrative
Adam Hodges

Digital Discourse: Language in the New Media
Edited by Crispin Thurlow and Kristine Mroczek

Leadership, Discourse and Ethnicity
Janet Holmes, Meredith Marra, and Bernadette Vine

Spanish in New York
Ricardo Otheguy and Ana Celia Zentella

Multilingualism and the Periphery
Sari Pietikäinen and Helen Kelly-Holmes

Discourses in War and Peace
Edited by Adam Hodges

Legal-Lay Communication: Textual Travels in the Law
Edited by Chris Heffer, Frances Rock, and John Conley

Speaking Pittsburghese: The Story of a Dialect
Barbara Johnstone

The Pragmatics of Politeness
Geoffrey Leech

Language and Superdiversity: Indonesians Knowledging at Home and Abroad
Zane Goebel

Language and Superdiversity
INDONESIANS KNOWLEDGING
AT HOME AND ABROAD

Zane Goebel

OXFORD
UNIVERSITY PRESS

Oxford University Press is a department of the University of
Oxford. It furthers the University's objective of excellence in research,
scholarship, and education by publishing worldwide.

Oxford   New York
Auckland   Cape Town   Dar es Salaam   Hong Kong   Karachi
Kuala Lumpur   Madrid   Melbourne   Mexico City   Nairobi
New Delhi   Shanghai   Taipei   Toronto

With offices in
Argentina   Austria   Brazil   Chile   Czech Republic   France   Greece
Guatemala   Hungary   Italy   Japan   Poland   Portugal   Singapore
South Korea   Switzerland   Thailand   Turkey   Ukraine   Vietnam

Oxford is a registered trademark of Oxford University Press
in the UK and certain other countries.

Published in the United States of America by
Oxford University Press
198 Madison Avenue, New York, NY 10016

© Oxford University Press 2015

All rights reserved. No part of this publication may be reproduced, stored in
a retrieval system, or transmitted, in any form or by any means, without the prior
permission in writing of Oxford University Press, or as expressly permitted by law,
by license, or under terms agreed with the appropriate reproduction rights organization.
Inquiries concerning reproduction outside the scope of the above should be sent to the
Rights Department, Oxford University Press, at the address above.

You must not circulate this work in any other form
and you must impose this same condition on any acquirer.

Cataloging-in-Publication Data is on file at the Library of Congress.

ISBN 978-0-19-979542-0 (pbk)
ISBN 978-0-19-979541-3 (hbk)

9 8 7 6 5 4 3 2 1
Printed in the United States of America
on acid-free paper

CONTENTS

List of Diagrams   vii
List of Figures and Tables   ix
List of Extracts   xi
Acknowledgments   xiii
Map   xv
Transcription Conventions   xvii

1. Orientations   1
   1.1. Introduction   1
   1.2. Communities and Competence   2
   1.3. Television, Demeanor, and Change   6
   1.4. Knowledging and Conviviality in Superdiversity   8
   1.5. The Multiple Functions of Talk and the Mundane   11

2. The Semiotic Figurement of Communities in Indonesia   13
   2.1. Introduction   13
   2.2. Communities and Enregisterment   15
   2.3. The Creation of Ethnicity in the Nineteenth Century   18
   2.4. Widening Social Domains in the Late Colonial Period   23
   2.5. Discourses of Nationalism in the Late Colonial Period   25
   2.6. The Japanese Occupation   32
   2.7. The Soekarno Period   34
   2.8. The New Order Period   42
   2.9. Conclusion   51

3. Representing Ethnicity and Social Relations on Television   53
   3.1. Introduction   53
   3.2. Approaching Television   56
   3.3. Television in Indonesia   58
   3.4. A Multimodal Approach to Comedic Soaps   60
   3.5. The Comedic Soap *Noné*   62
   3.6. The Comedic Soap *Si Kabayan*   74
   3.7. Representing Diversity: *Si Doel Anak Sekolahan*   85
   3.8. Conclusion   100

4. Ethnicity during a Decade of Political Reform and Decentralization 104
4.1. Introduction 104
4.2. Tensions Around the Idea of Ethnicity 105
4.3. Economic Crisis, Decentralization, and the Rise of *Adat* 108
4.4. Violent Ethnic Others: Conflict and Displacement 114
4.5. Recirculating Stereotypes via Other Forms of Localism 116
4.6. Conclusion 122

5. The Anchoring of Alternation to Place 125
5.1. Introduction 125
5.2. The Data 127
5.3. Anchoring Medium to Locale 128
5.4. Soaps, Stylized Alternation, and Place 135
5.5. Conclusion 141

6. Representing and Authorizing Linguistic Superdiversity 143
6.1. Introduction 143
6.2. Alternation, Knowledging, and Authorizing the Everyday 145
6.3. Representing Mobility and Diversity 155
6.4. Representing the Doing of Unity in Superdiversity 161
6.5. Conclusion 170

7. Talk and Conviviality among Indonesians in Japan 173
7.1. Introduction 173
7.2. Conviviality and Small Talk 174
7.3. Methods and Participants 177
7.4. Talk, Conviviality, and Meaning 180
7.5. Identities, Togetherness, and Meaning Revisited 191
7.6. Conclusion 199

8. Knowledging, Conviviality, Community, and Togetherness in Difference 201
8.1. Introduction 201
8.2. Community and Communicative Competence 202
8.3. Social Identification, Conviviality, and Community 205
8.4. Doing Togetherness in Difference and Knowledging 214
8.5. Conclusion 227

9. Conclusion 230
9.1. Introduction 230
9.2. Ideologies, Communities, Competence, and Superdiversity 237

Glossary 243
References 245
Index 265

LIST OF DIAGRAMS

5.2.1 Television stations recorded and medium representations in 2009   127
7.3.1 Transnational Indonesians watching television   179
8.3.1 Transnational Indonesians watching television and doing community   206
8.4.1 Transnational Indonesians watching television and doing togetherness   214

LIST OF FIGURES AND TABLES

Figures

3.5.1   Signs of place   64
3.5.2   Signs of social relations   64
3.5.3   Proxemics, body orientation, and unfamiliars   72
3.5.4   Proxemics, body orientation, and unfamiliars   72
4.3.1   Indonesian administrative hierarchy prior to May 1998   110
5.3.1   Subtitles as pointing to localness   131
5.3.2   Subtitling localness   132
5.3.3   Anchoring place through the use of a map   133
5.3.4   Anchoring place through the use of a map and text   133
5.3.5   Anchoring place through text in news reports   135
6.4.1   Representing Chinese-ness: Babah Liong with son   165
6.4.2   Representing Chinese-ness: Babah Liong with Melani   165
7.6.1   Meaning across time   200

Tables

7.3.1   Participant backgrounds   179
8.3.1   Participant backgrounds   205

LIST OF EXTRACTS

2.5.1 Associating linguistic forms with place in the novel *Sitti Nurbaya* 26
2.5.2 Outsider's reported talk in the novel *Si Doel Anak Betawi* 28
2.5.3 Insider's reported talk in the novel *Si Doel Anak Betawi* 29
3.5.1 The reading of a will 63
3.5.2 Indonesian and unfamiliars 65
3.5.3 Indonesian, other reference, and unfamiliarity 66
3.5.4 Talking about the material world 66
3.5.5 Names, gestures, facial expressions, and familiarity 69
3.5.6 Prosody and familiars 69
3.5.7 Sundanese usage, co-occurrence, and familiarity 70
3.5.8 A grandmother's warning 73
3.6.1 Proximity, Sundanese, and close interpersonal relations 75
3.6.2 Indonesian, strangers and interactional flatness 77
3.6.3 Familiars, animated talk, and Sundanese usage 79
3.6.4 Age mates talking about personal life-worlds 81
3.7.1 Being emotional and speaking Betawi 87
3.7.2 Building inter-group friendship through talk about personal life-worlds 90
3.7.3 Engaging in adequation 93
3.7.4 Representing knowledging 95
3.7.5 Knowledging and authentic social types 98
4.5.1 Celebrity fans posting on representations of ethnicity 120
4.5.2 Blogging and complaining about ethnic representations 121
5.3.1 Anchoring medium through story introduction 129
5.3.2 Interacting with locals and codeswitching 130
5.3.3 Sign alternation as the medium and linking medium to ideology 134
5.4.1 Soaps, signs of place, and local mediums 136
5.4.2 Stylized alternation anchored to Sundanese locales 138
5.4.3 Stylized alternation anchored to Javanese locales 140
6.2.1 That's what Sundanese call *munjungan* 146
6.2.2 I also know and can speak some Javanese 149
6.2.3 The authorization of adequating foreigners and mixing 151
6.3.1 Soap representations of the voices of poor mobile workers 156
6.3.2 Soap representations of the ethnic voices of affluent migrants 157
6.3.3 Using ethnic voices across lines of difference 159
6.4.1 Representing superdiverse neighborhoods 162

6.4.2	Representing older layers of diversity: Chinese-ness in Jakarta	166
6.4.3	Representing habitual linguistic superdiversity in Jakarta	169
7.4.1	From hearer-ship to engaged listening	181
7.4.2	From engaged listening to discourses of sameness	182
7.4.3	Repetition and the linking of language with place	184
7.4.4	Teasing and conviviality	187
7.4.5	From the serial: Another warning from Grandmother	188
7.4.6	Negotiating meanings and conviviality	189
7.5.1	Jointly constructing the meaning of *cipoa*	192
7.5.2	Naming languages, native speakership, and pursuing social sameness	194
7.5.3	It's uncommon Sundanese spoken by the elderly	195
7.5.4	The grandmother is just so Sundanese	197
8.3.1	Indexing membership in a public	207
8.3.2	Indexing participation in an ethnic community of practice	208
8.3.3	Solidifying participation in an ethnic community of practice	209
8.3.4	Identifying and evaluating medium usage	210
8.4.1	Recognizing signs and their associated medium	215
8.4.2	Iteung isn't very Sundanese	217
8.4.3	Were the protests because these two characters weren't Sundanese?	219
8.4.4	Wow, these guys have very noticeable accents	220
8.4.5	Knowledging and pursuing sameness in opinion	222
8.4.6	Alignment repetition	224
8.4.7	Knowledging as positive evaluation	226

ACKNOWLEDGMENTS

During the six years that I have been working on this research I have built up many debts. In this brief acknowledgment to the many people who have helped and supported me through this project, I offer my sincere thanks. I am very grateful to the series editors, Adam Jaworski and Nik Coupland, for initially giving the go ahead to my original book proposal. There are many people whom I would like to thank by name here, especially in the large community of Indonesians studying in Nagoya, Japan, whose permission, patience, help, and friendship made this research possible. However, some members of each group indicated on their consent forms that they preferred to remain anonymous, while others were happy for me to use their real names. Thus, for all participants I discuss in chapters 7 and 8, I have decided to use pseudonyms, as well as change some identifying information.

The initial research was made possible by a number of institutional grants from Nagoya University between 2008 and 2010 and a grant from the Japanese Society for the Promotion of Science (Grant No. C20520380). While in Japan, I was ably assisted by a team of Indonesian research assistants, including Eni, Riris, Inu, and Puji. To them I offer my sincere thanks. I am also grateful to the Institute for Human Security at La Trobe University for providing me with some teaching relief in 2011 to help me write chapter 2. I am also extremely grateful to the Faculty of Humanities and Social Sciences more generally for providing me with funding for a research assistant in 2011 to help me get through the data that I present in chapters 5 and 6. I would also be remiss not to thank Eni (my partner), who not only acted as a research assistant in Japan, but was willing to continue acting in this capacity while in Australia. Indeed, without her support, patience, and good humor and that offered by our two sons and our respective extended families, this book would not have been possible.

Some of this book builds on and refines my earlier work. With recourse to a wide range of secondary sources written by area specialists from various disciplinary backgrounds, chapters 2 and 4 significantly expand on ideas I first started writing about in Goebel (2008, 2010b). Chapter 3 fleshes out ideas I started to pursue in Goebel (2011b), while also incorporating current thinking in the area of language alternation and superdiversity. Chapters 7 and 8 expand analysis and arguments presented in Goebel (2011a, 2011c, 2012a, 2012b, 2013) by linking them with some of the book's main themes, namely, knowledging, superdiversity, togetherness talk, and the multiple functions of talk. The arguments presented in these chapters have also benefited from the generous feedback offered by conference audiences and anonymous reviewers of earlier material. Special thanks also needs to go to a number of journal editors, panel organizers, and panel participants for their feedback and encouragement, especially Asif Agha, Paul Manning, Alexandra Jaffe, Srikant Sarangi, Kuniyoshi Kataoka, Keiko Ikeda, Masataka Yamaguchi, Niko Besnier, and Jan Blommaert.

In its rewritten form, this book has benefited greatly from the feedback and guidance offered by Adam Jaworski, two anonymous reviewers, and Catherine Coyne. I am also indebted to copyeditor Bonnie Kelsey, and Brian Hurley and Hallie Stebbins at Oxford University Press, who expertly guided me through the whole process. As always, all errors and omissions remain my sole responsibility.

Zane Goebel
Melbourne, Australia, May 2014

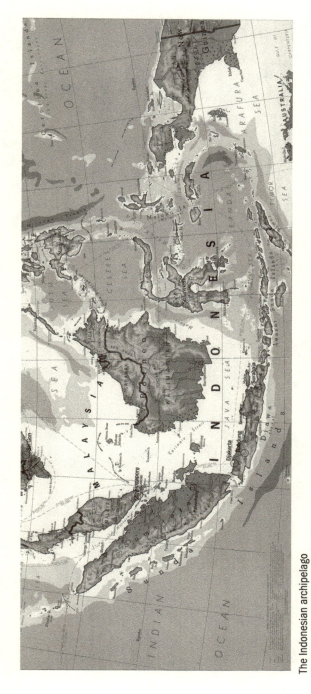

The Indonesian archipelago

Source: Adapted from Norton Ginsburg, 1968, Southeast Asia. Chicago: Denoyer-Geppert Company. Accessed May 4, 2014, at http://www.davidrumsey.com.

TRANSCRIPTION CONVENTIONS

Orthographic conventions are as similar as possible to the standard Indonesian spelling system set out by the Indonesian Department of Education and Culture (1993). Unless otherwise indicated in my analysis, I use the following transcription conventions:

Plain font	Indicates forms stereotypically associated with Indonesian.
Italics	Indicates ambiguous forms that are stereotypically associated with both Indonesian and regional languages.
Bold	Indicates forms stereotypically associated with Sundanese.
BOLD SMALL CAPS	Indicates forms stereotypically associated with Betawi.
BOLD CAPS	Indicates forms stereotypically associated with Javanese.
BOLD ITALICS CAPS	Indicates forms stereotypically associated with English.
<u>BOLD UNDERLINED CAPS</u>	Indicates forms stereotypically associated with Chinese.
BOLD ITALIC SMALL CAPS	Indicates forms stereotypically associated with Japanese.
. between words	Indicates a perceivable silence.
Brackets with a number (.4)	Indicates length of silence in tenths of a second.
=	Indicates no perceivable pause between speaker turns.
[	Indicates start of overlapping talk.
' after a word	Indicates final falling intonation.
? after a word	Indicates final rising intonation.
+ surrounding an utterance/word	Indicates raising of volume.

A hatch # surrounding an utterance/word	Indicates lowering of volume.
> at the start and end of an utterance	Indicates utterance spoken faster than previous one.
< at the start and end of an utterance	Indicates utterance spoken slower than previous one.
: within a word	Indicates sound stretch.
CAPS	Indicates stress.
Brackets with three? (i.e., ???)	Indicates word that could not be transcribed.
In extract words inside ()	Indicates a multimodal description.
In English gloss words inside []	Indicates implied talk or words used to make the gloss readable.
In English gloss words inside (())	Indicates implied background knowledge.
underline	Indicates the repetition of words or utterances between adjacency pairs.
broken underline	Indicates that the word or utterance was repeated in prior talk, although it may not always be in the immediately preceding turn.
Double underline	Indicates laughing while speaking.

Providing glosses of transcripts that are in other languages is always problematic, especially when what is represented is a conversation accompanied by multimodal information. In the following chapters there are many transcripts of this kind and I have tried to balance this challenge with typesetting constraints. The outcome of this is a compromise where glosses of transcripts cannot be interpreted as line for line equivalents.

Language and Superdiversity

1

Orientations

1.1 Introduction

In introductory and even advanced social-scientific accounts of Indonesia, we are told that Indonesia is made up of a population of over 240 million people who inhabit many of this archipelago nation's 18,000 islands (e.g., Cribb & Ford, 2009; Vickers, 2005). According to demographers, linguists, and political scientists, Indonesia's growing population is made up of hundreds of ethnic groups and their languages, all of the world's major religions, and a highly mobile and rapidly urbanizing population (e.g., Bertrand, 2003; Sneddon, 2003; Suryadinata, Arifin, & Ananta, 2003). In many domains within Indonesia, the ideology that language and ethnicity are geographically anchored to place continues to be a powerful way for understanding diversity in Indonesia.

The main aim of this book is to understand how this view of diversity has become so common and how a focus upon this can inform scholarship on superdiversity. I do this by detailing how ideologies about ethnicity came into existence in Indonesia, how these ideologies have been reproduced, and how they figure in everyday talk among a group of transnational Indonesians living in Japan. In examining how multiculturalism and multilingualism are imagined, represented, and enacted, I argue that it appears that language mixing is becoming institutionalized in Indonesia. I will show that this tendency sits in constant tension with other institutional and representational practices that reproduce ideologies about language that anchor it to place, forming ethnolinguistic communities in Indonesia. As with so much scholarship on language ideologies that tie the emergence and reproduction of them with ideas of modernity and capitalism (Errington, 2001; Heller, 2011; Inoue, 2006), it is a story that starts in the colonial era when a handful of islands were becoming the Dutch East Indies.

The tensions between ideas about compartmentalized multiculturalism and multilingualism on the one hand, and hybrid identities and codemixing on the other, can be regularly seen in everyday face-to-face talk in Indonesia, especially in urban areas that are characterized by diverse and transient neighborhoods (Goebel, 2010b). In many ways, these practices sit in direct contrast to other ideologies, especially Indonesia's state ideology about "unity in diversity," and the ideology that a standardized variety of Indonesian is the medium in which everyday acts of unity in diversity are carried out. The doing of unity in diversity can, of course, be interactionally achieved in many ways. A finding of the research reported in this book is that an unintended consequence of the processes that helped to sediment indexical relationships among language, place, and person to form "ethnicity" also facilitated a new way of representing and doing unity in diversity. In the following sections, I expand on each of these themes (ideology construction and reproduction, representational practices, and sociability) and the theories used to explore them, while introducing the chapters that engage with these themes.

1.2 Communities and Competence

The idea of community can be examined from four viewpoints. In line with work on membership category analysis (Antaki & Widdicombe, 1998), the first type of community is the outcome of situated face-to-face interaction. Another type of community is formed through a series of interactions across time in a locale. These types of communities are formed through the structuration process described in Gidden's (1984) and resemble a "community of practice" (Barton & Tusting, 2005; Eckert & McConnell-Ginet, 1999; Holmes & Meyerhoff, 1999; Wenger, 1998). As Bourdieu's (1984) work points out, the existence of multiple communities of practice (COP) also enables distinctions between different COP. The practice of making such distinctions helps to sharpen the boundaries between each COP (e.g., Barth, 1969; Bucholtz & Hall, 2004). "Publics" are another type of community that lives in the imaginations of media professionals, writers, and bureaucrats (Anderson, 2006 [1991, 1983]; Ang, 1996; Livingstone, 2005), and they are also constituted through acts of media consumption in living rooms and elsewhere, as well as lesson consumption in classrooms, lecture theaters, and other teaching venues. One of my concerns in this book is to show how each of these senses of community is produced, interrelated, and invoked in Indonesia and among transnational Indonesians living in Japan.

As we would expect, criteria for membership in each of these communities are different. In face-to-face interaction, there is a range of competences that can be involved, and these will be determined by membership in a particular COP. Sharing ways of speaking and the communicative competence (CC) associated with these ways of speaking are primary indicators of membership in a COP. In this case, CC is typically developed in a specific locale among a stable and often small, isolated population (Hymes, 1972a, 1972b; Ochs, 1988; Schieffelin, 1990; Wenger, 1998). These locales become a place where what is considered normative and deviant in interactional terms is regimented (Goebel, 2010b). In cases where there are members from multiple COP, membership in one COP or another is often determined through distinctions made between different ways of speaking (Bourdieu, 1984; Irvine, 2001). These ways of speaking and the locales that they are associated with thus represent a center within a system of multiple centers or a center within a "polycentric system" (e.g., Blommaert, 2010, 2013b; Blommaert, Collins, & Slembrouck, 2005a).

While there are often a limited number of members in a particular COP, publics typically have many more members. Membership in a public can be seen through competence to comprehend semiotic forms but often not to perform them. In this sense, the types of CC we find in a COP differ from the types of CC we find in a public. We can get a better sense of these differences if we start by looking at some of the groundbreaking language socialization studies of the late 1970s and early 1980s (e.g., Ochs, 1988; Schieffelin, 1990). These studies were often conducted in isolated communities. Those studied were a few novices involved in language socialization activities at any given moment—that is, a one-to-few participation framework (Agha, 2007). Those with the authority to model ways of speaking for these novices were also limited to older siblings, parents, elders, healers, and missionaries. Communicative competence in these types of COP was thus locally determined and reproduced. While it may have been straightforward to define the competences that one needed to be seen as a community member in these settings, an increasingly mobile and connected world has brought into focus distinctions in the ways of speaking of members from different COP, while also inviting scholars to reexamine the notion of CC (e.g., Blommaert et al., 2005a; Blommaert, Collins, & Slembrouck, 2005b; Kramsch & Whiteside, 2008; Warriner, 2010). Even so, a number of these studies were similar in their underlying assumptions about community and CC, namely that mobile persons were originally part of a community that was anchored to a locale, and members became communicatively competent through participation in one-to-one and one-to-few participation frameworks.

These small-scale language socialization settings and the CC developed within them contrast with large-scale language socialization situations where novices can range from a classroom full of students to a television audience. In this sense, large numbers of novices create a quantitatively different participation framework, namely a "one-to-many participation framework" Agha (2007: 74–77). The role of institutions is also different. For example, the institutions of family, extended family, clan, and so on that have in the past been primary socialization settings have increasingly been replaced by government institutions, the mass media, and so on (e.g., Giddens, 1990). The increasing role of government institutions and government-sponsored institutions has also meant a change in ideas relating to authority. For example, nowadays, those who have formal education often have more authority in terms of the ability to influence another's life trajectory than siblings, parents, elders, and so on. Authority is also much more dispersed, with many institutions having the authority to model and normalize particular ways of speaking (e.g., family and elders versus schools and media institutions). In terms of how those in positions of authority interact with novices, one-to-many participation frameworks are also increasingly common. In addition, while in small communities, linguistic forms are imbued with cultural value through interaction with siblings, parents, and elders (e.g., honorific forms, terms of address for elders, etc.), in larger urban contexts, government institutions and the mass media do much of this work (e.g., Agha, 2007; Inoue, 2006; Jaffe, 2003).

The ubiquitous nature of mass-mediatized semiotic forms in everyday life thus invites us to understand how publics are formed, the types of CC associated with these publics, and how these competences are used in face-to-face interaction to claim or disavow membership in locally emergent COP and other COP. In chapters 2–6, I examine how ethnic publics were formed and reproduced in Indonesia, starting from the early Dutch colonial period. To do this, I draw upon ideas about technology, circulation, and enregisterment before turning to how publics are invoked in face-to-face talk in chapters 7–8.

Studies of enregisterment examine how cultural value is associated with particular signs and social types over different timescales, and how the resultant constellation of signs—referred to as a semiotic register—are repeated across social domains to form situational, local, and stereotypical communities that have particular ways of speaking (Agha, 2007). In all cases, knowledge of particular registers becomes a defining feature of what it means to be a communicatively competent member of each of these communities (Hymes, 1972a, 1972b). As Agha (2007) points out, those registers that are situational or remain largely local are typically recirculated in one-to-few participation frameworks, while those that become widely known are often recirculated via one-to-many participation frameworks.

One-to-many participation frameworks are characterized by "one-way" types of communicative practices, in which one person—usually some "exemplary social type"—teaches or models ways of speaking to a large number of others, as in school classrooms, lecture theaters, television programs being viewed in multiple spaces, and so on. The ability and authority to not only model ways of speaking, but to also influence a person's life trajectory comes from a complex system of credentialism that has legitimized these exemplary social types as determiners and disseminators of social value (e.g., Agha, 2007; Bourdieu, 1991; Briggs, 2005; Inoue, 2006). In this sense, semiotic content that circulates in one-to-many participation frameworks also has some type of institutional authority. In the case of teachers, this situation is repeated on a mass scale in many corners of the world where curriculum and teacher training are standardized. I use "massification" as a working definition of the repetition of settings that involve one-to-many participation frameworks.

As Agha's (2007) work reminds us, while exemplary social types may act as models of ways of speaking and interacting, much of the semiotic content found in one-to-many participation frameworks provides competence to recognize this semiotic content, rather than to reproduce it. In cases where it is drawn upon or emulated, typically it consists of fragments or imperfect copies. Dispersed and multiple living quarters furnished with televisions, radios, magazines, newspapers, and computers represent other examples where one-to-many participation frameworks help to produce competence to comprehend semiotic content. The contexts surrounding the consumption of these semiotic forms are different from one-to-few participation frameworks because mutual orientation to semiotic form or content is often not a possibility (Agha, 2007: 74–77). Often, cases of contestation and the seeking of clarification about semiotic content happen in another time and place. When television and radio are concerned, this type of orienting behavior can take the form of letters to the editor, radio talkback sessions, parodies, and so on (e.g., King & Wicks, 2009; Loven, 2008; Miller, 2004). In cases when people emulate represented semiotic forms, usually this is also temporally and spatially distant from the initial representation (e.g., Cutler, 1999).

Repetition across multiple social domains creates not only possibilities of recognition and emulation of signs by a certain population; it also creates possibilities of evaluation. I refer to some instances of recognizing and evaluating signs at the interaction level as "knowledging." I return to this idea of knowledging in section 1.4. Large-scale repetition of one semiotic register inhabited by exemplary authoritative figures also creates a center of normativity that is often referred to and positively evaluated vis-à-vis another locale-specific register or registers. These types of distinctions (Bourdieu, 1984, 1991) set up what Blommaert (2005, 2008, 2010, 2013b) refers to as "orders of indexicality" whereby "standard languages" and their speakers occupy the top of this order while vernacular languages and their speakers sit below.

While part of chapter 2 is concerned with how the mobility of a primarily privileged and educated few figured in the construction and repetition of ideas of ethnicity, another part is concerned with the conditions that enabled the circulation of people and ideas. Thus, my accounts of the formation of ideas about communities of ethnic social types rely upon a close reading of historical, political, and economic accounts of Indonesia. I am especially interested in accounts that describe how different waves of technology facilitated, as well as came about through, the need to move and connect experts in the form of bureaucrats, soldiers, union bosses, political leaders, teachers, and so on throughout Indonesia on an increasingly larger scale.

While I take into account Castells's (1996: 5–13) cautions against making claims about technological determinism, I argue that since the nineteenth century, waves of new infrastructure have contributed to the speeding up of the circulation of ideas and people, often on a much larger scale. I refer to this increase of people and idea movement throughout the archipelago as "up-scaling." These new waves of infrastructure contributed and keep contributing to a compression of time and space (Harvey, 1989). This time-space compression in turn produced increasing levels of diversity along with new forms of sociability. In section 1.4, I relate these outcomes to more recent discussions about superdiversity (e.g., Blommaert & Rampton, 2011; Vertovec, 2007; Williams & Stroud, 2013).

I point out that up-scaling created new social domains for contact with and commentary about "the other." Such commentaries have been shown to be crucial for the formation and reproduction of semiotic registers and the stereotypes that are associated with these registers (e.g., Agha, 2007; Inoue, 2006). Following Agha (2007), I term these commentaries "metasemiotic commentaries" rather than "metalinguistic" or "metapragmatic" because they can include commentary on a whole host of signs rather than just linguistic ones. As I move through time, I connect the enregisterment of ethnic stereotypes with local, national, and global political and economic events. These events helped to index ethnic social types with different cultural value. This ranged from the positive associations of the early to mid-1990s to the negative ones associated with the period between the early 1950s and the early 1980s (chapter 2) and from 1999 onward (chapter 4). As the Indonesian developmentist state and its apparatus unraveled in the late 1990s, so too did many of the so-called harmonious interethnic relations that existed in many of Indonesia's provinces. As I point out in chapter 4, these events helped to associate ethnicity with a new type of cultural value. In particular, the stereotype of "ethnic troublemaker" also became linked to the stereotype of "victim of earlier development policy" and "empowered community supported by global actors."

1.3 Television, Demeanor, and Change

While chapters 2 and 4 only briefly discuss specific contexts and their connections with circulating ideas about ethnicity, I narrow my focus to the uptake of these ideas through a further examination of televised representations of ethnicity in Indonesia in chapters 3, 5, and 6. This seems important because though the study of televised representations is not new (e.g., Garrett & Bell, 1998; Johnson & Ensslin, 2007; Loven, 2008), little work has been done that investigates how such televised representations figure in adding embodied elements to circulating ideas about social types. In this book, I seek to develop this line of scholarship by using work on multimodality and "demeanor" (Goffman, 1967) to examine how ideas about ethnic social types have been indexically linked with an embodied image through television representations. In doing so, I seek to contribute to some of the discussions on language ideology formation by furthering the multimodal nature of such studies. Indeed, with a few recent exceptions (Bucholtz, 2011; Bucholtz & Lopez, 2011; Mendoza-Denton, 2011), most studies that look at how language ideologies are constructed and reproduced typically use and focus upon printed sources (e.g., Agha, 2003, 2011; Inoue, 2006; Inoue, 2011; Miller, 2004).

Chapter 3 starts to flesh out these ideas by focusing on television representations of ethnicity in the mid-to-late 1990s. I argue that these representations have helped form indexical links among particular ways of interacting, social relations, and ethnic social types. In so doing, I draw upon work on enregisterment discussed in chapter 2 to examine how these demeanors are repeated across several soap operas over time, while also starting to discuss how these representational practices relate to semiotic change more generally. In particular, I point to two contrasting processes of enregisterment. On the one hand, there are representational practices that continue to index linguistic forms with place and person that reproduce ideologies relating to ethnic communities and their languages. On the other hand, I show how some of these representations also question ideologies that have the formula of "Place + Person + Linguistic Signs = Ethnicity and Ethnic Language." Both practices, however, can also be viewed as evidence of semiotic change, especially when compared with the ethnic social types that had been circulating prior to the emergence of comedic soaps.

The delinking of place, person, and linguistic sign is done through the frequent representations of migrants and city dwellers engaging in a type of language alternation referred to as "alternation as the medium" (Gafaranga & Torras, 2002). In these representations, medium alternation resembles the following pattern (adapted from Auer, 1995): AB1 AB2 AB1 AB2 (the uppercase letters represent a particular medium and the numbers indicate speakers 1 and 2). I see these practices as alternation as the medium rather than crossing, which is the use of linguistic forms not normally associated with the speaker (Rampton, 1995). This is so because descriptions of televised representations of crossing elsewhere in the world are typically associated with liminality and spectacular performances (e.g., Androutsopoulos, 2007; Jaffe, 2000; Kelly-Holmes & Atkinson, 2007; LeCompte & Schensul, 1999), while the soaps examined here represent instances of alternation as typically unspectacular, mundane, and often habitual. In doing so, these televised representations also appear to be an example of the institutional authorization of code-mixing. This sits in contrast to other institutional practices in Indonesia and elsewhere in the world where the idea of multilingualism is commonly institutionalized and ideologized as a monolingual ability in two or more languages (Creese & Blackledge, 2011; Heller, 2007; Moyer, 2011).

The practice of representing ethnic social types who habitually engage in alternation became quite common on Indonesian television by the mid-1990s. These representations of alternation also provided alternate models of the doing of unity in diversity. These models sat in contrast to the state ideology that linked Indonesian to the doing of unity in diversity. In adding to work on linguistic diversity (Blommaert, 2010; Blommaert & Rampton, 2011; Jørgensen, Karrebæk, Madsen, & Møller, 2011), in chapters 5 and 6, I revisit Indonesian television to point out that representations of alternation were ubiquitous across a range of genres and television channels by 2009. In chapters 7 and 8, I move to looking at how televised representations are interpreted by viewers. In doing so, I explore the links among watching, talking, processes of enregisterment, and meaning-making. In particular, I point out that viewers' prior participation in authorized one-to-many participation frameworks (e.g., schooling, televised representations of ethnic social types) have enabled them to not only recognize ethnic stereotypes, but also to evaluate these ethnic stereotypes. I refer to this as "knowledging" and I expand on this concept below.

1.4 Knowledging and Conviviality in Superdiversity

Since submitting my first draft of this book in 2011 and then a revision in May 2012, the term "superdiversity" has continued to rapidly gain currency in sociolinguistics. Often attributed to Steven Vertovec (2007), the term is used as an alternative to terms like "multiculturalism" and "diversity." These terms are associated with simplistic notions of community, identity, and language along with ideologies that equate one with another, such as a language with a specific community (Arnaut & Spotti, 2014). In discussions about superdiversity, complexity is seen as the necessary starting point for understanding language practices along with the need for a new vocabulary set (Blommaert, 2013a). There are a number of themes covered in work on superdiversity, although here I focus on just two.

First, scholars generally agree that a characteristic of superdiversity is that intercultural contact occurs in more social domains and more frequently than in the past (Blommaert & Rampton, 2011; Vertovec, 2007). Typically, this is a result of the settlement of mobile or displaced persons in neighborhoods already associated with diversity and multiple languages. In such contexts, interaction among these strangers—who share few semiotic resources—is characterized by the use of just enough of another's language to be (mis)understood, to perform particular identities, or to enact particular positions vis-à-vis other participants (Blommaert, 2013a, 2013b; Blommaert & Varis, 2011). Notions like "bilingual" or "multilingual" do not adequately describe or account for this use of multiple linguistic fragments that are often not the first, second, third, fourth, etc., language of the participants, but rather part of a truncated repertoire that is a situationally constituted and emergent semiotic system (Blommaert, 2013a, 2013b; Blommaert & Backus, 2011; Goebel, 2010b). Superdiversity can thus be tentatively defined as a setting constituted by strangers from multiple backgrounds who never share the same language but only some semiotic fragments. These fragments are used in interaction to build common ground as part of efforts to create convivial social relations.

In chapters 2 and 4, we will see how different waves of technology, capitalism, and nation-building activities over the last 150 years related to the emergence of an uncountable number of locale-specific participant constellations, each with their own emergent semiotic registers. The emergence of this type of diversity also brought with it many opportunities to comment on such diversity. Chapters 3 and 6 add to work on linguistic superdiversity (Blommaert, 2010; Blommaert & Rampton, 2011; Jørgensen et al., 2011) by showing how superdiversity is represented on television, in this case, Indonesian television. In doing so, I point out that these representations provide models of the doing of unity in diversity that sit in contrast to the state ideology that links Indonesian usage to the doing of unity in diversity. There are, of course, other unintended outcomes of these practices, and part of the task of chapters 3 and 6–8 is to look at this hitherto underexplored area of superdiversity.

In these four chapters, I focus on the effect of increasing circulation and consumption of registers found in one-to-many participation frameworks (e.g., schooling, television and radio programming, etc.). In particular, I suggest that a further layer of linguistic diversity is added through participation in schooling and through the consumption of television programs, movies, radio programs, music, religious texts, Internet content, and so on. This extra layer is made up of "competence to comprehend" (Agha, 2007) and "competence to evaluate" semiotic fragments that do not normally form part of a person's habitually used semiotic repertoire. These two competences are added to a host of other competences, which together make up a person's "communicative competence" (Hymes, 1972a, 1972b). In chapter 8, I suggest that this ability to comprehend or evaluate semiotic fragments that do not normally form part of a person's habitually used semiotic repertoire—which I refer to as "knowledging"—also needs to be included in discussions about communicative competence. This is so because so much of a person's language socialization involves schooling and the consumption of semiotic forms from television and radio programming, films, the Internet, and other forms of one-to-many participation frameworks (Goebel, 2013).

While knowledging has parallels with other terms, such as "polylanguaging" (Jørgensen et al., 2011), "crossing" (Rampton, 1995), and "symbolic competence" (Kramsch, 2006; Kramsch & Whiteside, 2008), I argue that it needs to be treated separately for a number of reasons. First, knowledging is different because of the way in which we learn to associate semiotic forms with other. Accounts of polylanguaging describe performances without explaining how people learn the semiotic forms that help make up their performance. While access to one-to-many participation frameworks is partially used to account for performances of crossing—as in Cutler's (1999: 433–434) account of the role of the consumption of music videos and films in providing models of speech for her participant to emulate—in accounts of crossing and symbolic competence, participants' histories of interaction in one-to-one or one-to-few participation frameworks are used to account for their ability to engage in crossing and other mixed language practices. In contrast, the ability to engage in knowledging is solely an outcome of involvement in one-to-many participation frameworks. Second, polylanguaging, crossing, and symbolic competence are primarily concerned with performance, while knowledging focuses primarily, though not exclusively, on the receptive aspect of CC.

The idea of knowledging dovetails with another common question posed by those working in the area of superdiversity, namely how do people from very different backgrounds and with very different semiotic systems go about getting along (Ang, 2003; Goebel, 2010a, 2010b; Smets, 2005; Vertovec, 2007; Werbner, 1997; Wise, 2005). Knowledging as a social practice that engenders the doing of togetherness can be found in television representations and in actual face-to-face talk. In adding to work on superdiversity and the doing of togetherness, I focus on television representations of knowledging and their relationship to the doing of togetherness in difference in chapters 3 and 6. Knowledging is part of a type of sociability that is already well embedded in television producers' imaginations about their audiences. This is so because these media professionals produce such representations while seeming to expect their audiences to understand them.

In chapters 7 and 8, I continue to explore the links among knowledging, the doing of togetherness, and superdiversity by seeking to understand how a group of Indonesian sojourners from different backgrounds do togetherness while in Japan. The doing of togetherness in superdiverse settings is increasingly referred to as "conviviality" (Blommaert, 2013b; Williams & Stroud, 2013). The need to be convivial relates to the conditions of superdiversity, which often require and/or produce conviviality as a necessary interactional practice that helps in securing some goods, service, or employment in a setting, while producing locally emergent norms for interaction. While thus far, the idea of conviviality has been explored in fleeting interactional moments across lines of difference (Williams & Stroud, 2013), the idea of conviviality seems to also imply a move toward habitual use of particular semiotic features that help in establishing common ground among strangers. That the fleeting and the habitual are so semiotically and temporally different invites a more nuanced account of the range of language practices that can be described as convivial, and ultimately requires some sort of semantic distinction.

In adding to the work on superdiversity, I make this distinction in chapters 7 and 8 through my examination of the communicative practices of a group of Indonesian sojourners living in Japan. I use the term "conviviality" to refer to the doing of togetherness in difference in *INITIAL* face-to-face encounters, while I use the term "togetherness in difference" to refer to subsequent practices of *CONTINUING* to build common ground among the same group of people. In both chapters, we will see a whole gamut of language practices being used to build and reproduce conviviality and togetherness in difference. Some of these ways of speaking are often referred to as "small talk" in the literature. In both chapters, I am especially concerned with non-minimal responses, repetition, teasing, and the pursuit of social sameness.

1.5 The Multiple Functions of Talk and the Mundane

In looking at how a specific group of Indonesian sojourners goes about engaging in knowledging to build and reproduce convivial relations through talk, I also engage with a number of other areas. The first relates to the multiple functions and outcomes of talk. For example, we know that talk can contribute to the simultaneous development of identities and epistemologies (Goebel, 2010b; Wortham, 2006). In line with Bakhtin's (1981) and Vološinov's (1973 [1929]) ideas about the multiple meanings inherent in discourse, I add to this literature by teasing out the multiple and often simultaneous functions of talk that are evident in this group of Indonesians' talk while they watch comedic soaps.

In addition to building convivial relations, in chapter 7, I show how talk also relates to ongoing social identification and the assigning of meaning to an unknown word across two temporally adjacent speech situations. In particular, I examine the tensions around how this group jointly constructs the meaning of televised signs, while also contributing to the reification of one of the meanings of these signs, which in this case is a word. In chapter 8, I continue this theme, this time by following the talk of a different group across the course of two weeks. In so doing, I place my analysis into my earlier discussions about community and enregisterment by showing how this group of Indonesians interactionally indexes their participation in a number of communities while viewing television or while being interviewed.

In chapter 9, I conclude by pointing out some of the contributions that this study might make to sociolinguistics and Indonesian studies. In addition to engaging with sociolinguistic scholarship on language ideologies, superdiversity, community, and communicative competence, I also point out that for Indonesian area specialists, this book presents a story of the continued changing nature of the idea of ethnicity and how signs associated with this register are mobilized to do situated relationship work. The idea of ethnicity and its relationship with language has shown an ability to endure in the imagination and everyday activities of Indonesians. In some settings and under certain conditions, this idea can become associated with extreme difference and conflict (chapters 2 and 4). Even so, I hope that chapters 7 and 8 will show that an unintended consequence (Giddens, 1990) of the circulation of ideas of ethnicity is that it also enables the doing of togetherness through knowledging. While convivial talk is a hitherto road less traveled in studies of communal relations in Indonesia, nevertheless, what I offer in this book can complement the study of unity in diversity in Indonesia.

Finally, since the implementation of decentralization around 2001, we have seen a rise in the "symbolic" or "social" value (Bourdieu, 1991) of ethnicity, ethnic languages, and the mixing of ethnic languages with Indonesian. Evidence of this revaluation process is presented in chapters 3–6. In sociolinguistics-speak, this revaluing is an example of the reconfiguration of existing "orders of indexicality" (Blommaert, 2005, 2007, 2010). This revaluation process contests and reformulates hierarchies of language. For example, in the early 1990s, Indonesian was at the top; some ethnic languages such as Javanese, Sundanese, and Balinese were below it; and a mixing of Indonesian and ethnic languages was at the bottom. Since then, the increased presence of regional languages in the media, schools, and as topics of political discourse has created tensions in this hierarchy. Ethnic languages have edged closer to equality with Indonesian, and representations of language mixing are now commonplace. This revaluation that has been achieved through schooling and media has enabled the appropriation and mobilization of emblems of ethnicity. In the case I present here, I focus on the appropriation and mobilization of fragments of ethnic languages used together (often in the same utterance) with Indonesian. In chapter 3 and chapters 6–8, I point out that those who appropriate and mobilize these emblems are often those with no primordial claim to them. In doing so, I link a general process of appropriation and mobilization or "recontextualization" (Bauman & Briggs, 1990) of emblems of ethnicity to how recontextualization matters in political contexts too, such as in the political campaigning reported by Aspinall (2013).

2

The Semiotic Figurement of Communities in Indonesia

2.1 Introduction

Taking inspiration from scholarship in the broad area of language ideologies, this chapter looks at how ideas about the links among social types, regions, and linguistic forms have been circulated from colonial times until the early 1990s, forming what can be described as ethnolinguistic stereotypes. In building on my earlier work, which tended to oversimplify this picture (Goebel, 2008), I align with four sets of related ideas. The first is that tracing historical circulation of sign usage helps us understand how, over time, particular social types have become associated with a named language or a named register (Agha, 2007a; M. Inoue, 2006). In tracing the beginnings of this language ideology, I draw upon Errington's (2001a) insights about colonial linguistics, which discussed how early missionary work in Indonesia helped to erase and order linguistic diversity by naturalizing ethnicity as a category of personhood. In line with their mission to convert people within their territories, missionaries made written descriptions of previously indistinguishable languages, and assigned these languages to a named ethnic or tribal group, which often coincided with the territorial proclivities of missionaries rather than the speakers of these languages (Errington, 2001a). Through schooling and other processes, language became a widely recognized emblem of ethnicity in Indonesia.

The second set of ideas relates to trying to understand how this association process also involves a way of looking at what constitutes a language (Agha, 2007b; Errington, 2001a; Heryanto, 2007). For example, language planning and schooling in Indonesia has emphasized Indonesian as "a language" that is made up of certain syntax, words, morphological patterns, and so on that sit in contrast to these ethnic languages that also consist of certain syntax, words, and morphological patterns (e.g., Abas, 1987; Alisjahbana, 1976; Dardjowidjojo, 1998; Moeliono, 1986; Nababan, 1985, 1991). This perspective privileges an observer's view rather than a participant's and is grounded in a particular ideological view of what constitutes a language. While such a view recognizes multilingualism, typically the "multi" refers to multiple bounded languages, rather than the type of language mixing characteristic of everyday talk. In other words, in many respects, institutional ideologies of language in Indonesia are like those reported and critiqued elsewhere in the world (e.g., Blommaert & Rampton, 2011; Moyer, 2011).

The third set of ideas I align with is the general thrust of work in linguistic anthropology and the anthropology of migration that emphasizes diversity over simplification and focuses on superdiversity, multiple truncated competences, and the social value of the linguistic repertoires associated with these competences (Blommaert, 2010; Vertovec, 2007). Diversity and multiple truncated repertoires are a result of mobility and are an increasingly normal state of affairs in many settings. Not all repertoires are equal, however, and some linguistic repertoires have more symbolic value than others (Bourdieu, 1991). The different social values attached to different languages create what Blommaert refers to as "orders of indexicality" where the social value of a language changes as it moves from one setting or center to another (Blommaert, 2005, 2007, 2008, 2010). The fourth set of related ideas concerns the relationships between different waves of technology and how they have contributed to the up-scaling of the circulation of people—that is, the comprehension of time and space (Harvey, 1989)—while also creating new social domains for contact with and commentary about "the other" (Appadurai, 1996; Gershon, 2010). In doing so, I draw upon the work of economic historians of Indonesia who have convincingly argued for a perspective that looks at the interdependent nature of state formation and technological innovation.

In addition to pointing to some patterns, in what follows, I also flesh out the diversity and potential lives of many yet-to-be-researched sign systems, many of which are new centers with the potential to reconfigure existing orders of indexicality. I am especially concerned with pointing out how different waves of technology have contributed to the naturalization of links between linguistic signs, place, and person to form imagined communities of ethnic social types, while exploring how these processes contribute to superdiversity. For example, plantations, or the more recent settlement zones (created through internal government-sponsored migration) have produced new social domains for encounters with the other, and with it, many locally emergent sign systems and associated stereotypes. In linguistic-speak, mobility created new centers characterized by the emergence of a new language along with the norms of usage.

Following Agha (2007a), and wherever stylistically possible, I prefer to use "semiotic register" rather than "language" because it is underpinned by an idea of unlimited diversity rather than the relatively closed system implied by the word "language." A semiotic register, on the other hand, can be defined as a potentially unlimited constellation of signs—linguistic and nonlinguistic—that help constitute social types and their ways of speaking, while enabling one sign to implicate a register and its associated social type(s). In this sense, one sign used and ratified by two participants can be referred to as a language, as pointed out by Tannen (1989) in relation to married couples. Taking this approach avoids the slippery slope of trying to define a language, which is primarily an imagined object that is still too frequently essentialized and associated with a specific group of people living in a particular place and time. This also highlights the idea that there can be as many semiotic registers as pairs of speakers.

Thus, a major aim of this chapter is to point to the possibilities of a diverse, expanding, and sometimes overlapping mass of semiotic registers. In showing how the emergence of these registers is reliant upon the facilitation of people interacting with others from different backgrounds, I also describe how some registers have become more enduring and more socially valued. I start by fleshing out work on semiotic register formation (section 2.2), before taking a historical perspective that covers much of the colonial period (1800s–1942), the Japanese occupation (1942–1945), the Soekarno period (1945–1966), and most of the Soeharto period (1966 to the mid-1990s), respectively, sections 2.3 to 2.8.

2.2 Communities and Enregisterment

Across the humanities and social sciences, community is commonly discussed as both an imagined and real entity that is typically inhabited by exemplary social types, whether they be ethnic, gendered, classed, national, and so on (Anderson, 2006 [1991, 1983]; Appadurai, 1996; Z. Bauman, 2001; Gumperz, 1982; Hymes, 1972a; Labov, 1972; Putnam, 2000; Wenger, 1998). Concerns over whether community should be seen as real or imaginary tend to boil down to older debates over the relationship between action and social structure. Some people working in fields such as interactional sociolinguistics, conversation analysis, and educational ethnography discuss communities (as one type of identity), meanings, and social structures as things that are not fixed but rather negotiated and constructed in talk in a particular setting (Antaki & Widdicombe, 1998; Schegloff, 1991; Stevens & Hall, 1998; Wenger, 1998).

Even so, ideas about community and other identities do become sedimented in the minds of people, and these ideas are often used in face-to-face interaction. The sedimentation process became one of the focuses of Giddens (1984) and Bourdieu (1984), who argued that the routinization of social practices over space and time helped to produce knowledge about communities, identities, and the languages associated with them. Work by Goffman (1983), Bauman and Briggs (1990), Silverstein and Urban (1996), and others has shown us how this knowledge can be appropriated and reused in other settings.

Agha (2007a) has offered a recent clarification of these circular relationships. He starts from single communicative events and emphasizes that within these semiotic encounters, signs only become signs if those used by a sender are recognized by the receiver. In cases where receiver and sender interact with new participants using previously ratified signs and where negotiation of the meaning of these signs has *some* fit with prior meanings of these signs, then this series of interactions can be seen as a series of "speech chains" that figure in the widening of the social domain of a sign or signs (Agha, 2007a). If persons who have some link to the original interaction and signs interact with others while reusing these signs, then this allows for the formation of communities of practice (Wenger, 1998) or what Bourdieu (1984) terms *fields* within a larger *habitus*. As work on superdiverse settings has shown, this has typically resulted in locally emergent semiotic registers where insiders have different levels of competence in their ability to perform and comprehend signs (Blommaert et al., 2005a, 2005b; Goebel, 2010b). Within these types of settings, norms also emerge around how to use signs associated with these communities (Goebel, 2010b). This emergent normativity becomes one local "center" of normativity within a "polycentric" system (Blommaert, 2010, 2013b; Blommaert et al., 2005a). In other words, this center of normativity sits within a constantly changing system made up uncountable and constantly changing centers of normativity.

In addition to face-to-face encounters, signs can be repeated and circulated by other means in other social domains. For example, work in linguistic anthropology has shown how signs are repeated and circulated in one-to-many participation frameworks, such as school classrooms or mass-produced texts and artifacts like dictionaries, grammars, television shows, and so on (e.g., Agha, 2007a; Briggs, 2005; M. Inoue, 2006; Johnstone, Andrus, & Danielson, 2006; Miller, 2004). These are examples of the types of "discourses" discussed in Foucault (1978). One-to-many participation frameworks are different from one-to-few participation frameworks in a number of important ways, each of which help in making the semiotic forms that are mediated within these frameworks more widely recognized.

First and most obvious, is that sign repetition in one-to-many participation frameworks is, by definition, on a larger scale than in a one-to-few participation framework. Second, as Agha (2007a) points out, the way meaning is contested is different from how it is done in a face-to-face encounter, and often contestation is done in another time and space. For example, orienting behavior to semiotic forms that are mediated in one-to-many participation frameworks takes the form of letters to the editor, radio talkback sessions, parodies, curriculum and policy reviews, memos, and so on (e.g., King & Wicks, 2009; Loven, 2008; Miller, 2004). These types of commentaries are termed "metasemiotic" commentaries because they not only comment on the language being used, but also on the user and/or associated signs (Agha, 2007a). Just as importantly, the act of commenting not only recirculates signs, but it also helps these signs to become associated with other signs, moral dispositions, places, times, and so on. In short, these signs are imbued with symbolic value (Bourdieu, 1991), that is, they are "enregistered" (Agha, 2003, 2007a; Silverstein, 2003) and form centers of normativity that typically are more socially valued than local emergent centers of normativity, such as the norms that emerge through interactions among migrants in urban neighborhoods (Goebel, 2010b).

Third, while familial elders, older siblings, or kin have authority to model ways of speaking in one-to-few participation frameworks, in one-to-many participation frameworks, authority is dispersed both spatially and across time with one person being socialized by many different teachers, all of whom act as models of ways of speaking. People represented on television, radio, and the Internet (e.g., celebrities, athletes, politicians, scientists, and so on) also have some authority because they are represented as being experts of some type. Typically, speaking figures heavily in this doing of expertise, and thus these experts are also modeling particular ways of speaking that also become indexed with authority.

Whether and to what extent semiotic registers, social types, and communities are widely recognizable is also reliant upon changes in infrastructure that facilitate the up-scaling of people and idea circulation. By infrastructure, I am especially concerned with transport, communications, and large institutions (e.g., schools and universities, census offices, medical establishments, banks, and so on). Although changes in infrastructure can also mean a decrease in available infrastructure as found after war or economic depression, nevertheless, as Harvey (1989) and later Eisenlohr (2009, 2010) point out, in many cases, changes in infrastructure have also brought with them reduction in time and space between people or representations of difference and their reception. As those working on linguistics and media ideologies have pointed out (Barker, 2008; Gershon, 2010; M. Inoue, 2006; Weidman, 2010), the waves of new infrastructure introduced since the nineteenth century have facilitated the up-scaling of sign repetition, created new social domains for encounters with difference, and created or facilitated new forms of sociability.

Changes in infrastructure and the resultant up-scaling of the circulation of people that often accompanies these processes also help in the creation of multiple semiotic registers, social types, and communities. Thus, while there will always be dominant semiotic registers within a system of such registers—especially those that are authorized by schools and the mass media—there will also, necessarily, be competing semiotic registers. This is so because people participate in different speech chains, go to different schools, engage with mass-mediatized messages in different ways, and so on. In short, they have different trajectories of socialization (Bourdieu, 1984; Wortham, 2006) that create sociolinguistic diversity.

As work in sociolinguistics has continued to tell us, sociolinguistic diversity does not mean that different semiotic registers have the same social value

(Hymes, 1996; Labov, 1972; Philips, 1983). Indeed, as Bourdieu (1991) pointed out, these registers are hierarchically ordered. Blommaert (2005, 2007, 2008, 2010) refers to this ordering as "orders of indexicality." While a diverse population with fragmented understandings of more widely circulating semiotic registers and their social value is the norm, in any interaction, participants' familiarity with a semiotic register and its associated signs enables them to engage in practices of social differentiation whereby signs are perceived as similar to or different from ones that they have encountered in the past (e.g., Bucholtz & Hall, 2004a; Irvine, 2001; Tannen, 1993). In this sense, changes in infrastructure also set up the conditions for engaging in discourses about signs, stereotypes, and community.

In summary, the social domain of a sign that was ratified in a face-to-face speech chain can be repeated locally to form a local semiotic register and ideas about the normative use of signs associated with this register. This register can become more widely recognized through the circulation of fragments of this register in one-to-many participation frameworks: frameworks that are often facilitated by changes in infrastructure. This process also associates symbolic value with the register and its speakers, often to the extent that it becomes a widely recognized center of normativity. Typically, there are many simultaneous processes that produce multiple and hierarchically ordered semiotic registers, and populations that have varying levels of competence to perform or comprehend signs from these registers. For the linguistic anthropologist, this creates the desire to characterize this diversity in fine detail while also trying to avoid overgeneralization or essentialization of the community being described. In what follows, I try to walk this tightrope in the Indonesian context. On the one hand, I sketch out how linguistic forms, place, and person have been linked over the last 150 years or so to form ethnic stereotypes of differing social value. On the other, I point to the multitude of settings that were also likely to be sites of locally emergent semiotic registers, ironically creating the types of diversity and complexity that colonialists sought to understand and simplify (Errington, 2001). The formation of these spaces as sites has been facilitated by the same technological changes that have helped enregister ethnicity in Indonesia. I do this as a way of introducing the reader to the types of competence that the Indonesians that we will meet in subsequent chapters draw upon when interpreting televised sign representations.

2.3 The Creation of Ethnicity in the Nineteenth Century

While categories of difference among people living in the Indonesian archipelago existed well before the nineteenth century—especially through contact among royal courts, among merchants, traders, sailors, soldiers, pirates, and between royalty and their citizens (e.g., Goethals, 1959; Hefner, 2001; Ricklefs, 1981)—it seems that only after the arrival of the Dutch did ideas of ethnic difference start to circulate on a much larger scale throughout Indonesia. With each successive introduction of technology and/or political regime, there was a tendency toward increased circulation of people and ideas. This increased circulation directly influenced the rate and frequency of encounters with difference throughout the archipelago. In turn, this helped increase the circulation of ideas linking region, linguistic form, and person, while also creating new social domains and semiotic registers with differing social value. As will become apparent below, some of these associations solidified, while the meanings of some of these constellations were also multi-accentuated, in Vološinov's (1973 [1929]) sense.

Missionaries, colonial administrators, schoolteachers, medical personal, and scholars from the early to the late nineteenth century all contributed to the construction of ideas of language as emblematic of ethnicity in the then Dutch East Indies. Errington (2001: 20–24) points out that the (proto)linguistic work of missionaries helped to simplify and categorize linguistic diversity. This was done through written codifications that ethnolinguistically homogenized those living within the boundaries of a territory so that they became a tribe or ethnic group. In so doing, groups of linguistic forms and relationships became languages that where emblematic of ethnicity. This process also contributed to the social stratification of populations along the lines of literate versus non-literate (Errington, 2001: 25). This valuing of the indigenous Indies population along literate lines also coincided with, drew upon, and fed into another process of racial classing that emerged in one-to-few participation frameworks in Europe and the Dutch East Indies from the nineteenth century onward (Stoler, 1995b). This process of categorizing people emerged as part of discourses about how to police sexual relations in populations as a way of protecting European and Dutch bourgeois moral sensibilities and ideas about cultural purity and identity (Stoler, 1995b).

While language was not always seen as a locally important index of ethnic group membership in the Dutch East Indies (Davidson & Henley, 2007), in many cases, the production and distribution of print-based texts and schooling helped construct and spread notions that regional languages consisted of linguistic signs spoken by a community in a specific geographic space (Moriyama, 2005b). The spread of this ideology through schooling (one process of enregisterment) occurred at different rates across the archipelago. Moriyama (2005b: 2–5), for example, notes that the need to manage and administer coffee plantations in the western part of Java led to the introduction of Dutch-based literacy and schooling practices and machine-printed material at a much earlier time than in other parts of the Dutch East Indies.

In his study of the role of print literacy in the "modernization" of West Java, Moriyama (2005b) documents how the standardization of a regional language (Sundanese) and Malay, and the introduction of bilingual schools for the indigenous local elites figured in the preparation of local administrators who could fulfill an increasing need for mediators between the colonial administration and local populations. He points out how close collaboration between colonial administrators, European scholars, and local indigenous elites figured in the promotion of roman script over local Javanese and Arabic scripts, how Sundanese as found in print literature was a European construction that perpetuated place-based language ideologies, and how roman script and literacy increasingly became associated with morality, knowledge (in the case of Malay), and making money (Moriyama, 2005b).

As noted earlier, an important ingredient in the creation of semiotic registers is the creation of contrasts or distinctions (Bourdieu, 1984: 77). For example, the enregisterment of a language as standard-like and "good" typically requires many examples or commentaries about what is seen as substandard and bad, or just different. In the archipelago that was to eventually be known as the Dutch East Indies, there were many semiotic registers to choose from. There were various registers associated with Dutch. There were also various registers associated with literary Malay, as well as varieties of Malay associated with local communities. The semiotic registers that became socially valued ended up being called local languages, local varieties of spoken Malay (which were also to be found in written form in newspapers), and a variety of literary Malay.

Moriyama's (2005b) close documentation of language ideologies of particular administrators, educators, and scholars highlights how the links among ethnic group, language, culture, and geographic space were reproduced. These ideologies were so strong that by the late nineteenth century, Dutch colonial administrators had divided the archipelago into distinct ethnic groups (e.g., Sundanese, Javanese, Madurese), each with their own languages, cultures, and literary traditions (de Jong, 2009; Moriyama, 2005b: 3–18; Quinn, 1992: 2). For example, by 1872, the colonial administration had standardized Javanese (a variety from Solo), Sundanese (a variety from Bandung), and Batak (a variety from Mandeheling in Sumatra), and designated one of these along with Malay as the languages of education in their indigenous bilingual schools (Moriyama, 2005b: 23). These ideas were also in the process of becoming enshrined in law through the Dutch idea of *adat*, which encompassed ideas about custom, law, tradition, and territory (Burns, 2004; Fasseur, 1994).

While registers such as Sundanese were used in the earlier years of schooling (from around the age of ten years old) or in travelogues, as in the case of Javanese (Quinn, 1992: 6–8), increasingly, Malay was the register of school textbooks in the later years of schooling (Moriyama, 2005b: 75). Along with codification through a dictionary completed in 1877, the enregisterment of a form of spoken Malay from Riau continued through subsequent use of this variety in school textbooks, especially in the fields of math and geography (Moriyama, 2005b: 71–72; Sneddon, 2003: 87). In a sense, this was helping to link "advanced" knowledge with registers of Malay. At the same time, regional languages continued to be associated with the local through the use of school readers that had content primarily about the local.

While advanced knowledge, making money, privilege, and local elite initially had associations with Malay, by the late 1800s, increasing numbers of schoolchildren from a commoner background (i.e., not royal or wealthy) were allowed to enter Dutch schools (Moriyama, 2005b: 56–59). As Stoler (1995b) points out, these changes in schooling practices were in part driven by anxieties about the dangers that uneducated, poor, uncultured, and mixed-blood people posed to the colony. The point of this aside is that Malay was already losing its association with elite royal populations through a more heterogeneous make-up of schooling populations. In short, Malay was being revalued from the language of a privileged few to the language of a wider population while continuing to sit in a hierarchy with Dutch at the top, followed by Malay, and then ethnic languages, each with their own centers of normativity that prescribed and evaluated usage.

Schooling not only increased numbers of literate Malay-speaking indigenous colonial subjects, but in a real sense, it also helped in the imagination of a community of such social types who could buy and read newspapers (Anderson, 2006 [1991, 1983]). Even so, one of the differences between these subjects and the texts that they were imagined to read was that most of the newspapers that emerged across the archipelago from 1856 onward tended to use a register of Malay based on a local spoken register, rather than the type of literary Malay that was eventually to become the standard in colonial schools and documents (Cohen, 2006: 182; Moriyama, 2005b: 88; Sneddon, 2003: 89).

During the period between 1902 and 1910, the colonial regime standardized orthography and produced a grammar based on a literary form of Malay (Errington, 1998a: 273–274, 2000: 207–208; Moriyama, 2005b; Sneddon, 2003: 92; Teeuw, 1994). As this group of scholars has pointed out, material based on this literary standard was then disseminated through schools and in colonial training manuals, novels, and short stories that were published by the colonial publisher Balai Pustaka. This process contributed to further differentiation within a system of semiotic registers. For example, in contrast to literary Malay circulated by colonial machinery, the rapidly expanding newspaper industry also circulated written registers that were based on local spoken registers of Malay (Sneddon, 2003: 97). While the school textbooks on geography discussed by Moriyama may have alluded to "the other" in other parts of the Dutch East Indies, the travelogues discussed by Quinn imbued these places with social types including "others" who were different from the authors of these travelogues. The Javanese travelogues mentioned by Quinn emerged in the mid-1860s and were often about travels within the island of Java or to other parts of the archipelago.

Such travels were enabled through the building of road, rail, tram, telephone, telegraph, and electricity networks in Java between 1810 and 1900 (Å Campo, 2002; Dick, 1996; Mrázek, 2002). In addition, while other forms of oceangoing transport were certainly available before steamship companies began establishing inter-island networks in the 1850s (Á Campo, 2002; Reid, 1988), it seems worthy of note that the emergence of fiscal arrangements (in the form of banks, trading houses, insurance companies, and currency exchange treaties) and multiple, speedy time-regulated systems of transportation and communication described by Dick (1996) facilitated these travelogues. More generally, these new transportation systems sped up encounters with difference throughout the archipelago. Indeed, it seems that this time-regulated system of transport and the emergence of an increasingly dense road and rail system provided the conditions and infrastructure that enabled the setting-up of a plantation economy by the mid-1800s, the establishment of private mining companies, such as Billiton by the 1850s, the territorial defense of the Dutch East Indies from British incursions, and the subjugation of indigenous populations throughout the archipelago by the outbreak of World War I (Á Campo, 2002; Dick, 1996).

In summary, there were a number of interrelated processes that facilitated the (re)circulation of signs and semiotic registers during this period. On the one hand, infrastructure facilitated the circulation of people, social categories, and means for population surveillance at increased rates and on a larger scale, while creating new social domains for encounters with difference. In these encounters, there was a need to use any fragments of what one thought the other might know in terms of language: typically, fragments from some local register of Malay. The local character and forms associated with this semiotic register were repeated in local newspapers whose numbers were to increase remarkably in the future. For example, Sneddon (2003: 97) points out that between 1918 and 1925, newspaper titles increased from forty to over 200. On the other hand, encounters with difference together with the dissemination of ideas that indexed language with region (e.g., via schooling and travelogues) helped in the formation of other semiotic registers associated with local culture and, ultimately, ethnicity.

Contrasts between these registers helped to further their solidification. For example, differentiations between spoken and literary registers of Malay were to be found in newspaper commentaries about theater actors' language use (Cohen, 2006). Contrasts between Malay and local languages could be found in novels published by Balai Pustaka and the types of nationalist discourses that were to emerge by the early 1920s, both of which are discussed in the next section. This contrast was also increasingly one of social value, with the increasingly routinized circulation of literary and spoken Malay being positively associated with modernity, education, new "Western" knowledge, and the local (in the case of spoken and newspaper forms), while other languages were not only associated with regions and ethnicity, but with what were seen as "old" and "outdated" ways of thinking and being. In short, there was the emergence of two local orders of indexicality (Malay and ethnic languages), each with their own centers of normativity.

2.4 Widening Social Domains in the Late Colonial Period

Semiotic registers that had within their category of signs linguistic forms, region, and ethnicity continued to be recirculated in the early twentieth century. Among other things, this occurred as a byproduct of continued colonial practices that related to the administration and running of a plantation economy. Importantly, the mediation of these practices and discourses was made possible through the continued introduction of wave after wave of new technology during this period, each of which seemed to recirculate ideas relating to ethnicity and language, while also speeding up the rate at which encounters with sameness and difference occurred.

As with other European colonies (Weidman, 2010), we might expect that each type of technology also facilitated distinct encounters with sameness and difference. For example, Mrázak (2002: 17–18) points out that after World War I, lorries, motor vehicles, and buses that were increasingly common in Java also increased the speed in which encounters happened compared with older horse-and-cart technologies. This was also the case for electric trams in the cities, steam-powered boats and trains, and, importantly, their stations and stops. In addition, traveling theaters, circuses, radio, phonograph, and colonial expeditionary engineering surveys were all sites of encounters with sameness and difference (Cohen, 2006; Mrázak, 2002; Suryadi, 2006). These encounters resulted in metasemiotic commentaries of one type or another, which recirculated ideas about the links among linguistic forms, place, and social type.

In the case of the traveling theaters of the late nineteenth and early twentieth centuries, they not only regularly attracted audiences from all walks of life, but they also attracted commentaries and debates about social types and their language use (Cohen, 2006). Newspapers increasingly had commentaries about the (in)appropriateness of performers' language usage, commentaries about these shows' representation of ethnic and stratifiable "others," and commentaries about the moral characteristics of their audiences (Cohen, 2006). The promotion of phonographic "indigenous" music by traveling intellectuals also attracted commentaries in newspapers that linked these songs with regions and ethnic social types (Suryadi, 2006: 296). Thus, with the creation of new social domains (e.g., theaters, spaces for listening to and discussing music, and so on), there was a recirculation of ideas about ethnic social types speaking particular languages, while associating these social types with other semiotic forms, such as clothing and music.

An increase in discourses of difference through encounters with the "ethnic other" also increased in line with the increase of train and tram passengers. Between 1901 and 1909, there were in the vicinity of 900,000 passengers using these networks. An increasing number of passengers were also Muslims (Mrázek, 2002: 10–13). Some of their travel was to attend meetings in mosques about religion and nationalism that may have also involved those from linguistically different areas of Java and the archipelago. By 1932, the first indigenous radio station was established, and by 1941, there were twenty local radio stations with subscriber numbers growing to 100,000 (Mrázek, 2002: 165–182). These stations often played material associated with the ethnic other. For example, Mrázek (2002: 186–189) points out that in 1942, the sounds of Javanese shadow puppets and gamelan music performances were regularly aired on radio.

In addition to being dependent on telecommunications and transportation infrastructure, the running of a plantation economy was dependent on non-European labor and often systems of forced labor. Where Sumatran plantations were concerned, contract labor was imported from Java from 1905 until the end of the colonial period (Hardjono, 1977). For example, in 1905, just 155 Javanese families were moved to Lampung in South Sumatra, but by 1941, there were nearly 174,000 government- sponsored migrants from Java who were living in this area, and 23,600 living in Sulawesi (Hardjono, 1977: 16–18). In another area, the northeast coast of Sumatra, the population of Javanese migrant workers brought to work on the tea, rubber, and palm oil plantations increased tenfold from 50,000 in 1911 to 500,000 in 1930 (Stoler, 1995a: 30–35). As Stoller (1995a: 35–36) notes, many of the workers who were able to escape the exploitive indentured labor system did not return to Java. Instead, they lived and worked in marginal positions on the peripheries of these plantations, in nearby villages, or in the newly emerging towns and cities. Typically, they worked as unskilled laborers or sharecroppers for indigenous Malays, Bataks, or Chinese traders (1995a: 35–36).

In addition to aiding in the genesis of new locally emergent semiotic registers among people within these contact settings (Errington, 2001: 29), we might expect that the type of encounters between local indigenous populations and contract laborers may have also led to the production of discourses of difference. For example, the fights that broke out between Javanese migrants and Chinese contract laborers over Javanese women tricked into prostitution (Stoler, 1995a: 31–33) helped associate these registers with appropriate or normative ways of interaction in these communities. These conflictual interactions may well have resulted in the recirculation of ethnic stereotypes too. Whatever the case, the rapid increase in these migrant populations would have also significantly increased the visibility of difference, while also requiring the development of numerous local registers for communication that were based on fragments of linguistic forms used and ratified in these locales. While locally valued, these emergent registers were at the bottom of an emerging hierarchy of registers (e.g., Dutch, Malay, ethnic languages, local mixed language).

In summary, what seems to become clear is that with the introduction of each technology, new social domains emerged. Even so, it seems that each of these new sites had several factors in common. First, each new site facilitated encounters with difference. Second, the rate at which this occurred seemed to also increase. Third, each of these encounters had the potential to generate local registers, local centers of normativity, and discourses of difference, which in many cases would have helped recirculate ideologies that linked linguistic forms with conduct, region, ethnic social type, and social value. While these are questions awaiting future research, based on what we know about processes of enregisterment more generally (section 2.2), we can assume that the make-up of each semiotic register that resulted from these processes would have been quite different in each locale. For example, where indentured laborers were concerned, their discourses of difference may not have followed the language-ethnicity discourses being propagated by the Dutch colonial regime, those found in elite schools, or those found among transnational university students. In the following section, I look at some of these discourses as a way of tracing how signs from some of the emerging semiotic registers discussed thus far were recirculated during this late colonial period via oral and print-based mediums.

2.5 Discourses of Nationalism in the Late Colonial Period

A close reading of the work of Indonesia area specialists highlights the existence of many other social domains where such discourses of difference circulated, including schools and foreign universities. Elson (2008: 7–18) observes that during the period from 1912 to 1922, a handful of Dutch intellectuals, Dutch-educated Indonesians, Indonesian student groups studying abroad, and political parties started to discuss different unification systems, ethnic groups, and independence. In the case of overseas students, these discussions were made possible through the formation of self-help groups. Through interactions with other students, these sojourners discovered that there were other groups living in the Dutch East Indies (Elson, 2008: 21). Ethnicity as a category was thus reproduced through such dialogues, which differentiated ethnic states and regional-based ethnic groupings from the idea of Indonesia.

By 1920, these students, who were from royal and privileged backgrounds and typically knew both Dutch and Malay, were also involved in writing for and publishing their own journals (Elson, 2008: 25–26). In much of the writing found in these journals, the terms "Indonesia" and "Indonesians" started to be used, and these were contrasted with ethnic groups, such as Javanese, Minahasen, and so on. Although from 1912 on, there were many ethnic associations formed—including associations of people from Ambon, Sumatra, Jakarta, Sunda, and Madura—nevertheless, by 1920, thinking and writing about ethnic groups gave way to ideas about "one people" and "one nation" through discourses that noted the need to put an independent Indonesia on the political agenda (Elson, 2008: 31–32). In so doing, a new hierarchy was being created whereby citizens of an imagined Indonesia would become more socially valued than its ethnic components.

As Elson (2008: 38–46) goes on to note, these ideas were more widespread than in just intellectual circles, and by 1918, ideas about different ethnic groups were circulating in newspapers, while at the same time, Indonesia was constructed as a grouping of ethnic regions. These ideas could also start to be found across the political spectrum with figures from the nascent Indonesian communist party (PKI) also reproducing ethnic social types through writings that noted that a new Indonesian state would best be built upon autonomous local communities (Elson, 2008: 51).

Ideas linking ethnic social types, region, and language could also be found in some of Indonesia's first "modern" novels, which were published by small private publishers and the colonial publisher Balai Pustaka. One such novel—which according to Teeuw (1972: 117) later became the most loaned library book in pre-World War II Dutch East Indies—was *Sitti Nurbaya* written by Marah Roesli and published in 1922. In terms of ethnicity, the heroes of the story, Samsu and Sitti, were geographically anchored to an area called Minang, located in Sumatra. While most of their represented talk among themselves and with other characters was in literary Malay (as would be expected given Balai Pustaka's explicit goal of standardizing and propagating this register), there was some use of other linguistic forms that were anchored to place throughout the story.

For example, at the start of the story, eighteen-year-old Samsu grumbles at his carriage driver Ali, who is late picking up Samsu and Sitti on this occasion. Ali replies as follows (note that the orthography is not in use today; now the older forms "dj" and "nja" are respectively "j" and "nya"; boldface highlights the forms to be analyzed):

Extract 2.5.1 Associating linguistic forms with place in the novel *Sitti Nurbaya*

Engku muda djanganlah marah! Bukannja sengadja **hamba** terlambat.
Young boss don't be mad. **I** [your humble servant] wasn't purposely late.

(Roesli, 1965 [1922]: 6)

Roesli footnotes the term of address, *engku muda*, as a local term of address for persons of high social position or title. We can also see the use of the self-effacing term of reference, *hamba*, which although not specifically Minang, was different from other terms of reference used in other parts of Indonesia. Both terms of address and reference used above were also regularly differentiated from how Samsu and Sitti addressed each other. Typically, reference to the co-present other would be through the use of a shortened first name, *kau* or a suffixed form *mu*, while self-reference was *aku* or a suffixed form *ku*. Just as importantly, ethnic social types were explicitly tied to language in one of Samsu's letters to Sitti. In one of these letters, which was written when he first started studying at the Javanese Doctor School in Jakarta, he notes that there are Sundanese, Javanese,

Batak, Ambonese, Pelembangese, Madurese, Menadonese, and Jakartan students who sing all types of songs in all type of languages (Roesli, 1965 [1922]: 108). In addition to helping to enregister local ethnic languages through metasemiotic commentary, the primary use of Malay in the novel also helped to regiment its superior position to ethnic registers.

Signs from semiotic registers associated with ethnic social types continued to circulate in the 1920s and 1930s. This helped solidify these registers while also being indexed with new signs, especially nationalism (in the case of Indonesian) and a bounded geographic area increasingly talked about as Indonesia. At the same time, slightly negative associations were being made with regional ethnic registers and their speakers. Elson (2008: 59–64), for example, points out that from 1926 onward, more radical nationalist anti-colonial groups had solidified, and part of their discourse related to the way provincialism held back unity and an independent Indonesia. These groups became political parties whose membership increased toward 20,000 by the mid-1930s (Elson, 2008: 84–85). We might expect that with increases in membership and meetings there was also a widening of the social domain of these discourses.

At one such meeting—the 1928 Youth Congress—participants proposed that Indonesian should be the language of Indonesia and put it forth as the language of a growing anti-colonial movement and an independent Indonesian state (e.g., Abas, 1987; Alisjahbana, 1976; Anwar, 1980; Dardjowidjojo, 1998; Foulcher, 2000). Just as important, this pledge contrasted with an implied set of regional registers and their associated ethnic social types. At subsequent congresses and meetings involving some of the participants of the 1928 Congress, a register of Malay was increasingly seen as the appropriate means of public address (Foulcher, 2000). In 1938, the Greater Indonesia Party (PARINDRA) instructed its members to use only Indonesian when making public statements (Mrázek, 2002: 33). Of course, this distinction implied regional registers and thus also indirectly helped recirculate the idea of regional registers being spoken by ethnic social types. In addition, this distinction also helped to further regiment hierarchical relations between Malay and ethnic languages while also regimenting their relationships to different centers of normativity, in this case Indonesian with a privileged nationalist thinking elite and ethnic languages with those who were uneducated, indifferent, or against a unified non-Dutch Indonesia.

As Elson (2008: 65–66) points out, and as represented in Roesli's (1965 [1922]) novel, schooling opportunities in Jakarta also brought together people from throughout the archipelago. In these settings, the routinization of encounters with difference may have also contributed to the recirculation of ideas relating to Indonesian as the language of a nascent Indonesia and ethnic social types speaking a multitude of registers found in the regions. These settings would have also required the use and ratification of fragments of Malay and local registers among those of differing backgrounds. While we don't have any evidence of actual conversations in these school settings, reference to some of the novels of the early 1930s provides some representations of language use in these settings. For example, in the novel *Si Doel Anak Betawi* (Aman, 1971[1932]), the young male hero of the story, Doel, finally gets his wish to go to primary school. In this novel, Doel not only comments to his parents that the other kids are Sundanese and Javanese, but he talks of these kids using Indonesian with a Sundanese accent (Aman, 1971[1932]: 102–105), and he actually reports the Sundanese talk (in bold) of a Sundanese female student when speaking with his Javanese teacher, as in extract 2.5.2.

Extract 2.5.2 Outsider's reported talk in the novel *Si Doel Anak Betawi*

"**Abdi gaduh** adi **tilu**, entjik"
I have three siblings, miss (to the teacher)

(Aman, 1971[1932]: 104)

This particular story and the linguistic forms found within it deserve some more attention because of how it reproduces ethnic stereotypes, models distinction, and regiments hierarchical relations between local ethnic languages and Malay. Loven (2008: 17–18) points out that this Balai Pustaka novel was written by Aman, who migrated from West Sumatra to Jakarta and worked at Balai Pustaka. Aman was fascinated by the different lifestyle and language of his "Betawi" neighbors and noted that the source of his story was observations of one of his neighbor's children and their language usage (Loven, 2008). Indeed, Aman (1971[1932]: 5) specifically notes in his foreword to the novel that the dialogue involving the hero of the story, Doel, was in what he termed "Betawi language," and that he did this as a way of acquainting readers from outside of Batavia (now Jakarta) with the language of the Betawi community. In so doing, he not only recirculated ideas about the associations among linguistic forms, social types, and a specific geographical space, but he also differentiated Malay from a local named language (Betawi).

For example, he provides the following orthographic conventions: An open "a" becomes an "e" so that a word like *ketawa* (to laugh) becomes *ketawe*; the use of suffix "kan" becomes "in" so that *sediakan* (to prepare) becomes *sediain*; the verbal prefix "ber" becomes "be"; the time adverbial *udah* (already) becomes *ude*; and so on. There also appears to be specific vocabulary that is also regularly used in represented dialogues. These include words, such as the negator *tidak/tak*, which becomes *kagak*, and kin terms, such as *Babe* (father), *Engkong* (grandfather), *Njak* (Mother), and *Mpok* (older sister). Characters are indexically anchored to this neighborhood through reference to birth or their status as original inhabitants of this neighborhood, and all are represented as speaking in Betawi. I have reproduced an example of this below in extract 2.5.3 (which still uses the orthography described in the introduction to extract 2.5.1). In extract 2.5.3, Doel is represented as speaking with his mother (Betawi forms are in bold small caps).

Extract 2.5.3 Insider's reported talk in the novel *Si Doel Anak Betawi*

Nyak

1 Doeoel! Doel Hamiiid! Eh, KEMANE lagi   Doel! Doel Hamid! Gee WHERE IS
2 DIE? Barusan disini.   HE now? [He] was just here.

Doel

3 Ja NJAK!   Yes MUM!

Nyak

4 KEMANE LU? Udah sejak NJAK manggil,   WHERE ARE YOU? I have been calling
5 LU diam-diam ADJE. Pulang dulu DAHAR   [you], but you JUST haven't ans-
                                            wered. Come home now and EAT
6 nasi, nasi udah NJAK SEDIAIN!   some rice, I'VE already PREPARED it!

(Aman, 1971[1932]: 9)

Just as important, and in line with broader colonial policy on the need to imbue characters with colonial-sanctioned ideas about morality (Moriyama, 2005b), the characters in the story are associated with particular types of demeanors (Goffman, 1967), as well as economic abilities, social practices, and educational backgrounds. For example, Doel, his neighborhood peers, his late father, and his grandfather are all represented as hard-working, quick-tempered, and never afraid of getting into a fight. Doel and his late father are additionally represented as social types who are valorous, especially when defending their friends' honor. Doel's grandfather is represented as an "old-fashioned" Muslim and an "unkind" and "stingy" social type who will not allow his daughter to work in a shop where men come to buy goods. This is despite him not being willing to support his daughter financially after her husband's death. All people living within this neighborhood are also represented as poor and uneducated, but reasonably pious Muslims. This is especially the case for Doel, his parents, and grandparents. Both Doel and his mother are also represented as persons who obeyed the wishes of their parents even when these wishes were unreasonable.

There are a number of other contrasts throughout the story that also build upon emerging ethnic social types. For example, during the fasting month, Doel is represented as diligently fasting and studiously reading the Al-Quran while other Muslim neighbors do not. Doel's stepfather is also described as an outsider who speaks Malay, but whose accent is hard to place, possibly from Banjarmasin or Medan. The attitude of Doel's stepfather also contrasts markedly with that of his deceased biological father and his grandfather. The former encourages and supports Doel in his wishes to attend school, while the latter two see no utility in attending school. In summary, the association of place, morality, education, and economics with persons who speak in particular registers (in contrast to others who speak only in Malay registers) helped in the recirculation of ideas about ethnic social types who speak in regional registers. Social differentiation and the regimentation of social value to create orders of indexicality were achieved through the storytelling mechanisms used by the author whose representation of everything but the speech of characters was done in Malay.

This way of representing difference can also be found in other novels from the late colonial period. Brief reference to Teeuw's (1994) work on literature during this period shows at least three novels. The novel *Kintamani*, written by Iman Supardi and published by a private publishing house in 1932, is about a romance between a Javanese boy and a Balinese girl (Teeuw, 1994: 77). Many of the novels written in the 1920s and 1930s also had Minang people traveling to Java and/or marriage between people from different regions, as in the novel *Salah Asuhan*, written by Abdul Muis and published in 1928 (Teeuw, 1994: 69–71).

While it is clear that regional language and Malay language newspapers and magazines were circulating in areas such as Minangkabau in West Sumatra (Biezeveld, 2007: 212), more research is required to establish whether the type of regional language schoolbooks found in earlier colonial times continued to be used during this late colonial period. What is much clearer is that Malay and its association with modernity was continuing to be circulated not just via novels and newspapers, but also throughout the bureaucracy in the form of manuals and census practices (Sneddon, 2003: 97). While continuing to have less social value than Malay and those who spoke Malay (e.g., bureaucrats), the idea of ethnicity and by extension ethnic languages was further enregistered through census practices, such as the 1930 census that divided the population into sixteen ethnic groups, others, and Chinese (Suryadinata et al., 2003: 12).

Ideas about ethnic social types and their associated semiotic registers continued to be recirculated throughout the late 1930s through discourses about how to best go about forming a new nation. Elson (2008: 66–67) points out that by this time, it became increasingly clear to nationalist leaders that regional organizations were a manifestation of colonial policies of divide and rule. Yet, as he notes, there were also fears of unequal treatment at the hands of a Javanese majority in a new Indonesia. Citing a Minahasan reporter writing in 1938, Elson (2008: 68–70) points out how this reporter wrote about the importance of maintaining Minahasan language as a way of distinguishing Minahasans and their history from other Indonesians. At the same time, there were also calls for a federalist model that would recognize the differences within Indonesia and allow each region to govern itself. Groups of intellectuals and members of a literary movement (Pujangga Baru) also engaged in dialogue about how to make an Indonesian culture (Elson, 2008: 72). This, of course, allowed for essentializing contrasts between "Indonesian culture" and "regional culture," which also fit with the more general creation of orders of indexicality. Some Islamic movements were also active in talking about an Indonesian unity that was above place-based groupings. For example, in Islamic schools in Aceh, a conscious decision had been made to use a register of Malay as the language of schooling rather than another local register (Elson, 2008: 82).

Just as important, the large internal structural changes that were occurring in the Netherlands East Indies economy as a result of the 1930s depression also changed the way labor moved throughout the archipelago. Dick (2002: 160) points out that during the depression years, there was a collapse in the plantation industries of copra, sugar, tea, and rubber. Such a collapse would have slowed down the encounters with difference that characterized the earlier years of these industries described in the previous sections. At the same time, the textile industry in Java was booming, with some factories in Surabaya employing as many as 4,000 women by 1938 (Dick, 2002: 160–161). Similarly, in West Java during the late 1930s, the setting-up of automobile, shoe, tire, electrical goods, and food factories described by Dick (2002: 160–161) may well have brought together workers from different areas of Java, especially given the provision of transport infrastructure described in previous sections.

Like religious settings where religious scholars and leaders from throughout the archipelago met, these sites also produced labor movements that organized (Ford, 2008), perhaps with some members from around the archipelago coming together for congresses, meetings, and so on. Such settings would have represented new sites for encounters with difference. These encounters were all potential sites for the recirculation of the social types and semiotic registers discussed thus far. Such contact may have produced new locally emergent semiotic registers and centers of normativity that sat in contrast to the multiple centers of normativity associated with ethnic languages and varieties of Malay. As with contact among plantation workers in the early 1900s, however, this aspect of diversity requires future research.

In concluding this section, I should point out that speaking a regional language during the late colonial period was not always the only index pointing to an ethnic social type. The anthropologist de Jong (2009) points out that in places such as Sulawesi, ethnic groupings were in a continuous state of flux and were religiously based. For example, he points out that Calvinist missionaries in cooperation with the colonial administration and elites from areas of Central Sulawesi helped in the formation of one ethnic group based on Christianity. I should also point out that apart from the library-borrowing figures provided by Teeuw (1972), we know little about how readers interpreted the novels discussed in this section. While searches for commentaries about these novels in newspaper archives held in the Netherlands and Indonesia might go some way toward seeing whether and to what extent signs associated with these social types and semiotic registers were recirculated, this interesting aspect will have to be left until funding and time permit. Even so, I hope that my account so far paints a complex picture of the processes and infrastructure involved in the enregisterment of several competing semiotic registers and their associated social types. I also hope it has pointed out some of the continuities with earlier colonial times, especially the continuing association of linguistic forms with region and ethnic social type, Malay with knowledge, regime, and state, and the hierarchical ordering of these semiotic registers.

2.6 The Japanese Occupation

During the Japanese occupation, the idea of ethnic social types from the colonial period was recirculated (e.g., T. Inoue, 1986: 203). The policies, practices, and discourses of the Japanese and Indonesians working with them helped to recirculate ideas that associated language with region and ethnic social types, on the one hand, and nation with Indonesian on the other. As in the earlier colonial years, this was not in any way uniform and was partly a result of the Dutch East Indies being occupied by different sections of the Japanese military, with Sumatra and Java being controlled by different chapters of the army while the eastern parts of Indonesia were under the auspices of the navy (Elson, 2008; Reid & Akira, 1986; Ricklefs, 1981).

While variability in Japanese regulations about people movement did initially cause problems for students from the outer islands to continue or commence their education in Java, with the help of some Japanese administrators, this movement was facilitated in the later parts of the war (Shigetada, 1986: 264–265). In addition, as with the transmigration programs undertaken from 1905, the Japanese also moved approximately 150,000 Javanese around the archipelago (Colombijn, 1996: 394; Shizuo, 1986: 249–250), as well as approximately 2.6 million Javanese within the island of Java itself (Dick, 2002: 166; Shigetada, 1986: 258). Many of them were Indonesian women who were tricked or forced into being prostitutes for the Japanese army, and it was not uncommon to find Javanese teenage girls across the archipelago in places like Ambon (Vickers, 2005: 89–90). This system of forced labor and the circulation of people that it involved also resulted in interactions among insiders and outsiders, which may have produced metasemiotic commentaries about sameness and difference, as well as routinizing settings where local semiotic registers could emerge through interaction among those who may have only shared fragments of each others' semiotic repertoires.

There were also increases of between 25 and 30 percent in rural to urban migration during the Japanese occupation (Dick, 2002: 167). This was due primarily to the better conditions in the cities, which included regular meals and escape from forced labor (Dick, 2002: 167). According to Japanese sources, indigenous leaders from all around the archipelago were also located in Java (Shunkichiro, 1986: 117). As the war drew to a close, Japanese administrators sought to actively encourage Indonesian independence. This was facilitated by helping independence leaders, such as Soekarno and Hatta, travel to the outer islands, with Soekarno famously giving a speech in Bali where he noted that he was half Balinese (Shibata, 1986). These activities, the movement of people between areas, and the attractiveness of Jakarta, Semarang, and Surabaya as sites of political power all represent settings where there was potential for encounters with difference, the emergence of local semiotic registers, and metasemiotic commentaries about such encounters.

While these localized registers emerged, other Japanese policies and practices helped to circulate the idea of ethnicity more widely. For example, the administrative rule of thumb was to use existing organizations and structures, while also respecting local customs, religions, and feudal dynasties (Shunkichiro, 1986). Indeed, while they were opposed to most things Dutch, ironically, they tended to recirculate ideas of *adat* that closely resembled those of the Dutch (Bourchier, 2007: 116). These ideas linked *adat* with history, customs, locale, and authenticity (Bourchier, 2007: 116). It is also worthwhile pointing out that some of the short stories and novels published during this period reproduced ideas of region-based ethnic social types. For example, a book titled *Djangir Bali*, written by Nur St. Iskander and published as a serial in the newspaper *Pandji Pustaka* in 1942 (Teeuw, 1994: 108), presents a romance between two characters from different ethnic groups.

Japanese education policies also played a major role in the recirculation of associations between Indonesian and nationalism. For example, the Japanese banning of the public use of Dutch thrust Malay into prominence in public domains such as administrative reports, newspapers, and schooling (Alisjahbana, 1975 [1961]: 65; Sneddon, 2003: 111). Indeed, while the Japanese wanted Japanese taught and used for all communication, in the short term, it was communicatively expedient to use Malay. At the same time, access to schooling was expanded. For example, in places under navy control, such as Sulawesi and Bali, schools were opened to all levels of society and resulted in large increases in student numbers when compared to pre-occupation Indonesia (Okada, 1986: 154; Suzuki, 1986). In army-controlled Sumatra, however, education seemed more selective, with only certain students being allowed to study in Japanese-sponsored schools (Otsuka, 1986). The use of Malay for propaganda and as a language of instruction in some schools together with the increased use of Indonesian flags, the broadcast of an Indonesian anthem through local loudspeakers, and the circulation of newspapers written in local Malay continued to associate Malay with nationalism and ideas of a nation and a place called Indonesia (Elson, 2008: 101–103; Ricklefs, 1981: 190). Without archival research of newspapers published in this period or interviews with those who listened to or read these mediatized messages, it is hard to determine whether and to what extent there were actually readers and listeners. Indeed, given that competence to comprehend the different registers of Malay was fragmented and truncated—and primarily limited to intellectuals and those who acted as intermediaries between locals and the Dutch in prewar Indonesia—the social domain of these texts would have been quite small.

Leaving aside the important issue of reception, political discourses also continued to play a role in the recirculation of signs and their associated semiotic registers, especially those linking regional registers with ethnic social types and Malay with nationalism. As Elson (2008: 103) point outs, after September 1944, the Japanese premier announced Japan's intentions to grant Indonesia independence. These discourses and those that recirculated ideas about regions and Indonesia were repeated through deliberations at the committee for the investigation of independence (PBUPK) in May 1945, when they talked about whether an independent Indonesia should be a federation of regions (Elson, 2008: 105–106). News of the declaration of Indonesian independence on August 17, 1945 (an Indonesia that was to be made up of Java and the regions) was quickly circulated throughout the archipelago via the telegraph and radio network that had become heavily utilized during the Japanese occupation (Vickers, 2005: 97).

The 1945 constitution, which was drawn up during this period, respected and protected the traditions and rights of the regions (Elson, 2008: 114). This not only authorized links between a new named language, Indonesian, and a new Indonesia, but it also authorized links among ethnic social types, regions, and certain linguistic forms. For example, chapter 11 of the constitution was about regional governments; chapter 15 (article 36) was about the national language; and an addendum to article 36 related to the preservation of regional languages. The constitution also legalized an order of indexicality whereby regional languages were subordinate to the national language. Although these ideas were now enshrined constitutionally, it was only in force for around half of the period that Soekarno was president of Indonesia. More specifically, the Indonesian constitution was in force for the period between 1945 and 1949, and then not in force for ten years until 1959 (Ellis, 2002: 8).

2.7 The Soekarno Period

Similar to the time periods discussed in the previous sections, the period between 1945 and 1966 was characterized by changes in technology, infrastructure, and political relations, all of which figured in the recirculation of ideas linking linguistic forms with social types, place, and ultimately the formation and reproduction of orders of indexicality. This period has been characterized as one when infrastructure actually deteriorated in comparison to the prewar period (Colombijn, 1996; Ricklefs, 1981). Colombijn (1996: 394–395) points out that in West Sumatra, transport infrastructure declined and 80 percent of plantations closed down. At the same time, there was little investment in shipping and heavy industry, and this did not change until the mid-1960s (Dick, 2002: 188–189). Even so, these changes did create new social domains for encounters with difference and for the recirculation of ideas that linked region, language, and ethnic social types. As we will see, however, ideas about ethnicity were constructed and evaluated differently than in the past. In this section, I roughly follow the periodization used by many historians who generally break the time between 1945 and 1966 into three periods: the revolutionary period (1945–1949), parliamentary democracy (1950–1958), and guided democracy (1959–1966).

During the four-year period in which many autonomous groups of Indonesians fought their former colonial masters for a new independent Indonesia, there were changes in infrastructure that also changed the patterns of population circulation and ultimately the circulation of ideas and discourses about sameness and difference. Large-scale people movement among the islands was restricted because most of the modern ships used for inter-island trade had been sunk by the Allies during the war (Dick, 2002: 168). The only large-scale contact among peoples during this period were skirmishes in Sulawesi between Indonesian Republican soldiers and pro-Dutch Ambonese soldiers (Ricklefs, 1981: 221). As Dick (2002: 169) points out, the closing of factories and the reduction in the use of road and rail due to sabotage and movements of Indonesian independence fighters also meant that these sites were less likely to be sites of encounter, as they had been in pre-World War II times. This pattern continued due to increasing perversions in foreign exchange, black market operations, and a decreasing taxation base (Dick, 2002: 174–175). While there was a push for large industrialization projects such as cement factories, cotton spinning, and rubber re-milling, many of the migrants entering cities went into petty trade and hawking (Dick, 2002: 177). Although this produced different social domains for encounters with difference, the routinization of these types of encounters among particular groups of participants would also have produced locally emergent semiotic registers, together with commentaries about such registers and their speakers.

In the social domain of elite political discourses, ideas about what form a post-Japanese Indonesia would take came from Indonesian nationalists and the Dutch who wanted to re-colonize Indonesia. In so doing, there was often a recirculation of older ideas about regions and, with this, ideas about ethnic social types. One concrete manifestation of this ideology could be seen in the formation of the Komite National Indonesia Pusat (Central Indonesian National Committee), which was charged with advising President Soekarno and his cabinet. According to Kahin (1970 [1952]: 140), this committee included leaders of ethnic groups from the regions outside of Java because of concerns about representation. In addition, the predecessor of this committee, the Independence Preparatory Committee, decreed on August 19, 1945, that Indonesia be divided into eight provinces. These events and the subsequent administrative and military units that emerged as a result of this decree also contributed to the recirculation of earlier ideas relating to region (Kahin, 1970 [1952]: 141).

Similarly, the burgeoning number of political parties that formed at the end of 1945 often did so along religious grounds, which also indexed region and ethnicity. For example, the Christian parties had strong bases of support in Sumatra, Flores, Timor, and Ambon (Kahin, 1970 [1952]: 158). As issues of representation within the Central Indonesian National Committee reemerged in late 1946, Soekarno oversaw a fivefold increase in the number of members from the outer islands (Kahin, 1970 [1952]: 200–201). This helped keep ideas of region and ethnicity circulating in bureaucratic domains while also strengthening these regions as normative centers within a polycentric system. Large-scale encounters with difference also occurred in late 1947 as an estimated six million refugees from both West and East Java fled from Dutch military forces to republican-held areas in Central Java (Kahin, 1970 [1952]: 221; Vickers, 2005: 108). The routinization of encounters that would have accompanied this type of people displacement would also have produced many locally emergent semiotic registers along with metasemiotic commentaries about these encounters.

Between 1947 and 1948, the Dutch helped establish many states—including West Borneo, Madura, East Java, Pasunden, South Sumatra, and East Sumatra—which were to become part of a Dutch federal system of government (Legge, 1961: 4). The Dutch described Irian Jaya as having very different people than in other areas of the Dutch East Indies, and this was the basis for not including this area in any settlement with the Indonesian revolutionary government (Elson, 2008: 145). While within the revolutionary government there were differences of opinion and levels of resolve to include Irian in a new Indonesia (Elson, 2008: 146), what is important here is that these discussions helped to contribute to the recirculation of ideas linking language, region, ethnic social type, and difference.

In Yogyakarta, the sultan was promoting the use of Indonesian rather than Javanese as the language of official communication (Ricklefs, 1981: 208), which also reproduced orders of indexicality, with Indonesian sitting above Javanese. Legge's (1961: 29) account of governance also shows that in bureaucratic and legal domains, the promulgation of Law 22 of 1948, which related to powers of governance and autonomy at the provincial, *kabupaten* (district), and *desa* (village) levels, also helped keep the idea of "regions" and "local" circulating. Indeed, it was specifically designed to accommodate feelings of regional and cultural identity, while reducing grounds for fearing Javanese dominance in the fledgling state (Legge, 1961: 35).

As anti-Dutch sentiment rose throughout Indonesia in the 1950s, an increasing number of Dutch-owned businesses were taken over by local trade unions (Dick, 2002: 184). By 1958, over one thousand businesses had been taken over by primarily communist-dominated trade unions. The military fearing this economic dominance took over these enterprises, which essentially finished a process of nationalization (Dick, 2002: 185). In so doing, the army often inserted "ethnic others" into the local milieu of these enterprises (Ricklefs, 1981: 249). The majority of army officers, for example, were primarily from small cities around Java (Crouch, 1988: 36–37; Rinakit, 2005: 16). In West Java, the presence of army and air force personnel in villages also produced encounters in which villagers commented upon the odd behaviors of these outsiders (Palmer 1959: 48). Similarly, in places like Central Java, the presence of teachers and doctors described by Geertz (1960) may also have invited such metasemiotic commentaries.

New social domains for encounters with difference were also created in areas outside of Java with the increased presence of administrative and military units from Java (Legge, 1961: 39; Skinner, 1959: 4–5). These new social domains would have not only provided occasions for the recirculation of ideas about region, ethnic social types, and difference, but also the conditions necessary for the routinization of social interaction and with it the production of many locally emergent semiotic registers. For example, on the island of Sumbawa, the presence of bureaucrats from the central government helped set up a contrast between local and national (Goethals, 1959: 19). This distinction foregrounded regional-ethnic identity as compared with the Indonesian-speaking outsider bureaucrats, who made claims to a new type of identity: that of a modern Indonesian bureaucrat bent on developing the "underdeveloped" areas of Indonesia (Goethals, 1959: 19). In so doing, orders of indexicality were also being formed and reproduced in areas outside of the administrative and political center. The effects were similar in many ways to those found in Java, where an Indonesian-speaking elite positioned and evaluated themselves as exemplary models of Indonesian-ness while ethnic others were the opposite.

In addition to encounters with Javanese bureaucrats and military personnel, a fledgling transmigration program was also increasing the presence of outsiders in the outer islands. This program was an attempt to cope with the overpopulation problems experienced in Java and Bali where populations had grown by over 25 percent in ten years (Ricklefs, 1981: 225). While Hardjono (1977: 22–30) has characterized this program as largely unsuccessful and overoptimistic in terms of targets (often in the millions), nevertheless, between 1950 and 1965, there were nearly 400,000 farmers from Bali and Java who were moved to other areas of the archipelago under this scheme. As with the late colonial period, this transmigration would have created new social domains for encounters with difference and potentially for the (re)circulation of ideas about ethnic social types and the conditions necessary for the emergence of local semiotic registers. Similarly, rural-urban migration also created many opportunities for encounters with the other, and thus settings in which new local semiotic registers could emerge.

By the early 1950s, conflicts between the central government in Jakarta and its counterparts in the regions were increasingly frequent. These conflicts emerged around issues of how exports and imports were to be taxed (Dick, 2002: 180), and around issues of Islam and political representation (Ricklefs, 1981: 235). Within the regions, the sentiment ranged from a feeling of neglect by the center (Elson, 2008: 187) to suspicions of those in Jakarta and Java using this income for expanding the bureaucracy in Jakarta and for luxury consumption (Dick, 2002: 180). These sentiments developed into calls for regional autonomy and splits within the army in places such as the Mollucas, Sulawesi, and Sumatra (Dick, 2002: 180). With the covert support of the U.S., which feared the growth of the Indonesian communist party in Java, these splits developed into a full-blown rebellion by 1958 (Dick, 2002: 181). Calls for separatism also arose in Padang (Sumatra), although this was due to a fear of being overrun by Toba Bataks who were migrating from North Sumatra rather than because of unequal taxation arrangements (Elson, 2008: 167). This rebellion produced many refugees who settled across the archipelago taking up jobs as petty traders, food stall operators, and restaurant owners (Hedman, 2008b: 9–10). Similarly, in 1957, South Kalimantan was split in two—becoming South and Central Kalimantan—in order to diffuse separatist calls by Dayaks who felt that they were being overwhelmed by lowland Muslims (Miles, 1976).

Meanwhile, the Darul Islam movement, which consisted of loosely organized but connected rebellions that pushed for an Islamic state in West Java, Aceh, and South Sulawesi, also required military intervention from Jakarta (Ricklefs, 1981). In many cases, soldiers from Java were sent to these outer islands to quell the rebellions with force (Bruner, 1959: 52; Elson, 2008: 196; Ricklefs, 1981: 251). At the same time that military "others" entered primarily rural areas of West Java, the number of refugees who fled from these areas of conflict to urban areas increased, with numbers fluctuating between 50,000 to 300,000 persons a year between 1951 and 1962 (Hedman, 2008b: 9). Similarly, the Darul Islam movement in Sulawesi and Aceh displaced a further 350,000 people between 1953 and 1955 (Hedman, 2008b: 9). All of these mobilizations, confrontations, and displacements created further social domains for contact with difference on a large scale, while also attaching negative traits to the ethnic other.

For example, within village communities in Java, there was a strong sense of fear about escalation of these interethnic conflicts and tensions, and a fear of the ethnic other (C. Geertz, 1959; Palmer, 1959). During the early 1950s, interethnic conflicts were also developing in the major cities of Java where migrants were increasingly competing for scarce government jobs, with charges of ethnic favoritism and corruption being raised against different groups (Ricklefs, 1981; Skinner, 1959: 7–10; Vickers, 2005). It was thus not surprising to hear of villagers who perceived the city as a place of conflict where ethnic ties were to be used to get white-collar jobs (Palmer, 1959: 48–49).

This fear of the ethnic other, interethnic conflict, military mobilization, and people displacement was a constant theme in the 1960s. In the mid-1960s, Javanese soldiers were mobilized in the campaign for Irian Jaya and in the confrontation with Malaysia in Kalimantan (Ricklefs, 1981: 258–264). The confrontation with Malaysia, which was largely run from the cities of Sambas and Pontianak in West Kalimantan, set the stage for future conflict between indigenous Dayak and Indonesians of Chinese ancestry, and also conflict between Dayaks and Madurese migrants (Davidson, 2008). As Davidson points out, in the aftermath of the Malaysian confrontation, Indonesians of Chinese ancestry were forcibly moved by the military with the help of Dayak paramilitary forces that were trained to help in the confrontation period. The empty spaces left by the 75,000 people who were moved from rural areas to the city to help counter a perceived communist rebellion were then occupied by Madurese migrants, who from 1967 onward had frequent conflicts with local Dayaks over land and economic rights (Davidson, 2008).

Ideas about language and ethnic social types also continued to circulate within political parties and the bureaucracy during the 1950s, although the social value of ethnicity seemed to be contested. For example, regional leaders saw shared language as a sign of ethnic group membership that could be used to gather support for their efforts to gain more autonomy vis-à-vis the Jakartan political elite, while the Jakartan political elite (including Soekarno and then-Colonel Soeharto) saw ethnicity as a threat to the fledgling Indonesian state (Elson, 2008: 179–180; Feith, 1962: 522). Indeed, regionalism and ethnicity were matters for serious and sustained debate within the central government during the 1950s (Legge, 1961: 3). Within the provisional constitution of 1950, for example, a wide ranging autonomy was given to the regions (Legge, 1961: 9). In 1956, sustained debate culminated in Law 1 of 1957 that related to revisions of earlier regional autonomy legislation and laws (Legge, 1961: 60–61). This law remained in force until 1959 when Soekarno instigated a period of guided democracy (Elson, 2008: 218), which included the stationing of more Javanese bureaucrats in the regions (Legge, 1961: 60–61).

Liddle's (1972) account of the party system in northern Sumatra in the early to mid-1960s also shows how ideas of ethnicity, language, and religion were not only recirculated as part of party politics, but how these ideas became associated with particular political parties. For example, the modernist Islamic party, Masjumi, attracted many South Tapanuli Bataks, the Christian party (Parkindo) attracted and represented the interests of the North Tapanuli Bataks, while PNI and PKI attracted many of the Javanese migrants. As the Indonesian communist party continued its rise to political ascendency in Java in the early and mid-1960s, ideas about ethnicity and region were also circulated through its congresses and in literature published by those associated with the party. For example, in his 1964 book, the party leader, Aidit, pointed out that a unitary communist Indonesia would be made up of many nationalities (Elson, 2008: 202). The Islamic political party, Masyumi, and the nationalist party, PNI, regularly held all-Indonesia congresses (Ricklefs, 1981) that also represented another social domain in which contact with difference and the ethnic other was becoming routinized.

As with the prewar period, literature and the arts continued to circulate ideas that associated regions, linguistic forms, and ethnic social types. For example, there were regionally based novels and those that had the hero(ine) traveling throughout the archipelago, such as the 1955 novel by I Made Widadi, *Kembali kepada Tuhan*, which has the hero traveling in Bali, Lombok, and Timor (Teeuw, 1996). There were also novels that used regional languages when representing the talk of some of the characters, such as Firman Muntaco's series of newspaper short stories set in Jakarta in the 1950s and republished in the early 1960s as *Gambang Djakarté* (Tadmor, 2009). In addition, although the amount of novels written in a regional language, such as Javanese and Sundanese, decreased during the Soekarno period (Quinn, 1992; Teeuw, 1996), what did circulate nevertheless explicitly linked language, region, and ethnicity.

Indeed, within some organizations—such as the Peoples' Cultural Institution (LEKRA), which supported socialist- and communist-leaning arts in their broadest sense—there was support for regional literature, arts, and culture (and support for research into these areas), along with regular dialogue among artists from around the archipelago (Foulcher, 1986). In addition, there was the formation in 1947 of a government-sponsored language center that was eventually to be housed at the University of Indonesia in Jakarta (Dardjowidjojo, 1998: 39–40). Under the direction of various ministries with education and culture in their portfolios, this language center was responsible for the planning and circulation of regional languages, such as Javanese, Sundanese, and Madurese. In short, regional literature, regular meetings among artists and writers, and academic research in these areas represented further social domains in which ideas about the links among linguistic forms, region, and ethnic social types were recirculated during the Soekarno era. Of course, normative prescriptions about what represented good language and, by extension, exemplary social types who spoke good language may well have varied from one center to another (e.g., grassroot LEKRA circles and elite higher education).

The import of these ideas would have also been strengthened through contrasts with an emergent national language, Indonesian, which increasingly circulated as school participation rates increased, both in Islamic (*pesantren* and *madrasah*) and government schools (Ricklefs, 1981: 226; Soedijarto et al., 1980: 62). Increases in school participation rates were impressive despite issues of uniform access to schooling throughout the archipelago (Bruner, 1959: 53; H. Geertz, 1959: 28; Goethals, 1959: 20; Palmer, 1959: 47–48). While absenteeism and statistic reliability invite caution when viewing these figures (Soedijarto et al., 1980), between 1945 and 1960, the number of primary school and lower secondary school students increased from 2.5 million to 8.9 million and 90 thousand to 670 thousand, respectively (Bjork, 2005: 54).

Such massification also helped in the circulation of ideas about Indonesian and its relationship with Indonesia. Where schools and resources were available and where there were actually students, these schools represented two new social domains. The first was encounters among students or among students and teachers where new semiotic registers would have emerged. The second was one where ideas about ethnic social types, region, and difference were circulated, often implicitly through discourses of nationalism. Palmer (1959: 48), for example, points out that tolerance of other groups was promoted in schools through children's performances of other ethnic groups' dances. In Bali and Sumatra, on the other hand, it was distinctions between local ways of doing and being and newly introduced ideas of Indonesian ways of doing and being that helped in the circulation of ideas about ethnic social types (H. Geertz, 1959). Ideas about

Indonesian and its relationship to the nation also circulated on a mass scale from the mid-1950s through other forms of schooling, such as the grassroots literacy work of an increasingly popular and well-funded Indonesian communist party. This type of work was carried out primarily in rural East and Central Java among those who were nominally Muslim (Ricklefs, 1981: 236–237).

The import of ideas about the links among linguistic forms, region, and ethnic social types were also recirculated in the print media, especially as the circulation of Indonesian language newspapers, novels, serialized short stories, and poetry increased (Dardjowidjojo, 1998; Ricklefs, 1981; Teeuw, 1996). In the six-year period between 1950 and 1956, daily newspaper circulation increased from 500,000 to close to one million, and periodical circulation trebled to over three million (Ricklefs, 1981: 226), although from 1959 to 1961, newspaper circulation dropped to around 700,000 as political censorship increased (Ricklefs, 1981: 255).

A language center based in Jakarta was charged with the planning and circulation of a standard written Indonesian, with much of its activity focusing on the standardization of orthography, the creation of a grammar, and the coining of new vocabulary (Dardjowidjojo, 1998), while dictionaries, novels, and serials were sponsored and written by private individuals or enterprises (Sneddon, 2003: 117; Teeuw, 1996: 11). Although this language center and other centers that followed developed close to 400,000 new vocabulary items, these items were only circulated among intellectuals and those interested in language and culture (Sneddon, 2003: 118), the end result being that few of these new forms found their way into regular usage.

Since Indonesian independence, radio was also becoming an increasingly important medium for the circulation of ideas about Indonesia, with over a million licensed radios in operation by 1965 (Sen & Hill, 2000: 82). This figure massively increased in the Soeharto years, when there were around 32 million radio sets sold by 1995 (Sen & Hill, 2000: 91). While sports were still something done by urbanites in the 1950s (Vickers, 2005: 129), two events figured in their increasing popularity. First, there was the regularization of interprovincial sports competitions (*PON*) that started in 1948 and were held every four years from 1953 onward (Wikipedia, 2011). The circulation of athletes in interprovincial competitions represented one further social domain for encounters with difference and the circulation of ideas about regions, language, and ethnic social types. Second, the 1962 Asian Games held in Jakarta and aired as Indonesia's first television broadcast helped repeat ideas of sports competition involving the ethnic other and ideas of unity in diversity (Kitley, 2000: 23–24; Sen & Hill, 2000: 82), while also creating a new social domain for this repetition. As Kitley (2000: 24–25) points out, the then-minister for information, Maladi, argued that television could help facilitate national unity, and this idea of television as a vehicle for national unity continued during the New Order period (sections 2.8 and 3.3).

As in the 1940s and 1950s, conflict also displaced and moved people throughout the archipelago. With reference to scholarship on more recent conflict-based displacement (e.g., Herriman, 2010; Min, 2006; Sidel, 2008), it seems likely that discourses about difference circulated during some of Indonesia's darkest days in 1965–1966 when half a million or more Indonesians died through animosities between communist party sympathizers and right-wing Islamic and military forces (Cribb, 1990; Elson, 2008; Ricklefs, 1981; Vickers, 2005). The number of people displacements during this period is unknown (Hedman, 2008b: 16), though we can be much more certain that settlement in new areas produced locally emergent semiotic registers.

In sum, changes in technology, political and bureaucratic discourses and policies, encounters with the other through sporting events, conflict, migration, transmigration, and the introduction of schooling all figured in the creation of new social domains for the recirculation of ideas that associated language, region, and ethnic social types. Just as important, many of these social domains represented settings in which local semiotic registers emerged, contributing to an increase in centers of normativity and ultimately to sociolinguistic diversity within the archipelago. During this period, ethnicity was also associated with positive in-group membership among people living in the islands around Java. However, for many living in Java, ethnicity and the ethnic other had become associated with a negative trait: that of a "troublemaker." The circulation of these registers in particular social domains also formed and reproduced many centers of normativity while also (re)producing hierarchical relations among these registers.

In closing this section, I want to point out that much of the political work done during this whole period was around the notion of how to unify and keep unified such a diverse nation. Although these ideas had many similarities with the earlier nationalist thought of the 1920s and '30s, as Elson (2008: 105–108) points out, the idea of "unity in diversity" became institutionally enshrined in the state ideology of *Pancasila* (the Five Principles), which was formulated during the Japanese occupation. These Five Principles included (1) unity of the Indonesian nation; (2) humanitarianism; (3) a nation governed by representation, deliberation, and consensus; (4) social justice; and (5) belief in one supreme god (Elson, 2008: 105–108). While this ideology meant different things at different times during the Soekarno period, in the New Order period that followed, this ideology was espoused as the *only* national ideology by the Soeharto government (Elson, 2008: 242–243).

2.8 The New Order Period

The New Order period (1966–1998) was named as such because of the new ideologies espoused by Soeharto and his followers that contrasted with Soekarno's anti-West and socialist-leaning proclivities. Rejoining Western bodies, such as the IMF, World Bank, and the United Nations, was seen as necessary given the dire condition of the Indonesian economy (Ricklefs, 1981). This period can be characterized as one concerned primarily with "development" where there was large up-scaling in the mechanisms that facilitated the circulation of ideas linking language, region, and ethnic social types. In particular, transmigration projects, economic migration, investment in education, factories, transportation, and communications all facilitated the repetition of ideologies that had been constructed in the colonial period and recirculated in various forms until the start of the New Order period. In short, during the 1966–1998 period, linguistic forms became tightly associated with particular regions and equated with ethnic social types to the extent that when Indonesians talked of themselves as speaking a regional language, such as Javanese, Sundanese, or Balinese, this also frequently pointed to the same ethnic identity.

Similarly, although ethnicity was a taboo topic due to the separatism efforts of the late 1950s, people also talked of themselves as being Javanese, Sundanese, Balinese, and so on, which typically also pointed to an ability to use the regional language of the same name. At the same time, centers of normativity were strengthened with a clear bias toward those found within the island of Java. The indexical order that emerged during this period had Indonesian at the top, followed by a Yogyakartan variety of Javanese, Sundanese, and Balinese, followed by other regional languages spoken outside of Java, and then mixed language. As will be shown in chapters 7 and 8, these ideologies had become so widespread that those socialized during this period were able to perform and comprehend signs that had become associated with other ethnic social types. As with previous sections, here I take a roughly chronological view of some of the most important social domains that (re)emerged during the New Order period to figure in the circulation of these ideologies.

During the initial period of the New Order regime in the mid-1960s, perceptions about communism contributed to the continued circulation and association of negative traits with ethnicity (Schefold, 1998). For example, groups of people in places remote to central authority were constructed as ethnic social types with weak social organizations and strange primitive ways of life that could easily fall prey to communism. Some means of addressing this perceived communist threat in its neighborhood were military operations in West Kalimantan between 1967 and 1973, and the invasion of East Timor in 1975 (Hedman, 2008b: 16; Ricklefs, 1981: 278). In addition to the displacement of over 400,000 people in West Kalimantan and East Timor between 1967 and 1979 (Davidson, 2008; Robinson, 2008), military operations involving the mass mobilization of soldiers created new social domains for encounters with difference and the recirculation of ideas about ethnic social types. After the initial invasion of East Timor, some 40,000 Indonesian troops were deployed between 1977 and 1979 (Hedman, 2008b: 17). This pattern of conflict and military and civilian movement was repeated in the late 1980s and early 1990s in Aceh, where a small independence movement was countered with some 12,000 troops (Hedman, 2008b: 19).

Another means of addressing what was seen as negative aspects of ethnicity and of continuing population growth came in the form of a reinvigorated transmigration policy. Between 1969 and 1974, this program moved nearly 200,000 people from Java, Madura, Bali, and Lombok to the outer islands that were perceived as sparsely populated and underdeveloped (e.g., Hardjono, 1977; Hoey, 2003; Hoshour, 1997; Schefold, 1998). The primary receiving areas included Sumatra, Kalimantan, Sulawesi, Maluku, and the recently incorporated Irian Jaya (e.g., Hardjono, 1977; Hoey, 2003; Hoshour, 1997; Schefold, 1998). While transmigration had been seen as an ambitious but failed project in the early years of the Indonesian nation and during the Soekarno regime (Dawson, 1992), between 1973 and 1974, the new regime had managed to move well over 100,000 people, about the same number of people moved in the 1950–1966 period (Hardjono, 1977: 32–33). This figure increased to around 800,000 between 1979 and 1990 (Dawson, 1992). As with earlier people movement (section 2.4), transmigrants regularly needed to interact with locals to trade, work, and as part of their daily lives (Dawson, 2008). In this sense, interactions in local markets with traders, government officials, and so on represented sites for interacting with the ethnic other and thus also sites for the (re)production of ideologies about ethnicity and language. At the same time, they were also sites for the creation of new languages and norms for social conduct (semiotic registers).

In some places, such as South and Central Kalimantan, this transmigration program helped turn "host" communities into minority communities, with migrants from Java and Madura representing the third or fourth largest ethnic group by the time of the 2000 census (Suryadinata et al., 2003: 24). In other places, such as Aceh and Irian Jaya, significant numbers of ethnic others were found by the time of the 2000 census (Suryadinata et al., 2003: 15–29). In Maluku and East Timor, the coming of the ethnic other also brought significant changes in the religious make-up of populations and in the make-up of the military and the bureaucracy (Elson, 2008: 253; Sidel, 2008: 39; Suryadinata et al., 2003: 110–116). As is highlighted in chapter 4, these demographic and political changes all helped to set the stage for conflict in the late 1990s.

While transmigration was designed to develop the so-called underdeveloped and under-populated peripheries, it also was thought of as a further avenue for national integration, with transmigrants helping to "civilize" other groups of people living in the outer islands (Lenhart, 1997). At the same time, there were also other approaches to the populations living in the outer islands during the 1970s and early 1980s. These might be thought of as positively evaluating ethnicity, although they were motivated by other fears, this time of Islamic fundamentalism and Islamic opposition to an increasingly corrupt government (Ricklefs, 1981: 277; Schefold, 1998:273; Vickers, 2005: 177–178). For example, rather than encouraging the proselytization of members of these groups who entered into interethnic marriages with transmigrants, more leeway was given for members of these groups to continue to practice indigenous religious beliefs. In this way, ethnicity was again valued, although if only as a counterweight to the perceived threat of Islamic fundamentalism.

In addition to transmigration, an increasingly mobile bureaucracy also aided in the circulation of people throughout the archipelago and with it encounters with difference. Essentially, this reproduced the social domains for encounters with difference established in the early 1950s. Along with transmigration, this system of transferring bureaucrats and government workers such as healthcare personnel (Alesich, 2008) continued until the end of the New Order period. The movement of bureaucrats, transmigration, and spontaneous migration continued to contribute to the development of many new locally emergent semiotic registers and to diversity in Indonesia more generally. For example, in some cases, these registers and associated social types were less based upon language-ethnicity relationships and more upon interpersonal ties at the neighborhood level (Goebel, 2010b).

Transmigration was a component of a series of five-year economic development plans, REPELITA, which sought to develop not only Java but the outer islands. Indeed, in addition to having land available for appropriation, the success of the transmigration project was partly dependent on the availability and development of appropriate infrastructure. The 1970s, 1980s, and early 1990s were periods of rapid industrialization and heavy investment and growth in manufacturing, construction, mining, transportation, communication, and service industries (Booth & McCawley, 1981; Dick, 1996; McCawley, 1981; Thee Kian Wie, 2002). Dick (1996: 28) points out that during this period, inter-island trade rapidly developed in the archipelago. Other transport infrastructure projects that facilitated encounters with difference included the increased use of airplanes, the finishing of the trans-Sumatran highway in 1985, investment in railways and roads, and the expansion of inter-island passenger ferries between 1983 and 1994 (Colombijn, 1996: 396; Cribb & Ford, 2009a: 17; Thee Kian Wie, 2002: 209). Much of the land used for these projects was obtained under questionable circumstances and often without real permission from traditional landowners, which sowed the seeds for future interethnic conflict in the late 1990s (Katoppo, 2000; Kusumaatmadja, 2000; Sangkoyo, 1999).

Where air travel is concerned, by 1994, there were regular weekly return flights to Jakarta from the cities of Medan, Pekanbaru, Palembang, Tanjung Pinang, and Batu Besar (Colombijn, 1996: 396). This period was also one of increasingly sophisticated and regular census practices. These census exercises provided another social domain for the recirculation of ideas about the relationship among linguistic forms, region, and ethnic social types. For example, although census exercises prior to 1998 did not ask for information on ethnicity, census documents still had questions asking which regional language respondents spoke (see, e.g., Muhidin, 2002; Suryadinata et al., 2003). In a sense, this represented the recirculation of implicit and government-authorized discourses about regional language-speaking ethnic social types.

Demographers commenting on the late 1960s and early 1970s have pointed out that as transportation infrastructure and trade links developed among Indonesian provinces, there was substantial economic and education-related migration from some of the outer islands to Java (Suharsono & Speare, 1981). The so-called green revolution in agriculture that wasn't fully felt in Indonesia until the mid-1970s also meant that formerly labor-intensive rice harvesting could now be done with fewer people, pushing landless laborers to the cities (Vickers, 2005: 192), whose populations nearly doubled between 1970 and 1990 (G. Jones & Hull, 1997: 2). Unemployment in rural areas together with the lure of job and education opportunities resulted in large numbers of migrants moving from rural areas to the cities of Jakarta, Surabaya, Semarang, and Medan. Indeed, within these cities, rural-urban migration contributed to between 3 and 30 percent of their population growth (Suharsono & Speare, 1981: 297).

While some of these migrants settled and lived in urban neighborhoods (Bruner, 1974), many were short-term residents seeking education and work opportunities (Suharsono & Speare, 1981). Some of these migrants ended up working in the large factories that emerged across Indonesia's cities (Suharsono & Speare, 1981: 302). Others obtained work in an ever-expanding bureaucracy; this sometimes reproduced local ethnic cleavages in cities like Medan (Bruner, 1974). These migrants also often set up self-help and other associations (Goebel, 2000). In some areas, such as Bandung, historical migration of Javanese to this Sundanese heartland had resulted in new ways of emphasizing distinction, including an increase in the growth of Sundanese societies and groups (Bruner, 1974). As with earlier periods, however, these neighborhoods, factories, government offices, secondary and higher education institutions, and transport hubs all became sites of encounter with the other. In so doing, they also became potential sites for the (re)circulation of ideas about the links among linguistic forms, region, and ethnic social types. At the same time, these encounters also produced many local semiotic registers for communication among those of different backgrounds (Goebel, 2010b).

With memories of the regional tensions of the late 1950s still in mind (see section 2.7), the Suharto government also moved to look at identity, ethnic and otherwise, as multiple so that Indonesians were Indonesian citizens first and members of ethnic and religious groups second. Although these moves were meant to downplay ethnicity, they nevertheless assisted in the recirculation of ideologies that linked regions to ethnic social types. For example, the 1978 introduction of education programs for public servants about the state ideology, *Pancasila*, recirculated ideas about regions and ethnic groups through discourses relating to the need for inter-region harmony (Elson, 2008: 248–249). In a 1983 Department of Information publication, there was also explicit mention of ethnicity and the need for ethnic groups to be attached to the larger Indonesia (Elson, 2008: 253). This idea was exemplified in the motto "Unity in Diversity" that accompanied the state ideology plaque found in many government offices and schools during this period.

While the meaning of *adat* (customs, laws, and social structures) via its links with locale were recirculated through political debates about the naturalness of parliamentary democracy and the Indonesian-ness of guided democracy in the Soekarno era (Bourchier, 2007: 117–120), during the late 1970s and early 1980s, there was a move away from ethnicity as grounded in *adat* to ethnicity as grounded in *budaya* (culture). In addition to being anchored to linguistic forms, the new formulation was also associated with houses, artifacts, dress, and performance (with much continuity from earlier times). In this sense, *adat* became linked to art and display (Erb, 2007), while being delinked from "traditional" forms of social structures, laws, and regulations (de Jong, 2009). Where regional nongovernment radio was concerned, there were also new regulations that stipulated that programming should originate locally, be about regional cultures, be appropriate to local conditions, and be in a regional language (Sen & Hill, 2000: 86). As Sen and Hill (2000: 93–94) note, the government radio broadcaster (RRI) aired news in twelve regional languages and village agricultural programs in forty-eight regional languages.

The strengthening of associations of ethnicity with material signs and cultural performances continued with the marketing and commoditization of ethnicity for domestic and international tourists (Adams, 1984; Erb, 2007; Hooker, 1993; Parker, 2002). During the early 1990s, the sale of taped ethnic music recordings was around 15 percent of overall music sales in Indonesia (Sen & Hill, 2000: 170). For example, one Sundanese language recording, *Kalangkang*, sold over two million copies, and with the massive pirate industry, it may well have sold a further ten million copies (Sen & Hill, 2000: 170–171). Within other areas of Indonesia, some cottage industries recorded music for local audiences. This music included Western songs in a local language as well as local music (Sen & Hill, 2000: 173–174).

This marketing and commoditization process is perhaps best exemplified by the Mini Indonesia theme park in Jakarta that opened in 1975 (Vickers, 2005: 167) and was initially conceptualized as a model of unity in diversity. *Taman mini Indonesia*, as it is locally known, is in the shape of Indonesia and populated by houses, architecture, and distinctively dressed performers of named ethnic groups from around the archipelago (Hoon, 2006). In places such as Central Java, performances of high Javanese, which had in the past been indexically associated with royal courts and the "best" of refined Javanese culture, were increasingly becoming commoditized as a paid-for status- enhancing addition to wedding ceremonies (Errington, 1998b). In short, in addition to the domestication of ethnicity, ethnicity was commoditized in a way that strengthened indexical links among linguistic forms, regions, and ethnic stereotypes, while at the same time adding attire, housing, custom, music, and economic value to the semiotic registers associated with these stereotypes.

At the same time, Indonesian as the national language of Indonesia was vigorously planned based on Western models of development and nationalism, resulting in a semiotic register that included notions, such as development, truth, objectivity, evaluation, education, power, and so on (e.g., Errington, 1998a, 1998b, 2000). Just as important was Indonesian's role as a language of national unity by way of its function as a mediator of social relations among geographically dispersed ethnic groups with their own languages (e.g., Abas, 1987: 116; Dardjowidjojo, 1998; Lowenberg, 1990). This process of institutionalizing Indonesian as an exemplar of unity in diversity—via its role as a language of wider communication among those who are "ethnolinguistically different"—also allowed for the association of the "the other" or "stranger" with performances of Indonesian usage. In short, this implicit institutionally authorized metasemiotic commentary recirculated ideas that indexed linguistic forms with region and ethnic social type while indexing Indonesian with the idea of the doing of unity in diversity.

Although the quality of schooling and attendance rates were as variable in the New Order period as in earlier times, nevertheless, between 1975 and 1990, there was significant massification of education (Bjork, 2005; Soedijarto et al., 1980; Thee Kian Wie, 2002). For example, the number of primary school students in 1990 (24 million) was nearly three times that of 1960 (8 million), while the number of lower secondary school students had also increased from 1.9 million to over 5.5 million in this same period (Bjork, 2005: 54). During this period, successive central and regional government departments attempted to teach regional languages in primary and secondary schools (e.g., Arps, 2010; Lowenberg, 1992; Nababan, 1991; Soedijarto et al., 1980). While the success of such efforts was patchy (e.g., Arps, 2010; Kurniasih, 2007), these schooling practices (re)produced two social domains; the first was one that involved the recirculation of ideas linking linguistic forms to region and ethnic social types, and the second was one that involved the emergence of a local semiotic register.

In the case of the first social domain, Parker (2002) has observed that by the third grade of primary school, children can identify all the provinces in Indonesia along with their capital cities. This knowledge, together with the labeling processes that go with teaching, textbooks, and timetabled subjects, (re)creates a social domain for discourses of sameness and difference underpinned by children's understanding of linguistic forms as part of a whole language that is named and tied to particular geographical regions and signs from these regions, such as car license plates, architecture, and so on. Within this social domain, children can name the languages that they speak and imagine themselves as members of a particular group of people who are defined as such by way of residence and language usage (Nababan, 1991).

In other words, children's exposure to such discourses about regions, languages, and their users was another social domain in which ideas linking particular linguistic forms, regions, and ethnic social types were recirculated. These links are also implicitly repeated through the learning of Indonesian at school, especially when Indonesian is portrayed as the language of unity and communication among geographically dispersed ethnic groups with their own languages. For example, the propagation of Indonesian at schools as the language of national unity also brings into focus further criteria for defining communication with members of other ethnic groups as "a communicative practice requiring Indonesian." That is to say, Indonesian is required for communication with the ethnic other.

During this period, hierarchical relations solidified among Indonesian, ethnic languages, and mixed languages. Through its role as the language of education, development, and government, Indonesian sat at the top of this hierarchy, while some varieties of ethnic languages (e.g., Javanese from the royal centers of Yogyakarta and Solo) sat below Indonesian and were seen as important by way of their inclusion in the school curriculum (Dardjowidjojo, 1998; Errington, 1998a, 2000; Lowenberg, 1992; Nababan, 1985, 1991). Other ethnic languages sat below these standardized varieties and became marginalized and endangered (Florey, 1990; Kuipers, 1998). There were multiple, often overlapping, reasons for this, including their association with perceived backwardness, inadequate curriculum material, the value of Indonesian as a symbol of social mobility, mixed marriages, and so on (Jukes, 2010). During this period, the mixing of Indonesian with ethnic languages was also stigmatized (Errington, 1998b; Goebel, 2000), though as we will see in chapter 3, there were some institutional exceptions.

Spaces within schools and universities also produced a second type of social domain where interaction between those who were from different backgrounds required the establishment of a local semiotic register, as found in local Indonesian neighborhoods (Goebel, 2010b). Universities had another interesting mechanism for facilitating interaction across lines of difference. This system called *kerja kuliah nyata* (KKN; practical life experience classes), which started in 1971, was formalized by the 1990s and continues to the present day (Prastowo & Suyono, 2007). To graduate, all university students are required to complete KKN, which involves living in a rural village or poor community, often outside their home province, for a number of months. During this period, students learn from, help, and teach locals. My experience of KKN came secondhand through accounts from Indonesian university students in Semarang, my Indonesian brother-in-law's three-month stint in Bali, and my partner's neighbor's interaction with KKN students from Bandung. My brother-in-law, for example, was raised in Cirebon where he learned a local variety of Sundanese and Javanese. He then went to Semarang to complete a university diploma. In the process, he was a co-participant in the production of a local variety of Javanese, shared by him and his friends. He then went to a village in Bali to do his KKN where he again become involved as an ethnic other in the creation of a local semiotic register with locals in Bali. Similarly, in rural Cirebon, students from Bandung universities—who are often themselves from all over Indonesia—came to live in a farming village to learn from a local farming guru whose crops had never failed.

As with the Soekarno period, the printing and distribution of novels was a social domain in which ideas about the relationship among ethnic social types, regions, and linguistic forms also continued to circulate. There was the continuing publication of novels and serialized novels wherein the hero(ine) traveled throughout the archipelago, together with novels that were published in regional languages (Quinn, 1992; Teeuw, 1996). While only 500 Javanese novels were published in the 1980s, the introduction of other written genres, such as magazines and serialized novels published within them, helped take their place (Quinn, 1992: 28–30). In terms of the social domain of these Javanese language magazines, Quinn (1992: 38–39) points out that there were around 140,000 subscribers, with magazines regularly passing through the hands of neighbors and relatives. This trend away from printed books and toward magazines, radio, television, and the Internet could also be seen in the production and consumption of Indonesian language texts (Sen & Hill, 2000).

The introduction of television and the creation of a government broadcaster (TVRI) in 1962 also rapidly introduced a new social domain for the recirculation of ideas linking linguistic forms, regions, and ethnic social types, and for encounters with sameness and difference via televised representations. In the next chapter, I take a look at how television entered the lives of Indonesians from 1962 to 1998. While television was seen as one of the major tools for helping to unify Indonesia by representing an imagined and united community of Indonesian speakers from diverse backgrounds (Kitley, 2000), I am especially concerned with how the ethnic comedies that emerged in the earlier 1990s helped to associate embodied language with ethnic social types, as well as outsiders and hybrid social types.

In summarizing this section, we can say that during the New Order period, there was a massification and up-scaling of the mechanisms that facilitated the circulation of ideas linking language, region, and ethnic social types. For example, transmigration projects, migration, investment in education, factories, transportation, and communications all facilitated the repetition of ideologies that had been constructed in the colonial period and recirculated in various forms until the start of the New Order period. At the same time, other social domains that had been sites for regular encounters with Indonesians from throughout the archipelago during the Soekarno years, such as labor and literacy movements associated with the PKI (Ford, 2008; Foulcher, 1986), had been domesticated, monitored, changed, or eradicated during the New Order period. Even so, from 1966 to 1998, linguistic forms became tightly associated with particular regions and equated with ethnic social types to the extent that when Indonesians spoke of themselves as speaking a regional language, such as Javanese, Sundanese, and Balinese, this also frequently pointed to the same ethnic identity and stereotypical dress, housing, etc. The number of ethnic languages that had institutional centers of normativity also increased with at least forty-eight regional languages circulating in one-to-many participation frameworks like schools, radio, and television. At the same time, speaking Indonesian had become tightly associated with a whole host of ideas, but especially "Indonesian citizen," "knowledge," "education," "development," and doing "unity in diversity." In broad terms, the different social domains in which registers of Indonesian, ethnic registers, and mixed registers circulated also helped to regiment an order of indexicality where Indonesian was at the top, followed by some ethnic languages (e.g., Javanese, Sundanese, and Balinese), with other ethnic registers and mixed registers at the bottom.

2.9 Conclusion

Taking inspiration from a broad range of work, this chapter has been concerned with understanding the processes that have helped to index linguistic signs with signs of place and person to form ethnic social types in Indonesia over a period of about 150 years. I was especially interested in the role that new waves of technology had in these processes. On the one hand, I pointed out that these processes figured in the construction of regional languages, Indonesian, and their stereotypical speakers, while on the other hand, and in line with arguments put forward by those working in semiotic theory (Agha, 2007a), I suggested that these processes also produced an infinite number of registers in places receiving large numbers of migrants. As much of the writing in other areas of the humanities and social sciences has led us to expect, different waves of technology tended to up-scale and massify the circulation of people and ideas, while at the same time creating new domains for interaction with, and commentary about, the other.

Indonesian and regional languages were constructed as written entities made up of syntactic relations and words that underwent frequent (re)codification in word lists, dictionaries, and grammars that were produced by an academic elite and media professionals, and consumed in educational domains, by music lovers, and to a much lesser extent by television audiences (Kitley, 2000; Rachmah, 2006). While linguistic forms continued to be the most readily recognizable emblem of ethnicity, through the commoditization of ethnicity, other semiotic forms became new emblems that could index ethnic identity. A register of Malay eventually became a register of Indonesian, with the most widely circulating reproductions being found in the social domains of schools, bureaucracies, radio, television, and print media. While there were many genres, what seemed to be common to all was the use of literary written models for contexts that also involved the speaking of Indonesian. Another enduring theme was that this register of Indonesian was associated with the idea of a standard, new knowledge, education and development, authority (whether personal, bureaucratic, or political), expertise, nationhood, and the upper echelons of Indonesian society, while also being associated with citizens who could do unity in diversity through the use of Indonesian.

In contrast to the early colonial institutionalization of a diversity that included just a handful of regional languages, by the 1990s, there were forty-eight regional languages with institutionally supported centers that utilized one-to-many participation frameworks such as schools and media broadcasts. By the 1990s, there were also clear hierarchical relations within this polycentric system. Through its role as the language of education, development, and government, Indonesian sat at the top of this hierarchy, while some varieties of ethnic languages became standardized and valued (e.g., Javanese from the royal centers of Yogyakarta and Solo vis-à-vis Javanese from the peripheries) but sat below Indonesian. Other ethnic languages, especially those found in the islands outside of Java, became marginalized and/or endangered, while the mixing of Indonesian with ethnic languages was stigmatized.

Where interactional practice is concerned, the picture is one of increased interaction among strangers in an increasingly diverse and expanding set of domains. This superdiverse situation also required the development of local semiotic registers that were typically fragments of other local registers, and the more widely circulating ones. In a sense, an unintended consequence of the ideas and practices of development was increasing levels of diversity as people and ideas about "the other" circulated at ever-increasing rates and at ever-increasing scales, especially as one-to-many participation frameworks became the exemplary domains for learning and entertainment. An irony of this process, especially for those involved in language planning and the standardization of a national language, was that although Indonesian was strongly championed as the language that would assist in national development and unity, nevertheless, the people contact and idea circulation that were part of this development process ensured continued linguistic fragmentation whereby the language of interethnic encounters rarely matched national ideologies.

In taking a historical look at political, economic, and social events in Indonesia, I hope to have contributed to work on superdiversity (e.g., Blommaert & Rampton, 2011; Vertovec, 2007). In particular, while work on superdiversity provides fine-grained descriptions of semiotic practices in face-to-face encounters, we know less about the genesis and processes that produce superdiversity, especially in non-European contexts. In this chapter, I have mapped some of the conditions that have produced superdiversity in Indonesia, while showing how it sits in tension with standardizing processes that are outcomes of one-to-many participation frameworks (e.g., schooling and television programming consumption).

Finally, I should point out that while there were few examples of actual sign usage in this chapter, in the following chapters, I start to focus on televised representations of sign usage. More specifically, I examine how televised representations of ethnic social types have contributed to the indexing of linguistic forms to embodied practice. I also provide some examples of representations of interactions among ethnic social types (especially in urban settings) that mirror and model the unintended consequences of the massification and up-scaling of people and idea circulation. In particular, these examples of semiotic practice show that doing unity in diversity is not always characterized by Indonesian usage. Indeed, it seems that models of the doing of unity in diversity regularly include the use of fragments of semiotic registers associated with ethnic languages.

3

Representing Ethnicity and Social Relations on Television

3.1 Introduction

This chapter has three main aims. The first is to look at how personhood and social relations are represented in Indonesian comedic soap operas that were produced in the mid-to-late 1990s. These comedic soap operas were different from the genre of dramatic soap operas because they were not always set in the big city, and they did not always represent and imagine the lifestyles and language use of an Indonesian-speaking upper middle class (Rachmah, 2006). The second aim is to explore the relationships between ethnic stereotypes of the past and comedic televised representations. In doing so, I hope to contribute to an area of scholarship on language ideologies described in section 2.2. In particular, I seek to further the multimodal dimension of some of this scholarship by using television soaps as my data. While soaps are a relatively underutilized type of data in the study of language ideology formation—with most studies typically relying on archival, written, and printed sources (e.g., Agha, 2011a; Inoue, 2011; Miller, 2004)—their make-up provides rich metasemiotic commentaries that help in the construction of social types. The third aim is to start to develop a framework for understanding the type of language alternation practices found within these soaps.

In addressing these three aims, I undertake a multimodal analysis of interactions from three soap operas to explore how the televised representation of signs reproduces and reconfigures the semiotic registers described in chapter 2. In particular, I examine how the co-occurrence of specific words with embodied language (e.g., gesture, facial expressions, and prosody) and other signs—such as those of place (e.g., architecture, landscape), space (e.g., inside houses, proxemics in interaction), and situated activity (e.g., driving a taxi as opposed to being chauffeured)—help to produce ethnic social types with viewable and hearable "demeanors" (Goffman, 1967) that have varying degrees of interactional history and thus varying degrees of common ground (Enfield, 2006; Hanks, 2006). The lamination of demeanor and interactional history onto preexisting ethnic social types produces semiotically denser stereotypes.

There are also representations of social types who can engage in practices that resemble but are different in a number of respects from "crossing" (Rampton, 1995). Drawing upon Rampton's definition of crossing and later revisions of this term in discussions of "styling the other" (Rampton, 1999), here I define crossing as the use of linguistic forms or formulaic utterances that are typically not associated with the person using them through reference to the language habitually used by them with their grandparents, parents, and siblings. Crossing typically occurs as part of artful performances (often invoking another's identity) during liminal moments. Performances of crossing regularly attract commentaries by ratified participants in the communicative event in which crossing occurs. I suggest that representations of crossing-like practices in the soaps that we examine seem to offer an alternate model to the state ideology of doing unity in diversity through the use of Indonesian.

In carrying out my analysis, it will become clear that some of the constructed dialogues found in these recorded broadcasts are characterized by crossing and other language alternation practices. The classification of such practices is by no means straightforward. Accordingly, I start to flesh out a system for categorizing televised language alternation practices. This seems timely for two reasons. First, as noted above, the type of alternation found in these soaps is rather different from the type of alternation found in accounts elsewhere in the world. For example, much of this work has pointed to a global trend around the commoditization and popularization of multilingualism in the media (e.g., Androutsopoulos, 2007; Jaffe, 2000; Johnson & Ensslin, 2007b; Johnson & Milani, 2010; Kelly-Holmes & Atkinson, 2007; LeCompte & Schensul, 1999). What seems common in these studies is that representations of language alternation typically occur in liminal or spectacular interactional moments, similar in some respects to the situations where the practice of crossing (Rampton, 1995) can be found. In contrast to these studies, however, in this chapter, we find that representations of language alternation are typically unspectacular, mundane, and often habitual.

Second, despite an increasing interest in the media by sociolinguists (e.g., Agha, 2011b; Bell & Gibson, 2011; Gershon, 2010; Richardson, 2010) and a mountain of work on language alternation and code-switching more generally, there is little if any work that focuses on issues around the classification of representations of language alternation. My approach draws upon my earlier work on language alternation (Goebel, 2010), work on code-switching, especially Gafaranga's and Torras's (2002) and Auer's (1995) ethnomethodological approach to language alternation, and reflections on ethnomethodological approaches more generally (e.g., Francis & Hester, 2004; Liddicoat, 2007; Moerman, 1988; ten Have, 2007). For example, some treatments of ethnomethodology suggest that in order to carry out ethnomethodological analysis, the researcher needs to use external material accessed as part of their long period of immersion with those being studied (Francis & Hester, 2004). Thus, my representation and categorization of talk draw upon conversation-external information, such as that presented in chapter 2, my research assistant's classification of signs, my own knowledge about these signs, and a number of dictionaries.

In section 3.2, I start by grounding my analysis in the scholarly discussions surrounding television, while arguing that practices of representation directly contribute to what is often termed "language change." Section 3.3 presents a short history of television in Indonesia as a way of contextualizing the representation practices that are discussed in sections 3.5 to 3.7. Section 3.4 develops my earlier work on analyzing television representations (Goebel, 2008, 2011). This approach is a synthesis of scholarship in the broad fields of talk in interaction, ethnography of communication, semiosis, multimodality, and common ground (e.g., Agha, 2007a; Antaki & Widdicombe, 1998; Enfield, 2006; Goodwin, 2006; Hanks, 2006; Hymes, 1974; Kress & Van Leeuwen, 2001; Norris, 2004; Scollon & Scollon, 2003). Sections 3.5 to 3.7 introduce and then provide a multimodal analysis of three comedic soaps. Sections 3.5 and 3.6 provide examples of habitual language alternation, which, I argue, helps naturalize this practice. Section 3.7 also has examples of this type of alternation, but it has as well a representation of migrants and the big city. These representations contain examples of language alternation that resemble "adequation." Following Bucholtz and Hall (2004), I define adequation as the habitual pursuit of semiotic sameness in face-to-face interactions.

Some of the representations analyzed in section 3.7 also provide examples of what I referred to in chapter 1 as "knowledging." In brief, part of my definition of knowledging was that it related to a competence to recognize and understand signs that were indexical of "the other." I argued that this competence was gained through participation in one-to-many participation frameworks (e.g., schooling, consumption of newspapers, radio, and television) at multiple sites and across a person's lifespan. In some cases, this competence is manifested through performance, such as evaluations of televised ethnic representations, as in the cases we examine in later chapters. In this chapter, however, we will typically just examine cases of recognition by characters in a soap opera. Even so, what makes this interesting is that this practice is being modeled at all, especially given the widely circulating ideology that Indonesian is the language of interethnic interaction. In other words, in contrast to the state ideology of unity in diversity where Indonesian is the language of doing togetherness, in these representations, unity is done through using and understanding fragments of what are commonly referred to as regional languages. In a sense, we are seeing the representation of the unintended consequences of processes of enregisterment, processes that have been pushed along by technological innovation and ideologies about development.

3.2 Approaching Television

As Richardson (2010) points out, television is an area that has received sustained attention from a broad range of disciplines including cultural studies, linguistics, and anthropology. Much of the scholarship in the broad area of cultural studies focuses on television representations and how they are perceived (e.g., Ang, 1996; Hall, 2006 [1980]; Liebes & Katz, 1990; Morley, 1986). Some of this scholarship was in reaction to quantitatively driven work, which imagined audiences and consumption behavior while ignoring important factors, such as sociocultural context, gender, and so on. According to Ang (1996), this reactionary scholarship followed the ethnographic turn in many other humanities areas and focused on the local consumption of television, while keeping in mind that the interpretation of participants' viewing practices needed to consider broader ideological currents. Echoing Vološinov's (1973 [1929]) insights, a common theme to this work and also work coming out of the anthropology of the media was that the meaning of representations was situated and open to multiple interpretations by viewers (e.g., Ang, 1996; Ginsburg, Abu-Lughod, & Larkin, 2002; Liebes & Katz, 1990; Spitulnik, 1996).

Linguists from a wide range of paradigms have also had a keen interest in television. For example, some linguistic anthropologists and those working in social semiotics have focused on the representations themselves and their relationship to wider sociopolitical contexts (e.g., Fairclough, 1995; Meek, 2006). Another focus has been on the practices of producers, directors, financiers, actors, editors, advertisers, government departments, and so on and their roles in formulating how language and social relations are represented (e.g., Garrett & Bell, 1998; Johnson & Ensslin, 2007a; Kress & Van Leeuwen, 2001; Loven, 2008). Other streams of research have been concerned with audience engagement with and interpretation of these representations (e.g., Kulick & Willson, 2004 [1994]; Richardson, 1998), and how such representations are reused or repeated in other mediums (e.g., Clarke & Hiscock, 2009; King & Wicks, 2009), whether and to what extent representations of language use might relate to language change among viewers (Stuart-Smith, 2006; Stuart-Smith, Timmins, Pryce, & Gunter, n.d.), and how we might characterize and research television dialogue (Richardson, 2010).

I have two main points of departure from the above-mentioned work. First, I am interested in exploring how television creates personas that have both demeanors and interactional histories. This creation of semiotically dense stereotypes raises the question of how television representations might relate to discussions about semiotic change. Second, I draw upon work on enregisterment discussed in chapter 2 to look at how similarities among different soaps show how embodied language and interactional history have become widely circulating emblems of ethnic identity. I have discussed the theory behind this last point in chapter 2, so in the rest of this section, I want to begin to theorize the relationship between television representations and semiotic change.

The relationship between television representations and semiotic change has started to be explored by variationist sociolinguists, such as Stuart-Smith (2006, n.d.), who have set out to question assumptions that television has limited, if any, influence on language change among viewers (e.g., Chambers, 1998; Labov, 2001). Here I want to pursue a much more modest argument by pointing out that research on the practices of producers, directors, financiers, actors, editors, and so on shows that this group of media professionals plays a role in language change (or more precisely semiotic change), albeit only sign usage as represented on television.

As these studies have shown, such media professionals decide which signs and which practices will be foregrounded, backgrounded, co-occurring, and so on (e.g., Loven, 2008; Richardson, 2010). Richardson (2010: 45–46) notes that while television professionals try to represent "realistic" dialogues, typically, everyday features of conversation (e.g., overlap, false starts) are kept to a minimum or included to achieve a purpose, such as using overlap to show urgency in contrast to the everyday occurrence of overlap documented in the work of conversation analysts. In this sense, language change or, more precisely, semiotic change is achieved through the erasing of some of the features of everyday interaction.

Similarly, Richardson (2010: 110) points out that in contrast to the fine-grained conversational work people do in everyday interaction to manage social relations, typically, television drama foregrounds conflict and impolite behavior (Richardson, 2010: 110). Again, in these types of television representations, the erasure of "polite" behavior is an example of semiotic change that has been the outcome of media professionals' work. While these representations are designed to elicit reactions from an audience (Richardson, 2010: 128), another outcome of these representational practices is the association of a whole host of signs with social types to produce new social types, another example of semiotic change.

In the case at hand, recognizable emblems of identity associated with ethnic stereotypes (e.g., the formula of person, linguistic form, and place) are laminated with nonverbal signs and an interactional history to form semiotically denser ethnic stereotypes. The lamination of nonverbal signs to personas engaged in situated interaction helps to construct a "demeanor" (Goffman, 1967: 78). Representations of characters who share "common ground" create an image of interactional history that also projects the social relations that should exist between people displaying particular demeanors. Common ground can be defined as knowledge about referents in interaction that is jointly established as either shared or not among a participant constellation (Enfield, 2006; Hanks, 2006). Before taking a look at how semiotic density is constructed on television, I wish to look at television in Indonesia as a way of contextualizing these representations.

3.3 Television in Indonesia

The introduction of television and the formation of a government broadcaster, TVRI, in 1962 rapidly introduced a new social domain for the recirculation of a number of ideas. On the one hand, television circulated representations of encounters with sameness in the form of encounters with other Indonesian speakers. This (re)linked ideas of "Indonesian" with "Indonesian citizen" and "unity in diversity." On the other hand, television also circulated representations of encounters with difference, which (re)linked linguistic forms, regions, and ethnic social types. Putting aside the important question of reception (which is discussed in chapters 7 and 8), this section takes a brief look at the history of television in Indonesia. I point out that while the majority of programming was in Indonesian, nevertheless from the early 1990s onward, a series of events resulted in increasing amounts of regional languages finding their way into programming, especially in the area of soap opera.

The rate at which television entered the lives of Indonesians across the archipelago can be categorized into a number of stages. The first was the setting-up of regional infrastructure that enabled local production, programming, and broadcasting. According to Kitley (2000: 38), after the initial setup of a broadcasting unit in Jakarta in 1962, regional stations were setup in Yogyakarta, Central Java (1965), Medan, North Sumatra (1970), Ujung Pandang/Makassar, South Sulawesi (1972), Balikpapan, East Kalimantan (1973), Palembang, South Sumatra (1974), Surabaya, East Java (1978), and Manado, North Sulawesi (1978). The launch of the Palapa satellite in 1975 fueled an increase in television ownership and, by 1978, there were 900,000 registered television sets in Java and a further 200,000 in the outer islands (Kitley, 2000: 47).

As Ida's (2006) and Loven's (2008) studies of television reception have shown, in low-income neighborhoods, one television could attract a large audience including neighbors and family. Thus, the 1.1 million television sets may well have translated into five to ten million viewers. Indeed, I recall that during my time living in my partner's village in West Java in the early 1990s, her parents' small black-and-white television attracted audiences of well over twenty viewers in the late afternoons and evenings. I experienced a similar mass audience when doing my Ph.D. fieldwork in a low-income neighborhood of Semarang between 1996 and 1998. Programming also expanded in the sole television station, the government-owned-and-operated TVRI, although not at the rate of television purchases (Kitley, 2000: 42–62). For example, in 1979, TVRI broadcast from Monday to Saturday for 7.5 hours each day and Sunday was 6.5 hours (Kitley, 2000: 40).

During the early years, television was seen as a facilitator of education, especially for the teaching of the national language. Even so, there were some exceptions, such as the children's show *Si Unyul* (Unyul), which was broadcast between 1981 and 1993. This program had one of the main characters speaking Indonesian differently from other characters. This character, *Bu Bariah* (Mrs. Bariah), explicitly grounded her difference in terms of region through her commentaries about herself as someone hailing from Madura in East Java (Kitley, 2000: 112–137). According to Kitley, the only other notable exception to Indonesian language broadcasts was a series titled *Lenong Rumpi*, which had some local content and fragments from a regional language (Kitley, 2000: 98). In both cases, however, television became a new one-to-many participation framework that (re)circulated two sets of ideas. On the one hand, *Si Unyul* and *Lenong Rumpi* were representations that recirculated ideas about the relationship among linguistic forms, regions, and ethnic social types. On the other, the use of Indonesian on television helped solidify ideas about what Indonesian was, while continuing to link it with the nation, development, advanced knowledge, education, and political power. This was so because the majority of programming was in Indonesian and typically either educational or about ceremonies involving politicians and bureaucrats.

With the entry of commercial television in the early 1990s, local content and discourses about regional languages became increasingly common. For example, Sen and Hill (2000: 119) noted that the emergence of the first private television stations in Indonesia in 1990 was accompanied by programming and operating rules that stated that the language used by such stations should be standard Indonesian with regional languages being used only when suitable. During the period in which these authorized commentaries circulated, the entry of five new television stations in the period of 1990–1993 made it increasingly difficult for these stations to gain and maintain market share (Kitley, 2000: 150–153; Sen & Hill, 2000: 123–124). One of the ways in which private and public stations tried to do this was to include more local content, including increasing amounts of interaction in an imagined local language, especially in comedic soaps locally referred to as *sinetron* (e.g., Kitley, 2000; Loven, 2008; Rachmah, 2006; Sen & Hill, 2000).

In a bid to stem the tide of foreign films and unwanted Western influence on Indonesians, in late 1996, the government also ratified a law that would foster local content over international content (Kitley, 2000: 298). Televised representations of the local also occurred at a time of economic development (Vickers, 2005) and cheaper access to television sets that fueled a rapid increase in television ownership across Indonesia in the mid-1990s (Kitley, 2000), albeit typically in the middle-income segments of Indonesia society (Goebel, 2000). While the Asian economic crisis that hit Indonesia in mid-1997 and the rapid inflation that accompanied this crisis decreased Indonesians' ability to buy televisions, it did accentuate a move toward more local content. As Ida (2008: 97) notes, the economic crisis meant that local soap operas were much cheaper than foreign imports and broadcast content moved from 90 percent foreign in 1997 to 67 percent local in 1999, although the percentage of locally produced content dropped to 63 percent by 2001.

In sum, until the early 1990s, the New Order government's ideology about television was its function as a disseminator of Indonesian and of representations of Indonesians doing togetherness by using Indonesian. The emergence of new television stations in the early 1990s and the financial crisis that started in 1997 helped to provide an alternate to this ideology as regional languages increasingly found their way into television programming. This type of programming highlighted localism, ethnicity, and ethnic languages, while standing in contrast to the New Order's ideas about the importance of downplaying ethnicity and difference. In addition, some of this new programming modeled new ways of doing unity in diversity. From section 3.5 onward, I take a detailed look at some of the soaps from this period. Before doing so, however, I flesh out my approach to analyzing these soaps.

3.4 A Multimodal Approach to Comedic Soaps

When I recorded the three television serials that I present below, I did not record them with the intention of using them in the type of analysis undertaken here. The first one, an episode from *Noné* titled "*Cipoa*" ("Con Artist"), was recorded in Darwin at the then-Northern Territory University in 1995. The other two, *Si Kabayan* (Kabayan) and *Si Doel Anak Sekolahan* (Doel an Educated Lad), were recorded in Cirebon and Semarang in 1996 and 1998, respectively. Although the last serial was recorded as part of a larger linguistic-anthropological fieldwork project conducted in Semarang from December 1995 until August 1998 (Goebel, 2000), I didn't pay much attention to this data until much later (Goebel, 2008, 2010). Indeed, for a long time afterward, all of these serials were used as teaching material to help learners of Indonesian become acquainted with the type of variation that they would encounter in Indonesia (Black & Goebel, 2002, 2004; Goebel, 2002). In this sense, the three serials I use here were not originally gathered as part of an ongoing project that looked at the representation of ethnic social types. Even so, as I became increasingly interested in processes of enregisterment, I was drawn to televised representations of sign usage as one of the mechanisms that figured in the repetition of signs and the stereotypes that they helped construct.

In looking at these representations in more detail, two main methods seemed especially suited to the task. These include those offered in the broad field that looks at face-to-face interaction and embodied interaction (e.g., Antaki & Widdicombe, 1998; Goodwin, 2006; Gumperz, 1982; Haviland, 2004; Kendon, 1985; Tannen, 1984) and the ethnography of communication (e.g., Hymes, 1972). This combination is by no means new and has been fruitfully tried and tested by many scholars working in fields like language socialization and sign usage in interactions among those from different backgrounds (e.g., Ochs, 1988; Philips, 1983; Wortham, 2006).

Although Hymes's (1972) framework has been critiqued due to a lack of attention to interpretation processes relating to "norms" (e.g., Gumperz, 1982), nevertheless, his notions of speech events, speech situations, and his SPEAKING framework provide a useful guide for the systematic documentation of sign usage. SPEAKING is an acronym covering the minimal types of data that Hymes suggested are needed to understand what makes up participants' communicative competence. These include (S) Situation, (P) Participants, (E) Ends, (A) Act sequence, (K) Key, (I) Instrumentalities (or modes in the sense of those working in the area of multimodal interaction analysis), (N) Norms, and (G) Genre. In particular, it enables comparisons among each set of signs and a way of talking about how—when viewed as a whole social practice—these signs construct demeanors. Drawing on ethnomethodological insights allows us to provide a fine-grained description of represented conversational practices. Combining this analysis with Hymes's framework also allows us to see how such sign usage relates to other signs within a particular televised serial. In this sense, the methodology presented here falls within the type of multimodal analysis found in the work of Scollon and Scollon (2003) and Norris (2004).

While my analysis will focus on the use of multiple signs, I also need to be clear about two issues. First, I need to point out some of my ideological biases relating to transcription and classification (e.g., Ochs, 2006 [1979]). In particular, I need to provide a note about initial transcription procedures and how this figured in my classification of linguistic signs in these serials. Initial transcription was carried out by two Indonesian research assistants, both of whom reported to be from Sundanese-speaking West Java. Indeed, I chose them because their language background would enable them to transcribe the speech in two of the serials that I present here. I asked them to put in bold any forms that they considered were regional languages. Thus, part of my categorization of linguistic forms relied upon native-speaker judgments.

This presents some challenges insofar as while I draw upon Gafaranga and Torras's (2002) methods for helping categorize language alternation, I also relied upon conversation external judgments, the co-occurrence of other signs, my own knowledge of linguistic signs, and a number of dictionaries. While acknowledging that this approach has the potential to reproduce the ideologies I am trying to unpack, I need a starting point and thus beg the reader's indulgence for the moment. Second, many Indonesian words have been adopted from what has been labeled "Javanese" and "Sundanese," and the reverse is also true (e.g., Errington, 1998; Poedjosoedarmo, 1982). Indonesian also shares word order and affixation patterns with many local registers, such as those referred to as Javanese and Sundanese (e.g., Errington, 1998; Poedjosoedarmo, 1982).

Although Agha's (2007a, 2007b) work and my discussion in chapter 2 imply a need to write about language in semiotic terms, here and in the following chapters, I substitute more accurate descriptions, such as "linguistic signs stereotypically associated with Indonesian," "linguistic signs stereotypically associated with *ngoko* and *krámá* Javanese," "linguistic signs stereotypically associated with Sundanese," and "linguistic signs stereotypically associated with Betawi" for shorter ones: respectively, "Indonesian," "*ngoko* Javanese," "*krámá* Javanese," Sundanese, and Betawi. I use the term "medium," in Gafaranga and Torras's (2002) sense, to generally refer to Indonesian, *ngoko* Javanese, and *krámá* Javanese as defined above. This helps me separate linguistic sign usage in actual interactional practice from ideologies about such signs, which are often referred to as "language." I also prefer to use "medium" rather than "regional language" when looking at represented interactional practices because it does not presuppose the link between geographic place and language. In the context of the following analysis, it also allows the idea of "region" to emerge from the co-occurrence of signs of place and through the frames of difference set up by their contrast with other sets of signs.

3.5 The Comedic Soap *Noné*

Although not the first broadcast to include local content, the broadcast of the soap opera *Noné* (Missy) occurred at a particular historical juncture where reinterpretation of media laws, the emergence of new television stations, and the need to obtain market share all figured in a push for an increase in the use of signs stereotypically associated with regional languages in soap operas more generally (e.g., section 3.3). The data that I analyze is drawn from an episode titled "*Cipoa*" ("Con Artist") that was broadcast nationally in 1995 during the mid-afternoon time slot, which scholars of Indonesian media characterize as less popular because it attracts less advertising revenue (Loven, 2008; Rachmah, 2006). This comedic soap opera was broadcast by the commercial semi-educational television station TPI, one of the five commercial stations (Indosiar, SCTV, RCTI, and ANTV) that came online after television was deregulated in Indonesia in 1990 (Kitley, 2000).

This particular comedic soap is notable because of some characters' frequent alternation between Indonesian and Sundanese fragments and because of the representation of other signs that anchored this story geographically to West Java, an area associated with an imagined community of Sundanese speakers. This soap is also interesting because of the celebrity status of main actor, Nike Ardilla, who is represented as a speaker of Sundanese. She was a well-known and loved celebrity who was not only a pop singer but also a television and movie star. As a celebrity, Nike Ardilla fits into the category of an authorized speaker of this medium, which, as we will see in chapter 8, is a status bestowed upon her by viewers of this soap.

In representing the visual and spoken elements of these televised representations, I use a screenshot (frame) to exemplify embodied language usage, and starting from extract 3.5.4, a new frame is placed to the left of the dialogue where changes in gesture, posture, and facial expression co-occur with a change in participant constellations and/or a new speaker turn. The first extract of talk that I analyze (extract 3.5.1) is of an elderly woman narrating a letter that is read by the main character Dewi. One of my research assistants indicated that the two forms *aer* (water) on line 5 were Sundanese, which is indicated by bold font. (When necessary, I point to transcription conventions as I move through the analysis, but a full list of conventions can be found at the beginning of the book.) When talking with my other research assistant, however, she noted that the first instance was somewhere between Indonesian and Sundanese pronunciation, while the second occurrence was Indonesian pronunciation. Although the difference here is slight, the point here is that this pronunciation presents a sign that indexes the language background of the serial and the setting.

Extract 3.5.1 The reading of a will

Dewi's grandmother

1 dewi (1.7) kalau kamu baca surat ini   Dewi, if you are reading this letter, [then]
2 (1.3) mungkin nenek sudah menjadi   maybe Grandma has already become
3 tanah (1.8) jangan menangis (1.8)   dust. Don't cry.
4 nenek tidak mungkin hidup lagi (1.1)   It's impossible for Grandma to live again.
5 meskipun **aer** matamu sebanyak **aer**   Even if your **tears** are as much as the **water**
6 mata waduk jatiluhur (1.5) senyumlah   in lake Jatiluhur. Please smile.
7 (1.1) pandanglah mataku (2.0) kamu   Look into my eyes. You
8 harus berjuang seperti raden ajeng   have to struggle like Princess Ajeng
9 kartini . atau dewi sartika (1.1) karena   Kartini or Dewi Sartika. Because
10 semua wanita . harus sadar . bahwa   all women must be aware that
11 mereka harus bangkit dan berhasil   they must develop and be successful.
12 (1.0) kamu tidak boleh malas (0.9)   You aren't allowed to be lazy.
13 +janji+ (1.8) bagus (10.0) nenek   Promise! Good. Grandma
14 wariskan kepadamu . sebuah rumah   bequeaths you a house.

After Dewi finishes reading the letter that was written and narrated by her grandmother, the scene cuts to Dewi arriving at her inherited house. The house's colonial styling, expansive yards, and specific type of foliage may point to a place somewhere in mountainous areas of Indonesia. The scene then moves to another young woman who is riding in a taxi, which eventually stops in the driveway of Dewi's newly acquired house. These signs together with the exchanges that follow between the taxi driver and the passenger

(Susi), Susi and Dewi, and Dewi and the taxi driver all provide signs that may or may not disambiguate earlier signs about setting and which medium is being used.

In the talk that accompanies extract 3.5.2, the young woman (Susi) refers to the man (Ucup) as *Mang* (Uncle) and the man refers to Susi as *Neng* (Miss). The occurrence of another medium within a primarily Indonesian conversation may present signs of difference, but in isolation, these fragments may leave open the question as to just which medium. However, recourse to co-occurring signs enables the anchoring of these forms with geographic place. For example, the taxi's number plate is prefixed with a "D" meaning it is from Bandung, West Java, and the name of the taxi company, "Bandung Taxi Company," is at the bottom of the driver's door (figure 3.5.1). This sign of place not only anchors the whole serial to West Java, but it also presupposes a number of indexical relationships. For example, it points to the potential that those in the coming story may be of Sundanese ethnicity and by extension through indexical links among place, person, and language, Sundanese speakers who when involved in co-ethnic interaction stereotypically use ethnic languages if they are known to each other.

Just as important, representations of subsequent interactions may also provide further signs that help anchor these fragments with geographic place, while indexing embodied behaviors with particular mediums. Consider for example, the interaction that occurs around figure 3.5.2. In this interaction, Susi moves away from her interaction with Mang Ucup to ring the doorbell of the house. In doing so, this provides potential signs as to what the relationship might be between her and the occupant of the house. For example, we might read an unfamiliar or stranger relationship between Susi and the house's occupant because Susi has no key and rings the doorbell. Such a reading, however, is ambiguous without recourse to the interaction that ensues.

There are also other signs that offer particular readings about other aspects of character identities. For example, in the talk surrounding figure 3.5.1, Mang Ucup and Susi try to establish how Susi will pay for the fare. She offers a large

FIGURE 3.5.1 Signs of place

FIGURE 3.5.2 Signs of social relations

bill, which Mang Ucup says that he can't change, and that he doesn't earn that much in a day. Then Susi offers foreign currency—which Ucup doesn't want—so Ucup asks for her stuffed toy, which Susi notes is worth more than his taxi. All of this talk and the material artifacts involved offer readings of a "well-to-do" Susi. For such an identity to solidify, however, requires further interactional work.

Extract 3.5.2 Indonesian and unfamiliars

Susi
1   >ada orangnya nggak   Is anyone there or
2   sih di situ?> (1.1)   not?
3   [+heh+   Heh!
Dewi
4   [ya (1.3)   Yeah.

After ringing the doorbell again, Susi uses Indonesian in summoning the occupant. The occupant, Dewi, appears to orient to this Indonesian usage in line 4 with *ya* (yes). This co-occurs with long inter-turn pauses signaled by the number in seconds and tenths of seconds within parentheses (lines 2 and 4). The representation of this way of speaking with a potential stranger also models this social relationship and the ways of speaking that are appropriate to this type of social relationship. However, without recourse to subsequent interactions, such a reading is still only tentative. As the interaction unfolds, however, this stranger relationship continues to solidify.

At the start of this interaction, the door is opened as Susi asks again if anybody is at home (lines 5–6) in extract 3.5.3 below. The talk continues to be in Indonesian: notably without any terms of address or personal introduction. Inter-turn pause length also continues to be quite long, ranging from half a second to two seconds. In the two frames to the left of the text, we can also see that in terms of facial expressions, Dewi doesn't smile, as she does in her interactions in extracts 3.5.5 onward. What seems to be occurring across interactional time is the linking of unfamiliarity and the lack of smiles with Indonesian. We can also see that in terms of dress, Susi's leather coat and her expensive stuffed toy are noticeably different from that of Dewi, who is wearing a T-shirt and a sarong with a batik design. These differences may add to the potential differences in social status that seem to be implied through Susi's talk in lines 8–14 and the absence of introductions or terms of address.

Extract 3.5.3 Indonesian, other reference, and unfamiliarity

Susi

5	>ada orangny nggak	Is anyone there or
6	di situ?> (0.6)	not?

Dewi

7	ada (1.0)	Yes there is.

Susi

8	panggil (0.4) > eh	Call [the house
9	ada uang kecil	owner] eh, haven't
10	nggak?> (0.5)	got any change [have you]?

Dewi

11	+ha+ (0.5) kamar	What, is there a
12	kecil' (0.4) >ada tu	bathroom, yeah
13	di dalam> . masuk	there is one inside,
14	aja (2.0)	just come inside.

Indeed, as we will see, Susi initially assumes that Dewi is a maid. We can see some of this through what appears to be a false start (line 8) where Susi tells Dewi to call (*panggil*) someone (perhaps the house owner) before asking for change. What seems to be occurring across interactional time is both the solidification of stranger identities—which also help reproduce associations between Indonesian and unfamiliarity—and the emergence of classed identities based upon possession of material goods and money. After being invited inside (lines 13-14), Susi proceeds to comment on the aesthetics of the inside of the house primarily in Indonesian (extract 3.5.4).

Extract 3.5.4 Talking about the material world

Susi

15	wadu::h' (0.3) +oh **MY**	Wow, oh **MY**
16	**GOD**+ (0.3) bagus juga	**GOD** this
17	ini rumah ya? . ya tapi	house is great yeah. But
18	mesti diganti lagi sama	[we] need to change some
19	barang barang yang	of the things [furnishings] with more **TRENDY** ones.

20	lebih **TRENDI** (1.2)	Susi [i.e. "I"] doesn't like
21	susi nggak suka sama	colors like this, they are not
22	warna warna kayak gini	active enough. Yeah if its
23	(0.3) kurang aktif (0.4)	artists like us, right!
24	ya? . kita kan artis mesti	Yes, [we] need [to be]
25	**GLAMOR** gitu' . eh	**GLAMOROUS** right.
26	(0.3)	
27	tolong dong dibayarin	Eh, please pay the taxi first,
28	taksi dulu . +itu tu+	that one, the one outside,
29	yang di luar ya? (9.0)	yeah.

In the above talk, we see that Susi identifies herself as an artist (at this stage, this might mean either screen or music). While artists who practice traditional forms of entertainment could have associations with moral deficiencies (Hanan, 1993), people like Susi who practiced more contemporary styles of music were often associated with a lack of morality because of the scantily dressed youths found in Western MTV music videos of the 1990s (Kitley, 2000; Rachmah, 2006). One interesting aspect of this talk, which only comes out through comparison with subsequent talk, is that the topic of above talk is primarily about the material world (lines 15–25). In short, because this talk is also primarily in Indonesian, Indonesian also becomes linked with talk about the material world. This talk also helps to further disambiguate the "stranger" relationship between Dewi and Susi insofar as Susi appears unfamiliar with the house. In addition, while there are two mediums used in this talk—linguistic signs associated with English (bold italic caps) and those associated with Indonesian—most of Susi's talk is in Indonesian. In using primarily an Indonesian medium between strangers, the association between Indonesian and strangers also solidifies.

Even so, Susi's use of English also invites analysis. From a microanalytic point of view, such usage might initially fit into three categories found in the literature on language alternation (Auer, 1995; Gafaranga & Torras, 2002; Rampton, 1995). The first is "alternation as the medium," which resembles the following pattern (adapted from Auer, 1995): AB1 AB2 AB1 AB2 (the uppercase letters represent a particular medium and the numbers indicate speakers 1 and 2).

Often, alternation as the medium has associations with habitualness, and individual moves from one medium to the other often do not have indexical meanings, but rather the overall pattern can index a particular community of practice (e.g., Alvarez-Cáccamo, 1998; Franceschini, 1998; Goebel, 2010; Swigart, 1992). The second and third could be code-switching or crossing, which are typically liminal with the alternation carrying further indexical meanings. These types of alternation can be illustrated with the pattern A1 A2 B1 A1 A2 (adapted from Auer, 1995).

In examining talk between Susi and Dewi throughout this soap, it becomes clear that alternation between English and Indonesian is not habitual, and indeed it only occurs on this occasion. Thus, this rules out alternation as the medium. It seems that this usage resembles code-switching in the sense offered by Gafaranga and Torras (2002) because it engenders a sense of "interactional otherness" in comparison to Susi and Dewi's other talk, which is in Indonesian. In supporting the interpretation that the use of English-like words has some sort of meaning, I suggest that it contributes to a solidification of Susi's moneyed-class identity insofar as English usage may suggest an ability to engage in overseas travel, to study overseas, or to take special courses within Indonesia. All of these practices are expensive and, during the mid-1990s, out of reach of the type of low-income Indonesians who made up the majority of Indonesia's population. As the interaction continues, Susi's moneyed-class identity appears to further solidify together with Susi's interpretation of Dewi as a maid. Susi's interpretation of "maid" is made more explicit when Susi asks Dewi to go and pay the taxi (lines 27–29). Interaction between Dewi and Ucup contrasts markedly with other interactional pairs, such as Susi and Ucup, and Susi and Dewi. This too helps solidify their emerging identities.

In extract 3.5.5, we see that Mang Ucup appears to recognize Dewi, as evidenced through reference to her name, as she is standing at the door. Looking at the two frames to the left of the text, we can also see that Ucup's facial expression, which ends in a smile, is reciprocated by Dewi when she appears to also recognize Mang Ucup. In other words, the smile appears to become a mutually recognized and ratified sign of familiar interpersonal relations. This embodied language co-occurs with increased body movement (e.g., the movement of Dewi's arm into a pointing gesture) and the use of Sundanese fragments (in bold font) as their medium. In so doing, it begins to link this medium with embodied signs.

Extract 3.5.5 Names, gestures, facial expressions, and familiarity

Ucup
30 **neng** dewi? (1.1)   **Miss** Dewi?

Dewi
31 **mang** (1.0) heh (1.0)   **Uncle**? Huh! **Uncle**?
32 **mang** (1.0)

The sign usage in extract 3.5.5 also contrasts considerably with the earlier interaction between Susi and Dewi, which was not characterized by the use of terms of address, names, and smiles as it is here. In short, what we have here is the representation of an intimate type of social relationship that has also been geographically anchored to a particular region through sign usage. As with the previous interaction, however, the identities that such sign usage point to are still ambiguous, but as we follow the interaction, an increasingly close, intimate interpersonal social relationship emerges through the co-construction of common ground (in this case, knowledge of personal names), as in the following extracts.

Extract 3.5.6 Prosody and familiars

Ucup
33 **neng** dewi (0.3)   **Miss** Dewi. **Miss!**
34 **+neng+** hehe (0.5)   Laughs.

(*continued*)

Extract 3.5.6 (Continued)

Dewi
35 mang . +mang [a::: Uncle, Uncle, a:::
36 mang+   Uncle

In extract 3.5.6, we see that Ucup appears to be sure that the young woman is in fact the Dewi that he knows through the use of her name again. This also co-occurs with further smiling, Ucup jumping up and down and waving his arm (the first frame to the left of the text), continued use of Sundanese terms of address (in bold font), together with raised volume (indicated by the "+" surrounding an utterance or word) and laughter (line 34). Dewi orients to this sign usage by continuing to use the same medium (primarily terms of address), smiling, running toward Ucup (the second frame to the left of the text), and raising the volume of her talk (lines 35–36). In doing so, the identity of "familiars" continues to solidify. The co-occurrence of these new embodied behaviors is also linked or indexed with the medium being used. This medium usage becomes even heavier as the interaction ensues, as can be seen in extract 3.5.7. This medium usage co-occurs with the continued use of embodied language, including smiling, laughter, and pointing at each other, as can be seen in the three frames to the left of the text.

Extract 3.5.7 Sundanese usage, co-occurrence, and familiarity

Ucup
37   [>
38 (laugher) ini **teh neng**   Laughter. You're Miss Dewi
39 dewi **téa**>=   **aren't you**?
Dewi
40   = >+ ya **mang**   Yes **Uncle**.
41 [(laughter)+>
Ucup
42 [>+**euluh euluh euluh**   Gee gee gee
43 **mani** sudah besar begini   **wow you're** already grown
44 ah+> . masih ingat **ka**   up. Do [you] still remember
45 **mang** coba . he. =   **Me**, try [and remember].

Dewi

46	= >+ya	Yeah
47	masih **atuh** ini **teh**	**of course** you [are]
48	**mang+>** ma::ng	Uncle, Uncle,
49	>kéheula kéheula	hang on, hang on,
50	kéheula kéheula> .	hang on, hang on,
51	ma:::ng >mang ucup =	Uncle, Uncle Ucup.

Ucup

52	=	Wow right.
53	>+ wah betul+> =	

Both

54	=	
55	simultaneous laughter =	Simultaneous laughter.

Ucup

56	=	
57	**damang neng'**=	How are [you] Miss?

Dewi

58	= +SAÉ?	GOOD,
59	**mang+**	Uncle.

In beginning my analysis, we can start by comparing these participants' use of social space with the use of social space by two other pairs, Susi-Ucup or Susi-Dewi (figures 3.5.3 and 3.5.4). There appears to be much less space between Dewi and Ucup (extract 3.4.7) when compared with the pairs Susi-Ucup or Susi-Dewi (figures 3.5.3 and 3.5.4). This difference in the use of social space is also mirrored in how they orient their bodies. For example, by comparing the frames in extract 3.5.7 and figures 3.5.3 and 3.5.4, we can see that Dewi and Ucup directly face each other, while the pairs of Susi-Ucup and Susi-Dewi do not.

In the interaction represented in extract 3.5.7, Dewi repeats Ucup's propensity for jumping up and down (the second frame). This potentially indicates a mutual recognition of this activity as a sign of familiar interpersonal relations. Just as important, we also see mutual orientation to a new set of signs from lines 37–59. These include overlap (the start of which is indicated by a square bracket "["), latching (i.e., no perceivable pause between turns indicated by "="), rapid speech (indicated by a ">" surrounding words/utterances), and touch (the last frame).

We also see that Dewi confirms that she is indeed the Dewi that Ucup thinks he knows (lines 40–41) and that Dewi is able to remember Ucup's name

FIGURE 3.5.3 Proxemics, body orientation, and unfamiliars (Susi and Ucup)

FIGURE 3.5.4 Proxemics, body orientation, and unfamiliars (Susi and Dewi)

(line 51). In line 57, Sundanese is used to ask about personal life-worlds as compared with earlier Indonesian usage that was about the material world (extract 3.5.4). All of this sign usage helps further solidify the identities of Dewi and Ucup. In this case, it is now clear that they are Sundanese-speaking familiars whose affective stance toward each other can be characterized as one of rapport (in the sense offered by Tannen, 1984, 1989) or intimacy. It is also apparent here that Sundanese and Indonesian are alternated on lines 38–39, 40, 42–44, 44–45, and 47–48 within an intonational unit (i.e., where there is a pause between utterances). That both engage in alternation that involves Sundanese fragments, both here and elsewhere in the soap, suggests some sort of habitualness, while contrasting with sign usage in the participant constellations of Susi-Dewi and Mang-Susi. There is also Ucup's lowering of his body (the last frame of extract 3.5.7) and Dewi's use of what can be classified as a "politeness" form—*saé* (good/well), which are all signs of hierarchical social relationships. (To keep from making my analysis too complex, however, I will not analyze this usage here.)

As the story continues, another young woman, Ayu, arrives responding to the same "room for rent" advertisement that attracted Susi. In contrast to Susi, she introduces herself to Dewi. In so doing, she makes it clear that they are strangers. She, like Susi, is represented as a city woman who is lazy and lacking in morals. In thinking about whether she should invite either of these Indonesian-speaking women to rent a room, an image of her grandmother reappears for the third time in the show. Her grandmother is pictured sweeping the yard in a traditional *kebaya* and frequently using Sundanese fragments (in bold), as illustrated in extract 3.5.8.

Extract 3.5.8 A grandmother's warning

Dewi's grandmother

1 dewi? (0.8) uang **teh** perlu (0.5) tapi	Dewi, money is important. But
2 kamu jangan jadi mata duitan (0.7)	don't you become obsessed with it.
3 +kalo bangun tidur . >jangan suka	When you get up in the morning, don't
4 bengong> (0.9) **sok beberes** .	be lazy. **Tidy up,**
5 **bebersih+** (0.9) kalo pekarangan sudah	**clean up**! If everything is already
6 bersih . baru kamu boleh mengerjakan	tidy then you can do
7 yang lain? (1.4) **yeuh** . kalo pekarangan	other things. **Go on**! If the yard is
8 itu bersih . itu **hiji** tanda . bahwa	clean, that is **a** sign that you are also a
9 kehidupan kamu juga bersih . **+ngarti+**	clean-living person. [You]
10 (0.8) **+aeh aeh** . >jangan seperti orang	understand! **Oh my, oh my** don't be
11 lain> . **atuh**? . +>baru pegang sapu	like other people, **really**! [They] have
12 sudah merasa capai>+ (1.0) **yeuh** (1.0)	just picked up the broom and already feel tired. **Go on,**
13 +>**sok geura beberes . geura sasapu** .	**tidy up, do the sweeping, sweeping,**
14 **jung>+**	**hurry up!**

In the above represented talk, we can see Dewi's grandmother's Sundanese usage co-occurs with her animated way of speaking (some of which can be seen through my representation of prosody, volume, and pause), all of which contrast sharply with the ways of speaking between the unfamiliars represented in this soap (Susi-Ucup, Susi-Dewi, Ayu-Dewi), while mirroring the ways of speaking between familiars (Ucup and Dewi). For example, there are regular changes in tempo that can be seen by looking at the use of ">" in the extract. Dewi's grandmother also frequently varies her volume (see, for example, my use of "+," which represents rising volume). While nowhere in the serial do characters explicitly note where this story is set, we do get some insights into character identities.

For example, after briefly leaving the house with Ucup and his taxi, Susi comes back. At this time, Ucup provides Dewi with an alternative to having to get paying housemates to help her look after her large house and gardens. He suggests that as a way of repaying his debt to Dewi's grandmother (who put him through driving school), he could live there and help look after the house and grounds. In this sense, he provides a commentary about the type of intimate social relationship that exists, which has thus far been represented only through sign usage. By the end of the comedic soap, it also becomes clear that both young women are not who they claim to be and instead of being well-moneyed, generous, and good tenants, they are represented as people who only pretend to be like this. The grandmother refers to this undesirable trait as *cipoa*. What is also interesting here is that the alternation engaged in by Dewi's grandmother adds to our earlier interpretation of this practice as habitual between intimates.

In summary, we can say that the mediums discussed thus far were associated with region, social types, and specific types of interpersonal relationships. This process was one that relied not only upon narrative progression and explicit commentaries about social relationships, but also upon contrasts of sign usage from one speech event to the next. In doing so, these encounters indexed a new set of signs with semiotic register users and usage that can be equated with demeanor. On the one hand, Indonesian speaking was being indexed to stranger relationships, city folk, worldliness, and those with access to substantial financial resources. On the other hand, the use of Sundanese was indexed to local poor folk (Mang Ucup, the taxi driver). In short, we are seeing the modeling of orders of indexicality with Indonesian sitting above regional languages. Even so, it is also interesting to point out that in the case of Sundanese usage, we are also seeing the authorization of models of language alternation. This is so because what is represented is the use of Sundanese fragments alternated with Indonesian in a habitual way in settings associated with intimates.

In the following sections, I focus on series that were seen as more popular. In line with scholars of the Indonesian media (Loven, 2008; Rachmah, 2006), I define popular here as simply occupying a prime-time slot (between 6–9 p.m.) and as being part of a sequel (in the case of films) or a new season (in the case of soaps). In the first of these, *Si Kabayan*, there are also explicit statements by characters as to the geographic anchoring of the story.

3.6 The Comedic Soap *Si Kabayan*

The persona of *Si Kabayan* has been circulating on television and in feature-length films since the early 1970s, and in short stories and novels since the 1930s. Typically, the narrative revolves around the daily life of Kabayan, his friends, love interest, and potential in-laws. The television rendition that I look at here is from the series *Si Kabayan*, which was broadcast nationally by the commercial broadcaster SCTV in early 1996. The episode I focus on is titled "*Bukan Impianku Bag: 1*" ("It wasn't my dream: Part 1"). As with "Noné," what is striking in this episode and serial is the contrast in Sundanese usage among Kabayan and his peers and Indonesian usage among a stranger, Kabayan, and other characters. From a purely quantitative view, for example, over 20 percent of the tokens Kabayan used were Sundanese, while the stranger used only Indonesian. What I will do in the rest of this section is show how this usage co-occurs with proximity, gesture, facial expressions, and prosody and interactional histories to produce semiotically denser models of Sundanese-ness and of Indonesian-speaking strangers.

The first interaction that I look at, extract 3.6.1, occurs after two scenes. The first scene is of a group of children observing the main character, Kabayan, kneeling and practicing what he wants to say to his girlfriend's father. His talk is peppered with Sundanese tokens. The scene then moves to a house and its surrounds where a male, the father in question, has finished exercising to the astonishment of two female onlookers (his wife and daughter) who are sweeping the yard and drying rice cakes. Bold indicates Sundanese, plain font indicates Indonesian, and bold italics indicate ambiguous forms (i.e., those that could be either Indonesian or Sundanese).

Extract 3.6.1 Proximity, Sundanese, and close interpersonal relations

Abah

1 kenapa **ambu** .   What's up **Mum**?
2 melihatnya sampai   **Gawking** at me like that,
3 **melongo** begitu (0.5)   as if you were looking at
4 kaya? melihat *kebo'*   a *buffalo*.

Ambu

5 he::ran . **abah teh** udah   [I] don't understand. **Dad**
6 puluhan tahun? tidak   [you] haven't done any
7 pernah *olahraga* (0.5)   *exercise* **for years, why**
8 >naha ayeuna *olahraga*   **are** [you] **now taking up**
9 **deui atuh'**>   *exercise* **again**?

(Talk deleted: Abah explains that what he is doing is Taiso, which the Japanese taught him during the occupation. Abah then notes that Ambu can also do this as well, although it is a dance version, which he parodies.)

Ambu

10 +bo::hong iteung .   [He's] fibbing Iteung,
11 bohong+ >**si abah mah**   [He's] fibbing, it's just
12 biasa aja> lah' . **sok aya**   like [your] **dad**, [he's]
13 **aya waé**   **always talking nonsense**

(*Source:* Petet, 1996)

The first onlooker is referred to with the term *Ambu* (Mother) on line 1, while the other is referred to in the subsequent talk with Iteung (a person's name) on line 10. Although the forms in bold font are not explicitly named as Sundanese, they are potential indexes of ethnicity by way of their being spoken in a setting that also presupposes close interpersonal relations. For example, the physical location of the interaction—which is in the front yard of a house surrounded by gardens—hints at potential family and thus intimacy. Such a reading is further supported with recourse to signs of speaker age, where both speakers seem to be of the same age and much older than Iteung (the person in the middle). Together and over the course of the interaction, this set of signs starts to provide "indexical focus" (Agha, 2007a: 24) that not only frame the interaction as intimate, but also as potentially ethnic because intimacy can presuppose ethnicity.

As their talk continues, we also see Iteung and Ambu move their bodies so that they are standing side-by-side. This closeness also co-occurs with some touching and the mention of a proper name, Iteung, which also presupposes some level of familiarity (i.e., a shared interactional history). They then face each other while laughing and proceed to carry out the highly animated talk in lines 11–13. It is animated in relation to the prior talk because of regular touching between Ambu and Iteung (frame 3) as Ambu refutes Abah's parody of her. Ambu also raises her voice (indicated by the "+" signs surrounding the text) and changes her tempo (indicated by ">" signs surrounding the text). As with the interactions described in section 3.5, it is also worthwhile to point out that the topic of talk and Abah's decades of physical inactivity (lines 6–10) are about personal life-worlds, which also presuppose a history of close interpersonal relations (i.e., to say that someone hasn't exercised for ten years presupposes that you have known them for ten years). All of these signs continue to provide an indexical focus that points to intimate social relations between the participants. The import of this representation is how it adds other signs to the doing of intimate social relations and thus also increases the semiotic density of these models of personhood and the social relations that exist between them.

As with interactions between Dewi and Ucup in section 3.5, we also see that much of the talk represented here can be characterized as alternation as the medium and indeed, in interactions between locals, this is typically the pattern throughout this soap. As the story continues, these interactions and the linguistic signs described thus far begin to be anchored with geographical region. In extract 3.6.2, which represents a stranger's entrance into a rural setting, we see that this stranger's semiotic practices are interactionally "flat" when compared with interactions between those who have been represented as intimate. This interaction is preceded by a shot of Kabayan lying down in a field tending his buffalo and then the buffalo returning to Kabayan's home. As the story cuts to Kabayan's home, we find one of his friends, Diran, and two strangers, a driver of a car sporting a Bandung license plate, and a well-dressed and well-fed man who is standing and holding a briefcase in Kabayan's front yard.

Extract 3.6.2 Indonesian, strangers, and interactional flatness

Diran

1	mau cari siapa pak (1.1)	Who are you looking for Sir? Maybe I can help.
2	barangkali bisa saya	
3	bantu (1.2)	

Stranger

4	begini pak (1.4) saya	It is like this Sir, I came here with the purpose of meeting and accompanying Mr. Kabayan [to...]. Earlier the stall owner said his [Kabayan's] house is here.
5	datang ke mari (0.5)	
6	maksudnya mau menemui	
7	dan membawa saudara	
8	kabayan (0.8) tadi:: . kata	
9	tukang warung:: .	
10	>rumahnya di sini> .	
11	katanya .	

Diran

12	iya . betul pak (0.3)	Yes, that is right Sir.

Stranger

13	he he he he' (0.5)	Laugh.

Diran

14	membawa . >maksud	To accompany, what do you mean Kabayan will be brought where?
15	bapak . kabayan mau	
16	dibawa ke mana> .	

(*continued*)

Extract 3.6.2 (Continued)

Stranger

17	o:::h . bukan membawa	Oh [I] don't mean bring
18	(0.5) maksud saya:? .	[as a prisoner] what I
19	saya hanya ingin	mean is that I only wish
20	menemuinya' (0.6) ada	to meet with him. There
21	masalah penting (1.0)	is an important matter.

Diran

22	itu tadi . kerbaunya baru	Earlier his buffalo just
23	saja masuk (0.5) biasanya	came home, usually
24	. kabayan di belakangnya	Kabayan is right behind
25	pak .	him, sir.

(*Source:* Petet, 1996)

By taking a comparative perspective of the above embodied talk with that represented in extract 3.6.1 and section 3.5, there are a number of similarities and differences. First of all, we see that although the represented space is a house, at least one of the people does not belong to this intimate setting. This is so because Diran's act of asking "who are you looking for" together with his use of the terms for you ("Pak" instead of Pak + name) presuppose unfamiliar social relations. Second, unfamiliarity with locality is explicitly stated by the stranger in lines 8–11, when he checks whether the person he is looking for lives at the house. In this sense, participants are represented as jointly establishing that they do not share common ground about locale. As the interaction unfolds, there is also a notable difference in proximity between speakers (compare, for example, the last frame of extract 3.6.1 with the frames in 3.6.2).

We also do not see any of the body language (touching and smiling), animated talk (e.g., laughter and changes in volume and tempo), or use of emphatic forms, such as *teh, atuh*, and *mah* (lines 5, 9, and 11) found in the earlier interaction represented in extract 3.6.1. The difference in the use of space, gesture, touch, and facial expressions also co-occurs with patterns of pause that are typically longer than those found in extract 3.6.1. The talk itself is also very much about the material world and the whereabouts of one person (Kabayan) and contains no talk that indicates a sharing of common ground (e.g., about locale). Taken together, all of these signs help to provide an indexical focus that points toward a stranger relationship among these participants.

This stranger relationship is further supported by the existence of another sign, namely the car license plate (see the first frame in extract 3.6.2), which helps anchor the interaction to a region, in this case somewhere in West Java, which is stereotypically known as a Sundanese-speaking area. More specifically, the "D" on the car license plate in figure 2 indicates "registered to the Bandung area of West Java." This plate helps to solidify the emergent stranger identities through a number of other indexical relationships. On the one hand, it anchors the whole serial to West Java and thus these speakers as potentially of Sundanese ethnicity and, by extension through indexical links among place, person, and language, Sundanese speakers. Second, and following on from this, co-ethnic speakers stereotypically use ethnic languages if they are known to each other. That they do not seem to speak in the same way as those in extract 3.6.1 points to unfamiliar social relations.

After the initial conversation, Diran and the stranger sit down in front of the house pictured in extract 3.6.2 to wait for Kabayan. Diran then introduces himself as Kebayan's good friend, which anchors Diran to the location. The stranger introduces himself and notes that he is a lawyer. This talk further reinforces stranger social relations because the act of introducing oneself makes it clear that they are strangers. As the talk proceeds, it becomes clear that they are strangers who do not live in the same locale because the stranger names his place of origin (Bandung, which is a big city rather than a rural village like the one represented here). Their talk also continues to be similar to their earlier talk, both in form and content, and it contrasts with the talk in extract 3.6.3, which occurs after Diran says he will go and look for Kebayan. Once out of sight, Diran proceeds to run to the house represented in extract 3.6.1. Diran's approach and talk with Iteung and her mother (referred to as Ambu) are represented in extract 3.6.3 and are again characterized by the interactional patterns and Sundanese usage found in extract 3.6.1.

Extract 3.6.3 Familiars, animated talk, and Sundanese usage

Diran

1 **tulung** (1.5) **tulung** (0.6)   **Help! Help Miss** Iteung.

2 **nyi** iteung . **tulung** .   **Help Mrs. Help!**

3 **ambu** (1.4) **tulung** (6.7)

(continued)

Extract 3.6.3 (Continued)

Ambu

(Running to the front of their house where Diran has sat down on the bench in front of the house)

4 ada +apa+ (0.5)   What is up?

Iteung

5 kenapa **kang** diran? =   What is the matter **Brother** Diran?

Ambu

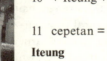

7   =   **Gee, gee, what is the**
8 **eleuh eleuh .+ kunaon**   **matter? What is the**
9 **kunaon +** .   **matter?**

10 + Iteung + ambilkan **aer**   Itueng quick go and fetch
11 cepetan =   some **water**.

Iteung

13   = iya (1.1)   Yes.

Ambu

14 **kunaon** pak (1.4)   **What is the matter** Sir?

(*Source:* Petet, 1996)

There are a number of distinctive features that contrast with the previous interaction between Diran and the lawyer from Bandung (extract 3.6.2) and Diran and the two women in extract 3.6.3. First of all, Diran's level of familiarity with locale and those who inhabit this locale is presupposed by Diran's knowledge of how to get from Kabayan's house to Itueng's house. This familiarity with locale and those who inhabit it is further solidified through the use of personal names (Iteung and Diran) in lines 2 and 5, respectively. In contrast to the interaction represented in extract 3.6.2, we can also see large differences in distance between speakers and the use of gesture and touch. In the last three frames of the interaction in extract 3.6.3, all three participants are spatially close and Ambu frequently touches Iteung and Diran. This use of space, gesture, and touch also co-occurs with changes in prosodic patterns (in this case, increased volume in lines 8–10) and emphatic particles (e.g., *eleuh* in line 8). As with the earlier interactions, there are examples of alternation as the medium (lines 5 and 10–11), as well as whole turns that are in Sundanese (lines 1–3 and 8–9). Together, all of these signs provide an indexical focus that points toward familiar social relations among these participants.

As with extract 3.6.1, these participants go on to talk about personal life-worlds; in this case, they are puzzling over why the lawyer from extract 3.6.2 wants to see Kabayan and how this might relate to previous events and interactions at the local level. Again, this talk about local history also continues to point to familiar social relations among these participants by way of them sharing common knowledge about events within the locale. This focus on personal life-worlds in interactions among Sundanese- speaking intimates is very much foregrounded in the following interaction that occurs after three scenes (1. Kabayan, Iteung, Diran, and another friend of Kabayan, Armasan, meeting with the lawyer at Kabayan's house; 2. Iteung's mother and father discussing with Iteung Kabayan's suitability to be her husband given his million-dollar inheritance; and 3. Kabayan worrying deeply over needing to leave his village, friends, and animals to organize his inheritance in the big city). In extract 3.6.4, the scene now cuts to Iteung where she is spatially located back in her yard at home where she is preparing and eating spicy fruit salad with some of her neighbors, who are age mates and friends.

Extract 3.6.4 Age mates talking about personal life-worlds

Iteung's Friend 1
1 **ih** (0.5) kamu **mah mani**   Wow you **are so happy**
2 **resep nya nyi** (0.4)   **younger sister aren't you**?

Iteung
3 **resep** apa (0.4)   Why am [I] **happy**?

(*continued*)

Extract 3.6.4 (Continued)

Iteung's Friend 1

4	**heueuh eta** (0.4) >pan	Yeah, that matter **right**?
5	**kang** kabayan **teh**	**Older brother** Kabayan
6	sebentar lagi> . punya	will soon own a textile
7	pabrik tekstil? . PAST:I	factory. Later if you
8	>nanti **teh** kamu kalo	marry him, **I can imagine**
9	kawin> . >**kacipta** tujuh	[there will be a wedding
10	hari tujuh malam> .	ceremony that lasts]
11	+**euy**+ (0.5)	seven days and seven nights, **right**!

Iteung's Friend 2

12	iya yah . >pasti bakal ada	Yeah, right? There will
13	**golek** asep sunarya> (0.7)	surely be a **puppet**
14	#ih# (0.4) kamu **mah**	**performance** by Asep
15	beruntung **nyi** . pilihan	Sunarya (a famous
16	kamu TEPAT? (0.5)	puppeteer). **Wow**, you are **so** lucky **younger sister**. You made the right choice.

Iteung's Friend 1

17	sebetulnya' . kamu **teh**	Actually [to be honest]
18	milih **kang** kabayan (0.5)	why did you choose **older**
19	+apanya **nyi**+ (while	**brother** Kabayan,
20	smiling and raising	**younger sister**?
21	eyebrows) (0.5)	

Representing Ethnicity and Social Relations on Television 83

Iteung
22 emang apanya gitu' (0.6)   Why do [you] think?

Iteung's Friend 1
23 >yang jelas **mah . kang**   What is clear is that **older**
24 kabayan **teh . jaba**   **brother Kabayan is not**
25 **bageur** .   **just nice and polite**,
26 **jaba pinteur . jab::a** > but also **smart**, and also
27 (0.4) eh . **ai** sekarang **teh** ... ah ah now in addition
28 ditambah lagi? (0.3)

Iteung Friend 2
29 ditambah apa gitu =   What else?

Iteung's Friend 1
30   =
31 **+beunghar+** (0.6) kaya   **Rich**, rich.
32 (0.3)

Iteung
33 y:a >kalo memang   Yes if [he] is indeed my
34 jodoh> . mau bilang   destined partner, then
35 apalagi **atuh** =   what can I say, right.

Iteung's friends
36   = adu:::h.   That's great.
37 (followed by a spoken
38 version of a whistle)

(*Source:* Petet, 1996)

As with extracts 3.6.1 and 3.6.3, locale presupposes intimacy insofar as it is in Iteung's neighborhood. That participants seem to know about Iteung's history (lines 1–11), Kabayan's name (line 24), and Kabayan's characteristics (lines 24–31) also presupposes that the two other participants are locals and thus have some degree of shared interactional history. In contrast to talk about the world in extract 3.6.2, in extract 3.6.4, the whole conversation is about personal life-worlds—in this case, Iteung's love interest, Kabayan, and why she chose him. The discussion about personal life-worlds continues well after line 38 when Iteung is asked when she will marry him, as well as the dangers of letting him go to the big city before getting married.

Participants also appear to be age mates who wear similar clothing (e.g., T-shirts and batik dresses) that is different from Iteung's mother's clothing. Sameness in clothing choices further points to similarities among these three women and thus to potentially intimate social relations. Although the participants do not use personal names, they do use terms of other reference, *nyi* "younger sister" (lines 2, 15, and 19) and *kamu* "you" (lines 1, 8, 14, 16, 17), which are also stereotypically linked with intimate personal relations. The social activity of chatting while eating together also points to the existence of intimate social relations among these three women. In short, in this extract, there are many signs that produce an indexical focus that points toward intimate social relations that are occurring in a Sundanese-speaking locale.

Importantly, these social relations, the participants, and the linguistic forms they use are also linked with demeanors through the co-occurrence of other signs. For example, in their talk, we also see many of the features found in the embodied talk represented in extracts 3.6.1 and 3.6.3, including changes in the prosodic features of the talk, the frequent use of smiles and body language, and the frequent use of emphatic particles. For example, there are regular changes in tempo of talk (indicated by the ">" surrounding talk) in lines 4–14, 23–26, and 33–35. In addition, there is regular stressing of words (indicated by CAPS) as in lines 7 and 16, together with the raising of volume of talk (indicated by "+" surrounding talk) in lines 11, 19, and 30. In terms of facial expressions, the three women regularly move between smiles and other facial expressions. These facial expressions sometimes co-occur with other embodied language. For example, in reaction to her friends' teasing in lines 36–38 and their subsequent teasing about when Iteung will marry Kabayan, Iteung stands up and stamps her feet and insists that she doesn't yet have any plans or a set date to marry Kabayan. As with the earlier interactions between intimates, their talk is characterized by alternation as the medium with most Sundanese fragments typically being kin terms or affective particles.

In sum, taken together, all of these signs help to further differentiate interaction among Indonesian-speaking strangers and Sundanese-speaking familiars, while laminating them with particular demeanors and interactional histories. These representations continue to situate linguistic sign usage as emblematic of ethnicity (in this case, Sundanese-ness) while also being indexed with other signs to form denser semiotic models of ethnicity. Just as important, the representations examined here also repeat many of the signs associated with the ethnic stereotypes found in other comedic soap operas, including the ones discussed in the previous section and the ones discussed in the next section. Typically, representations of Sundanese usage have been representations of Sundanese fragments used in alternation with Indonesian. Producers of soaps, such as those who produced *Si Doel* (discussed below), note that this strategy provides enough fragments to give a local flavor but not so much as to make it difficult for an Indonesian audience to follow (see, e.g., Loven, 2008). While this tends to authorize alternation as a common and natural interactional practice, it also provides an example of a producer's role in semiotic change.

In closing this section, I should point out that much of this comedic soap was about rural-urban differences. For example, there is overlap between the representation of ways of speaking of ethnic intimates who live in a rural area and speak an ethnic language with their representation as mostly poor and not sophisticated in their views about the world. This representation of ethnicity and ethnic language users contrasts markedly with the entry of a wealthy urban lawyer who speaks Indonesian. In a sense, these types of representation also help to reinforce orders of indexicality where Indonesia is at the top followed by ethnic languages.

3.7 Representing Diversity: *Si Doel Anak Sekolahan*

Up to this point, I have explored continuities between televised representations of sign usage and users and how this relates to the reproduction of semiotic registers and associated stereotypes where language use continues to be emblematic of ethnicity. I have paid particular attention to how linguistic signs are indexed with embodied language on the one hand and interactional history on the other to reproduce ethnic stereotypes while adding semiotic density to these stereotypes. Although the types of television representation described in sections 3.5 and 3.6 no doubt also provide insights into the diversity found in Indonesia, in this section, I look at a more explicit representation of diversity as it relates to migrants living in the city. In particular, I show how representations of sign usage and users can also contribute to the production of what might be seen as a competing semiotic register where ethnic languages aren't always emblems of ethnicity. Associated with this competing register are migrants or ethnic others who are represented as learning local ways of speaking to the extent that they can engage in practices of "crossing" (Rampton, 1995), "adequation" (Bucholtz & Hall, 2004), and "knowledging" (Goebel, 2013).

Although I defined these terms in section 3.1, it is worth repeating these definitions here. Crossing is the non-habitual performance of linguistic forms or formulaic utterances that are typically not associated with the person using them through reference to their ethnolinguistic background. Adequation is the habitual pursuit of semiotic sameness in face-to-face interactions, while knowledging is the ability to recognize and evaluate linguistic forms stereotypically associated with another ethnic group that is not one's own. Representations of these three practices also seem to offer an alternate model to the state ideology of doing unity in diversity through the use of Indonesian.

I focus upon a long-running popular series, *Si Doel Anak Sekolahan* (Doel an Educated Lad) originally broadcast by RCTI at the local level in Jakarta (Sen & Hill, 2000: 123), but later broadcast nationally by SCTV. Like the serial *Si Kabayan, Si Doel* is based upon an interpretation of an earlier novel titled *Si Doel Anak Betawi* (Doel a Betawi Lad) and a number of earlier television serials and feature-length films (e.g., Loven, 2008), some of which I discussed in section 2.3. I recorded this particular episode in mid-1998. This serial is different from *"Noné"* and *Si Kabayan* because it offers representations of sign usage and users that both reproduce the idea of ethnic social types who speak a certain ethnic language, act in certain ways, and are geographically anchored, while also offering representations of those who engage in adequation, which tends to sit in contrast to this first semiotic register.

This series is also different insofar as the music accompaniment—a song that starts with *Anak Betawi...* (A child of the Betawi area...)—and the co-occurring Betawi fragments, panorama shots showing skyscrapers (mainly found in Jakarta), shots of Jakarta's famous port (*Sunda Kelapa*), and other landmarks suggest that what follows is ethnic and geographically anchored in Jakarta. It is also striking in that the producer, Rano Karno, reported specifically producing this series to convince older Indonesians of Betawi background that education is important:

> Lewat Si Doel Anak Sekolahan, misi yang ingin saya sampaikan pada orang-orang tua Betawi yang masih kolot itu, bahwa sekolah penting demi mengangkat harkat dan martabat keluarga. Saya ingin memperkenalkan kepada Indonesia, bahwa inilah kultur masyarakat Betawi yang sebenarnya (Tabloid Jelita/Dv/Idh, [n.d.]).
>
> [What I wanted to convey via *Si Doel Anak Sekolahan* to *Betawi* elders, who were still traditional in outlook, is that schooling is important for raising family welfare and prosperity. I wanted to show Indonesians that this was the true authentic culture of the Betawi.] (Author's translation)

Both the semiotic framing of the show and the above commentary provide implicit and explicit commentaries about ethnic social types as linked with particular social practices and particular geographic spaces.

The following scene, which is taken from the third season from the episode entitled *"Meniti Batas Mimpi"* ("Walking along the Edge of a Dream"), occurs after a brief argument between Doel (the main character) and his uncle Mandra. Doel, Mandra, and Doel's sister Atun all live with Doel's mother Leala. In this interaction, Mandra is inside their home and getting ready to go and ask for his girlfriend's hand in marriage. After finding out that Mandra hasn't yet asked his girlfriend's parents if they are prepared to meet them, Leala (Mandra's older sister) tells Mandra what he should do.

Extract 3.7.1 Being emotional and speaking Betawi

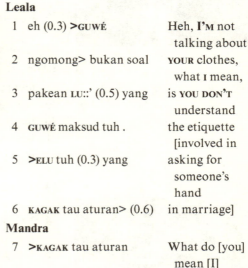

Leala

1 eh (0.3) >GUWÉ   Heh, I'M not talking about
2 ngomong> bukan soal   YOUR clothes, what I mean,
3 pakean LU::' (0.5) yang   is YOU DON'T understand
4 GUWÉ maksud tuh .   the etiquette [involved in
5 >ELU tuh (0.3) yang   asking for someone's hand
6 KAGAK tau aturan> (0.6)   in marriage]

Mandra

7 >KAGAK tau aturan   What do [you] mean [I]
8 +bagaimana+?> (0.6)   DON'T understand?

Leala

9   >lah . iya dong> (0.5)   Yeah [you don't
10 ELU ngajak GUWÉ   understand] silly. YOU
11 ngelamar ke si munaroh?   asked me to come with you
12 (0.3) >di sana dah tahu:>   to propose to Munaroh. Do
13 . BELON?   they know [that we are coming] or NOT?

(*continued*)

Extract 3.7.1 (Continued)

Mandra
14 ya::? . +udah jelas   Yeah [they] already know,
15 TAHU:: . dong + . >+kan   I've already asked Munaroh
16 saya dah boleh MESEN>   to ask, you know.
17 sama si munaroh' (0.7)

Leala
18 (cut to Doel who is
19 outside cleaning his
20 motorbike before cut
21 back to Leala) >#mesen   Asked
22 munaroh#> (0.5) enak   Munaroh [to do it]? You are
23 AJÉ ELU (0.5)   JUST too much! A marriage
24 NGELAMAR . kayak   proposal like buying a
25 orang beli karcis .   ticket,
26 >+bisa dipesen+> .   as if it can be ordered!
27 (abruptly turns away and
28 goes behind curtain)

This interaction shares many of the features represented in interactions among intimates in the previous two sections. For example, we have the co-occurrence of Betawi fragments (bold small caps) with facial expressions, regular changes in the prosodic features of the talk, and discussions of personal life-worlds. More specifically, extract 3.7.1 shows characters using a large range of muscle movements around the eyes, forehead, and mouth. Often, these expressions co-occur with verbal features including stress (indicated by CAPS) or increased volume (indicated by "+" surrounding the talk), as in lines 8, 14–16, and 24. These prosodic features also occur together with regular changes in tempo: for example, the speeding up of speech (indicated by ">" surrounding the talk) in lines 1–2, 4–6, 7–9, 11–12, 15–17, 21–23, and 26. Just as important, these features also occur in talk that is peppered with Betawi fragments: typically, terms for I (*guwé*) and you (*elu*). As with representations of medium usage in the previous sections, we can also see that alternation as the medium is represented as the way in which participants interact. In so doing, this can also be seen as authorizing alternation.

Leala abruptly turns away from Mandra after line 26 and moves away from him. Mandra follows her, addresses Leala as *mpok* (older sister), while raising his voice further. Leala then responds in a softer voice and in talk now peppered with Betawi fragments. She says that the correct way to ask for Munaroh's hand in marriage is to first go and ask her father when his family might be ready to receive a visit from Mandra and Leala about the proposed marriage. Mandra feels that this way is just too complicated. Following this, the story briefly cuts to Doel, who is still outside cleaning his motorbike. He is shown to be now intently listening while shaking his head as Leala scolds Mandra for not listening to an elder's advice. Mandra then notes that Munaroh has been previously married so this is not like her first marriage. Leala, who has recently lost her husband, suddenly emerges now screaming at Mandra who hastily steps back from the curtain and sits down before asking for forgiveness. Immediately afterward, this whole interaction—which has been visibly and audibly one of conflict—is then metapragmatically framed as such by Doel, who directly scolds his uncle for arguing with Leala, saying that she deserves respect as Mandra's older sister.

In short, up to this point, the characters have not only been represented as ethnic social types geographically anchored to a particular place, but also as Betawi-speaking social types with particular demeanors made up of a complex mix of facial expressions, prosodic patterns, body language, and views about how interpersonal relationships should be conducted. The discussion of personal life-worlds, in this case, Mandra's wedding plans, also presupposes shared common knowledge about referents (e.g., Munaroh and where she lives) and thus also points to shared interactional histories between Leala and Mandra. The combination of demeanors and interactional histories thus adds semiotic density to the Betawi stereotypes represented here.

In the scene that follows the above interaction, we see the development of a friendship between two young women who both see themselves as romantic prospects for Doel. There is Sarah, who in season one and two was introduced as an anthropology student from a wealthy cosmopolitan background (Loven, 2008). Through her anthropological study of a Betawi community in Jakarta, she becomes increasingly infatuated with Doel, who is also represented as poor but also the first in his family to get a university education. Although it is increasingly Sarah who becomes the object of Doel's affections, in the past, he has had a romantic interest in Zaenab, the daughter of a wealthy Betawi neighbor.

In this particular interaction, Zaenab, who has just found out that her mother is not her biological mother, is found by Sarah wandering aimlessly on a road. Sarah invites Zaenab to spend the night at her house, and in the morning, she offers Zaenab some clean clothes to wear before they engage in some more intimate talk about personal life-worlds and their conversation from the night before (extract 3.7.2). What is interesting in this extract is that their developing relationship is represented in a semiotically different way from other interethnic relationships in this series. In so doing, it also provides representations of the diversity of ways of speaking that can develop between those from different backgrounds. At the same time, these representations also provide contrasts that help regiment an order of indexicality where cosmopolitan, educated, and wealthy Indonesians speak Indonesian, while poorer and uneducated Indonesians speak an ethnic language (e.g., Mandra and Leala).

Extract 3.7.2 Building inter-group friendship through talk about personal life-worlds

Sarah
1 kok belum ganti baju:: Gee [you] haven't yet
2 nab (0.7) heuh (0.4) changed your blouse Nab, yeah!

Zaenab
3 ah . iya . >nanti deh sar> Ah, yes, [I'll do] it later
4 (Sarah walks over to sit Sar.
5 down on the floor with
6 Zaenab) (4.4)

Zaenab
7 sar = Sar.

Sarah
8 = heeh (while sitting Yes.
9 and turning to look at
10 Zaenab) (3.4)

Zaenab
11 maaf ya (1.2) aku: . Sorry yeah. I'm
12 >selalu aja ngerepotin just always imposing on
13 kamu> (0.4) you.

Sarah
14 #ngerepotin apa si::h'# [You] haven't put me out at all.
15 (while touching Zaenab
16 on the shoulder and
17 smiling) (2.2)

Representing Ethnicity and Social Relations on Television

Zaenab

18 iya: ngerepotin kamu'   Yeah imposing on you,

19 (0.5) ngelibatin kamu ke   involving you in my own

20 masalah pribadi aku:'   personal problems.

21 (1.4)

Sarah

22 #ngak apa apa kok'# (3.4)   It's no problem at all, really.

Zaenab

23 da::n (0.5) makasih juga   And, thanks also for last

24 yah (0.6) >semalem kamu   night when you listened

25 mau dengerin cerita   to my story.
26 aku:'> (1.7)

Sarah

27 #udah deh na:b . kamu   Please don't worry Nab,

28 tuh sekarang ngak usah   now you don't need to

29 mikir yang ngak ngak   worry about what-ifs

30 lagi::# (0.3) yah (1.1)   anymore, yeah?

31 #yang jelas sekarang .   What is clear now is that

32 kamu tuh musti tabah dan   you need to be strong and

33 tega:r'# (said while   persistent.
34 stroking Zaenab's
35 shoulders and back) (3.3)

The embodied encounter represented in extract 3.7.2 above is also interesting when compared with the encounters represented in extracts 3.7.3, 3.7.4, and 3.7.5 (which we will look at shortly). What stands out here is the lack of Betawi fragments, the high use of truncated names not preceded by a kin term, the facial expressions, touch, the maternal prosody of Sarah's talk, the discussion of personal life-worlds, the social activity being engaged in, and the use of personal space. For example, in contrast to earlier interactions among strangers where facial expressions were fairly unchanging, Sarah (the person on the left) shows a large range of muscle movements around the eyes, forehead, and mouth. Often, these expressions co-occur with touch as in lines 14–17, 23, and 27–35 and verbal features including a drop in volume (indicated by "#" surrounding the talk). These prosodic signs also occur in talk that is characterized by frequent self references and other references. Typically, terms for "I" are *aku* (e.g., lines 6, 20, and 26), while terms for "you" are either *kamu* (e.g., lines 13, 18-19, 24, 27, and 32) or a truncated form of the person's name (e.g., lines 2–3, 7, and 27).

Sarah and Zaenab's talk is also very much about personal life-worlds as can be seen through discussions of clothing and adoption. Indeed, as their talk continues, it is primarily about life-worlds, including what each other has learned about life and how to cope with its ups and downs. In this sense, they are not only sharing personal life-worlds, but establishing the common ground needed to further build positive interpersonal relations. Similarly, the talk occurs within the intimate and personal social practice of getting ready within one's home (e.g., Zaenab changing her blouse), and both Sarah and Zaenab's bodies are spatially very close throughout the whole interaction. It is also interesting to note that after Sarah takes Zaenab to her grandfather's house, she then visits Zaenab's mother to tell her where her daughter is. During this talk, she frames her and Zaenab's relationship as "good friends." In short, the interaction represented in extract 3.7.2 contrasts with the interactional flatness seen in other interactions characterized by Indonesian usage. This is done by mirroring the types of features used in intra-ethnic encounters (e.g., extracts 3.5.5–3.5.7, 3.6.1, 3.6.3, 3.6.4, and 3.7.1).

The features used in the above interaction, which is represented as between people of different ethnic backgrounds, can be further contrasted with the following two extracts. The first has a migrant, Karyo, engaging in adequation, while the second is a representation of both knowledging and social differentiation through the use of Javanese in a setting where the use of Betawi is common. The first scene occurs after that represented in extract 3.7.2 and is preceded by a shot of Karyo raising a birdcage up a pole beside Leala's house. He then moves to Leala's nearby *warung* (a small canteen type of construction selling food and home necessities), where Karyo starts his conversation with Leala. I don't focus on the visual aspects here becvause they are basically just Karyo talking while walking toward the *warung* with Leala inside and out of sight. The rest of the interaction occurs with Karyo facing the front counter of the *warung*, but barely visible in the shadows. What is interesting here, however, is his ability to comprehend linguistic signs associated with Betawi social types and also use some of these forms.

Extract 3.7.3 Engaging in adequation

Karyo

1	MAK nyak . BANG mandra sudah jalan	MUM, OLDER BROTHER Mandra has
2	*toh'* (0.4)	already gone *heh*?

Leala

3	*u:::+dah+* (0.5)	*Yeah.*

Karyo

4	*kok tumben loh* pagi pagi' (0.5)	*Gee that's unusual* [for him to get up] so early.

Leala

5	IYÉ mau ke rumahnya munaroh' (1.3)	YEAH, [he] wants to go to Munaroh's house.

Karyo

6	ke rumah munaroh .	To Munaroh's house?

Leala

7	iya =	Yeah.

Karyo

8	= *ngelamar* ya' (0.3)	[He] wants to *propose* [marriage] yeah?

Leala

9	ng::gak . >cuma mau *nanyain* . kapan	*No*, [he] only wants to *ask* when
10	lamarannya bisa DITERIMÉ::> *gitu*.'=	[is the best time to propose so that] it is ACCEPTED [by his girlfriend's parents].

Karyo

11	= o:h .	Oh
12	>jadi belum ya MAK ya>' =	so not yet heh MUM yeah?

Leala

13	= ya BELON	*No of course* NOT YET.
14	*dong* . (laugh) (0.4)	

Karyo

15	atun ada MAK .	Is Atun around MUM?

Leala

16	ada NOH lagi sarapan'	Yeah, THERE having breakfast.

(*Source:* Karno, 1998)

What sets this extract apart from the previous extracts is that Karyo is portrayed as an ethnic Javanese who on occasion uses and is spoken to in Betawi in an interethnic interaction where we might expect to hear Indonesian. For example, Karyo uses the kin terms *mak* (mum) and *bang* (older brother) in lines 1, 12, and 15. We also see that he appears to comprehend the Betawi fragments spoken by Leala (e.g., lines 6 and 12). This representation suggests that accommodating to one's new linguistic environment is not unusual and perhaps desirable. It is important to note here that such usage is situational. In other parts of the serial, Karyo uses and is spoken to in Indonesian in interaction with those he doesn't have close social relations. He only appears to use Betawi fragments when interacting with familiars. Thus, while Karyo's Betawi usage here is situational, by looking at wider interactional patterns, we find it also represents a habitual pursuit of semiotic sameness through the alternation of Betawi and Indonesian. In other words, what we see here resembles adequation (e.g., Bucholtz & Hall, 2004) carried out in a way that actually denaturalizes the type of language-ethnicity links described thus far. It is also important to point out that this representation alternation in an interethnic interaction among participants who have little formal education also sets up a further contrast with earlier and later participant constellations. This contrast also helps reproduce another register to be situated within the orders of indexicality discussed thus far, though its placement within this hierarchy can only be implied with reference to the stigmatization of mixed languages more generally (e.g., section 2.8).

Representations of knowledging as a social practice are also found in subsequent interactions and episodes where we see Karyo interacting with Atun (his Betawi girlfriend) and other Betawi in utterances containing Javanese fragments. These are examples of knowledging insofar as Atun is represented as someone who understands and follows Javanese talk. In other words, she is represented as someone who has an ability to comprehend linguistic signs associated with Javanese. Taken together with Karyo's practice of engaging in adequation, we can say that in these contexts, identity relates less to an essentialized ethnic identity and more to a situated "community of practice" (Wenger, 1998), where new ways of speaking and new identities develop simultaneously in an ongoing interaction. Ethnic social types are thus represented here as situated rather than static. Just as important, the interaction represented in extract 3.7.3 provides an example of doing unity in diversity that starts to contrast with earlier models whereby social relations among those from different backgrounds were ideologized as being conducted in Indonesian, though it is important to note that this type of activity seems only to be engaged in by poorer and "uneducated" folk.

Extracts 3.7.4 and 3.7.5 provide striking representations of Mandra's ability to comprehend linguistic signs. The scene occurs at the end of this episode. It is preceded by Mandra meeting with his girlfriend Munaroh, who tells him that they had best wait to get married until he has a more secure job. Mandra then returns home early, and feeling depressed, he goes to lie down under a jackfruit tree outside Leala's house. When asked what is up, he says nothing to his sister Leala, his niece Atun, or his nephew Doel. Karyo then enters the scene while Mandra is examining a small jackfruit. After asking how he is and not getting an answer, Karyo briefly teases Mandra about the size of his lips before asking how his marriage proposal went. Upon hearing that it was unsuccessful, Karyo comforts him by saying that his day has been bad too because his lack of a Jakartan identity card had led to an unsuccessful credit application.

Extract 3.7.4 Representing knowledging

Karyo
1 **MAS** (0.8) **OPO**   OLDER BROTHER,
2 **SAMPEYAN** juga punya   DO YOU also have one?
3 **TOH**? . >KTP Jakarta'>?   A Jakartan identity card.
4 =

Mandra
5 = (nods head) =   Yes.
Karyo
7   = bene::r   Really?
8 (0.3)

Mandra
9 (Nods head) =   Yes.

Karyo
10   = (laughs) .
11 >boleh ndak> . kalo saya   What do [you] think if I
12 pinjem' =   borrow [your KTP]

Mandra
13   = (Looks up and
14 sighs) =

(*continued*)

Extract 3.7.4 (Continued)

Karyo

15	= buat ngajuin	to put in a finance application.
16	#KREDIT# (0.7) nanti	
17	kalo kriditnya kelua:r .	Later if it is successful
18	(while touching Mandra	
19	on the shoulder)	
20	**SAMPEYAN TAK**	I'LL GIVE YOU [a]
21	**KASIH #KOMISI::?# =**	commission.

Mandra

22		=
23	(turns gaze toward Karyo	
24	and then takes out his	
25	wallet from his back	
26	pocket and proceeds to	
27	take out his identity card	
28	"KTP") =	

Karyo

29	= ha:duh (2.1)	
30	ha:: la::h ini? . >ktp	Wow, this is it, the Jakartan identity card that I'VE been looking for
31	Jakarta yang	
32	**TAK** cari cari (while	

33	patting Mandra's ktp). ya	Ya this is the one
34	ini loh **MAS>** . +a:	**OLDER BROTHER,** yes! I've already
35	**WIS?+** . **KELAKON**	
36	kredit **AKU MAS . SI:P** .	**GOT** finance **OLDER BROTHER, GREAT!**

37	e::::h . waduh? .	Eh, wow [You are really]
38	**GANTENGÉ**	**HANDSOME IN THE**
39	**PHOTONÉ** (1.7)	**PHOTO**.

(*Source:* Karno, 1998)

What sets this extract apart from the previous one is that now Karyo is using linguistic fragments that are stereotypically associated with Javanese (in bold caps) in his encounter with Mandra. Mandra is also represented as comprehending these fragments by his responses in lines 5 and 22–28. As with earlier representations, this talk is characterized by alternation as the medium, at least on the part of Karyo. What also stands out here is that while Karyo referred to Mandra as *Bang* Mandra (older brother Mandra) in his earlier conversation with Leala (extract 3.7.3, line 1), when talking with Mandra here, he chooses the Javanese form for older brother, *mas* (lines 1, 34, and 36) and the second- person pronoun *sampeyan* (lines 2 and 20).

Taken together with Karyo's alternation practices, we are also starting to see the modeling of representations of diversity from a number of perspectives. First, we see that Jakarta is made up of migrants, and second, that such migrants have several different types of linguistic competence including the ability to engage in knowledging. In a sense, this representation offers a model of doing unity in diversity or togetherness that doesn't exclusively involve Indonesian. There are also many similarities with previous representations of ethnic social types and interactions among those who are intimate, especially the use of space, facial expression, gesture, touch, prosody, and talk about personal life-worlds. For example, in addition to the use of Javanese fragments, Karyo and Mandra are seated close together, Karyo touches Mandra's shoulder (lines 18–19), and Karyo's facial expressions and gestures change in each frame. Indeed, Karyo uses many of the features that were found in the intra-ethnic encounters examined in sections 3.5 and 3.6. These features include stress and volume (lines 16 and 21), tempo (e.g., changes in speed of delivery in lines 1–3 and 29–34), and vowel elongation (lines 7, 17, and 21).

It is also interesting to highlight the social practice engaged in by Karyo, where his talk is something like "preparing to ask a big favor" and "asking a big favor." Karyo starts this sequence by explaining his problems (i.e., not having a Jakartan identity card), then asking if Mandra has a Jakartan identity card, followed by the promise of some money. The combination seems to work because Mandra hands over his Jakartan identity card. As we follow the interaction, however, things turn sour (extract 3.7.5).

Extract 3.7.5 Knowledging and authentic social types

Karyo

40	#loh# (2.7) (while	What!
41	slapping Mandra on the	
42	shoulder) +is::+ (0.8)	Hey!
43	+>ini masa berlakunya .	This card is expired, you
44	sudah ABIS gini>+ loh	know.
45	(0.5)	
46	+>**SAMPEYAN** ni **PIYÉ**	**WHAT IS UP WITH**
47	**TOH>+** (1.9) (Mandra	**YOU!**
48	turn away and is slapped	
49	again on the shoulder by	
50	Karyo)	
51	+>ini loh **MBOK** diliat	Here have a look!
52	tu>+ (while pointing to	**DIDN'T** [you] see this!
53	card) (0.7)	
54	+masa BERLAKU+ .	Valid until the 5th of
55	lima februari . sembilan	February 97, that means it
56	tujuh . +>berarti telat	has [already been
57	setau::n>+ (0.7)	expired] for one year!
58	+>**SAMPEYAN KUDU**	**YOU MUST** go to the
59	ngurus ke kelurahan lagi	local government office
60	ini>+ . +>sudah ndak	again. [This one] is
61	laku::?>+ =	already expired!

Mandra

62	= (turns gaze	
63	toward Karyo) >sini>	Give it here!
64	(grabs grabbing card from	
65	Karyo's hand) (1.1)	
66	>emangnya GUWA	It doesn't matter, I'M not
67	pendatang kayak ELU?>	a newcomer like YOU!
68	(0.6)	
69	(waving hand and card	
70	toward his chest)+>GUWA	I'M
71	betawi asli:?>+ (0.9)	a genuine Betawi!
72	>biar gak punya ktp . juga	Even if [I] don't have an
73	gak apa apa . ngak bakal	identity card it is OK. I'll
74	ditangkap> . (pointing to	never be arrested [by the
75	Karyo) >emangnya kayak	police]. Not like YOU.
76	ELU> . +>ditangkep LU>+	YOU'LL be arrested if you
78	>kalo ngak punya ktp	don't have a Jakartan
79	jakarta> . +tolol+ (while	identity card, idiot!
80	hitting Karyo on the knee)	

(*Source:* Karno, 1998)

In the above interaction, Karyo continues to use Javanese (bold), as in lines 46–47, 51, and 58. Mandra continues to be represented as a Betawi-speaking social type (lines 66–71), who nevertheless understands the gist of what is being said from his responses from line 62 onward. While thus far, we have seen that some forms of touch, gesture, facial expression, and prosody are characteristic of friendly social relations between intimates, here we also get to see not-so-friendly relations between intimates, where intimate can be defined as "a relationship developed over frequent and sustained interactions." In this case, the relationship is not just framed through reference to prior interactions between the two, but also through the metapragmatic commentary of Mandra who positions Karyo as a non-Betawi outsider (lines 62–78) who is also an idiot (line 78). Despite this characterization, we also see that Karyo is represented as someone who understands Betawi fragments (bold small caps), in this case, the use of terms for "I" and "you" (lines 66–67, 70, and 76).

In sum, the extracts in this section have shown not only how embodied features and interactional histories are attached to Betawi and Javanese stereotypes to produce denser stereotypes, but they have also provided representations of the semiotic diversity to be found in the city. Part of the model offered in these representations was an apparent ability to comprehend and/or use languages that are not one's own. Importantly, these examples model the doing of unity in diversity, which can also be achieved through the use of fragments of a regional language. These practices of adequation and knowledging thus far seem to be reserved for interactions among those from the low socioeconomic segments of Indonesian society. This helps place alternation between ethnic languages and Indonesia on a par with or below the use of ethnic languages in an emergent indexical order that has Indonesian at the top.

3.8 Conclusion

This chapter sought to explore how personhood and social relations were represented in Indonesian comedic soap operas in the mid-to-late 1990s. This was done with an eye to identifying continuities between these representations and the circulating ideologies about ethnicity and the broader indexical orders discussed in chapter 2, while contributing to some of the scholarship on language ideology formation. Taking inspiration from work on media and television more generally (section 2.2), I went on to point out that these comedic representations were the outcome of particular historical circumstances as they related to the emergence of television and local soaps (section 3.3). In general, television programming was produced by and for an emerging middle-income Indonesia. After outlining my multimodal approach (section 3.4), in sections 3.5 to 3.7, I analyzed three comedic soaps. In particular, I showed how the co-occurrence of lexical items with embodied language (e.g., proxemics, gesture, facial expressions, activity type, and prosody) and common ground helped to laminate ethnic stereotypes with viewable and hearable "demeanors" (Goffman, 1967) and interactional histories.

Through these televised representations, the ethnic stereotypes discussed in chapter 2 were linked with signs of place and intimate interpersonal social relations in all three soaps. In contrast, representations of the Indonesian-speaking subject became indexed with facial expressions and prosody, although these typically become signs of a lack of intimate interpersonal social relations. The locally emergent registers that developed as part of contact between those of different backgrounds described in chapter 2 were also laminated with many of the signs found in representations of intra-ethnic interactions, while also helping to index interactional practices in settings characterized by diversity with social types who can engage in adequation. At the same time, the representation of poor, rural, and uneducated personas who typically spoke ethnic languages was regularly contrasted with wealthier, urban, and educated types who spoke Indonesian. In so doing, these representations also helped to regiment centers of normativity associated with Indonesian and ethnic languages, while modeling and/or reproducing the emergent orders of indexicality described in chapter 2.

Fragments of local mediums were commonly found in all three soaps, although this was typically alternated with Indonesian in a way I refer to as "alternation as the medium." This representation of alternation thus also appears to be authorizing mixing in settings that do not have a close fit with descriptions of alternation elsewhere in the world, which are typically in the form of crossing (e.g., Androutsopoulos, 2007; Jaffe, 2000; Kelly-Holmes & Atkinson, 2007; LeCompte & Schensul, 1999). In contrast to crossing, which is typically represented as part of liminal and spectacular performances, the instances of alternation I have examined are typically unspectacular, mundane, and often habitual. For a number of political and economic reasons (section 3.3), this practice of representing ethnic social types who habitually engaged in alternation had become quite common on Indonesian television by the mid-1990s. Indeed, as television moved into the late 1990s and early 2000s, this practice continued as comedic soaps became increasingly popular (Loven, 2008; Rachmah, 2006).

The work in this chapter contributes to some of the discussions on language ideology formation by furthering the multimodal nature of such studies. More specifically, with a few recent exceptions (Bucholtz, 2011; Bucholtz & Lopez, 2011; Mendoza-Denton, 2011), most studies that look at how social types and social relations are constructed while being associated with particular signs typically use and focus on printed sources (e.g., Agha, 2003, 2011a; Inoue, 2006; Inoue, 2011; Miller, 2004). Yet printed sources can only represent certain modes of communication in comparison to the wider array of signs represented in moving picture formats, which constitute an increasingly ubiquitous one-to-many participation framework. In addition, the extra modes found in soap format also offer implicit metasemiotic commentaries that help in the construction of social types, such as the introductory song and pictures to the comedy *Si Doel,* which indexed the comedy as local and ethnic.

Some of the representations analyzed in section 3.7 also modeled a practice I refer to as "knowledging." Part of what constitutes knowledging is what Agha (2007a) refers to as competence to comprehend semiotic fragments that do not normally form part of a person's habitually used semiotic repertoire. Knowledging has parallels with other terms, such as "polylanguaging" (Jørgensen, Karrebæk, Madsen, & Møller, 2011), "symbolic competence" (Kramsch, 2006; Kramsch & Whiteside, 2008), and "crossing" (Rampton, 1995). However, polylanguaging describes performances of knowledging but does not account for them.

Work on crossing does to a limited extent account for an ability to engage in knowledging (Cutler, 1999), but it does not treat knowledging as something separate from crossing. As with polylanguaging, work on crossing typically focuses on the performance aspect. If we turn to the idea of symbolic competence (SC), there are also some clear differences when compared with knowledging. The most obvious is that symbolic competence is accounted for by participation in one-to-few participation frameworks, whereas an ability to engage in knowledging is best accounted for with reference to participation in one-to-many participation frameworks. Put slightly differently, SC is developed in very similar ways to how communicative competence (CC) is reported to be developed in studies of language socialization in small group settings (e.g., Ochs, 1988; Schieffelin, 1990). The difference between CC and SC is that work on SC shows how some of these competences are brought to and applied in new settings by mobile participants. Knowledging, on the other hand, usually involves exposure to modeling practices that are carried out by non-familial experts of some sort or another (as compared with elders and older siblings), and it is often done simultaneously in multiple sites (e.g., in school or when watching television, etc). In a sense, the ability to engage in knowledging represents a semiotic reflex of the unintended consequences of increases in the circulation of people and ideas in Indonesia.

Representations of knowledging also provided models of the doing of unity in diversity that sit in contrast to the state ideology that links Indonesian to the doing of unity in diversity. In adding to work on superdiversity and polylanguaging (Blommaert, 2010; Blommaert & Rampton, 2011; Jørgensen et al., 2011), in chapter 6, I revisit these ideas and show that the types of representations of diversity and knowledging that were starting to become part of Indonesian mediascapes by the mid-to-late 1990s were by 2009 ubiquitous across a range of genres and television stations. In chapters 7 and 8, we will also see that the doing of unity in diversity through knowledging is also common in face-to-face unmediatized interactions.

Richardson's (2010) insight that media professionals erase or foreground polite behaviors led me to suggest that these professionals are agents of semiotic change. The lamination of demeanors and interactional histories onto preexisting ethnic stereotypes is another example of semiotic change. In comparison to ethnic social types who spoke particular ethnic languages and hailed from a particular region, in these soaps, they now audibly spoke and visually acted in particular ways that had a semiotic fit with their represented interactional histories. The representations of adequation and knowledging also contribute to semiotic change through the modeling and authorization of new hybrid social types (e.g., Karyo using Betawi and Mandra understanding Javanese in section 3.7). Even so, as with ethnic languages and their stereotypical speakers, hybrid social types who mix tend to be those from the lower levels of Indonesian society, thus helping to reinforce orders of indexicality where Indonesian is at the top, followed by ethnic languages, and finally mixed languages. More generally, such soaps also provide explicit representations that seem to naturalize the types of diversity found in Indonesia's cities. These themes will be taken up further in chapters 5 and 6. Finally, because this book is also very much concerned with ideas of circulation and the widening of the social domain of ideas about ethnic stereotypes, we should also ask how such representations are interpreted by Indonesians. In chapters 7 and 8, I address questions of audience interpretation.

4

Ethnicity during a Decade of Political Reform and Decentralization

4.1 Introduction

As highlighted in chapters 2 and 3, by the mid-to-late 1990s, there was a widely circulating ideology that Indonesia was made up of ethnic communities that resided in certain areas. Membership in these communities was indexed by emblems such as linguistic forms, attire, dress, housing, food, music, religion, and so on. While ideologies about ethnicity were largely associated with positive social relations and recirculated in a myriad of social domains across the archipelago, the idea of the "ethnic other" was also increasingly indexed with negative traits from the mid-1990s onward. Continuing to draw inspiration from work on language ideologies and enregisterment, the main aim of this chapter is trace how the idea of ethnicity became associated with these negative traits. In exploring this issue, I am especially interested in tracing how and why these ideologies were circulated, while also showing how these processes have tended to reproduce and reify earlier ideologies about ethnicity.

In section 4.2, I trace how the circulation of ideologies about ethnicity relates to the appropriation of land for logging, mining, and transmigration projects on the islands outside of Java. The economic migrants that these projects attracted were increasingly perceived as unwelcome ethnic and religious others by indigenous populations in Kalimantan, Sulawesi, Aceh, and Irian Jaya. They were unwelcome because they were perceived as not only taking part in the illegal or unfair appropriation of indigenous land, but also because they did not wish to assimilate into local ways. Similarly, in areas that had high levels of work-related in-migration, such as Bali, these ethnic and religious others were also unwelcome newcomers who were increasingly associated with criminality.

As I point out in section 4.3, these issues were compounded by the severe economic downturn that started in 1997 and continued for over ten years, producing millions of unemployed Indonesians. This downturn tended to shrink the number and size of social domains where interactions among those of differing backgrounds had occurred during the relatively prosperous years of the early-to-mid-1990s. For example, many working in factories, offices, malls, street kiosks, and so on in the large cities had little or no work and, when possible, returned home. In a real sense, opportunities for intercultural dialogue decreased. This economic uncertainty produced social unrest across Indonesia leading to the fall of the Soeharto regime. In its place came cases of localism and the politicization of ethnicity, which picked up steam through political and fiscal decentralization.

Decentralization together with feelings of localism turned into interethnic or interreligious conflicts between "indigenous locals" and (trans)migrants in places such as Kalimantan, Sulawesi, Maluku, Aceh, and Irian Jaya. While each conflict had specific local reasons, some of the recurring and interrelated causes of this violence included land rights and just compensation for land used in transmigration, logging, and mining projects; elite power struggles that followed the political and fiscal decentralization of 2001; an increasingly fragmented and weakened central government; and the revival of ideas of tradition. What is important for this chapter and this book is that these conflicts not only facilitated the recirculation of ideologies about ethnicity, but the massive population displacements that were part of these conflicts also created new social domains for encounters with the ethnic other. Section 4.4 takes up these issues.

While ethnic conflict and scrambles for political power were also part of numerous "tradition" revivalist movements, these movements also involved more benign discourses of tradition that related to language and cultural loss, as well as revival. Some of these discourses morphed into more concrete practices including increasing amounts of locally produced television media, pop, and artwork; renewed local language curriculum in a number of regions; and Ph.Ds. aimed at documenting endangered languages. These discourses and practices also recirculated ideologies of ethnicity, while helping to reproduce links with linguistic signs. At the same time, this revaluing of ethnicity and ethnic languages also helped to produce new centers of normativity that at the same time helped to reconfigure existing orders of indexicality. This reconfiguration involved increases in the social domains where ethnic language use was valued. In section 4.5, I examine these issues in further detail before I conclude by fleshing out the interrelationships among each of these issues with an eye to showing how these events and processes have helped maintain the circulation of ideologies about ethnicity and the signs associated with them. In particular, I argue that while ideas of the hybrid social types still circulated, older ideas about ethnicity seemed to get the most attention.

4.2 Tensions Around the Idea of Ethnicity

This section seeks to connect broader global and economic events with their local consequences, especially as they relate to an increasing tendency to index negative signs with ethnicity. These processes and the politicization of ethnicity helped to set the scene for large-scale interethnic and interreligious conflicts that occurred between 1999 and 2005. I will point out that some of the recurring causes of these tensions related to land rights and just compensation for land used in transmigration, logging, and mining projects. Before 1998, these tensions were primarily local and emerged through face-to-face interactions or altercations between locals and outsiders at the local level. In this sense, the circulation of negative associations with ethnic social types was also primarily local and on a small scale (i.e., it occurred in one-to-few participation frameworks).

With the introduction of new foreign investment, mining, and forestry laws in 1967 (Laws 1, 5, and 11), the state appropriated large tracts of land in places such as Kalimantan, Sulawesi, Aceh, and Irian Jaya/Papua (Resosudarmo, 2005: 2–3). While land rights and just compensation were already well-known problems by the early 1960s (Hardjono, 1977: 39), these appropriations typically delivered few socioeconomic benefits for locals (Henley & Davidson, 2007; Resosudarmo, 2005). Sangkoyo (1999: 173), for example, points out that in the twenty years between 1973 and 1993, land appropriation actually helped increase the landless poor in Indonesia by about two million people.

These land appropriations also produced environmental degradation and an influx of outsiders seeking work and business opportunities (Henley & Davidson, 2007; Resosudarmo, 2005). For example, between 1970 and 2000, some 780,000 people had come to Irian Jaya/Papua (220,000 as transmigrants), changing the demographics to the extent that outsiders now constituted roughly 35 percent of the overall population (Chauvel, 2008). In the cities, migrants made up nearly 70 percent of the population. There was resentment toward both groups of migrants, but especially toward economic migrants, who were primarily from South Sulawesi and Moslem. This resentment emerged for a number of reasons. On the one hand, migrants were employed in industry instead of the locals whose land had been appropriated for these industrial projects. On the other hand, migrants rarely interacted with locals and tended to view them as primitive and backward.

A similar situation occurred in Aceh where over 180,000 transmigrants had arrived from Java and Bali since 1975 (Aspinall, 2008). These transmigrants were typically settled in "homogenous" villages. Despite many of these migrants marrying locals and having children in Aceh, they were seen as outsiders who were getting the best jobs in industries that were built on locals' land without appropriate compensation. At the same time, these transmigrants were also perceived as major contributors to environmental degradation and economic recession (Aspinall, 2008). Increased funding for development projects in West Kalimantan also brought with it large numbers of Madurese economic migrants (Davidson, 2008). This exacerbated preexisting tensions and conflict between Dayak locals and Madurese migrants that had emerged out of the confrontation with Malaysia in the 1960s. These conflicts were typically blamed on these migrants' perceived unwillingness to assimilate and interact in locally appropriate ways (Davidson, 2008).

In Central Sulawesi, the situation was different, but tensions between insiders and outsiders were also on the rise. Sidel (2008) points out that lowland wealthy Bugis Moslems moved to upland Christian areas of Poso to buy land for farming because prices for copra and coffee began to boom. This influx of Moslem outsiders was also fed through the staffing of government offices by outsiders and an influx of landless and unemployed youths who were the victims of the economic and environmental crisis that befell Indonesia from 1997 onward (Sidel, 2008). In Maluku, one of the islands to the southeast of Sulawesi, in-migration also brought with it changes in religious demographics and tensions over land rights and religious issues (Sidel, 2008). In Bali, tensions also arose for different, but related, reasons (Vickers, 2002; Warren, 2007). Warren (2007) notes that these tensions came about due to investment in the building of large hotels despite popular protests, the large influx of migrant workers, the disempowerment of local customary laws vis-à-vis local government laws, and instances of crime that were blamed on outsiders.

At the same time that these tensions arose around issues of land rights, economic rights, and negative perceptions of outsiders, international conservation movements funded and assisted a new cadre of student activists in forming local NGOs in Kalimantan (Katoppo, 2000; Kusumaatmadja, 2000). By the mid-1990s, these NGOs had successfully raised local and international attention around issues of land rights and just compensation for land used in transmigration, logging, and mining projects (Henley & Davidson, 2007; Katoppo, 2000; Kusumaatmadja, 2000; Resosudarmo, 2005). In effect, these movements had helped strengthen and circulate ideas about local identities, while contrasting them with outsiders. The issue of the local was also coming to the fore in the field of political contests. For example, during the early-to-mid-1990s, there were increased disaffections with the central government's choices of outsiders as regents (*bupati*) and district-level bureaucrats (*camat*) despite local candidates being locally favored (Malley, 2003: 108). This disaffection could be found in places such as West Sumatra, Southeast Sulawesi, Central Kalimantan, North Sumatra, East Kalimantan, East Sumba, Irian, and what used to be called East Timor (now Timor Lesté). In a real sense, locality was also being associated with local identities.

In summary, before 1998, tensions about ideologies of identity revolved around issues of insiders and outsiders and in many senses were an outcome of state developmentist policies. These policies directly contributed to massive influxes of outsiders—including economic migrants, transmigrants, administrators, police, and military personnel—over a short period of time. As Inoue (2006), Coppel (1983), and Collins and colleagues (2000), among others, have pointed out, such rapid increases in the visibility of strangers or outsiders are one of the preconditions for the construction of social types with negative characteristics.

These tensions were primarily local and sometimes emerged through face-to-face interactions or altercations between locals and outsiders. In this sense, the circulation of negative associations with certain identities was primarily local and on a small scale. These identities related primarily to earlier ideologies of ethnicity that were grounded in locale. However, the effects of an ongoing currency crisis, an extended drought, rising dissatisfaction with the New Order government from all levels of Indonesian society, and the decentralization of power and fiscal arrangements from 1999 helped set the stage for the circulation of ideologies about ethnicity on a much larger scale.

4.3 Economic Crisis, Decentralization, and the Rise of *Adat*

The end of the Cold War in the early 1990s had a number of implications for the way Indonesia handled issues of development and governance. During the Cold War, there were agreements about allowing import protectionism in exchange for a staunchly non-communist regime, but by the early 1990s, this gave way to increased pressures from the U.S. and other countries for trade liberalization and human rights (Vickers, 2005). This occurred in a context where the Indonesian development program had already produced disparities between urban and rural areas, as well as between the rich and the poor (Vickers, 2005). These disparities were especially felt in the regions outside of Java (Henley & Davidson, 2007).

By 1998, the economic growth rates of earlier years had dramatically dropped. There were several reasons for this, including a rapid decrease in the exchange rate for the Indonesian rupiah, which decreased from 2,300 rupiah per U.S. dollar to around 10,000 rupiah per dollar between 1996 and 1998 (Ikhsan, 2003). This plummeting exchange rate was compounded by a severe El Niño drought that brought crop failure and the need to import food, falling oil prices that reduced government revenues, an International Monetary Fund (IMF) push to reduce fuel subsidies, and a doubling of inflation rates (Thee Kian Wie, 2001). These events crippled most businesses with foreign loans, resulting in bankruptcy, business closures, a doubling of the unemployment rate, and a doubling of the number of people living under the poverty line (Ikhsan, 2003). If they could afford the increasingly expensive bus fares, many of the construction and finance workers who lost their jobs in the big cities returned to their villages (Booth, 2000; Silvey, 2004). On the one hand, this mass exodus made cities, such as Jakarta, less diverse and reduced the social domains where interaction across lines of difference could occur. On the other hand, as found in the novels of the early twentieth century, homecomings to rural areas, such as where my partner's parents lived, were often accompanied by stories of encounters with difference, thus recirculating ideologies of ethnicity.

During this period, demonstrations about rising costs of living and the need for political reform became common and often violent (Mietzner, 1999). These demonstrations were supported by layers of Indonesian society that had previously been apolitical. This visible loss of support for the government came with a loss of support from different factions within the military and from Islamic organizations. The end result was the resignation of President Soeharto in May 1998 after his thirty-two-year reign as the head of government (Mietzner, 1999). His vice president, B. J. Habibie, was installed as Indonesia's third president. Very soon after Soeharto's resignation, media censorship laws were increasingly ignored, and there were increasing numbers of calls for independence coming from many of the regions outside of Java (Aspinall & Fealy, 2003; Bourchier, 2000; McGibbon, 2003).

While these calls for independence were linked with the development practices noted in the previous section, it was also the case that with Soeharto gone, the vast patronage networks that had been set up during his reign started to unravel (Bourchier, 2000). This resulted in many local struggles for power and resources, which were often linked with calls for independence (Bourchier, 2000; Lindsey, 2001). In the islands outside of Java, some of these struggles involved military officers who—with a weakened central command—started to act autonomously, sometimes instigating or supporting interethnic and interreligious violence (Mietzner, 2001). Seeking to differentiate himself from the former regime, while hoping to keep Indonesia as a united nation, President Habibie instigated a wide range of reforms in 1999 (Elson, 2008: 281). These reforms included new press freedom laws, free political parties, new election procedures, decentralization legislation, and a referendum for East Timor (Aspinall & Fealy, 2003; Chauvel, 2001; Elson, 2008; Kitley, 2001).

Of particular relevance was the introduction of two new laws in May 1999, Laws 22 and 25, which devolved political and fiscal powers to the third level of government shown in figure 4.3.1. While this third level initially included 360 cities and districts, the number would swell to nearly 490 in the years to come (Bünte, 2009: 116). More specifically, Law 25 related to a new system of fiscal arrangements whereby districts and cities were to receive a much larger share of revenues earned within their borders (Aspinall & Fealy, 2003: 3). Law 22 devolved authority to these districts and cities in the areas of education, health, environment, labor, public works, and natural resource management, while the central government retained authority in the areas of foreign policy, defense, security, monetary policy, the legal system, and religious affairs (Aspinall & Fealy, 2003: 3).

It is important to note here that decision-makers chose to focus on autonomy at the district and city level rather than at the provincial level (level two) because it would set up districts as competitors for resources, while not making them large enough to think of separatism (Aspinall & Fealy, 2003: 4). This approach was seen as especially important because of the history of separatist movements (see, e.g., chapter 2) and the recent separatist calls (Aspinall & Fealy, 2003: 4). Put in semiotic terms, these political discourses about regions and ethnicity helped reproduce categories of ethnicity and their linguistic and social practices, while anchoring them to region. While these discourses primarily circulated among bureaucrats and politicians, nevertheless, they also helped to highlight and recirculate ideologies of ethnicity and associated emblems of ethnicity in several social domains.

For example, in the provincial city of Bandung, West Java, the decentralization of decision-making affected issues of town planning, which increasingly involved citizen groups (Antlov, 2003). In rural areas, decentralization at the village level meant that there were now 10–13 elected members coming together in the 52,000 or so villages across the archipelago with an estimated number of meetings around 520,000 in 1999 alone (Antlov, 2003). In addition, there was the development of networks and associations of village councils that acted collectively to pressure district-level politicians (Antlov, 2003).

Large federations also formed, such as a number of farmer federations in West Java (Antlov, 2003). Some of these were the product of the unification of smaller federations, as in Solo where some twenty associations of marginalized groups made up of pedicab drivers, prostitutes, domestic workers, hawkers, and so on unified to become an association claiming 20,000 members (Antlov, 2003). This expansion of networks mirrored the nationwide explosion in the number of trade unions, which before 1998 were strictly controlled and few in number (Ford, 2004, 2008). Within unions, there were opportunities to attend training, national forums, and congresses, which in the case of national congresses, were attended by Indonesians from throughout the archipelago (Ford, 2008: 21–27),

Level 1: Central Government

Level 2: Provinces (*propinsi*)

Level 3: Regencies (*kabupaten*) **and cities** (*kota*)

Level 4: Districts (*kecematan*)

Level 5: Sub-districts (*Kelurahan*)

Level 6: Neighborhood (*rukun warga*)

Level 7: Ward (*Rukun Tetangga*)

FIGURE 4.3.1 Indonesian administrative hierarchy prior to May 1998

thus increasing opportunities for interactions with ethnic others. These new social domains were not just a result of local pressures, however. As Ford (2008) points out, many of these unions were supported by the International Labor Organization (ILO) and the IMF.

During this time, there was an increase in other types of NGOs that had similar influences on people and idea circulation. In some cases, NGO literature directly contributed to the (re)anchoring of social types with region and language. For example, during the 1999 election campaign, NGOs concerned with women's rights published posters on voting in a regional language in South Sulawesi (Baso & Idrus, 2002: 202), thus reproducing the idea that linguistic forms were linked with region, and by indexical association, emblematic of ethnicity. In semiotic and interactional terms then, all of these new organizations and their activities represented new social domains for encounters with sameness and difference, which all potentially involved the recirculation of ideologies about ethnicity.

The promise of decentralization also brought with it some unintended consequences that also contributed to the recirculation of ideologies about social types and their association with region and ethnicity. For example, Quinn (2003) notes that Javanese-speaking Banten, which was originally part of the province of Sundanese- speaking West Java, successfully became a new province in 2000. The reasons for this were based on economic grounds, claims of religious, linguistic, and cultural differences, and claims about political underrepresentation at the provincial level. The emergence of a new province with a revalued ethnolinguistic identity represents an emergent center of normativity that helped reconfigure existing orders of indexicality. In essence, within this new province, Banten Javanese was vying for co-equal status with other varieties of Javanese. While future research is required on how this new social value is manifest in schooling practices in Banten, reference to research in Banyuwangi (Arps, 2010) suggests that should Banten Javanese enter the school curriculum, then there is potential for a widening of the social value of Banten Javanese throughout this province.

The antecedent discourses about Banten identity and the subsequent granting of provincial status impacted on the way other areas thought about their identity and political status. This new province was seen by some as a threat to Sundanese identity, whose territory no longer encompassed all of West Java, and not even the most western parts (Quinn, 2003). This led to calls for a name change of the province to something that included the term "Sunda." This in turn raised eyebrows in the area of Cirebon, which is part of West Java but has many Javanese speakers. Calls for new provincial status and district status also came from towns within Java, such as Solo in Central Java, and from the island of Madura located above Surabaya in East Java (Quinn, 2003).

In the outer islands too, there were calls for new provinces and districts, as well as increasingly strong calls for political recognition and land rights, which helped to recirculate ideologies of ethnicity at the national and local level. Within districts in Riau in Sumatra, for example, there were new tensions over which groups were entitled to political power and economic spoils and whether this province should be split (Ford, 2003). This atomization of territory was common to the extent that by mid-2003, the number of districts had gone from 360 to 416, and the number of provinces had increased from twenty-seven to thirty (Jones, 2004). By early 2007, this number had increased to 487 districts (Bünte, 2009: 116). This territorial fragmentation continues, as pointed out by Aspinall (2011, 2013). NGOs that had a history of working on land rights issues played a role in this atomization helping to produce numerous *adat* communities. Eight hundred representatives of these communities came together in 1999 at the first *Aliansi Masyarakat Adat Nusantara* (Alliance of *Adat* Communities of Indonesia) conference (Acciaioli, 2007).

This body started to act as a mediator between government and *adat* communities about issues of land rights, compensation, and environmental degradation (Katoppo, 2000). For example, these groups aided in the local registration of tracts of land on the part of a community, and these maps became (re)associated with *adat* communities across the archipelago (Kusumaatmadja, 2000: 207). In so doing, old ideologies linking region to person and language were being reproduced. In some cases, this was more explicit than others. For example, some branches of *Aliansi Masyarakat Adat Nusantara* (AMAN) in Sulawesi defined an *adat* community as a group of people willing to follow guidelines put forth by elders (Acciaioli, 2007: 301). As many elders have limited ability in Indonesian, local language is thus implied in these types of formulations. In addition to helping recirculate ideologies of ethnicity via media reports of this conference and via the work of AMAN branches pursuing land rights, face-to-face encounters among conference attendees may also have reproduced ideas of difference and ethnicity.

From 1999 onward, *adat* had a very fluid and situation-specific meaning, including history, land, law, authenticity, community, harmony, order, justice, and/or a combination of these (Henley & Davidson, 2007; Tyson, 2010). Ultimately, as these and other scholars explain, in the period from 1999 onward, the term *adat* became associated with two sets of meanings. The first, which had loose associations with law and justice, developed as an alternative to law and justice associated with an increasingly dysfunctional military and police force, as well as militias that had developed initially as peacekeepers but eventually morphed into partisan troublemakers (Crouch, 2003; Henley & Davidson, 2007). In this sense, *adat* was a way of negotiating the insecurity of a turbulent and unpredictable present and future through recourse to practices of the past (Henley & Davidson, 2007). Second, there was the meaning recirculated by AMAN, which emphasized rights to territory based on historic links (Bourchier, 2007). The idea of historical rights to territory was used by one group—often but not always one associated with elites—to marginalize, victimize, or appropriate resources from another group (Biezeveld, 2007; Henley & Davidson, 2007; Jones, 2004; Li, 2007; Ramstedt, 2009; Sakai, 2003; Tyson, 2010; Van Klinken, 2007b).

Such marginalization occurred between those living within close proximity of one another (Resosudarmo, 2005: 7; Warren, 2007: 186). Fox and colleagues (2005: 94–95) provide examples of disputes over fishing grounds erupting between two sub-districts within a single district in Pontianak in Kalimantan. In Bali, tensions were just as much about differences in social practices in the north and south, with hierarchy and Hinduism dominating in the south, while the north had a much longer history of pluralism (Ramstedt, 2009: 357–358). There were also tensions among different strata within Bali, with elites lamenting that decentralization had produced fragmented communities and fragmented notions of what it meant to be Balinese (Ramstedt, 2009: 329–330).

In other places, such as Sambas in West Kalimantan, local Malays felt disadvantaged by the way *adat* had been mobilized by internationally funded Dayak groups to gain greater economic spoils and political representation (Davidson, 2008). In particular, there was a revival of sultanates and sultans as a way of claiming authenticity and entitlement, especially because it added to political candidates' chances if they had a link with these "old" sultanates (Van Klinken, 2007b). Unlike Dayak movements, the Malay movement had no support from AMAN, but it did draw upon some of the meanings associated with *adat*, especially tradition, authenticity, and entitlement (Van Klinken, 2007b). As Davidson (2008) points out, ultimately, this contest led to tensions between Malay groups and Dayak groups, but more important, it created major problems for Madurese migrants (see section 4.4).

As Henley and Davidson (2007) point out, from 1999 onward, *adat* also increasingly became an issue of insiders and outsiders. Crouch (2003: 30), for example, points out that with the granting of special autonomy to Irian Jaya/Papua in 2001, the new local parliament passed legislation that made it necessary to seek permission at the local level before any further transmigrants would be allowed to enter Irian. In West Sumatra, Aceh, Kalimantan, Sulawesi, and the Moluccas, distinctions about land rights were made on the basis of whether one was "ethnically" local and behaved in accordance with local customs or whether someone had migrated several generations earlier (Aragon, 2008; Aspinall, 2008; Biezeveld, 2007; Bouvier & Smith, 2008; Davidson, 2008; Sidel, 2008; von Benda-Beckmann & von Benda-Beckmann, 2009). As we shall see in the next section, in many cases, lack of indigeneity, inauthenticity, and/or difference in social practices became reasons for forcibly displacing these migrants. In other cases, from 1999 to around 2004, indigeneity became the criterion for hiring in local governments (Aspinall & Fealy, 2003: 6; Carnegie, 2010: 130; van Klinken, 2007a: 7).

In linking the above discussion with the circulation of ideologies relating to ethnicity, it is important to point out that these contestations over land, rights, authenticity, and so on regularly attracted the gaze of local and national media, as well as major political figures. Discourses about the potential problems of decentralization including localism, *adat*, and ethnopolitics circulated in 2001 and 2002 in local and national newspapers (Aspinall & Fealy, 2003: 7). Often, these stories were reports of presidential or vice presidential opinions (Aspinall & Fealy, 2003: 7) that leant authority to such discourses. Local issues often found themselves on the national stage, as Erb (2007: 268) points out in relation to *adat* disputes in Flores. In places such as Bali, there also seemed to be some audience for these news reports. For example, migrants complained that media reports relating to the push to strengthen Bali *adat* privileged Balinese while marginalizing migrants (Warren, 2007: 174).

In summary, economic and political crisis, decentralization, and *adat* revivalism all helped recirculate older ideologies that linked region to ethnicity. As in other places around the world (Collins et al., 2000; Poynting, Noble, Tabar, & Collins, 2004), the preexistence of stereotypes coupled with economic and political uncertainty, a highly visible group of outsiders, and media reportage about rights and entitlement assisted in the assigning of negative associations to ethnic social types in certain areas of Indonesia. One outcome of these interrelated processes was that deviance was increasingly mapped onto people who were migrants, replacing earlier, more neutral readings of ethnicity. The consequences of this were the worst cases of communal violence and population displacement since the events surrounding regime change in 1965–1966 (van Klinken, 2007a).

4.4 Violent Ethnic Others: Conflict and Displacement

Hedman (2008b: 4) points out that by 2001, Indonesia had the world's highest number of refugees due to conflict, numbering around 1.4 million people. Among other things, this circulation of people also helped to recirculate ideologies about ethnicity in new social domains and on a large scale. In this section, I look at scholarship on this topic to highlight some of these social domains, as well as to point out some of the discourses that these people movements created in their new, temporary homes.

In 1999, a long history of animosity between Dayak groups and Madurese economic migrants in West Kalimantan erupted yet again into violence that continued sporadically to 2001 (Davidson, 2008). As part of this violence, around 50,000 people were displaced. Many of them were moved to various holding camps in Pontianak or boated to Madura and Surabaya in East Java. These refugees received little local support, and in the media they were increasingly blamed for crimes that occurred in the cities that had become their temporary homes (Davidson, 2008). In 2001, close to 150,000 Madurese living in Central Kalimantan were displaced (Bouvier & Smith, 2008: 231). Dayak groups that participated in this large-scale forced displacement of primarily Madurese economic migrants were media-literate, networked and financed by the Ford Foundation (Bouvier & Smith, 2008: 244). This allowed them to more effectively circulate stereotypes about Madurese who had none of these advantages and could not counter these negative stereotypes effectively (Bouvier & Smith, 2008: 244). At subsequent peace conferences that were held in Jakarta and East Java, organizers focused on intercultural differences and the lack of assimilation on the part of Madurese, while neglecting the role of political elites, military, and criminals (Bouvier & Smith, 2008: 246).

During the same period, hundreds of thousands of people were displaced in North Maluku, Maluku, and Central Sulawesi because of interreligious violence (Sidel, 2008: 29). In Ambon, the capital of Maluku, for example, around 70,000 people had fled by March 1999. By the end of 2000, nearly double that number were seeking refuge in other areas of Maluku, while tens of thousands were seeking refuge in other parts of Indonesia (Sidel, 2008: 49). As Sidel (2008: 49) points out, this flood of people brought with it stories and rumors that helped start interreligious violence in the areas where they had sought refuge. In the nearby island of Lombok, an Islamic rally led to some of the radical attendees attacking Christian homes, businesses, schools, and churches (Sidel, 2008: 52). Three thousand Christians fled to neighboring Bali, Manado, and Papua.

This large-scale circulation of refugees, paramilitary, and military personnel was common throughout the archipelago during this period, resulting in the creation of new social domains for encounters with difference and new opportunities for the generation of stories about such encounters. This was especially the case in places with long histories of separatist movements, such as Aceh, East Timor, and Irian Jaya. Aspinall (2008) points out that between 1999 and 2003, around 130,000 Javanese and those of Javanese descent were forced to leave Aceh by the free Aceh movement (GAM) or its sympathizers. This displacement of people and people movement was to pale in significance to what occurred as a result of the December 2004 tsunami. In the aftermath of this disaster, 500,000 people were displaced and tens of thousands of volunteers from around the archipelago came to the aid of survivors (Hedman, 2008a). In East Timor after the UN sanctioned and observed the Independence vote in 1999, the actions of paramilitary militias (which were trained by the Indonesian military) displaced some 400,000 East Timorese people (Robinson, 2008). Of these, 250,000 moved across the border to West Timor or to neighboring islands (Robinson, 2008: 99–100). In Irian, people displacement was also common as were clashes between locals and migrants, although typically this was on a smaller scale in comparison to Aceh and East Timor.

As in earlier times (see chapter 2), Indonesian military personnel who were involved in people displacement were drawn primarily from Java or from regions other than where conflict was occurring. For example, the military crackdown in 1999 involved primarily troops from Java (Bourchier, 2000). In 2001–2002, an estimated 22,000 military personnel and a further 11,000 police were deployed to Aceh (Crouch, 2003). Similarly, in places were communal violence was occurring, such as Poso, some 4,000 troops and police were deployed (Crouch, 2003). In addition to military personnel, there were also paramilitary personnel who moved throughout the archipelago and were often recruited in Java to provide medical, communications, and paramilitary support (Crouch, 2003; Sidel, 2008). For example, the radical Islamic group *Laskar Jihad*, which formed in 2000 (and was supported by some elements within the military), sent between 3,000 and 4,000 of their members to areas of interreligious conflict, including Maluku, Poso (Central Sulawesi), Aceh, Irian Jaya/Papua, East Kalimantan, and South Sulawesi (Crouch, 2003; Sidel, 2008).

Encounters between locals and personnel from the military and police also helped recirculate ideologies of ethnicity and difference. For example, in 2003, a reporter who traveled with the military reported that soldiers complained that people they talked to in Aceh always answered in a local language and wouldn't use Indonesian unless forced (Aspinall, 2008: 141). Such reports point to different views about orders of indexicality, with soldiers of the Indonesia state trying to regiment Indonesian at the top of the hierarchy while locals appeared to place their local language at the top.

As with the struggles over resources noted in section 4.3, from 1999 onward, the separatist conflicts in Aceh, Irian, and East Timor (now Timor Lesté) also attracted increasing media attention, especially as new freedom-of-the-press laws came into effect (Kitley, 2001; Sen & Hill, 2000). For example, between November 2003 and September 2004, the escalation of military operations in Aceh produced almost daily news reports of separatist (GAM) casualties (Aspinall, 2005: 28). Presidents, vice-presidents, and parliamentarians also frequently commented in the media about these conflicts (Chauvel, 2001). This increased level of reporting, often authorized by those with the highest authority in the land, thus helped to further recirculate ideologies linking ethnicity with regions.

To summarize this section, the most important points are that population displacement and military involvement across the archipelago created many new social domains for encounters with difference and for the generation of stories about such encounters. Such encounters occurred in refugee camps, in interactions among military personnel, aid workers, locals, and refugees. During this time, there was also a large increase in the mediatization of conflicts involving those of different ethnic backgrounds, at both the local and national levels. As with earlier times, registers associated with ethnic social types were regaining negative associations through both one-to-many participation frameworks and one-to-few participation frameworks (e.g., face-to-face talk). In addition, further unintended consequences of earlier developmentist nation-building ideas and processes continued to work against ideas of unity in diversity (e.g., chapter 2). In the following section, I focus on some language-specific examples of the impact of decentralization and *adat* movements from the early 2000s onward.

4.5 Recirculating Stereotypes via Other Forms of Localism

In this section, I look at some of the other social domains where ideologies about ethnicity were circulated as a reflex of regionalism and practices relating to ongoing decentralization. I point out that, in the period from 1999 onward, there was a recirculation of ideas about ethnic social types mentioned in section 2.8 and chapter 3. In particular, it seems that in the areas of education and the media, decentralization clearly helped to strengthen associations among region, language, and ethnicity in some places. This helped create emergent centers of normativity that in turn helped to reconfigure existing orders of indexicality. In this section, I start by looking at some education and training practices before moving to the media and the Internet.

A close reading of Arps's (2010), Moriyama's (2005, 2012), Quinn's (2012), and Ramstedt's (2009) work suggests that since decentralization, the rise of regionalism and *adat* has facilitated the recirculation of links among language, region, and ethnicity in East Java, West Java, and Bali. These links have been authorized through policy documents, seminars, the production of grammars, dictionaries, school textbooks, and the contrasting of different varieties of language with those being used/proposed in local school curriculums. Arps (2010) for example, points to efforts in standardizing and including in local school curriculums a Javanese dialect in the Banyuwangi area of East Java. Ramstead (2009: 360) points out that the governor of Bali allocated a budget for local languages, customs, and knowledge systems to be included in school curriculums from 2004 onward. Moriyama (2005) points out that in 2003, some government offices within West Java introduced laws mandating the use of Sundanese in the office. During fieldwork in Semarang in 2003–2004, I also read newspaper articles about similar initiatives in district government offices within Central Java.

Part of the justification around the use of Sundanese and Javanese in government offices related to the fear of losing a particular honorific variety of the language. While this fear of loss is typically articulated by older-generation speakers who are in senior and/or powerful positions—a situation common to discourses surrounding language change more generally (Aitchison, 1996; Blommaert, 2010; Inoue, 2006)—these fears of loss also came at a time when Indonesia started to seriously invest in improving the skills of its academic workforce and requiring Indonesian academics to engage in global academic discussions through the use of English. For example, in 2007 the Indonesian Directorate General of Higher Education (DIKTI) decreed that all university lecturers should have a minimum of a master's qualification (Direktorat Jenderal Pendidikan Tinngi, 2010a, 2010b).

DIKTI has facilitated this policy by offering large amounts of funding for completing master's and doctorate studies. In turn, this impetus has provided resources to primarily mid-career academics to study endangered local languages and, in so doing, reproduce language-region-ethnicity links. However, whether or to what extent scholarly theses will translate into district-level policies and school curriculums, as was the case in Arps's (2010) study, is still an open question. For example, Sudarkam Mertono's (2014) Ph.D. work suggests that while language loss is important in places like Palu, Sulawesi, decentralization of education hasn't meant that local languages uniformly enter the curriculum. Instead, it appears that local languages compete for a place in the curriculum with international languages and IT.

As in the 1990s, the circulation of authorized discourses linking languages to regions and ethnic social types continued via the mass media. Moriyama (2005: 6) observes that where print media is concerned, there appears to be an increase in Sundanese language magazines. Media professionals involved in the setting-up of regional television stations across Indonesia articulated hopes that such stations might also increase interethnic understanding and ease the interethnic tensions that had emerged in Indonesia (Loven, 2008: 45). The increase in regional television stations was facilitated by a new broadcasting bill (No. 32/2002, Article 36, point 2) that stipulated that 60 percent of television broadcasts should be local (Rachmah, 2008: 97). By 2004, there were sixty private local stations, and a further fifty-three had filed applications to start broadcasting (Rachmah, 2006: 42).

As with the content found in the broadcasts of the mid-to-late 1990s, some of the language used was local, again helping to reproduce the idea that language was emblematic of ethnicity and region. For example, Rachmah (2006: 82), Yuyun Surya (2006), and Moriyama (2005) report that news programs were broadcast in a local language, and Ida reports of soap operas being dubbed in a local language rather than Indonesian. Barkin (2008) points out that travel shows became increasingly popular from 2000 onward. A common theme from the producers' perspective was the need to have a focus on "exoticism" as a way of highlighting differences between the viewer and the travel location. In some cases, this involved asking locals to put on "authentic" clothes (Barkin, 2008). As with the commoditization of ethnicity that had been occurring in the 1990s, this practice linked region, clothing, and social practice. Similarly, among the many different genres of soap operas, comedies often exploited ethnic differences (Rachmah, 2006: 67–68). As we shall see in chapters 5 and 6, these comedies also continued the practice of representing the local through the use of fragments of local languages. Even so, in chapter 6, we will also see a number of examples that index ethnic difference while showing that doing unity in diversity doesn't necessarily mean a need to use Indonesian.

At the same time, concern for market share continued to influence content in ways different from the 1990s. For example, Rachmah (2006: 43–44) notes that television station managers' rhetoric relating to having varied programming that catered to a heterogeneous market did not match their actual practices. Instead, "sell-well" programs were imitated by other television stations producing homogeneous programming. This practice, the fact that one production house produced 80 percent of local soap operas, and patterns of media ownership that had three stations owned by one company often led to very similar content across several television stations at various times of the day and week (Rachmah, 2006: 51–58, 101–102). In chapter 5, we will see that trends toward homogeneous programming seemed to continue into 2009 when we look at the content of eleven television stations.

During the mid-to-late 2000s, media news reports also helped to recirculate ideologies about ethnicity. For example, between 2006 and 2008, the introduction of anti-pornography legislation attracted much controversy because of fears that it would criminalize expressions of local ethnicity while authorizing Islamic-influenced dress codes (Bush, 2008: 178). Controversy surrounding Inul, a female *dangdut* singer, whose onstage moves offended various Islamic groups and older famous male *dangdut* singers, also ended up creating regional rivalries (Heryanto, 2008: 23). In particular, after being involved in a demonstration against new anti-pornography legislation, one Jakarta-based group purporting to also be Betawi (*Forum Betawi Rempug*) went to Inul's business address and residence to intimidate her and demand that she leave Jakarta. Her supporters in East Java responded by threatening to force Betawi living in Surabaya to leave (Heryanto, 2008: 23).

The rise of regionalism and decentralization also had other less dramatic, yet important effects on the circulation of people and ideas. Mietzner (2009: 139) notes that the election campaign for governor in North Sulawesi was in part run on candidates' credentials for being good conflict mediators who were well positioned to handle the ethnic and religious heterogeneity in the province. In Irian Jaya/Papua, decentralization had brought with it increases in spending on infrastructure, including bureaucracies, schools, and hospitals (McGibbon, 2003: 201). Although these bureaucracies were local and often locally staffed, there were still many cases of interaction across differences. For example, while during the New Order period, medically trained midwives often came from Java or from the big cities, in the decentralized period, midwives came from small cities in the outer islands. These midwives were transferred to other areas within their districts (Alesich, 2008). Often, these transfers were to districts where the language was different and where establishing trusting relationships required some knowledge of local practices (Alesich, 2008). The midwives were transferred every five years and, in many ways, they can be held up as exemplars of multicultural and multilingual Indonesians living in and creating superdiversity.

Thus far, I have covered just a few of the most obvious social domains where ideas about ethnic stereotypes can be recirculated. Notably, I haven't spent any time on the role of the Internet. This is so because scholarship on the Internet has not been able to keep abreast of the many ongoing changes. Here, I will just sketch out a few of these changes. During my fieldwork in the mid-1990s, this technology was primarily used by a small number of affluent urban Indonesians who had fixed telephone lines in their homes. Hill and Sen (2005: 56) point out that even in 2000, only 3.6 percent of Indonesia's population had phone lines, and of the seven-and-a-half million telephones, nearly half were in Jakarta, with few in rural areas and places outside of Java. With the emergence of Internet cafes in the late 1990s, access to the Internet became less reliant upon fixed phone lines and increasingly affordable to a wider section of society (Hill & Sen, 2005).

By 2009, the burgeoning urban mobile phone usage that was evident during my 2004 fieldwork in Semarang (Central Java) had also become common in rural West Java. Some phone companies even offered access to the Internet via these mobiles, although at a price that could be afforded only by affluent people in these rural areas. By 2009, there were magazine and television advertisements for phones and phone services that offered direct access to the Internet, although these goods and services seemed primarily aimed at those living in Jakarta. By 2012, youths in rural West Java also had access to the Internet via their mobile phones. They, like their urban contemporaries, thus also became potential producers and consumers of ethnic stereotypes in multiple emergent social domains, such as celebrity fan sites of the type exemplified in extract 4.5.1.

Extract 4.5.1 presents an example of one such domain. It is taken from a section on entertainment from the forum *Lautan Indonesia* (Indonesian Seas). This forum had a total of ten brief posts about the soap opera *Jiran*, which we will be introduced to in section 5.4. Extract 4.5.1 is the fourth commentary made on August 11, 2009. The commentaries that precede it were all made on August 10. Those making the posts discussed their excitement and anticipation upon seeing the trailer; one joked about Titi Kamal who plays the main character as crying a bucketful of tears in the first ten minutes while pondering what type of dance other characters were doing in a particular scene. Another applauded the setting, which was also in Malaysia, while pondering whether it might attract protests from Malaysians.

Extract 4.5.1 Celebrity fans posting on representations of ethnicity

Patzzi

1	seru episode pertama..jiran logatnya sunda	The first episode was exciting. Jiran has a very Sundanese accent. As usual, Titi Kamal's role is a sobbing and tortured one, but it can be differentiated from her other role as Muslimah [in the soap titled Muslimah].
2	abis . . . tikam meski perannya mewek n	
3	teraniaya tapi bisa beda dari muslimah	

Meme koe

4	^gua sempat nonton sbntar . . . scene merit	I had a chance to watch for a while. The marriage scene where the people played by Titi and Didi were witnessed by the husband of the actress played by Titi. And the scene [when] Didi knocked on Titi's door and asked if [she] was ready to go home to his home (in Malaysia, right??)
5	tokoh yg diperankan Titi & Didi disaksikan	
6	cowo yg suaminya tokoh yg diprenkan Titi	
7	trus scene Didi ketuk pintu kamar titi minta	
8	siap2 ke mau plg ke kampungnya	
9	(Malaysia ya??).	
10	Iya oatzz . . . logatnya titi sunda bgt	Iya???. Titi's accent is very Sundanese. By the way, what is the name of the character played by Titi? Hehehe. Good luck for the soap Jiran.
11	btw, nama peran titi di sini apa??	
12	hehehe . . . good luck buat sinetron Jiran.	
13	[original text]	

Source: www.lautanindonesia.com/forum/index.php?topic=43128.50. Accessed on January 31, 2012.

In this Internet domain, it is representations of an ethnic stereotype by a particular actor that attracts commentary while also recirculating emblems of ethnicity, in this case, accent. In lines 1 and 2, Pattzi positively evaluates Jiran's Sundanese accent. This post by Pattzi gets a response from Meme koe some two hours later on the same day (lines 4–12). This response is also positive and ratifies Pattzi's comment about Jiran's Sundanese ability (line 10). In another commentary (extract 4.5.2), it is the Sundanese-ness of the soap as a whole, rather than the language practices of a particular actor, that appear to be evaluated. This commentary titled *Sinetron Jiran Hina Orang Sunda* (The soap *Jiran* denigrates Sundanese) was posted on a magazine-like blog spot *jurnalbogor* (Bogor Journal) on September 4, 2009, by Jayadi (electronic identity) and apparently authored by Kosasih Kadra (line 26).

Extract 4.5.2 Blogging and complaining about ethnic representations

1	Saya sangat prihatin ketika mengamati	I was very concerned when
2	tayangan sinetron JIRAN di Indosiar,	I was looking at the soap *Jiran*
3	dimana pemain utamanya adalah Jiran dan	on Indosiar where the main
4	Pendi yang di simbolkan sebagai orang	actors, Jiran and Pendi, are
5	Sunda yang digambarkan sangat bodoh,	represented as Sundanese who
6	dungu dan nyaris tanpa moral. Mem-blow	are very backward, idiotic and
7	up karakter seperti itu sah-sah saja sebagai	almost without any morals. To
8	arena hiburan.	exaggerate characters is fine in the entertainment arena.
9	Tapi yang sangat disayangkan adalah	But what is very unfortunate
10	adanya upaya penistaan dan pendiskreditan	are the efforts to denigrate and
11	terhada etnis Pasundan yang begitu	discredit Sundanese, which is
12	menonjol.	very obvious.
13	Terusterang saya sebagai orang Sunda	To be frank, as a Sundanese
14	merasa tidak nyaman dan menganggap hal	myself I feel uncomfortable
15	tersebut sebagai pelecehan. Dan tentu saja	and consider this matter as an
16	kita berharap hendaknya para produser	insult. And indeed we hope
17	tidak hanya berorientasi hiburan dan rating	that the producer doesn't only
18	atau prof it semata, tetapi juga	focus on entertainment and
19	pertimbangkan perasaan, kultur dan budaya	profit, but also a consideration
20	Sunda secara adil dan proporsional.	of the Sundanese sensitivities and culture in a fair and proportional way.
21	Pertimbangkanlah perasaan kami warga	Please consider our feeling as
22	Pasundan atau etnis manapun yang	Sundanese or in fact any other
23	dijadikan obyek cerita. Lebîh arif lagi	ethnicity that becomes the
24	apabila tayangan tersebut dihentikan dan	focus of a story. It would be
25	direvisi. [original text]	even better if you stop this soap and revise it.
	Kosasih Kadra	Kosasih Kadra

Source: http://www.jurnalbogor.com/?p=50136. Accessed on January 31, 2012.

In extract 4.5.2, it is the social traits of the characters that attract commentary. This commentary is from someone who self-identifies as a Sundanese (line 13) and then as a member of a community of Sundanese social types (lines 21 and 22). The commentary focuses upon a number of related issues. The first relates to the negative representation of Sundanese intelligence and morality (lines 4–6). Second, the author sees these representations as a direct attempt to denigrate those of Sundanese ethnicity (lines 10–12). This idea of a community of Sundanese social types is further solidified through their membership in a wider community of ethnic social types (lines 21 and 22). While there is no mention of episodes or specific language and social practices, with reference to the first episode (see section 5.4), we can guess that these impressions relate to a number of indexical associations. For example, in the first episode, we were introduced to Jiran's husband who had a propensity to drink, gamble, associate with thugs, and eventually sell his wife. All of these characters were represented as speaking a medium other than Indonesian. The speech was associated with Sundanese provenance through a number of mechanisms, including the speaking of subtitled language by multiple characters living, working, and socializing in the same area and a number of cars with license plates that point to a setting in and around the city of Bandung in West Java, and finally to a character's reference to Jiran as Sundanese.

In closing this section, we can say that many of the stereotypes, social domains, and representation practices described in section 2.8 and chapter 3 were also present in the period from 1999 onward. On the one hand, decentralization has clearly helped to strengthen associations among region, language, and ethnicity in some places, especially in the broad area of language education. In some cases, television news broadcasts, which in New Order Indonesia were in Indonesian, can now also be found in regional languages, and ethnic comedies are still a popular form of television entertainment. Political discourses too often indirectly or directly point to the existence of ethnic social types, thus reproducing this category of personhood. In short, in some places, the revaluing of local ethnic languages had gained powerful institutional support and the one-to-many participation frameworks characteristic of such institutions represented new centers of normativity. In turn, the existence of these new and emergent centers helped to reconfigure hierarchical relations between Indonesian and ethnic languages.

4.6 Conclusion

As many Indonesianists have pointed out, the period from 1999 onward was one of major change. During this period, ideologies of ethnicity continued to circulate in one-to-many participation frameworks and one-to-few participation frameworks. Ideologies that linked languages with regions were recirculated via schools (Arps, 2010), the media, and government artifacts such as census forms that now included ethnic categories (Suryadinata, Arifin, & Ananta, 2003).

During this period, the social value of ethnicity along with ethnic languages underwent some major semiotic reconfiguration in the wake of major social, political, and economic changes. In many areas of the archipelago, negative traits were increasingly indexed with ethnicity (especially those who were seen as migrants), the ideology of ethnicity as a particular social category became strongly (re)linked to region, and new centers of normativity emerged that helped to contest and reconfigure older orders of indexicality.

In exploring the genesis of what amounted to the criminalization of certain ethnic groups, in section 4.2, I started by looking at state developmentist policies of the New Order period. These policies directly contributed to massive influxes of outsiders over a short period of time to the islands outside of Java. These outsiders were primarily economic migrants, transmigrants, administrators, police, and military personnel. I pointed out that such rapid increases in the visibility of outsiders were one of the preconditions for the construction of social types with negative characteristics. These tensions were primarily local and sometimes emerged through face-to-face interactions or altercations between locals and outsiders. In this sense, the circulation of negative associations with certain identities was primarily local and small scale, typically circulating in one-to-few participation frameworks.

While tensions between locals and migrants were initially locale-specific, their co-occurrence with an ongoing currency crisis, rapid political change, decentralization, tradition revivalist movements, and increasing media coverage about rights and entitlement assisted in the mapping of deviance onto migrants more generally (section 4.3). One serious consequence of this process was some of the worst cases of communal violence and population displacement seen in Indonesian since the mid-1960s. In section 4.4, I described how this population displacement and military involvement across the archipelago created many new social domains for encounters with difference and the generation of stories about such encounters. Such encounters occurred in refugee camps and in interactions among military personnel, aid workers, locals, and refugees. During this time, there was also a large increase in the mediatization of conflicts involving those of different ethnic backgrounds, at both the local and national levels. In a real sense, and as with earlier times, registers associated with ethnicity were now regaining negative associations not just in the regions but also in Java where there were almost daily newspapers reports of violence perpetrated by one ethnic group against another.

In the final section (4.5), I pointed out that in a number of regions in Indonesia, decentralization has also clearly helped to strengthen associations among region, language, and ethnic social type while reconfiguring existing orders of indexicality. As in the past, one-to-many participation frameworks, such as school classrooms, television, and radio, all assisted this process, which also helped to revalue ethnic languages vis-à-vis Indonesian. Ethnic comedies that had their beginnings in the early 1990s continued past representation practices and continued to be broadcast on a national scale, as we will see in chapters 5 and 6. In particular, we shall see that there were representations of ethnic social types speaking ethnic languages, as well as hybrid social types who engaged in knowledging more generally.

In relating chapter 4 to discussions about superdiversity, what seems striking is that while superdiversity was primarily a benign and unintended outcome of processes of massification during the New Order period, it also helped set the scene for the creation of even more diversity. As economic and political conditions deteriorated, areas with large populations of migrants became plagued by interethnic conflict resulting in the displacement of millions of Indonesians throughout the archipelago. In doing so, diversity was layered upon diversity, especially in cities receiving refugees. At the same time, this situation set the scene for the creation of further diversity and further cycles of displacement. For example, locals often unjustly blamed refugees for local crime and forced them to relocate yet again.

5

The Anchoring of Alternation to Place

5.1 Introduction

In this chapter, I start to examine some of the 400 hours of television that I recorded in 2009. Drawing on the theoretical orientations laid out in chapters 2 and 3, I highlight how representation practices in this television footage have continuities with past practices. In particular, I focus on the tension between how these representations help to naturalize language alternation on the one hand, while continuing to "anchor" (Irvine, 2005) this alternation to locale. In so doing, this practice recirculates older ideas about ethnic social types, their language practices, and their links to place. In effect, these practices have reproduced while also altering some of the signs found in semiotic registers from the past. While I point out that this recirculation occurred across a number of genres including soap operas, variety shows, on-the-spot news reports, and commercials, I focus primarily on news reports, children's shows, and soap operas.

What is striking about this data is that this alternation was represented as habitual across many genres, time slots, and television stations. Although this represents a continuity with the practices described in chapter 3, the increase in genres containing alternation produces multiple centers of normativity that challenge and reconfigure existing orders of indexicality. The representation of habitual alternation also offers a different case of the type of alternation found in accounts elsewhere in the world. For example, where television representations are concerned, alternation typically occurs in liminal or spectacular moments (e.g., Androutsopoulos, 2007; Jaffe, 2000; Johnson & Ensslin, 2007b; Johnson & Milani, 2010; Kelly-Holmes & Atkinson, 2007; LeCompte & Schensul, 1999). Just as important, the mixing in my data offers a different case from other cases where multilingual practices are ideologized in institutions. This is so because what is typically found in institutional ideologies about multilingualism is the idea that it equals talk being carried out in two or more neatly bounded languages, where one utterance is one language and the next utterance is another, rather than one utterance containing fragments from multiple languages (e.g., Creese & Blackledge, 2011; Heller, 2007; Moyer, 2011).

More specifically, in section 5.2, I introduce the data gathered while pointing out that in all of the eleven television stations, recorded alternation between Indonesian and other mediums could be found on any day of the week and in any time slot. In section 5.3, I turn to news reports and children's variety shows that contained unscripted dialogue that was framed in a way that fits ideas about reported speech. I start by showing how this reported speech is characterized by alternation. Participants do not make commentaries about each other's alternations, nor do they engage in medium repair. This suggests a type of habitualness that is further foregrounded through the existence of a community of speakers engaging in similar alternation practices. I argue that while these representation practices helped to naturalize alternation, paradoxically, the use of linguistic signs that anchored them to place also reproduced older place-based language ideologies.

The signs that helped to anchor this alternation to place included explicit commentary by a narrator or newsreader, subtitle-like text, the use of maps, subtitles, communities of speakers using similar mediums in a particular setting, the explicit naming of a language, and the use of other signs of place (e.g., car license plates). These other signs that help anchor linguistic signs to place can be viewed as metapragmatic commentaries (Jaworski, Coupland, & Galasiński, 2004; Johnson & Ensslin, 2007a) or, more accurately, "metasemiotic commentaries" (Agha, 2007a) about the linguistic forms being used, the choice of the latter term being motivated by the multimodal nature of these commentaries.

In section 5.4, I point out alternation practices similar to those described in section 5.3. With reference to other represented signs, I argue that this alternation is represented as part of more habitual social relations between characters. These other represented signs include subtitling practices and the presence of a community of speakers who apparently share the same ways of speaking. As with the conclusions reached in relation to televised talk in section 5.3, I point out that these soaps help naturalize alternation while assisting in the reproduction of older associations between medium and place. I also point out that there are instances when the use of fragments from different mediums is much less than what is found in the subtitled cases. I differentiate these cases (extracts 5.4.2 and 5.4.3) by referring to them as "stylized alternation." In the concluding section, I point out that while the type of analysis I carry out in this chapter is different from the one used in chapter 3, it represents a move toward foregrounding the importance of engaging with ideas about semiotic registers versus ideas of language (Agha, 2007a, 2007b). In doing so, I model a method for examining such ideas in practice. For the case at hand, I suggest that this type of minimal multimodal analysis can assist in teasing out the tensions and multiple messages inherent in any representation (Johnstone, 2011).

5.2 The Data

My data consists of around 400 hours of recordings that were made in August 2009 in Cirebon, West Java. These television broadcast recordings covered a sample of eleven of the twelve television stations that were broadcasting at the time. Of these eleven stations, one was local (RCTV), while the rest were Jakarta-based commercial broadcasters. I recorded each station for a minimum of a day, and often up to four days when broadcast reception was good. These recordings were made starting at around five in the morning and usually finishing at one the following morning. Thus, while what I present here is not a perfect sample, nevertheless, it does provide enough data to point out some patterns of broadcast content and representational practices.

Diagram 5.2.1 provides a calendar-type summary of which television broadcasts were recorded, along with information on when they were recorded and how much content contained linguistic fragments that are stereotypically associated with regional languages (in italics), which I have been referring to as "medium" in previous chapters. In the fifteen-hour period between 10 a.m. and 1 a.m. on August 5th, I identified around 1.75 hours of talk that contained alternation between Indonesian and fragments of regional languages. As can be seen in this diagram, the representation of these mediums was common on any day of the week. While some material, such as on-the-spot interviews found in news timeslots, contained whole utterances in

AUGUST 2009						
Sun	Mon	Tue	Wed	Thur	Fri	Sat
						1
2	3	4	5 TRANS7 10am–1am *1.75 hours*	6 TRANS7 5am–1am *1.3 hours*	7 TRANS7 6am–1am *2.8 hours*	8 TRANS 5am–1am *1.1 hours*
9 RCTV 10am–12pm *2.5 hours*	10 RCTI 6am–1am *2.5 hours*	11 RCTI 6am–1am *3.25 hours*	12 RCTI 5am–1am *3.4 hours*	13 GlobalTV 6am–1am *2 hours*	14 GlobalTV 5am–1am *3.8 hours*	15 SCTV 6am–1am *2.1 hours*
16 ANTV 8pm–1am *1 hour*	17 ANTV 5am–1am *0.75 hour*	18 SCTV 3am–1am *0.9 hour*	19 Indosiar 6am–1am *1.9 hours*	20 Indosiar 5am–1am *2 hours*	21 TransTV 6am–1am *2 hours*	22 TransTV 3am–1am *5 hours*
23 TVOne 4pm–1am *2 hours*	24 TVOne 5am–4pm *0.5 hours*	25 TPI 4am–1am *3.75 hours*	26	27	28	29
30	31					

DIAGRAM 5.2.1 Television stations recorded and medium representations in 2009

these mediums, typically, the soap operas, variety shows, and commercials only contained a couple of fragments, usually kin terms or short utterances. When compared with Kitley's (2000) reports of language use in the early days of Indonesian television (i.e., when Indonesian was the primary language found in such representations; section 3.3), we can see a clear move away from the use of Indonesian on television. In addition, ethnic comedies are no longer the sole genre that represents language alternation, as was the case in the 1990s (sections 3.4–3.7). In chapter 4, I noted that a reconfiguration of older orders of indexicality was underway, and the data I present in this chapter provides some linguistic evidence of this reconfiguration.

As I moved through these recordings, it was also evident that while this type of material could be found in almost any timeslot between five in the morning and one the next morning, the representation of alternation as the medium was most common in the timeslots between 7–11 a.m., 12–3 p.m., and 5–11 p.m. As can be seen from diagram 5.2.1, programming containing these mediums was more common on some stations and on particular days. For example, on Friday, GlobalTV had the most representations of these mediums. This was perhaps because Friday was imagined to be a day with a potentially larger audience as it was a short working day for many of Indonesia's majority Moslem population.

As with data in chapter 3, my initial classification of linguistic sign representations was carried out by an Indonesian research assistant. I checked these classifications drawing upon my knowledge of Indonesian and other mediums gained through fieldwork and other visits to Central and West Java since the early 1990s. However, as pointed out in section 3.4, there are a number of factors that complicate this categorization. For example, I pointed out that Indonesian words have been adopted from what has been labeled "Javanese" and "Sundanese," and the reverse is also true. Indonesian also shares word-order and affixation patterns with many of these mediums, especially Javanese and Sundanese. Similarly, as found in sections 3.5–3.7, kin terms and pronouns from these mediums are often found in otherwise Indonesian utterances, as are question words, demonstratives, and particles used to indicate affective stance. In the rest of this chapter, I will engage with these problems using a minimal type of multimodal analysis of televised talk.

5.3 Anchoring Medium to Locale

In this section, I focus on children's shows and news broadcasts. I show how representation practices help anchor medium to place, which in turn reproduces the idea of language as emblematic of ethnicity. Some of the mechanisms that facilitate this anchoring are explicit commentaries about place by a narrator or newsreader, the use of subtitle-like texts that state place, the use of maps, the subtitling of talk, and the presence of a community of speakers whose speech also requires subtitles. The representational practices also help frame this talk as a type of reported speech, although typically this is a report of the actual talk, rather than a report that constructs talk, as found in analysis of reported talk elsewhere (Holt & Clift, 2007; Tannen, 1989).

The first extracts and figures I look at are drawn from a couple of children's shows, *Cita-Citaku* (*My Dreams*, extract 5.3.1) and *Si Bolang Bocah Petualang* (*Bolang the Adventurous Child*, extract 5.3.2). These shows were screened in the 1 p.m.–3 p.m. slot on Trans7. During the three days from which I have footage, there were seven different stories that were anchored to Ohoidertawun in Maluku, Bogor and Sumadang in West Java, and Semarang and Bantul in Central Java. There were a number of mechanisms that helped anchor the story and linguistic signs to a particular region, including explicit mention by the child of where they were or through the presentation of a map of Indonesia that pinpointed where the story occurred. After these initial anchoring processes, the stories are then typically narrated by a child in Indonesian. This practice contrasts with interactions between groups of local children or local children and local adults, which are carried out in a local medium. These conversations are either accompanied by subtitles or translated by the narrator.

At the start of extract 5.3.1, the narrator Bambang is shown lying down on the front porch of his house while drawing. As with my earlier transcripts, my initial classification relies on my own judgments, those of my research assistant, and sometimes a number of dictionaries. (This same caveat applies to all other transcripts in this chapter and the next.)

Extract 5.3.1 Anchoring medium through story introduction

Bambang

1	aku sedang melukis pemandangan di	I'm drawing the scenery in my
2	desaku (0.8) oh ya . namaku bambang (0.8)	village, oh yes, my name is
3	lengkapnya . bambang nuriswanto (0.4)	Bambang, [my] full name [is]
4	saat ini . aku duduk di kelas enam . sd jati	Bambang Nuriswanto. At the
5	sari . semarang jawa tengah	moment I'm in Grade 6 at the
		Jati Sari Primary School in
		Semarang, Central Java.

Source: Trans7, Cita-citaku, Thursday, August 6, 2009 (2–3 p.m.)

As can be seen in extract 5.3.1, the narrator Bambang anchors the story and interactions within it to place by naming where he goes to school: "Jati Sari Primary School in Semarang, Central Java" (lines 4–5). This narration, which is in Indonesian (plain font), is contrasted with interaction between Bambang and his friend Eko, who is introduced as a local via reference to him attending the same school as Bambang (line 9 in extract 5.3.2). The talk in extract 5.3.2 occurs immediately after the talk in extract 5.3.1.

Extract 5.3.2 Interacting with locals and codeswitching

Eko

6 he bang .   Hi Bang (shortened form of Bambang).

Bambang

7 hou .   Hi.

Eko

8 **RENÉ** ko .   **COME HERE** Ko (shortened form of name, Eko).

Bambang

9 eh. itu kan eko . teman sekolahku .   He, that [person] you know, is Eko my school friend.

Eko

10 *lagi* **OPO KOWÉ** =   **WHAT ARE YOU DOING** *at the moment*?

Bambang

11   = *nggambar* =   *Drawing.*

Eko

12   = *nggambar* **WHAT ARE YOU** *drawing*?

13 **OPO** =

Bambang

14   = *nggambar* **OPO KI** =   **WHAT AM** [I] *drawing*?

Eko

15   = **KOWÉ**   Wili **AND** Eki [are]

16 **WIS DIENTENI** eki **BAI** wili . **NING**   **WAITING FOR YOU**

17 *lapangan*   **AT** *the field.*

Source: Trans7, Cita-citaku, Thursday, August 6, 2009 (2–3 p.m.)

In extract 5.3.2, the two friends are interacting in a local medium, in this case, a local Javanese medium (bold caps). This localness is signaled through the use of subtitles (figure 5.3.1), which point to the talk being in a different medium from what has just occurred (e.g., lines 1–5 in extract 5.3.1 and line 9 in extract 5.3.2). We can also see that from lines 10 to 17, Bambang and Eko alternate between ambiguous forms, that is, forms that can be either classified as Indonesian or Javanese (italics) and Javanese. We also see that one participant orients to another's medium choice at each transition-relevance place (TRP) (i.e., they ratify this alternation by engaging in alternation themselves). Following conversation analysis understandings of TRPs (Liddicoat, 2007), I see these TRPs as signaled through the utterance being intonationally complete, complete as

FIGURE 5.3.1 Subtitles as pointing to localness
Source: Trans7, *Cita-Citaku*, August 6, 2009 (1–2 p.m.)

a social action, and grammatically complete. That change in speaker does not occur with medium repair (i.e., a move back to an Indonesian medium) points to the habitualness of this type of alternation between these boys. According to Gafaranga and Torras (2002), this type of alternation can be classified as "alternation as the medium." This type of alternation can be represented with the following pattern (adapted from Auer, 1995): AB1 AB2 AB1 AB2 where the uppercase letters represent a particular medium and the numbers indicate speakers 1 and 2.

Alternation as the medium sits in contrast to Bambang's alternation between Indonesian (line 9) and their local medium (which is alternation as the medium). This interactional otherness is further indexed by way of its co-occurrence with a change in activity type (narration > interaction) and participant constellation (Bambang and the audience > Bambang and Eko). This alternation thus seems to assist in the signaling of "change in activity type" and "change in participant constellation." Accordingly, the type of alternation on line 9 fits Gafaranga and Torras's (2002) idea of codeswitching, which was characterized in chapter 3 as A1 A2 B1 A1 A2, where the uppercase letters represent a particular medium and the numbers indicate speakers 1 and 2 (adapted from Auer, 1995). Just as important, I also suggest that the anchoring to place helps associate the exchange in lines 10 onward with a particular place. In doing so, it also adds information

FIGURE 5.3.2 Subtitling localness
Source: Trans7, *Si Bolang Bocah Petualang*, August 6, 2009 (1–2 p.m.).

about the provenance of the local medium. This metasemiotic commentary helps reproduce and set up contrasts between two semiotic registers. The first register is made up of ethnicity, a local medium, and local life-worlds, while the second is made up of the voice of a reporter who reports about a life-world in Indonesian.

The practice of subtitling was common in other children's programs, including *Si Bolang Bocah Petualang* (*Bolang the Adventurous Child*), as can be seen in figure 5.3.2. As with *Cita-Citaku*, in *Si Bolang Bocah Petualang*, all of the stories are introduced as being in a particular area. In *Si Bolang Bocah Petualang*, however, the narrator is a cartoon character (Bolang). For example, in the first adventure, the cartoon character introduces the first destination as Ohoidertawun within the province of Maluku. This is followed by actual children introducing themselves in a local medium, as in figure 5.3.2.

The subtitle reads "I'm Puing a kid from Ohoidertawun, [I'm] happy to meet you." (I haven't produced an extract here as it is in a local medium that neither I nor my research assistant is familiar with.) The children in this story are shown engaging in fishing and boating. At the end of this first story, a series of maps are shown. Figure 5.3.3 is of the map before the island of Maluku starts to turn red and then grow. The map represented in figure 5.3.3 is then followed by a large shot of the island with the cartoon character in a glider superimposed over it with the text "Maluku."

Bolang is then shown flying across the archipelago to a new place, this time Petir Village in the Darmaga district of Bogor, West Java (figure 5.3.4). There are then a number of shots of a rural setting that are accompanied by a type of flute music that is commonly associated with West Java and Sundanese personhood (similar in many ways to the types of music found in the *Si Kabayan* series discussed in chapter 3). Bolang then introduces the place and a new set of children, who are again shown interacting in a local medium while catching birds and playing tug-of-war in an agricultural land. Many of these exchanges are also accompanied by subtitles.

In all of the children's' shows discussed thus far, a further mechanism that helps reproduce associations between linguistic signs and place is the movement from one story to the next. Often, each story occurs in a different part of Indonesia

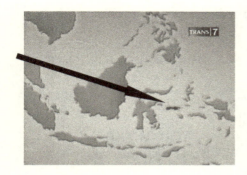

FIGURE 5.3.3 Anchoring place through the use of a map

Source: Trans7, *Si Bolang Bocah Petualang*, August 6, 2009 (1–2 p.m.)

and is inhabited by local medium-speaking Indonesians whose mediums are different from one setting to the next, as are the social practices engaged in by each group of children. These contrasts thus also help to indirectly reproduce ideas that these local mediums are also spoken by local social types from a particular region. The mechanisms described so far for anchoring linguistic signs to place and person could also be found in other genres, such as human interest stories and on-the-spot news reports. For example, human interest stories that looked at the life of impoverished young and elderly Indonesians often grounded the story to place in introductory narratives (which were subtitled), or by highlighting that the person had lived in a particular place all of their life. In the series *Minta Tolong* (*Asking for Help*) (RCTI) and *Dengarlah Aku* (*Listen to Me*) (Trans7), interviews were subtitled, which also helped to associate this local medium with the place where the interaction occurred. Similarly, some news broadcast programs were entirely in a local medium, as in the case of RCTV Cirebon.

On-the-spot news reports were also another common language practice that helped reproduce links between linguistic signs and region. Extract 5.3.3 is a report about a public transport minibus that caught fire. This talk occurs after shots of a burning public minibus are shown, and the newsreader's report notes that the bus caught fire after breaking down. Here the driver, who appears to be in his late fifties or early sixties, is being interviewed by a series of reporters.

FIGURE 5.3.4 Anchoring place through the use of a map and text

Source: Trans7, *Si Bolang Bocah Petualang*, August 6, 2009 (1–2 p.m.)

Extract 5.3.3 Sign alternation as the medium and linking medium to ideology

Reporter 1

1   *mati* **TEKO KENÉ** *pak . mati* =   [It] *broke down* **HERE** *Sir*?

Minibus driver

2   = *mati* .   [It] *broke down* [here].

Reporter 2

3   **ONO::** . **ONO** *punumpangÉ pak* =   **WERE THERE, WERE THERE** *passengers, Sir*?

Minibus driver

4   = **ORA**   **THERE**

5   **ONO RA** *pak* =   **WEREN'T, NONE** *Sir*

Reporter 2

6   = **ORA ONO** .   **THERE WEREN'T.**

Reporter 3

7   **OPO** *pak gara gara***NÉ** *pak* =   **WHAT** *Sir* **WAS THE** *cause, Sir*?

Minibus driver

8   = **RA** *ngerti*   *I* **DON'T** *know Sir*, **THE** *cause*

9   *aku pak . gara gara***NÉ IKU** *mas*   *Younger Brother.*

Source: GlobalTV, Berita Global, Friday, August 14, 2009 (4–5 p.m.)

In starting our analysis, we can see that the talk consists of both ambiguous forms (italics) and Javanese forms (bold caps). Each participant appears to orient to each other's utterance at each TRP (i.e., they continue to alternate between ambiguous forms and Javanese forms rather than change into another medium such as Indonesian). This suggests that this alternation is classifiable as alternation as the medium. In this sense, alternation as the medium becomes the local medium. As with the previous extracts, signs of place not only anchor this local medium to place, but they also suggest the provenance of this local medium. For example, the presence of a number of reporters who all seem to speak the same medium as the bus driver suggests that they are from the same place and are part of the same community of speakers.

Just as important, as with the majority of these types of news story, the story is introduced by the newsreader as occurring in a particular place. In the case at hand, this is Probolinggo, East Java, which has been historically linked to Javanese-speaking social types. The place is again repeated by a text at the bottom of the screen that reads "*Probolinggo, Jawa Timur*" (see figure 5.3.5) followed by two more mentions of place by the on-the-spot reporter, first in the introduction to the story and second as the reporter signs off. In a sense, alternation is naturalized through the existence of a community of speakers who habitually alternate between Javanese and ambiguous forms, and through the practice of noting the location of an event. At the same time, however, they also seem to help reproduce older ideologies where language, in this case, fragments of Javanese, is linked to region.

FIGURE 5.3.5 Anchoring place through text in news reports

Source: GlobalTV, *Berita Global*, August 14, 2009 (4–5 p.m.)

In summary, so far we have looked at how linguistic signs are anchored to place through a number of practices that are a type of metasemiotic commentary. Typically, a number of these practices co-occurred in a way that helped solidify the provenance of the local talk. These practices included explicit commentary by a narrator, newsreader, or a subtitle-like text, and the use of maps, subtitles, and communities of speakers using similar mediums in a particular setting. As with many of the examples in chapter 3, most of the talk examined here could be characterized as alternation as the medium. Participants oriented to this alternation without engaging in medium repair, and this suggests a type of habitualness that was further foregrounded through the existence of a community of speakers engaging in similar alternation practices. I suggested that while these representation practices helped to naturalize alternation, paradoxically, the use of signs that anchored linguistic signs to place also reproduced older language-place ideologies. The practice of medium alternation and the anchoring of this alternation to place were pervasive in other genres, especially soaps. This talk was often scripted or at the very least performed, and in the next section, I examine some examples of this.

5.4 Soaps, Stylized Alternation, and Place

As with the 1990s, representations found in a number of the 2009 soap operas also reproduced links between linguistic signs and regions. Unlike the subtitled interactions in children's programs or between reporter and victim in on-the-spot news stories, however, typically, these links were less explicit and relied on other modes. For example, the use of vehicles and their license plates often anchored the story and thus the dialogue to a certain region. On other occasions, this type of sign of place is reinforced by the representation of all the cast speaking a local medium or through other narrative devices that help establish a character's background. Typically, and in line with Richardson's (2010) observations about television dramatic dialogue in general, these signs are scripted to occur in the early part of the story to help quickly create a setting. In this section, I continue to point out the ubiquitous nature of representations of medium alternation, while also drawing out the tensions between this increasingly common way of representing interaction and older ideologies that link linguistic forms to place, person, and a named language. At the same time, I want to reiterate some earlier observations by Loven (2008) and Richardson (2010) that point out that even within soaps and dramas, the level of scripting and stylization varies from scene to scene, with actors having a lot of freedom to improvise in their performances. In what follows, I start with what appears to be a less scripted and stylized performance before contrasting it with more stylized performances.

Extract 5.4.1 is taken from the first episode of the soap *Jiran*, which was produced by Sorayaintercine Films and broadcast on Indosiar. Sundanese is in bold, Indonesian is in plain font, and italics indicate ambiguous forms that can be classified as either Sundanese or Indonesian. This particular interaction occurs at the very start of the episode and is set in a marketplace surrounded by greenery and mountains, all of which point to a rural setting. Jiran is working carrying the goods of wholesalers and shoppers in the market.

Extract 5.4.1 Soaps, signs of place, and local mediums

Male client 1

1   atos *rapih* **neng** .   [You're] **already** *done* **Younger Sister**?

Jiran

2   *Iya* .   *Yes*.

Male client 1

3   **tah ieu nya** (giving Jiran money) (5.0)   Here is [your pay].

Jiran

4   **nuhun** (16.0) (while walking towards next   Thanks.
5   customer who arrives in a van with a D
6   number plate visible)

Jiran

7   **akang** (0.5) mau dibawakan . barangnya =   **Older brother**, can I carry your goods for you?

Male client 2

8   =
9   oh **tiasa** atuh **neng tiasa** . eh antosan nya   Oh **of course** [you] **can Younger Sister**, yes [you]
10   . **yeuh** bayaran **anu ayeuna neng** . (gives   **can**. Eh, **wait a moment**
11   money) *dua rebu* . **tah ku akang**   **OK**, Here is the payment
12   **ditambihan deui sarebu** (0.5)   for now **Younger Sister**, two **thousand** (rupiah). Here, **Older Brother will give you one more thousand**.

Jiran

13	nuhun kang =	Thanks Older Brother.

Male client 2

14	= neng . tong hilaf enjing ka	Younger sister, don't forget
15	dieu deui nya . sok atuh angkut *barang*	to come back here tomor-
16	*barang*na . hati hati **nya neng nya**	row OK. Please take *the goods*, be careful **OK Younger Sister OK**.

Source: *Jiran*, Sorayaintercine Films, broadcast on Indosiar

The subtitling of the talk represented in extract 5.4.1 signals that it is not Indonesian, as is the rest of the interaction that occurs in the market. If we look at the dialogue, we can see that all participants orient to each other's usage, which for clients 1 and 2 is primarily in a Sundanese medium peppered with some Indonesian and ambiguous forms. There does not appear to be any medium repair (i.e., where participants move from one medium to another). In a sense, this type of alternation is represented as habitual, and we can thus characterize it as alternation as the medium. While this representation helps to naturalize alternation, as with extract 5.3.3, other signs also help to reproduce older associations between linguistic signs and place. In this case, the talk is anchored to region by the presence of a number of small vans and trucks that have a highly visible "D" preceding a series of numbers on their license plates. This prefix is the one used for Bandung, located in West Java. The anchoring of this dialogue to region and implicitly to Sundanese-ness is also reinforced by the occurrence of other dialogues in this setting that are also subtitled. This suggests a community that speaks the same local medium.

As the story continues, other characters are introduced, including Jiran's money-hungry husband, who has a drinking and gambling problem, and his friend, who has just returned from working in Malaysia. In their interactions and interactions with other locals, they also use Sundanese. However, increasingly, this usage is just fragments stereotypically associated with Sundanese, as in extract 5.4.2. In these instances, no subtitles appear. As the story continues, we find out that Jiran's husband is paid to have Jiran marry a wealthy young Malaysian sultan on a contract basis. Jiran and her husband go to the city where all the cars, motorcycles, and buses have license plates with a "D" prefix, which suggests that this part of the story is now set in Bandung, the capital of West Java. Any ambiguity about the actual name of the medium is removed (at least for those who watch the whole episode) in the last few minutes when a servant of the sultan explains to two of his other wives that Jiran addressed them with the term *Teteh* because it is a term of address used in Indonesia, and specifically Sundanese for "older sister." In the episode that I recorded in August 2009, none of the explicit signs found in extract 5.4.1 were present. In this setting, Jiran's husband (Pendi) is at a telephone exchange trying to call Jiran while speaking to himself and to the service officer. As with extract 5.4.1, Sundanese is in bold, ambiguous forms are in italics, and Indonesian is in plain font.

Extract 5.4.2 Stylized alternation anchored to Sundanese locales

Pendi

1	eh . **gancang atuh** subhan di angkat	Eh. **quickly come on** Subhan
2	*telepon***na** . **heeh** ini **mah** darurat . **sia teh**	pick up the *phone*. Heeh,
3	**jeung noan** tidak angkat telepon . **aing teh**	this is an emergency **right**
4	lagi butuh uang untuk kimoterapi si putri	**here right now. What are you**
5	(dials another telephone number)(12.0)	**doing**, [you] aren't picking up the phone. **Here I am** really needing money for Putri's chemotherapy.
6	ah **sarua waé** . sengaja apa si subhan **teh**	Ah **it's just the same** [no
7	(1.0) tidak mau angkat telepon dari **urang**	answer], are you doing it
8	(3.0)	on purpose Subhan, [you] don't want to answer a call from **me**.
9	ah si brengsek **mah** si subhan . si jiran	Ah **that** Subhan is an idiot.
10	**mah** sama **waé** (2.0) di sini **mah** lagi perlu	That Jiran is also the **same**.
11	uang banyak buat bayar kimoterapi si putri .	Here [I] need a lot of money
12	belum buat makan . belum buat kartu uh	to pay for Putri's chemo-
13	(slams down telephone) (3.0)	therapy, not to mention food, not to mention playing cards.

Telephone booth attendant

14	(stands up) **atuh kang** . jangan di banting	**Gee Older Brother**, don't slam
15	banting teleponnya .	the phone.

Pendi

16	**ieu mah** telepon **blegug. teu** bisa	**This** telephone **sucks**, it
17	nyambung nyambung .	**doesn't** ever connect.

Telephone booth attendant

18	telepon sananya yang **blegug** . telepon sini	It's the receiving telephone
19	**teh** . bener semua . ini telepon baru semua	that **sucks**, the phones here
20	**akang** . huh dasar	are **really** good, they are all new **Older Brother**, huh fool.

Source: Jiran, Sorayaintercine Films, broadcast on Indosiar, Thursday, August 20, 2009 (7–8 p.m.)

As with the talk in extracts 5.3.2 to 5.3.5, there is a lot of medium alternation, although this time, the amount of Sundanese is much less than in the first episode (see extract 5.4.1). Both participants orient to this type of alternation and there is no medium repair, which implies that this alternation is habitual and thus can also be classified as alternation as the medium. As with the other representations we have looked at, there is also a broad range of word classes, many of which have Indonesian cognates and most of which neatly fit the word order found in Indonesian talk. For example, there are affective particles (*atuh*), focus/emphasis particles (*mah, teh*), terms of address (*akang* and the shortened form *kang*, "older brother"), terms for self (*aing* and *urang*, "I") and other references (*sia*, "you"), modifiers (*waé*, "just"), negators ([*hen*]*teu*, "no"), question words (*naon*, "what"), conjunctions (*jeung*, "with"), and adjectives (*gancang*, "quickly" and *blegug*, "sucks").

Unlike the talk represented in extract 5.4.1, no subtitles accompany this talk. This talk and setting are contrasted with the prior Malaysian setting primarily by way of participants being involved (e.g., Jiran, the sultan, his other wives, and servants) and the subtitles that go with the dialogue that is represented as occurring in Malaysia (and contains Malay and English mediums). In a sense, the medium being used in the telephone booth is anchored to place by a movement to a rural setting together with the movement from subtitled to no subtitles. When the alternation in extract 5.4.2 is analyzed in light of these contrasts, it seems that this type of representation is part of the producer's toolkit for quickly providing a change in geographic setting and participant backgrounds. When compared with the talk of clients 1 and 2 in extract 5.4.1, this talk seems much more stylized insofar as it assumes that the use of fragments or "just enough" (Blommaert & Varis, 2011) linguistic forms will be sufficient to invoke a change in place. In a sense, we are also getting a glimpse of the producer's and actors' perception of their imagined audience's ability to engage in knowledging. In other words, and in line with Bell and Gibson's (2011) work, we can suggest that the success of such stylized alternation is dependent on the imagined audience's knowledge of the "voices" (Hill, 1995) of widely circulating Sundanese stereotypes.

The occurrence of stylized alternation was very common in the Indonesian television soaps that I recorded in August 2009. Over the three-week period, there were the following soaps that had these types of representation: dramas set in Indonesian and Malaysia: *Tangisan Isabela* (*Isabela's Tears*) and *Amira* [a woman's name] (Indosiar) and *Maharani* [a woman's name] (TPI); the comedy *Suami-Suami Takut Istri* (*Husbands Afraid of Their Wives*) (TransTV); the dramas *Bunda* (*Mother*) and *Dimas dan Raka* [two men's names] (TPI) and *Inayah* [a woman's name] (Indosiar). Extract 5.4.3 represents one more example of stylized alternation, although there are even fewer local fragments.

This extract is taken from the soap *Inayah* produced by Sorayaintercine Films and broadcast on Indosiar. The story revolves around the main character Kadjeng Doso, his many wives, and the family intrigues that occur as some of his wives attempt to get their hands on his gold. In this clip, one of the wives, Shinta, and her brother Tedi have just located Kadjeng Doso's treasure, which they plan to steal.

Extract 5.4.3 Stylized alternation anchored to Javanese locales

Shinta

1   ayo . fotoin dulu sama emas emas **IKI** =   Come on, photograph me with **THIS** gold.

Tedi

2   = oh
3   **IYO** . kenang kenangan **YO** mbak =   Oh **YES**, a souvenir **YES** Older Sister.

Shinta

3   = **IYO**   YES.

Source: Inayah, Sorayaintercine Films, broadcast on Indosiar, Wednesday, August 19, 2009 (8–9 p.m.)

In the above talk, there is no medium repair (i.e., both participants orient to each other's alternation between Javanese forms [bold caps] and Indonesian ones [plain font]). This thus falls into the category of alternation as the medium while also suggesting habitualness. This habitualness is reinforced through the actors' usage of alternation as a medium in other settings. As with extract 5.4.1, this episode also explicitly anchors this medium to Yogyakarta in Central Java through a car license plate that is prefixed by "AB." In addition to these Javanese fragments, pronunciation is stereotypically Javanese. Typically, all participants in the story also use one or both features, although where lexicon is concerned, there is typically only a few fragments of this medium in each utterance, including adverbs indicating the stage of completion of an action, interrogatives, demonstratives, affect particles, and kin terms. As with my analysis of extract 5.4.1, the representation of multiple participants who are not related yet use these same features also points to a local community that uses a local medium, all of which assists in the anchoring of story to place.

In summary, as with other televised talk examined thus far, much of the dialogue in soaps was also characterized by alternation as the medium. The habitualness of such alternation was assisted by a number of other signs, including the use of subtitles and the presence of a community of speakers who apparently share the same ways of speaking. Where the use of subtitles was concerned, this typically occurred at the start of a soap or prior to a change in setting. Both practices typically assisted in the anchoring of a participant constellation to a locale and a local medium (e.g., extract 5.4.1). There were also instances where the use of fragments from a medium was much less frequent than what was found in the subtitled cases. I differentiated these cases (extracts 5.4.2 and 5.4.3) by referring to them as "stylized alternation." As with the conclusions reached in relation to televised talk in section 5.3, what we are seeing here is the naturalization of alternation as the medium. Yet, this sits in tension with the occurrence of other signs, such as car license plates, subtitles, and dialogue, which help to reproduce older associations between medium and place. In short, representations of alternation as the medium are increasingly becoming a new imagined version of Sundanese and Javanese.

5.5 Conclusion

In this chapter, I started to analyze some of the 400 hours of television that I recorded in 2009. Drawing upon the theoretical orientations laid out in chapters 2 and 3, I focused upon the tension between how televised representations helped to naturalize alternation as the medium on the one hand, while continuing to anchor this alternation to locale. While I pointed out that these practices occurred across a number of genres including soap operas, variety shows, on-the-spot news reports, and commercials, I focused primarily on news reports, children's shows, and soaps. What was striking about these representations of alternation as the medium was that it was represented as habitual across many genres, time slots, and television stations. In a sense, alternation as the medium continues to offer an alternative case to the type of alternation found elsewhere in the world, where alternation typically occurs in liminal or spectacular moments. Moreover, that these representations were institutionally authorized also seems to sit in contrast to the institutionalization of alternation practices in other parts of the world, where multilingualism is compartmentalized as the ability to monolingually speak two or more languages.

The habitualness of these practices was also assisted via anchoring practices, which I argued also assisted in the recirculation of older ideas about ethnic social types, their language practices, and their link to place. Anchoring was achieved through explicit commentary by a narrator or newsreader, or by metasemiotic commentaries, such as maps, subtitles, communities of speakers using similar mediums in a particular setting, the explicit naming of a language, car license plates, and so on. I differentiated between two types of alternation practices found in soaps, where the first contained large amounts of a local medium, while the second, which I refer to as stylized alternation, contained just a couple of fragments from a local medium.

In concluding, I wish to make four points. The first relates to the type of minimal multimodal analysis that I have used from section 5.3 onward. While this approach is different from the one used in chapter 3, nevertheless, it represents a move toward foregrounding the importance of engaging with ideas about semiotic registers versus ideas of language (Agha, 2007a, 2007b).

In particular, it offers a method for looking at language ideology formation through a multimodal lens. In doing so, it extends scholarship on language ideology formation in a number of ways. Similar to my analysis in chapter 3, the analysis presented here contributes to a scarce literature that is starting to focus on the role of non-print-based mediums (e.g., television and movies) in the formation and reproduction of language ideologies, especially those relating to stereotypes and their associated semiotic registers (Bucholtz, 2011; Bucholtz & Lopez, 2011; Mendoza-Denton, 2011).

Second, and again in line with points made in the conclusion to chapter 3, the extra modes found in the soap format help us to extend our analysis of the use of metasemiotic commentaries that can help assign cultural value to particular linguistic signs. In the case presented here, the idea of cultural value relates to ideas of ethnic identity, and the metasemiotic commentaries that are used to help index this value include subtitle-like text, maps, subtitles, communities of speakers using similar mediums in a particular setting, the explicit naming of a language, the use of signs of place (car license plates), and so on. Third, as the modeling of alternation as the medium becomes increasingly ubiquitous on Indonesian television, there is a clear reconfiguration or revaluation of ethnic languages vis-à-vis Indonesian, especially when compared with representations during the first twenty-five years of Indonesian television when Indonesian was the sole medium. Finally, the representation of multiple semiotic registers in multiple social domains points more generally toward the diversity found in Indonesia, which is the topic of the next chapter.

6

Representing and Authorizing Linguistic Superdiversity

6.1 Introduction

This chapter shows how representations of linguistic diversity and knowledging that were starting to become part of Indonesian mediascapes in the early 1990s were by 2009 ubiquitous across a range of television stations and genres. We will see that this authorization of alternation and diversity also often sits in contrast to the practices described in chapter 5 where linguistic forms were anchored to ethnic social types and/or region. In this sense, these representational practices not only denaturalize the language-place-ethnicity links that I have described throughout this book, but they also provide insights into one of the unexpected consequences of the long-term processes of enregisterment described in chapters 2–4, namely the addition of one further layer of linguistic diversity to an already diverse situation. In addition, these representational practices have also modeled and authorized the doing of unity in diversity on a larger scale than in the 1990s. In particular, and in contrast to ideologies about doing unity in diversity, unity is done through the use of fragments of what are often referred to as "regional languages." (I have referred to these throughout this book as "mediums" in order to deemphasize the idea of language and foreground the idea of semiotic register.) More generally, the representations I will be looking at mirror the doing of social relations in settings typically described as "superdiverse" (e.g., Blommaert & Rampton, 2011; Vertovec, 2007).

A major aim of this chapter is to contribute to discussions about superdiversity more generally. While superdiversity is something that has been around for a long time (Vertovec, 2007), what is important is that complexity and diversity are increasingly acknowledged as the necessary starting points for understanding the interface between human social relations and language practices. There are a number of themes covered in work on superdiversity, although here I just focus on two that are relevant to the ideas and arguments put forth in previous chapters. First, scholars generally agree that a characteristic of superdiversity is that intercultural contact occurs in more social domains and more frequently than in the past (Blommaert & Rampton, 2011; Vertovec, 2007). Typically, the settlement of mobile or displaced persons is in neighborhoods already associated with diversity and multiple languages. In a sense, this helps layer diversity over diversity (e.g., Blommaert, 2010; Blommaert & Rampton, 2011; Rampton, 2011; Vertovec, 2007). We have seen how this has occurred across the Indonesian archipelago for the last 150 years or so, and how it relates more generally to the emergence of an uncountable number of locale-specific emergent semiotic registers.

Even so, an under-theorized area of work on superdiversity is the effect of increasing circulation and consumption of registers found in one-to-many participation frameworks. In particular, we can say that a further layer of diversity is added through the consumption of different types of mediums, such as television programs, movies, radio programs, music, religious texts, Internet content, and so on. Consumption of these mediums adds to the multiple repertoires and truncated competences that people develop through face-to-face interactions (e.g., Blommaert & Backus, 2011; Blommaert, Collins, & Slembrouck, 2005; Jørgensen, Karrebæk, Madsen, & Møller, 2011). In short, consumption of television and other media enables people to develop varying degrees of competence to comprehend and an ability to engage in knowledging. The idea of knowledging brings us back to a second observation relating to studies of superdiversity, namely that the condition of superdiversity requires new ways of understanding how people from very different backgrounds and with very different semiotic systems go about getting along (Ang, 2003; Goebel, 2010a, 2010b; Smets, 2005; Vertovec, 2007; Werbner, 1997; Wise, 2005). With an understanding of the mechanisms that enable people to engage in knowledging, we can come to a more nuanced understanding of people's actual interactional practices that involved knowledging. This topic will become part of the discussion in chapters 7 and 8.

The Indonesian soaps that we will examine provide examples of superdiverse Indonesian neighborhoods, while also modeling interactional practices in such settings. We will see that ideas about superdiversity seem to have entered into the imaginations of those who produce these television shows in such a way that knowledging on the part of characters within television shows is represented as everyday and mundane, while also implying that the producers of these shows imagine their audiences to also engage in knowledging. More specifically, section 6.2 focuses on understanding representations of alternation practices that are stylized and those that resemble adequation. As with some of the representations found in the soaps described in chapter 5, alternation often involves fragments that have associations with ethnic communities and locales. Typically, these fragments are terms for self and other reference, terms for thanking, and affective particles. In contrast to the televised material covered in chapters 3 and 5 where we had the representation of multiple voices anchored to different parts of Indonesia, in the talk I examine in section 6.2, these voices are now represented as spoken in settings associated with the city. I also examine an interesting case of a foreigner engaging in practices of adequation, which included appropriating and using Indonesian voices and voices associated with ethnic social types.

In section 6.3, I examine how mobility and diversity are represented through the use of a few fragments from widely circulating semiotic registers associated with the voices of imagined ethnic communities. I provide examples of interactions among those who are represented as sharing similar trajectories and similar ethnic voices. I also provide examples of the use of ethnic voices across lines of difference where participants are represented as understanding each other's talk. The representations in this section also differ in important ways from the representations found in section 6.2. First, there are no metasemiotic commentaries that anchor linguistic signs to geographic space or a named language. Second, as with the representations discussed in chapters 3 and 5, here the representation of linguistic diversity is also done in a non-spectacular way, suggesting habitualness across a number of social domains inhabited by social types from multiple backgrounds. In this sense, alternation as the medium is presented as common, as well as institutionally authorized.

In section 6.4, I look at representations of doing unity in diversity, which are done in similar ways to the representation of diversity that we examine in section 6.3. In concluding, I bring these sections together by relating them back to my discussion on superdiversity, especially the issue of understanding how one-to-many participation frameworks help to increase linguistic diversity. As we will see in chapters 7 and 8, recourse to the notion of one-to-many participation frameworks enables a more nuanced understanding of the linguistic practices of a group of transnational Indonesians living in Japan.

6.2 Alternation, Knowledging, and Authorizing the Everyday

This section focuses on understanding representations of alternation practices that are stylized and those that resemble adequation. As with some of the representations found in the soaps described in chapter 5, alternation often involves fragments that have associations with ethnic communities and locale. I point out that these practices are accountable with reference to notions of enregisterment. In contrast to the material examined in the previous chapter, the talk I examine here is represented as spoken in settings associated with the city. In looking at all of these practices, I suggest that what we are also seeing is an authorization of superdiversity where models of doing unity in diversity are increasingly ones that involve fragments of regional languages, rather than Indonesian as was common in the New Order period.

Extract 6.2.1 is taken from the quiz show *Siapa Lebih Berani* (*Who Is Braver*), which was aired each day between seven and eight in the morning on RCTI. Like many of the same genre, this show has household items and cash as prizes. This show elicits participants for subsequent shows by advertising for them during each show. Teams of around twenty participants are chosen and then presented with general-knowledge questions and survey results. This show is often themed, and on this occasion, contestants are wearing pajamas, dressing gowns, hair rollers, and other things stereotypically associated with the practice of sleeping. During this episode, there are five groups of around fifteen to twenty participants. Midway into the quiz, the hosts announce which members of the group have won household items because their individual guesses about survey results were closest to the actual results. At the end of each sequence of prize-giving, one member from each group is selected to compete for the major prize, which is a television.

While the female presenter, Alya Rohali, uses fragments of many mediums throughout the show, her usage increases as she greets each of these five people. As can be seen in extract 6.2.1, she refers to herself and addresses some of the chosen contestants with Sundanese fragments (in bold), while also speaking to the male host using Betawi fragments more generally (bold small caps). This interaction occurs after the male host invites the winner from group A.

Extract 6.2.1 That's what Sundanese call *munjungan*

Alya

1 ayo sayang =   Come on honey.

Helmy

2   = ayo .   Come on.

Alya

3 GUÉ jadi ingat masa kecil GUÉ =   It makes ME remember the
                                                  time I was young like her].

Helmy

4   = GUÉ juga   ME too.

5 =

Alya

6 = mirip kan . ok silahkan . ayo   Similar right! OK please go
                                                  ahead, please go ahead.

Lines deleted. Helmy goes through list of winners for group B before announcing the next contestant.

Alya

7 **mangga neng** . ke depan ya   **Please younger sister**, to the front.

Lines deleted. Helmy announces next contestant, who comes down and greets Helmy and shakes hand without doing so with Alya.

Helmy

8 siapa nama ELU =   What is YOUR name?

Contestant

9   = nando (shakes Helmy's   Nando.
10 hand and walks straight to podium) =

Alya

11   =
12 cuekin GUÉ mutus (1.1) awas ya =   Ignore [me] I will ignore [you], look out.

Helmy

13   = ya =   Yes, [look out].

Alya

14   = soal   I'll make your questions hard.
15 kamu saya susahin =

Helmy

16   = dia . dia soalnya tidak   She, the issue is she doesn't
17 melayani tanté . nggak tanté lah ya .   respond [if called] Auntie, it's not Auntie OK [everyone].

Alya

18 **teteh** . gila   [Everyone call me] **Older sister**, got it.

Lines deleted. Contestant from group D is called up. He first greets Helmy and then Alya.

Contestant

19 halo tanté =   Hi Auntie.

Alya

20   = **munjungan** . kata orang   [That greeting he just per-
21 sunda **munjungan**   formed] is a **greeting** which Sundanese call **munjungan**.

Source: Siapa Lebih Berani broadcast on RCTI, Tuesday, August 11, 2009 (7–8 a.m.)

In the above extract, Alya alternates between Indonesian and a number of widely circulating forms that are stereotypically associated with Sundanese (lines 7, 18, 20, 21). This alternation is marked for a number of reasons. First, the primary medium seems to be Indonesian forms alternated with forms stereotypically associated with being Betawi or living in Jakarta (lines 3 and 12). Typically, these Betawi forms (bold small caps) are terms of self and other reference. For example, on line 12, Alya moves between the form *gué* (I) stereotypically associated with talk about oneself, personal life-worlds, and intimate interaction among either Betawi social types or city social types of similar status and age, and *saya* (I) on line 15, which is more commonly associated with social relations among unfamiliars, those where there are inequalities in status, and official contexts associated with schooling and expertise.

Second, Alya also uses a number of terms associated with Sundanese (7, 18, 20, 21). In cases where there is potentially an interactional slot where a contestant could become the next speaker, as in line 7, her alternation is not reciprocated and her co-host then moves on to announcing the next contestant in Indonesian. Similarly, her play with the idea that Auntie (*Tanté*) should be replaced with Older Sister (*Teteh*) on line 18, presumably because she felt that she was not yet old enough to be an Auntie, is not oriented to by the next contestant on line 18 who also uses the term *tanté*. While what we are seeing here seems to resemble medium repair, Alya's continual use of words associated with Sundanese and her metapragmatic description of some of these words as Sundanese, as in her commentary about the provenance of the word *munjungan* (lines 20 and 21), suggests she is engaging in a practice that resembles the stylized alternation discussed in section 5.4.2.

What makes her alternation above even more interesting is a comparison with her performance the following day, when she uses a form stereotypically associated with intimate social relations among Javanese (in bold caps). On this occasion, the groups are much more mixed in terms of age, although much more homogeneous in terms of gender. There are three groups of women (whose ages appear to range between early twenties and forties), a group of younger men (perhaps in their twenties and thirties), and a mixed group of people in their late teens and early twenties. Of interest is the later part of the show, where all five group representatives are brought to the front and invited to guess the identity of a famous person. One contestant, Agus, presses the buzzer and the following interaction ensues (extract 6.2.2). Indonesian is in plain font and Javanese is in bold caps.

Extract 6.2.2 I also know and can speak some Javanese

Agus

1	mel lisen =	Mel Lisen

Helmy

2	= mel salah .	Mel is wrong.

Alya

3	**SOPO** sih agus . [melan **SOPO**	WHO do [you] think it is Agus? Melan **WHO**?

Helmy

4	[mel **SOPO** . ngerti	Mel **WHO**? [I] understand,
5	bukan mel shandy [chintami sini aja	it's not Mel Shandy. Chintami come here
6	(saying while summoning chintami with	please.
7	hand)	

Agus

8	[melan =	Melan.

Alya

9	= melan apa	Melan or
10	mican	Mican?

Talk deleted (A number of wrong guesses until the correct one. Then nine new questions all in Indonesian. This is followed by a commercial break before the next round of short questions)

Agus

11	surabaya =	Surabaya (name of capital city of East Java).

Helmy

12	= surabaya =	Surabaya.

Alya

13	= surabaya =	Surabaya.

Helmy

14	= betul	Correct, yes [correct].
15	ya	

Source: *Siapa Lebih Berani* broadcast on RCTI, Tuesday, August 12, 2009 (7–8 a.m.)

In the above extract, Alya alternates from Indonesian to a widely circulating form that is stereotypically associated with Javanese (line 3). This alternation is marked in this show because it sits in contrast to the primary medium in the preceding and subsequent talk, which is Indonesian. Indeed, as can be seen in lines 9, 14, and 15, Alya and Helmy repair this medium by reverting back to Indonesian in their subsequent talk with Agus. As with extract 6.2.1, the above talk also suggests that the presenters imagine their audience as having some familiarity with the mediums used. When taken together with her previous performance, we get a picture of a person who appears to either engage in a type of stylized alternation for the fun of it or perhaps to orient to the particular ethnic identities of contestants. For example, although no talk made these identities explicit here, they may well have been built up to in the off-air interactions between hosts and contestants. Although this last point is purely speculation, what is clear is that this type of stylized alternation is an institutionally authorized practice. This representation of addressing both a local audience (the contestants) and a national one in Indonesian and fragments from a number of other mediums (typically associated with regional languages) gives further weight to circulating models for the doing of unity in diversity that don't exclusively involve Indonesian. Indeed, it seems to assume that those who may not speak Sundanese or Javanese may nevertheless understand bits and pieces of these registers.

Just as important, although there are some aspects of the last two extracts that resemble contexts where crossing is found (i.e., liminal moments, during performances, at initial stages of an interaction), what sets this apart from the type of crossing described in Rampton (1995) is that these people do not know each other. It is also likely that those whose linguistic forms are being appropriated will find out about this type of appropriation (e.g., the potential for some of the contestants or audiences being Javanese or Sundanese). As noted above, it also resembles but is not the same as the stylized alternation discussed in section 5.4. This is so because alternation is either not oriented to by the person being addressed or there is no interactional slot for such orientation (e.g., Alya's comment about *munjungan* on lines 20 and 21 of extract 6.2.1). Knowledging thus seems a better way of describing Alya's practice here insofar as she appears to be using her knowledge of fragments of widely circulating mediums to perform her alternation. This interpretation also fits with what we know of Alya who was born in 1976 and was thus potentially a participant in processes of enregisterment that facilitated the circulation of this type of knowledge (e.g., chapters 2 and 3).

While we know nothing about Alya's interlocutors' backgrounds, other genres provided much richer representations. Often, as with the one I focus on in extract 6.2.3, these representations seem to sit in contrast to the processes of enregisterment described so far (i.e., the anchoring of language to a social type living in a particular region). For example, in the case I examine below, Sacha Stevenson, who self-identifies as a Canadian, appropriates not only an Indonesian voice but also a Javanese one. Extract 6.2.3 is taken from the skit that occurred in the comedy entitled *Acara Saatnya Kita Sahur*, which I awkwardly translate as *A Show for Us while We Are Eating prior to the Daily Fast*. This show was aired on TransTV each day during the fasting month between three and four in the morning.

The interaction represented in extract 6.2.3 occurs between two people who are friends of a third person, Komeng, who has phoned them and asked them to get his suitcase, which he has left behind. These two people are standing and practicing English with the aid of dictionaries in an airport waiting room somewhere in America. Their wordplay and mixing of English and Indonesian are interrupted when an unknown young woman, Sacha, arrives unexpectedly. The two men act confused and start using fragments of English before then suggesting that Sacha may be Spanish and thus needs to be addressed with an appropriate term for "you." This linking of nationality to linguistic form continues to include Italian, French, German, Arabic, and Dutch, often with the actors using the forms and saying she must be French, Dutch, and so on. After engaging in self-repair (of each medium), the two give up in despair and start speaking what is later named as Javanese. Until this use of Javanese (in bold caps), Sacha acts increasingly confused but says nothing.

Extract 6.2.3 The authorization of adequating foreigners and mixing

Participant 1
1   ORA *usah* =   DON'T *worry about* [it].
Participant 2
2   = ah =   Ah.
Participant 1
3   = WIS lah . *aku* . *aku* RA   [We're] DONE. *I, I* DON'T
4   *ngerti mesti* diapain =   *know* what [we] *should* do.
Participant 2
5   = SAMI KARO *aku* =   [That] IS THE SAME AS *Me*.
Participant 1
6   =
7   [*aku*   *I*.
Participant 2
8   [MBUH RAK *ngerti* =   DON'T KNOW, DON'T *know*.
Participant 1
9   = MBOTEN   [I] DON'T
10 NGERTOS lah . capai lah =   KNOW, [I'm] tired of this.
Participant 2
11   = MULIH   [Let's] GO,
12 MULIH . MONGGO MONGGO =   [Let's] GO, EXCUSE ME
                                                          [Mrs.] EXCUSE ME.

(continued)

Extract 6.2.3 (Continued)

Participant 1

13	= WIS	We are **DONE**, [let's] **JUST**
14	kita **MULIH WAÉ YO . MONGGO**	**GO COME ON, EXCUSE**
15	capai *aku* (0.5)	**ME** [Mrs.], *I'm* tired [of this]

Sacha

16	o::::::h **SAMPEAN IKI NGOLEKI** *kopor*	Oh, **YOU ARE LOOKING FOR** *a suitcase*
17	**TOH** (0.5) **KOPERÉ ONO NING**	**RIGHT? THE SUITCASE OVER**
18	**KONO** .	**THERE.**

Participant 1

19	wa:::h o::::::::h bulé apa =	Wow! What sort of white foreigner is this?

Participant 2

20	= ya ngomong	Yeah say so
21	kalau bisa ngomong jawa . ngomong (0.8)	if you can speak Javanese, say so.

Participant 1

22	ini mah . ini mah . bulé istrinya pak **LIK**	This is, this is, this white foreigner is our **YOUNGER UNCLE'S** wife.

Talk deleted

Sacha

23	**IKI OPO** (pointing to chocolate that	**WHAT IS THIS?**
24	Participant 1 wiped on her mouth) =	

Participant 1

25	= **IKI**	**WHAT IS THIS?**
26	**OPO** . haha **IKI OPO . WIS PANGANÉ**	(Laughs). **WHAT IS THIS? ITS FOOD,**
26	**PANGANÉ**	**ITS FOOD.**

Source: TransTV, *Acara Saatnya Kita Sahur*, Saturday, August 23, 2009 (3–4 a.m.)

There are a number of striking features of the talk in extract 6.2.3. First, we see that alternation is common (e.g., lines 3, 4, 13–15, and 22) with the two males alternating among forms stereotypically associated with Javanese (bold font), forms stereotypically associated with Indonesian (plain font), and ambiguous forms (italics). They also do not engage in medium repair. Thus, this practice can be characterized as alternation as the medium and habitual. As with chapters 3 and 5 and extracts 6.2.1 and 6.2.2, this alternation is publically authorized by way of its being broadcast nationally on television. In so doing, the one-to-many participation framework of television helps to naturalize language alternation, while also naturalizing superdiversity more generally.

Second, we have a person, Sacha, whose white Caucasian appearance has the actors orienting to her perceived difference through talk that associates her with all types of foreigners. Nevertheless, this framing as foreign is thrown into disarray as she speaks Javanese to these two actors. In so doing, she performs what might on the surface look like crossing. This is so because her Javanese usage is not initially reciprocated, but rather attracts metasemiotic commentary (line 19) as participant 1 wonders just what type of white foreigner she might be. What makes Sacha's use of Javanese different from crossing is that after initially showing surprise—which is initially done in Indonesian and thus a type of medium repair—shortly thereafter, Sacha continues in Javanese on line 23. Her usage is subsequently reciprocated by participant 1 on line 25. While this alternation is not habitual in the same sense as the interaction between participants 1 and 2, nevertheless, the subsequent orientation to this usage from line 22 onward suggests that her ability to use Javanese is not only ratified but also locally accountable. For example, her unusual ability is quickly explained by noting that she is the wife of someone they refer to as *Pak Lik* (younger uncle) on line 22.

It is these actors' explanation that moves what might have otherwise fit into the category of crossing into a practice associated with adequation. This is done by linking Sacha's ability with her everyday activities and life-world of being the wife of someone whom they know is Javanese. The Javanese-ness of her husband is made explicit by indexical links with the Javanese kin term *Pak Lik* (younger uncle) when referring to the non-present spouse on line 22. In this sense, it also pushes the boundaries of normal definitions of crossing because Sacha is represented as someone authorized to speak Javanese. Indeed, this representation fits with more common practices of adequation found among internal migrants in Indonesia (Goebel, 2010b). Finally, as with the naming practices discussed above and in chapter 5, Sacha's talk and the other actors' talk is given the name "Javanese" (line 22) and by extension anchored to Java, thus reproducing older ties between language and region.

The language practices exemplified in extracts 6.3.1 and 6.3.2 were quite common in a number of other genres including travel shows and culinary shows and across a number of broadcasters. As with the above interactions and with some of the representations found in the soaps described in chapter 5, these were typically terms of self and other reference, terms for thanking, and affective particles. Unlike other analyses of these types of genre (Jaworski, Thurlow, Lawson, & Yälnne-McEwen, 2003), however, crossing does not seem to be an appropriate way of categorizing the alternation practices found in these Indonesian genres or the talk represented in extracts 6.2.1–6.2.3.

Instead, we can account for this type of stylized alternation with reference to knowledging (i.e., participation in processes of enregisterment that occurred on a mass scale from 1966 onward). As with the television representations analyzed in chapters 3 and 5, the representations of alternation in this section are also institutionally authorized insofar as an institution, in this case, a government-sanctioned television station, is broadcasting models of language and social relations.

In summary, in contrast to the televised material covered in chapter 5, where we had the representation of multiple voices anchored to different parts of Indonesia, in the extracts above, these voices are represented as spoken in settings associated with the city. As with section 3.7, we also were provided with models of doing unity in diversity that involved the use of fragments of regional languages rather than solely Indonesian. We also had foreigners engaging in practices of adequation, which included appropriating and using Indonesian voices and voices associated with ethnic social types. This practice was quite common with celebrities, such as Sacha Stevenson, appearing in other shows that were aired in primetime (in the 8–9 p.m. timeslot), such as the comedy *O.K.B* (*Orang Kaya Baru*, or *The New Rich*). On this occasion, Sacha performed in an Indonesian voice while also noting to her surprised interlocutors that she could also do so in Betawi if they wished. In a sense, what we are seeing in the above extracts are authorized representations of adequation and linguistic superdiversity. In the following sections, I address the theme of superdiversity.

While representations of alternation and adequation are a reflection of what was happening on the ground in the mid-1990s (Goebel, 2010b), and most likely during the colonial period as well (see chapter 2), these representations, as well as the processes of enregisterment that I have discussed thus far, have helped set up the conditions for these practices. In this chapter, this has meant that both actors and producers have represented this practice as everyday and normal while imagining their audiences as having an ability to comprehend linguistic fragments from mediums that they would not normally speak. In a sense, processes of enregisterment have helped produce a new form of sociability, which in turn contributed to even more linguistic diversity (i.e., when people engage in knowledging or adequation) in settings already characterized by linguistic diversity. Finally, the authorization of alternation and adequation also suggests the continued emergence of a center of normativity that began in the late 1990s with representations in soaps such as *Si Doel*. The authorization of these practices also suggests a continued reconfiguration of orders of indexicality, with Indonesian losing ground in the social domain that involves doing unity in diversity.

6.3 Representing Mobility and Diversity

Most of this book has alluded to a diverse range of ethnic social types found throughout the Indonesian archipelago. These social types and their voices have typically been anchored to regions through the representation of identifiable signs, such as car license plates, buildings, and other metasemiotic commentaries. In the previous section and section 3.7, we also saw that there were representations that pointed to mobility, the type of ethnolinguistic diversity one finds in Jakarta, and models of doing togetherness using fragments of mediums other than Indonesian. In this section, I want to examine how representations of migrants and their linguistic practices can help contribute to an increase in the social value of linguistic diversity. We will see that, typically, the representation of linguistic diversity is done in non-spectacular ways, suggesting habitualness across a number of social domains that are inhabited by social types from both poor and affluent backgrounds.

These cases differ from the other extracts of talk in section 6.2 insofar as they are anchored to the city as a locale. As with the representations examined in much of this book, many of these interactions are characterized by alternation that is semiotically linked with everyday mundane interactions and social relations. Typically, ethnic voices are represented by the use of linguistic fragments that are associated with ethnic social types from the imagined heartlands of Sundanese speakers, Betawi speakers, Javanese speakers, and so on. While there are many genres that contained these types of linguistic practices, in this section, I focus on soap operas.

The first one is *Indahnya warna pelangi* (*How Beautiful Are the Colors of the Rainbow*), which was aired by Trans7. The central theme of this soap was a political message about the need to follow one's own preferences in the upcoming elections and not those of one's boss, spouse, friend, or financial patron. In addition to this explicit political message, which was aired during the run-up to the 2009 presidential elections, there are a number of other interesting things happening in this soap. For example, as with many of the other representations we have examined, this soap was anchored to Jakarta by way of car license plates and via travel to other places where the medium being used was different. Extract 6.3.1 was taken from this soap and occurs at the very beginning when a boy on a bicycle delivers papers to an affluent household where the household's driver is washing one of their many cars and the household's gardener is nearby working on a hedge. When the paperboy arrives, the older driver asks the gardener to get the paper, but the gardener says he can't because he has dirty hands. The driver then asks the paperboy to put the paper on the fence.

Extract 6.3.1 Soap representations of the voices of poor mobile workers

Driver

1	**jang** . **sok jang** tolong taro sana dulu **jang**	**Son. Please son** help put [the
2	=	newspaper] there for the moment **son**.

Paper boy

3	= ya pak (proceeds to place paper on top of	Yes Sir.
4	fence and then walks back to bicycle)	

Driver

5	makasih ya **jang** ya	Thanks yeah, **son**, OK.

Source: Trans7, *Indahnya warna pelangi*, Friday, August 7, 2009 (9–10 a.m.)

In the above talk, we see that the driver speaks to the paperboy alternating between fragments of Sundanese (in bold) and Indonesian (plain font) in lines 1 and 5. We also see that the paperboy apparently understands these fragments through his ratification of the driver's request (lines 3 and 4). Jakartan suburbia is thus represented as not only a diverse place, but one where alternation as the medium is common and where understanding this type of alternation is normal. This practice was common within this soap, especially in interactions among the driver, the gardener, and the maid. In these interactions, talk was often peppered with linguistic fragments stereotypically associated with Sundanese-ness, including kin terms (*kang*, "older brother"), particles indicating stance (*teh, mah*), and so on. In this sense, this alternation is also represented as a habitual practice in certain social domains among certain participant constellations.

As with the representations of talk discussed in chapter 5, here the representation of alternation sets up three tensions. On the one hand, in general, this alternation between Indonesian and Sundanese helps to further denaturalize ideologies that link region to linguistic signs and ethnic community. On the other hand, the frequent representations of multiple social types who engage in alternation as the medium among themselves tend to reproduce ideologies about social types belonging to communities of ethnic social types who use ethnic languages. Third, that these representations are broadcast to a linguistically diverse audience presupposes or imagines that all viewers are familiar with fragments from these mediums.

The practice of alternation was not just one that associated the city with ethnic voices from low-income migrant social types. In extract 6.3.2, we will see these people's employers alternating in other social domains; in this case, alternation involves fragments of Javanese (in bold caps) in interactions among family members in their home during meals. In the talk that precedes extract 6.3.2, the husband and wife (who are the employers of the domestic help involved in extract 6.3.1) are in the process of discussing which presidential candidate is best and how each platform relates to the provision of free education.

Extract 6.3.2 Soap representations of the ethnic voices of affluent migrants

Bapak

1 bukannya iklannya yang ada di mana mana
2 (0.4) apa mungkin . anak seorang sopir
3 angkot bisa menjadi seorang pilot . kalau
4 sekolah gratis cuma sampai smp . lah untuk
5 masuk sma . dan sekolah pilotnya . **SOPO**
6 **SING** bayar **DIDOL** angkut pun . nggak
7 bakalan nutup ma

Isn't it that [free education] is [just] in advertisements that can be found anywhere? Is it possible that the child of minibus driver can become a pilot. [At the moment] schooling is free only until junior high. So for senior high and pilot school **WHO IS IT THAT** will pay? Even **SELLING** the minibus won't be enough to pay the fees, Mum (here a term used to refer to his wife).

Mama

8 bapak ini keterlaluan banget sih ya . bener
9 bener nggak punya etiketa (0.5)

You are a bit over the top you know, you really don't have any etiquette.

Bapak

10 loh . kok mama jadi marah beneran

Wow, gee Mum you are actually angry.

Source: Trans7, *Indahnya warna pelangi*, Friday, August 7, 2009 (9–10 a.m.)

As can be seen in the talk in lines 5 and 6, there are a number of fragments stereotypically associated with Javanese (bold caps). As with extract 6.3.2, here it appears that Mama understands such usage though she does not engage in alternation. In a sense, this practice also resembles the type of stylized alternation discussed in section 5.4, though here it seems to function as a quick way of providing character background. For example, together with the use of other linguistic fragments associated with Javanese (such as the kin terms *Mas*, "older brother," and *Pak Dé*, "older uncle"), this use of fragments was enough to help portray the family's background, with the father being a Javanese migrant who had settled and obviously done well in Jakarta.

The above type of representation of migrants living, working, or studying in Jakarta was very common in soaps across all broadcasters and across most timeslots. For example, GlobalTV aired *Bukan Sinetron* (*This Is Not a Soap*) in the 6–7 p.m. timeslot. This particular soap represented the main characters as migrants who typically used Indonesian and Javanese fragments among themselves, such as *endi*, "where," *opo*, "what," *wis*, "already," and so on. Typically, these fragments were mixed with Indonesian in a way that represented alternation as the medium. While extracts 6.3.1 and 6.3.2 represent talk from soaps where ethnic voices were found in different social domains within the city—for example, the boss spoke Javanese while the domestic help spoke Sundanese—there were also soaps, comedy sketches, and live televised comedy performances that brought different ethnic social types together within one setting. In these settings, the doing of unity in diversity or togetherness continued to be represented by a combination of Indonesian and regional languages, rather than just Indonesian.

In these settings, actors used their ethnic voices with those who were represented as not being of the same ethnic social type as they. In other words, these voices were shown to be used across lines of difference, as was the case with extracts 3.7.4 and 3.7.5. Extract 6.3.3 provides an example of this type of representation. The extract is taken from the comedic soap *OB* (*Office Boy*), which is set in an office in Jakarta. Some of the main actors have voices associated with ethnic social types from West Java (Sundanese) and Jakarta (Betawi). In the extract below, Ipul is interacting with two others (Susi and Saodah). Ipul is represented as a Sundanese through his use of linguistic fragments stereotypically associated with Sundanese-ness (in bold), Susi and Saodah are represented as having links with either the city or Betawi social types by their usage of linguistic fragments stereotypically associated with Betawi social types (bold small caps). Forms that are ambiguous in terms of being classifiable as Indonesian or Betawi are in italics. This interaction occurs after one of the office staff asks Susi to guard the female toilet door while he is using the women's toilet (the men's toilet is engaged). Susi is getting bored with waiting when Ipul walks up the corridor and the following conversation ensues.

Extract 6.3.3 Using ethnic voices across lines of difference

Susi
1   o:: lama banget sih pak hendra .   Gee, why is Pak Hendra taking so long?

Ipul
2   (???) (???) (while humming and playing   (???) (???)
3   with his hair and approaching Susi) .

Susi
4   a:: ha ha (slaps Ipul on the arm) kebetulan   A [here is someone to take my place] as it happens
5   LU datang ha . *gantiin* GUÉ ya .   YOU have come by, *replace* ME yeah!

Ipul
6   Eh . *gantiin* **naon teh** .   Eh *replace* **what Older Sister**?

Susi
7   ndak jangan kebanyakan nanya (while   Stop, don't ask too many questions.
8   grabbing shirt and moving around Ipul and
9   pushing him in front of toilet door) nah LU   Now, YOU just stay
10 diam aja di sini . berdiri di sini . ya =   here, stand here, OK?

Ipul
11   =
12 (doesn't say anything and looks at Susi   (No affirmative response)
13 with confused expression) =

Susi
14   = ntar kalau   Later, if for example a
15 misalnya ada cewek yang mau masuk .   woman comes to use the toilet,
16 jangan dikasih . ngerti KAGAK . ya itu pun   don't let them in. Understand or NOT? That is
17 kalau LU KAGAK mau *dimarahin* . ngerti   if YOU DON'T want to get in *trouble*. [Do you] understand
18 nggak (0.5)   or not?

Ipul
19 **enya enya atuh enya** =   Yes, yes, OK, yes.

Susi
20   = bagus (puts up   Great.
21 thumb and walks off) (0.6)

(continued)

Extract 6.3.3 (Continued)

Ipul

22 (puts up thumb) **alus enya** (3.9) Ok, **great yes**.

Saodah

23 (exits a door located nearly opposite the (exits a door located nearly opposite the
24 toilet door guarded by Ipul) toilet door guarded by Ipul)

Ipul

25 wah ah (puts up two hands) **punten teh** . Gee, **I'm sorry Older Sister**,
26 kata **teh** susi nggak ada yang boleh masuk **Older Sister** Susi said that no one is allowed to go in.

27 (0.7)

Saodah

28 e:: siapa juga yang mau masuk . GUÉ justru What? Who wants to go in? I actually
29 mau minta LU *pijitin* GUÉ . badan GUÉ want YOU to give ME a *massage*. MY whole body
30 udah pegel semua nih is very stiff.

Ipul

31 e:: tapi kata **teh** Susi (while pointing) Oh, but **Older sister** Susi said.

Saodah

32 (Grabs Ipul and pushes him in front of her (Grabs Ipul and pushes him in front of her
33 through the door into the common room.) through the door into the common room.)

Source: RCTI, *OB* ("Shift 2"), Monday, August 10, 2009 (3–4 p.m.)

In the above talk, we see that all the actors use and expect each other to understand linguistic fragments that are associated with particular imagined ethnic communities. Susi and Saodah are represented as communicating across lines of difference while understanding Sundanese forms. For example, Susi is represented as understanding Ipul's use of Sundanese interrogatives (*naon*), kin terms (*teh*, the shortened form of *teteh*), and the word *enya* ("yes") in lines 7–10, 19 and 20. Similarly, Soadah is shown as understanding Ipul's Sundanese usage in lines 28–30. In short, Susi and Soadah are represented as able to engage in a form of knowledging. On the other hand, Ipul is represented as understanding forms associated with Betawi. For example, in line 6, Ipul is shown to understand local terms for self and other reference (*lu* and *gué*), while he is also represented as understanding Sodah's use of terms for self and other reference in lines 28 and 29. Ipul's practice is a little different from Susi's and Soadah's, however, insofar as his residence in Jakarta implies that he has learned these forms through local interactions rather than through participation in one-to-many participation frameworks (e.g., schooling, media consumption) that have enabled the large-scale circulation of fragments of other mediums. In other words, he is represented as engaging in adequation while Susi and Soadah are represented as engaging in knowledging. Both cases, however, present models of doing unity in diversity that do not exclusively require Indonesian.

In summarizing this section, we have seen that the representation of mobility and diversity is done through the use of a few fragments from widely circulating semiotic registers associated with the voices of imagined ethnic communities. I provided examples of interactions among those who were represented as sharing similar trajectories and similar ethnic voices (e.g., extracts 6.3.1 and 6.3.2), and representations of the use of ethnic voices across lines of difference where participants were represented as understanding each other's talk (extract 6.3.3). The representations in this section also differ in important ways from the representations found in extracts 6.2.1 and 6.2.2. First, there were no metasemiotic commentaries that anchored linguistic signs to geographic space or to a named language. Second, as with the representations discussed in chapters 3 and 5, here the representation of linguistic diversity is also done in a non-spectacular way, and it is done among those who already know each other, suggesting habitualness across a number of social domains inhabited by social types from multiple backgrounds.

Alternation could be further differentiated when we started to account for abilities to engage in alternation. On the one hand, there were those whose backgrounds suggested that interaction in one-to-few participation frameworks enabled them to habitually engage in alternation. I referred to this as adequation. On the other hand, there were those who still habitually engaged in alternation, but their ability to do so was more appropriately accounted for in terms of their participation in one-to-many participation frameworks. In this sense, alternation is represented as natural and thus provides one further repetition of the idea that alternation is normal. These representation practices also provide further support for the idea that orders of indexicality are in the process of being reconfigured, with alternation increasingly competing for coequal status with Indonesian in settings involving the doing of unity in diversity. Indeed, the type of representation found in extract 6.3.3 was common in many of the soaps in my database. In the following section, I focus on just one of these soaps to flesh out how linguistic superdiversity is also being naturalized through such representations.

6.4 Representing the Doing of Unity in Superdiversity

In this final section, I want to look at representations of not only talk across lines of difference, but also representations of habitual use of features associated with the multiple voices of imagined communities of ethnic social types. I refer to these representations of social life in Jakarta as representations of linguistic superdiversity. In doing so, I continue to point out how this practice sits in contrast to other models of doing unity in diversity that are linked solely with Indonesian. I focus on an episode (*"Banyak orderan banyak masalah,"* "Plenty of Orders, Plenty of Problems") from the comedic soap *Bukan Romeo Juliet* (*It's Not Romeo and Juliet*), which was broadcast on ANTV.

This comedy is geographically anchored to Jakarta via shots of the multiple elevated highways found only in Jakarta, the skyscrapers lining the skyline, and the streets full of cars with "B" license plates. There are also other signs that anchor this story to place. These include the occasional appearance of *bajai*, two-person taxis powered by motorcycle engines (which are found only in Jakarta), music that has interdiscursive links with ethnic comedies anchored to Jakarta, such as *Si Doel* and *Bajai Bajuri* (*Bajuri's Bajai*; see section 3.7), and of course the representation of multiple unrelated people all using linguistic forms stereotypically associated with Betawi ethnic social types. The talk in extract 6.4.1 occurs as Sutini is tending her coffee shop and Melani arrives. Sutini remembers that Melani is the ex-girlfriend of the boy next door, and the following talk ensues. As with the previous extracts, Javanese is in bold caps, ambiguous forms (i.e., those that are both Indonesian and Javanese) are in italics, English is in uppercase bold italics, and Indonesian is in plain font.

Extract 6.4.1 Representing superdiverse neighborhoods

Melani

1 *MORNING mbak* sutini (while smiling) =   MORNING *Sister* Sutini.

Sutini

2   =
3 (while smiling) e::: ***GOOD MORNING*** .   Oh, ***GOOD MORNING***,
4 (while pointing) u:::m *mbak* melani kan =   um [you are] *Sister* Melani right?

Melani

5   =
6 (while putting two thumbs up and smiling)
7 betul (0.5)   Yes.

Sutini

8 lah . (while smiling) mesti ke sini cari *mas*   So, [you] must have come here looking for *Brother*
9 alung =   Alung.

Melani

10	= iya dong (while smiling) . habis	Of course.
11	*aku* [kangen sih *mba::k* =	I miss [him] so much, you know, *Sister*.

Sutini

12	[(stops smiling) = lo::h *mba::k*.	What *Sister*?
13	*YOU* kan udah tahu . kalau **MISALÉ** *mas*	*YOU* already know right, that **FOR EXAMPLE** Brother
14	alung dah ada **GIRLFRIEND**nya . [nanti	Alung already has a **GIRLFRIEND**. Later if
15	**MISALÉ** rebut lagi kaya waktu itu **PIYÉ**	**FOR EXAMPLE**, [you both] fight again like before, **THEN WHAT?**

Melani

16	[	(Is represented as being upset about what
17	(smile turns to sad face as she turns body	Sutini has said.)
18	away from Sutini and sits down) (2.0)	

Sutini

19	(confused look) aduh *mbak* . maksud *I AM*	Gee *Sister*, *I* didn't mean
20	nggak gitu loh . a:: ndak usah =	it like that. Um [you] don't need

Melani

21	= udah udah . ndak apa apa *mbak* . ndak	[It's] ok. [It's] ok, [it's] alright *Sister*,
22	apa apa (1.1)	[it's] alright

Source: ANTV, *Bukan Romeo Juliet*, Sunday, August 16, 2009 (8–9 p.m.)

The talk in extract 6.4.1 is striking for a number of reasons. First, we see that both Melani and Sutini are represented as using and understanding fragments of English (e.g., lines 1, 3, 13–22). This practice is typically in the form that resembles alternation as the medium (i.e., it occurs with fragments of other mediums within an intonational unit and usually does not result in a change of medium). Second, Sutini also uses fragments that are stereotypically associated with Javanese (bold caps) in lines 13 and 15. As with her use of English, her usage is represented as being understood by Melani. In addition, we see that her usage of Javanese forms co-occurs with Indonesian and English within the same intonation unit (e.g., lines 13–15). In other words, this alternation can be categorized as alternation as the medium, though this usage does result in a medium change by Melani in line 21.

As Sutini continues, she uses other Javanese forms, as well as some English with another neighbor, who also works as the local neighborhood security guard, although this time, English fragments are by themselves within an intonational unit. Sutini continues to interact with the rest of the cast, including Wan Abud and Babah Liong, who are both keen to date her. Wan typically uses Indonesian mixed with a few Betawi terms of other reference (e.g., *enté*, "you"). Sutini is represented as understanding such usage, although she does not use these forms. This contrasts with Wan's talk with his family. In these situations, he typically also uses other Betawi forms, including *kenapé* ("why"), *bagaimané* ("how about"), *kagak* ("no/not"), *sané* ("there"), and combinations of these forms. Wan Abud and his family are also linked to Betawi social types by his family's surroundings and practices. For example, his house door is of the slat type associated with Betawi, as is the green color of the doors that is also indexically linked with Islam. Wan and his family are also represented as Moslems by their greetings. As pointed out in chapter 3, by themselves, such signs are ambiguous, but when they co-occur with the other signs, they produce an indexical focus that points to Wan and his family as Betawi social types. In short, as the story unfolds, we are provided with pictures of different participant constellations with habitual patterns of sign exchange.

As with extract 6.3.3, we can also differentiate Sutini's ability to understand Betawi forms from Melani's ability to understand Javanese forms. Living in Jakarta in a neighborhood inhabited by Betawi social types implies that Sutini is being represented as someone who has learned to comprehend these forms from participation in local social life. Melani, on the other hand, seems to be represented as engaging in knowledging. That is, she is more likely to have learned to understand Javanese through participation in the type of one-to-many participation frameworks described in chapters 2 and 3. Where the use of English fragments is concerned, as a low-income stall owner, Sutini's ability to use English fragments is locally accountable in terms of the ubiquitous character of English in Indonesians' everyday life (e.g., English medium films and television programming), some school English subjects, and perhaps some study in one of the many short English courses found throughout Indonesia. As someone represented as much better off economically, Melani's ability to understand English forms is locally accountable by a trend whereby overseas study options are often taken by Indonesians who can afford them or who are lucky enough to get scholarships (see also section 4.5). As with the representations analyzed in section 3.7 and extract 6.3.3, here we are also seeing models of doing unity or togetherness that do not exclusively involve Indonesian.

This soap is exemplary in its representation of complexity because, in addition to having Javanese migrants who speak Javanese and English and understand Betawi, there are also representations of those of Chinese ancestry who use many different ways of speaking. In this soap, there are in fact three types, all of which have received sustained attention in the literature on

FIGURES 6.4.1 AND 6.4.2 Representing Chinese-ness: Babah Liong with son and Melani
Source: ANTV, *Bukan Romeo Juliet*, Sunday, August 16, 2009 (8–9 p.m.)

Chinese Indonesians (e.g., Coppel, 1983; Goebel, 2009, 2010b; Hoon, 2006; Purdey, 2006; Suryadinata, 2004a, 2004b; Wolff & Poedjosoedarmo, 1982). These three types include (1) those who have been referred to locally and in the literature as *peranakan* (Chinese Indonesians who have lived in Indonesia for many generations) (in this case, Melani is represented as peranakan; she is seated in figure 6.4.1); (2) those who have been referred to locally and in the literature as *totok* (Chinese who are first- generation migrants to Indonesia) (in this case, Babah Liong, who is the man standing in figure 6.4.1); and (3) the children of *totok* Indonesians (in this case, Alung who is the son of Babah Liong; see figure 6.4.2). Representations of these social types rely on emblems that have indexical links with them. At the same time, such representations help recirculate these emblems and their indexical links to these social types.

For example, as can be seen in figures 6.4.1 and 6.4.2, Babah Liong (Mr. Liong) is visually represented as a *totok* Chinese in a number of ways. These include his dress and appearance (e.g., a thin moustache, a colorful cap, and a pigtail), his work activity (as a shop owner), his workplace (which doubles as his home), and furnishings (including a picture of a dragon in his shop, a table with a candle below this dragon, another table draped with a red cloth in his guest room, and red walls and drapes. He is also frequently referred to as *babah*, a term stereotypically used for addressing older Indonesians of Chinese ancestry.

Just as important, we hear Babah Liong and Melani engaging in a number of language practices that offer noticeable contrasts. For example, when speaking with his son's former girlfriend Melani (who is represented as a *peranakan*), Babah Liong uses Indonesian that is disfluent and grammatically, morphologically, and phonologically marked, as in extract 6.4.2 below. This interaction occurs after Melani asks for a bit more advice from Sutini about how to handle her love life (discussed in extract 6.4.1 above), though she does not wait to listen to the response. Instead Melani leaves Sutini's coffee shop to visit the home of her ex-boyfriend Alung, where she meets Alung's father, Babah Liong. Forms associated with Chinese-ness are in underlined bold caps, and forms associated with Indonesian are in plain font.

Extract 6.4.2 Representing older layers of diversity: Chinese-ness in Jakarta

Babah Liong

1 melani . kalau **LU** olang masih . suka ma si Melani if **YOU** a person still likes Alung,
2 alung . coba kamu kembali lagi . terus it is enough to come back. And
3 kamu belusaha . jangan putus asa::h . you try, don't give up,
4 **OWEH** yakin kok alung masih suka sama **I'M** certain that Alung still likes
5 kamu . [dan yang lebih penting . itu you. And even more important is
6 bagaimana caranya . si alung bisa jauh ama what is the way Alung can be separated
7 si zaenab dan putus . terus ah . **OWEH** from Zaenab and break up. And ah, **I**

Melani

8   [(starts to move body away from
9 Babah Liong then puts up hand) **SUK SUK** **FATHER, FATHER,**
10 (takes deep breath) um . um boleh melani um, um, may I be left alone
11 ditinggal sendirian nggak **SUK** . or not **FATHER**?

Babah Liong

12 a::h . ah bisa . dan **OWEH** yakin . kamu Ah, ah yes, and **I** am certain, you
13 mungkin mau befikir yang jerni . telus . maybe want to think clearly, and
14 a::h . [menyusun bagaimana kata kata ah about how to best put your words to win
15 melaih si alung back Alung.

Melani

16   [(starts shaking head and puts up
17 hand) bukan . No.

Babah Liong

18 huh . What?

Melani

19 ah bukan itu **SUK** . Ah, not that **FATHER**.

Babah Liong

20 ah ah .   Yes, go on.

Melani

21 ah. soalnya dari tadi . melani . um maaf   Ah, the problem is that ear-
                                                lier, I, um forgive [me]

22 **SUK** ya .   **FATHER** yeah

Babah Liong

23 ah ah .   Yes, go on.

Melani

24 kaya . ah ada hawa hawa gimana gitu **SUK** It's like, ah there is a smell
                                                or something you know
                                                FATHER,

25 ya . ada kaya yang lupa . gosok gigi (puts yeah it is like
26 hand over mouth) =   someone forgot to clean their
                                                teeth.

Babah Liong

28   = (looks around with a
29 confused look) ah siapa ya . cuma bedua   Ah who could it be, yeah? It
                                                is just the two
30 [(points back and forth to himself and   of us.
31 Melani)

Melani

32 [(low laugh while pointing at Babah Liong   It is you.
33 and nodding head)

Babah Liong

34 [(puts hand up to mouth and smells breath)
35 ah . ya **OWEH** . **OWEH** sudah seminggu . Ah, yes **ME**. It's been a week
                                                since **I** last
36 tidak gosok gigi .   brushed my teeth.

Source: ANTV, *Bukan Romeo Juliet,* Sunday, August 16, 2009 (8–9 p.m.)

There are interesting aspects of this talk that point to linguistic superdiversity via characters' competence to comprehend and their use of a diverse set of semiotic features. Starting with terms of self and other reference, we can see that in comparison to extract 6.4.1 where Melani used the terms *Mbak* (sister) and *aku* (I), here Melani uses *suk* (father/elder) for other references (lines 9, 11, 19, and 24) and her own name for self reference (lines 10 and 21), while also understanding *lu* (you) and terms for I (*oweh*) on lines 1, 4, 7, 12, and 35. Just as often as not, we can also see that these kin terms are used within an intonation unit with features associated with Indonesian, thus pointing to alternation as the medium.

As with many of the previous representations we have examined, here alternation and superdiversity are being naturalized through institutionally authorized representations.

In contrasting intonation units, we also see that Babah Liong's talk is represented as rather different from Melani's, insofar as sometimes his talk is not grammatically complete in an intonation unit. For example, we could expect his talk in lines 1 and 2 ("*kalau lu olang masih . suka ma si alung*") to occur without the pause after *masih*. When compared with Sutini's and Melani's talk in extract 6.4.1 and Melani's talk here, we are left with an impression of disfluency. We also see that on occasion, Babah Liong's talk is marked by word repetition. For example, in line 1, he uses a term of address *lu* (you) and then the person classifier *orang*. In this soap, he is the only person represented as engaging in this type of repetition. In addition, he is represented as pronouncing the liquid alveolar /r/ differently from Melani and Sutini. For example, Melani consistently trills her /r/ in the words *sendirian* (line 11) and *dari* (line 21), as does Sutini in the words *cari* (line 8) and *rebut* (line 15) in extract 6.4.1. Babah Liong, on the other hand, is represented as either deleting /r/ altogether in words such as *bel/fikir*, "to think" (line 13) and *bel/dua*, "us/together" (line 29), or lateralizing /r/ to become /l/ in words like *olang* (line 1), *belusaha* (line 3), *telus* (line 13), and *melaih* (line 15). Alone, each of these features are quite ambiguous, but when taken together with the visual representations, the practices engaged in by Babah Liong, and the narrative, we see the construction and reproduction of a Chinese social type who is represented as being very different from other Indonesians in the soap.

As we shall see below, in representations of talk with his son Alung (extract 6.4.3), we can also say that these representations also position Babah Liong as an exemplar of the type of superdiversity one finds in mega-cities such as Jakarta. In this extract, we see Babah Liong now fluently speaking with his son using a mix of Sundanese, Javanese, and Indonesian. In this setting, Melani has returned after being escorted out by Alung, who is worried that his new love, Zaenab, may mistakenly think that he is still dating Melani. However, as with Melani's earlier visit (extract 6.4.2), Alung's father, Babah Liong, encourages Melani to stay and talk with Alung because he will benefit financially from his son's marriage to her. (Earlier, Babah Liong also made it clear to Alung that he did not like him dating Zaenab.) Some of the unspoken reasons here also include Babah Liong's competition with Zaenab's father for the affections of Sutini, whom we met in extract 6.4.1. As Babah Liong goes back into his shop hopefully leaving Alung and Melani to rekindle their romance, the following talk ensues.

Extract 6.4.3 Representing habitual linguistic superdiversity in Jakarta

Alung

1   mel . nggapain di sini .　　　　　　　Mel, why are you here (again)?

Melani

2   (smile changes to shocked look and moves
3   body away from Alung)

Babah Liong

4   (comes back through curtain separating his
5   shop and sitting room) hei **gélo** . kalau　　Hey **dummy**, if
6   ngomong dengan **awéwé** . (points at　　　you talk with a **woman you**
　　　　　　　　　　　　　　　　　　　　　　　(do it)
7   Alung) [**SING** sopan **atuh sia**　　　　　**WITH** etiquette, **ok**!

Alung

8   　　　[(moves body backward, then nods　Yes.
9   and moves shoulder down while smiling.)

　　Source: ANTV, *Bukan Romeo Juliet*, Sunday, August 16, 2009 (8–9 p.m.)

The talk in extract 6.4.3 exemplifies linguistic superdiversity in Indonesia for a number of reasons. First, we see that Babah Liong, who through his usage is represented as a recent migrant to Indonesia, uses linguistic signs from three different semiotic registers, including Javanese, Sundanese, and Indonesian. Second, we see that he uses these forms within an intonational unit, thus representing alternation as the medium. Third, his usage here is not primarily Indonesian and disfluent, as in his interactions with Melani and Sutini (e.g., extracts 6.4.1 and 6.4.2) and other neighbors. Fourth, he habitually speaks with his son using these features. The contrasts in usage among different participant constellations also helps add to the idea that each participant constellation has some sort of habitual register usage. In short, Babah Liong is represented as a social type who uses different sets of fragments from different semiotic registers depending on participant constellation. As with Sutini, here Babah Liong's alternation and linguistic superdiversity are more generally represented as common and everyday.

　　In sum, we have seen that the representation of linguistic superdiversity is done in similar ways to the representation of diversity that we examined in section 6.3. In the case of mediums other than Indonesian, typically, this is done through the use of a few fragments or features from widely circulating semiotic registers associated with the voices of social types belonging to imagined ethnic communities. In the case of the ability to use or understand English fragments, this was locally accountable by what we know about the ubiquitous nature of

English in Indonesians' everyday lives, and for the more privileged segments of Indonesian society, by their ability to pay to study abroad. Differences in trajectories of socialization also helped differentiate practices of adequation from practices of knowledging. Adequation was typically associated with learning locally, while an ability to engage in knowledging was more likely to be an outcome of participation in the types of one-to-many participation frameworks described in chapters 2 and 3.

Both representations of diversity and superdiversity were rather common in my 2009 database and could be found in a range of soaps and other genres. For example, I identified similar practices in the long-running comedy sketch *Sri Mulat*, which was aired on Global TV in the 9–10 p.m. slot; the comedy sketch *Acara Bebas Stres Seger*, aired on ANTV in the 7–8 p.m. slot; the comedy series *Lupa Lupa Ingat*, aired on TPI in the 7–8 p.m. slot; the music show *Acara Inbox*, aired on SCTV in the 8–9 a.m. slot; the celebrity gossip show *Obsesi*, aired on Global TV in the 9–10 a.m. slot; and so on. As with section 6.3, the representations in this section are also different than those discussed in section 6.2 because there were no metapragmatic commentaries that anchored linguistic signs to geographic space or a named language. However, in some cases, as with Babah Liong and Wan Abud's family, these signs were anchored via their association with metasemiotic commentaries, such as those offered through the co-occurrence of other visual signs, such as dress, appearance, furnishings, activity type, and so on. Even so, Babah Liong was not represented as Sundanese or Javanese, and Sutini's Javanese-ness was only implied by her habitual usage of Javanese fragments. Finally, some of the representations in this section added to what seems to be the continued institutional modeling of a type of sociability wherein talk involving those from different backgrounds is rarely conducted in a medium that is exclusively Indonesian. That these representations also presupposed an audience that understood them also helps to circulate ideas about the commonness or naturalness of linguistic superdiversity.

6.5 Conclusion

In this chapter, I started to more directly engage with scholarship on superdiversity by showing how representations of linguistic superdiversity and knowledging that were starting to become part of Indonesian mediascapes in the early 1990s (chapter 3) were by 2009 ubiquitous across a range of television stations and genres. In doing so, I pointed out how the representation of alternation and superdiversity contrasted with the representation practices described in chapter 5, where linguistic forms were anchored to ethnic social types and/or region. I suggested that the representational practices examined in this chapter not only denaturalize the language/ethnicity links that I have described throughout this book, but they also provide insights into the outcomes and enabling potentials of processes of enregisterment (i.e., one-to-many participation frameworks and the up-scaling of people and idea mobility described in chapters 2–4). In particular, I point out that in contrast to the New Order period, the doing of unity in diversity is no longer an activity that is ideologized as something done solely in Indonesian. Alternation and adequation are increasingly common in representations of doing unity in diversity. These representations thus point to a process of revaluing whereby the make-up of orders of indexicality is changing domain by domain.

More specifically, section 6.2 focused on understanding representations of alternation practices that were stylized and those that resembled adequation. I pointed out that alternation often involved fragments that had associations with ethnic communities and locale. I suggested that these practices were accountable with reference to notions of enregisterment. Participation in processes of enregisterment that occurred on a mass scale from 1966 onward also provided the fragmented competence needed to engage in acts of knowledging described in this chapter and in chapter 3. In contrast to the televised material covered in chapters 3 and 5 where we had the representation of multiple voices usually anchored to different parts of Indonesia, in the talk I examined in section 6.2 onward, these voices were now represented as spoken in settings associated with the city.

In section 6.3, I examined how mobility and diversity are represented through the use of fragments that are associated with widely circulating semiotic registers that have voices of imagined ethnic communities within their constellation of signs. I provided examples of interactions among those who were represented as sharing similar trajectories and similar ethnic voices, and representations of the use of ethnic voices across lines of difference where participants were represented as understanding each other's talk. In section 6.4, I went on to look at representations of superdiversity. In contrast to the representations examined in section 6.3, typically, representations include a number of fragments. Each individual fragment had an association with a widely circulating semiotic register that in turn had associations with the voices of social types belonging to imagined ethnic communities. I pointed out that in cases involving representations of the social pursuit of linguistic sameness (adequation), this was typically associated with learning locally, while an ability to engage in knowledging was more likely to be an outcome of participation in the processes of enregisterment described in chapters 2 and 3.

In engaging with some of the common themes surrounding the theorizing and study of superdiversity (Blommaert, 2010; Blommaert & Rampton, 2011; Rampton, 2011; Vertovec, 2007), we can say that work on superdiversity has typically been concerned with the type of diversity found in one-to-few participation frameworks. Here I have extended this scholarship by looking at representations of superdiversity in one-to-many participation frameworks. In addition, and again as with my observations in chapter 5, the long-term unintended consequence of processes of enregisterment in Indonesia is that they have enabled the layering of diversity over diversity, in this case, by facilitating a new type of sociability that I have described as adequation and knowledging. This type of sociability seems to already be part of television producers' imaginations about their audiences because they produce such representations as mundane and everyday and expect their audiences to understand them.

Another contribution to scholarship on superdiversity relates to how people do togetherness in difference in superdiverse settings (Ang, 2003; Goebel, 2010a, 2010b; Smets, 2005; Vertovec, 2007: 1045; Werbner, 1997; Wise, 2005). Typically, work to date focuses on doing togetherness in difference in face-to-face encounters, rather than representations of such encounters, which has been the focus of this chapter. Indeed, a primary focus here is how Indonesian television has provided models of people doing unity in diversity. In many ways, these representations are quite accurate portrayals of what happens on the ground in some places in Indonesia. As we will see in chapters 7 and 8, representations of knowledging also resemble the type of practices Indonesians engage in when involved in face-to-face interaction. For example, in chapter 8, we find Indonesians using their knowledge of ethnic stereotypes and the linguistic signs associated with them to evaluate particular representations of ethnic stereotypes. Often these evaluations sit in contrast to how another co-present viewer, who has socially identified him/herself as a member of the represented group, evaluates these representations.

7

Talk and Conviviality among Indonesians in Japan

7.1 Introduction

The central aim of this chapter relates to understanding how a group of transnational Indonesians from different backgrounds do togetherness while in Japan. In adding to more general scholarship about how people do togetherness in difference in settings characterized by diversity (e.g., Ang, 2003; Brettell, 2003; Vertovec, 2007; Werbner, 1997; Wise, 2005), I focus on the communicative practices that figure in the building and reproduction of what have been described as convivial relationships (Blommaert, 2013b; Williams & Stroud, 2013). The idea of conviviality relates to fleeting interactional moments across lines of difference. The need to be convivial, it is suggested, relates to the conditions of superdiversity, which often require and/or produce conviviality as a necessary interactional practice that helps in securing some good, service, or employment in a setting where norms for how to interact are locally emergent.

Even so, theorization about the idea of conviviality seems to also imply the habitual use of communicative practice across lines of difference. That the fleeting and the habitual are so semiotically and temporally different invites a more nuanced account of the range of language practices that can be described as convivial and ultimately requires some sort of semantic distinction, which I make in section 7.2. In short, here I use conviviality to refer to the pursuit of common ground in fleeting moments of interaction among strangers, while I use the term "togetherness in difference" to refer to subsequent practices of conviviality among those who have just become acquainted. In this chapter, I focus on how conviviality is interactionally achieved among a group of transnational Indonesians living in Japan during two temporally close speech situations. In contrast, in chapter 8, I examine how language practices figure in the building of togetherness in difference across a number of temporally distant speech situations. Section 7.3 introduces some of these Indonesians and provides some background as to why conviviality is necessary for what is largely a struggling group of postgraduate students and their families.

In both chapters, we will see a whole range of language practices being used to build and reproduce positive interpersonal relationships. Some of these ways of speaking are often referred to as "small talk" in the literature. In this chapter and in chapter 8, I am especially concerned with non-minimal responses, repetition, and teasing. I draw out the relationship between these practices and conviviality in section 7.2. We also know that the type of talk we will examine here has multiple functions. For example, we know that talk can contribute to the simultaneous development of identities and epistemologies (Wortham, 2006). In line with Bakhtin's (1981) and Vološinov's (1973 [1929]) ideas about the multiple meanings inherent in discourse, this chapter adds to this literature by teasing out the multiple functions of talk in a particular setting. In addition to showing how talk figures in the building of convivial relations in sections 7.4 and 7.5, I also show how talk relates to ongoing social identification and the assigning of meaning to an unknown word.

7.2 Conviviality and Small Talk

Anthropologists and cultural studies scholars have made strong arguments about the need to focus on the communicative practices of mobile and displaced persons as a way of understanding how togetherness in difference is done in settings characterized by diversity (e.g., Ang, 2003; Brettell, 2003; Vertovec, 2007; Werbner, 1997; Wise, 2005). Sociolinguists have provided us with the tools to examine how togetherness and/or conflict are achieved in face-to-face talk across lines of difference (e.g., Gumperz, 1982; Rampton, 1995; Tannen, 1984). Rampton's (1995) work on crossing and more recent accounts of similar practices (e.g., Blommaert et al., 2005a, 2005b; Goebel, 2010b; Kramsch & Whiteside, 2008; Williams & Stroud, 2013) provide exemplary approaches for investigating how the doing of togetherness in difference can be manifested linguistically in face-to-face interactions in settings where multiple mediums are commonly used.

In looking at performances of linguistic superdiversity in standup comedy and hip hop performances, Williams and Stroud (2013) emphasize that these performances help to transcend ideas that linguistic features belong to any group in particular and help to model a particular type of sociability they refer to as "conviviality." They see conviviality as the productive points of contact between mobile and often displaced persons (i.e., those who inhabit and constitute a superdiverse setting) during the course of their mundane everyday activities. They emphasize that the idea of "productive" encompasses not just positive interpersonal relations but the struggles, contestations, and negotiations that produced these positive relations. While the idea of conviviality seems to involve face-to-face interaction and longer-term social relations, I want to suggest that it needs to be differentiated from subsequent and emergently habitual practices of conviviality, which I refer to as the doing of togetherness in difference. In doing so, I want to emphasize a move from fleeting interaction to longer-term social relationships. This is because the idea of conviviality, as developed by Williams and Stroud (2013), seems to be built on fleeting moments of interaction and does not follow up on subsequent interaction in a number of ways.

First, their work focuses on the production of linguistic superdiversity by standup comedians and hip hop performers, and thus we do not get to see how these practices of conviviality are interpreted by audiences. Second, for many reasons, people do go beyond fleeting interactions to regular habitual interaction that can lead to long-term social relationships (Goebel, 2010b). In multilingual settings where there are habitual social relations, there can be a move from engaging in crossing in face-to-face interaction to adequation (i.e., the linguistic pursuit of social sameness; Bucholtz & Hall, 2004a). In this sense, crossing and conviviality can be seen as interrelated practices, as well as precursors to more habitual conviviality where crossing becomes so common that talk is best described as language alternation as the medium (e.g., Alvarez-Cáccamo, 1998; Gafaranga & Torras, 2002) and ultimately can be considered as a new locally emergent semiotic register, as discussed in chapters 2 and 3. In other words, in cases of habitual interaction, some of the defining features of crossing disappear, and habitual crossing is better defined as something like adequation.

Convivial relations can be interactionally achieved via a whole gamut of practices. Classic anthropological and sociological works show that convivial relations are built through practices of reciprocity (e.g., Goffman, 1971; Malinowski, 1996 [1922]; Mauss, 1966 [1925]). Within anthropology, the idea of reciprocity continues to be used to understand convivial practices across lines of difference, as can be seen in Wise's (2009) work. In this work, Wise suggests that the giving and receiving of food, offers of assistance, recipes, lessons, and so on, build convivial relations because these practices represent an important display of mutual recognition. If we look at some of the work on small talk, we also see that reciprocity seems to be an underlying feature of displays of recognition.

Studies of small talk show that recognition is done through the giving and receiving of compliments, the exchange of a joke for laughter (Ryoo, 2005), repetition (Tannen, 1989), the pursuit of sameness in states of being (Ryoo, 2005), teasing (Strachle, 1993), non-minimal responses (McCarthy, 2003), and so on. McCarthy's (2003) work, for example, shows how a single response token (e.g., "yes") indexes hearer-ship while the use of non-minimal responses (e.g., "yes, yes, heem") can index engaged listening. The former practice can be seen as displaying a basic type of conviviality, while the latter starts to move conviviality toward relationships more commonly labeled as friendships, or what I referred to earlier as togetherness in difference.

Non-minimal responses are part of larger set of interactional practices referred to as repetition and more recently the "social pursuit of sameness" (Bucholtz & Hall, 2004b). As Tannen (1989), Berman (1998), Bjork-Willen (2007), and others have shown, repetition of others' words, utterances, or embodied practices can index and produce positive interpersonal social relations. When interactants know little about each other, showing that you have similar linguistic repertoires, dispositions, opinions, and so on seems to not only provide interactional recognition of the other, but also tacit approval of their ways of speaking, while also establishing common ground on which future interactions can be based (Enfield, 2006). Enfield (2006: 422) defines common ground as "knowledge openly shared by specific pairs, trios, and so forth." Common ground is achieved through participants' ability to jointly agree on referents in interaction (Enfield, 2006; Hanks, 2006). These referents have typically been the subject of prior interaction. Even so, humans' pro-social proclivities (e.g., Boyd & Richerson, 2006; Enfield, 2006; Levinson, 2006; Liszkowski, 2006; Tomasello, 2006) also help those who do not have a history of prior interaction to nevertheless move toward sharing common ground.

Like practices of reciprocity, the interactional pursuit of common ground is both a form of conviviality and an investment in future social relationships (Blommaert, 2012; Enfield, 2006, 2009). In transnational settings and those characterized by diversity, the pursuit of conviviality is typically done among strangers rather than kin (Bunnell, Yea, Peake, Skelton, & Smith, 2012; Wise, 2009) and is ultimately about securing resources needed to survive in a new environment (Blommaert, 2013b). Knowledge about housing options, employment options, the least expensive or best shops, and so on (e.g., common ground) can only be established if such strangers can successfully interactionally negotiate what constitutes conviviality. In what follows, I suggest that the type of small talk discussed earlier seems to help establish common ground while also acting as a form of conviviality among strangers.

As the building block of social relationships more generally, talk is also a major factor for the doing of identity work. While there have been a plethora of book-length treatments and articles on identity in the last twenty-five years or so (e.g., Antaki & Widdicombe, 1998; Auer, 2008; Georgakopoulou, 2007; Le Page & Tabouret-Keller, 1985), Wortham's (2006) work requires special mention. On the one hand, he has shown the utility of tracing participants, signs, and meanings across speech situations. The importance of viewing someone's interactional trajectory also underpins why I think conviviality in fleeting moments needs to be differentiated from more habitual types of conviviality. On the other hand, Wortham has shown how social identification is intimately tied to other activities, such as learning. Here I draw upon these insights to show how conviviality is intimately tied with the social identification of participants over time and the assigning of meaning to a particular linguistic form.

Throughout this book, I have looked at the semiotic make-up of ethnicity (e.g., language, place, and social practice) and how this make-up has changed and been revalued over time. Another more modest aim of this chapter is to provide a situated interactional example of this process by focusing on how just one word becomes indexed with a named ethnic language. I will draw upon Vološinov (1973 [1929]), who pointed out that while words and utterances do have some brought-along meanings, often meanings are constantly negotiated and contested among participants involved in interactions. Vološinov (1973 [1929]: 81) referred to the multi and dialogical nature of word meaning as "multiaccentuality." In drawing out the tension between multiaccentuality and fixedness, I draw upon the work on enregisterment discussed in chapter 2 to show how particular associations can become enregistered over a number of speech situations while highlighting how this all relates to broader revaluing processes.

7.3 Methods and Participants

The data that I use in this and the next chapter is drawn from a project that didn't start out as one that was interested primarily in conviviality and small talk. Instead, I was interested in how Indonesians interpreted and talked about televised representations of ethnicity. Although an anthropological study of television viewing in Indonesia would have been ideal, without leave from university teaching and administration in Japan, I could not make the long-term time commitment that such a study required. Instead, I drew upon work on language attitudes and ideologies in interactional sociolinguistics and social psychology (Lambert, 1986 [1967]; Rampton, 1995; Tannen, 1993) to set up a type of focus group study that would enable me to gain insights into participants' ideologies about sign usage through the use of audio-video recordings. In this sense, my methods differ from that used in much of the work on small talk and social relations, which focused on less laboratory-type contexts. Even so, this type of context offers a number of opportunities to focus on how people do conviviality through talk.

Importantly, although most of these participants knew each other to varying degrees through their involvement in support networks, bringing them together in this setting required talk that would build and/or reproduce interpersonal relations, as well as talk that would figure in the social identification of participants. In looking at the backgrounds of the seventeen participants in this study, I'll start by pointing out some of the similarities in their trajectories of socialization before moving on to the differences. These Indonesians were all from a highly mobile middle-income population. They were primarily graduate students and/or the spouses of graduate students studying at a university in Nagoya. Many had lived abroad on several occasions with their parents when they were younger and some had lived abroad later in life while pursuing graduate degrees.

Most had lived in at least two Indonesian provinces where they had learned local semiotic registers, frequently referred to as named regional languages (*bahasa daerah*). All participants had a trajectory of socialization that included repeated exposure to fragments of these registers and their associated signs, as well as exposure to a semiotic register that has become associated with a named language, Indonesian. Some of the primary contexts in which this occurred included interactions with other Indonesians from a different background—though as I have shown elsewhere, this set of semiotic registers is locale-specific (Goebel, 2010b)—and through their participation in the Indonesian education system. Typically, this started with primary school in the early 1970s and ended with graduation from an Indonesian university in the mid-1980s.

While this group of Indonesians clearly fits into what is essentially middle-class Indonesia, nevertheless, like many postgraduate students across the world, they were not wealthy and lived frugal lives while in Nagoya. Although many benefited from the increased push by the Indonesian government to increase the number of postgraduates working in government offices and universities (see section 4.5), typically, their scholarships were small by Japanese standards, with most taking on part-time jobs to support themselves and their families. As I became part of the Indonesian network in Nagoya, because of my long-term interest in Indonesia and also because of my Indonesian spouse, I learned that most of these Indonesian students lived in the old, yet-to-be-made-earthquake-proof public housing located on the outer fringes of Nagoya. In many ways, a comfortable life in Nagoya was made possible by the support networks that had emerged through their own and their predecessors' efforts. One such network was the Nagoya branch of the Indonesian Student Union of Japan (PPI Japan).

This network provided lists of people who knew Japanese; lists of people who knew the least expensive places to buy furniture, clothes, appliances; information about where and when houses may become vacant; and how to work with (or around) bureaucracy to ensure that you had a place to live. This network also organized access to labor and vehicles for moving furniture and so on for new arrivals and for those returning; monthly worship gatherings; practice sessions for cultural performances at multicultural festivals; the Saturday school for Indonesian children; committees that facilitate these support activities; and so on.

These Indonesians all voluntarily responded to an advertisement seeking participants for this study, which was advertised as being concerned with how people understood representations of characters and events in soap operas. With the help of a couple of Indonesian research assistants, we divided respondents into viewing groups of four to five people and invited them to attend four viewing and interview sessions over four weeks. Each viewing session lasted between one and two hours. Sessions started with some informal chatting to participants about the research project and questions about participants' backgrounds. Following this, a comedic soap opera or film was screened (lasting twenty-five to ninety minutes).

These sessions were audio-recorded. In order to help me transcribe participants' talk, I also videotaped them while they watched the screenings. Following the screening, I interviewed participants. Questions included those that had arisen as a result of participants' talk during the viewing session, whether they had seen the soap or film before, what they thought about it, what they thought the relationships were between characters and why they thought so, and where they thought the characters were from and why. What I will present in my analysis is the talk that occurred between one of the four groups of participants during their first viewing session. During this screening, they watched an episode – *Cipoa* (*Con Artist*) – from the comedic soap opera *Noné*, which was discussed in section 3.5. A summary of participant backgrounds is presented in table 7.3.1.

This group of participants consisted of five people, myself, and an Indonesian research assistant. Diagram 7.3.1 shows where each participant

TABLE 7.3.1
Participant backgrounds

Name	Age	Relationship with other participants	History of mobility		Education	Language abilities
			Years	Place		
Desi (S)	35	Familiar	27	Bandung	MA	Indonesian
			3	Solo		Sundanese
			5	Japan		Japanese
						English
Lina	23	Familiar (Slamet's spouse)	8	Pekan Baru	BA	Indonesian
			3	Jakarta		Japanese
			9	Padang		
			1	Japan		
			1.5	Padang		
			0.5	Japan		
Slamet	33	Familiar (Lina's spouse)	21	Irian	MA	Javanese
			5	Bandung		Indonesian
			0.5	Jakarta		English
			2	Japan		
			4	Padang		
			0.5	Japan		
Gun (S)	37	Familiar	19	Cirebon	PHD	Javanese
			6	Bandung		Sundanese
			4	Jakarta		Indonesian
			8	Japan		Japanese
						English
RA	39	Familiar	27	Solo	BA	Javanese
			10	Jakarta		Indonesian
			2	Japan		Japanese
Me	41	Familiar with RA only.	35	Australia	PHD	Indonesian
			3.5	Semarang		Javanese
			0.5	Cirebon		Sundanese
			2	Japan		English

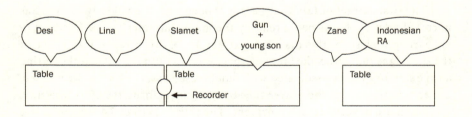

DIAGRAM 7.3.1 Transnational Indonesians watching television

was seated (all names are pseudonyms). All of these participants knew each other through their interactions within the Indonesian community in Nagoya. However, Slamet and Lina, a husband and wife couple, had only recently arrived in Japan and were not well acquainted with the other participants who had all lived in Nagoya for a number of years. Gun had brought his little boy along, and he sat on Gun's lap during the screening and subsequent interview. As can be seen in table 7.3.1, most participants were highly multilingual. With the exception of Desi and my research assistant, they were also rather mobile. Participants were also of similar age (the exception being Lina), and all were highly educated.

In sum, we can say that the research design of the project brought together a number of groups of Indonesians to view recordings of televised Indonesian comedies. This context represents one further setting where participants needed to build and/or reproduce convivial relations. It is important not to underplay this aspect, especially given that as transnationals, each person needed to get along with other Indonesians in Nagoya in order to access the informal support networks there.

7.4 Talk, Conviviality, and Meaning

Throughout the viewing of this soap opera, the use of non-minimal responses (e.g., "yes, yes, heem") and repetition figured in the building and reproduction of common ground and convivial relations among this group. At the same time, their talk also categorized the represented semiotic world and the audience in terms of ethnolinguistic identities. We also see how the social domain of the meanings of a word, *cipoa*, widens through repetitions of prior utterances by an increasingly large number of participants over interactional time.

The first extract of talk that I analyze occurs after an elderly woman has narrated a letter that is being read by the main character Dewi. As noted in my earlier analysis of this dialogue (extract 3.5.1), this piece of talk is one of the first signs that index the language background of the serial and the setting as one stereotypically associated with Sundanese-ness. Even so, as we will see, understandings about the provenance of a linguistic form, the story's setting, and so on are negotiated and emergent. The talk in extract 7.4.1 occurs after a series of images that show a house situated on expansive grounds. (As the analysis proceeds, I will introduce any new transcription conventions, though the majority of conventions remain the same as those used in the previous chapters.)

Extract 7.4.1 From hearer-ship to engaged listening

Gun (S)
1 <u>vila</u> ya (1.0) <u>vilanya</u> si nike (1.0)   It's a <u>villa</u> yeah? Its Nike's <u>villa</u>.
Slamet
2 <u>vila</u> (0.8)   [Yes] a <u>Villa</u>.
Desi (S)
3 kaya <u>rumah</u> di <u>kuningan</u> [laughs   Like <u>houses</u> in <u>Kuningan</u>.
All
4   [(laugh) =   (Laugh).
Desi (S)
5   =
6 <u>kuningan</u> sih (??? ???) =   [In?] <u>Kuningan</u> (??? ???)
Gun (S)
7   = heem . ya:: gitu.   Heem, yeah like that.

About a minute after seeing the images of the house and yard, we see that the topic of residence is ratified by three participants through repetitions (indicated by an <u>underline</u>) of *vila* ("villa") and its rephrasing as *rumah* ("house") in lines 1–3. In engaging in repetition (or the reciprocal exchange of linguistic forms), each participant is showing the other that they recognize the referent (villa), and thus they also begin to start sharing common ground. We also see that in lines 3 and 6, Desi notes that the house is like those found in Kuningan (an area located in West Java). The repetition that occurs on lines 1–3 and 6 shows how common ground and hearer-ship are established. Gun's non-minimal response in line 7 shows that he has recognized the referent (Kuningan) and is listening to Desi with his first "heem." The subsequent use of *ya gitu* ("yeah, like that") repeats this information in a way that suggests engaged listening.

While the establishment of common ground and the use of non-minimal responses suggest a reproduction of convivial relations, we need to see how the interaction proceeds. (For Gun and Desi, I use "reproduction" rather than "build" because these two participants know each other through engagement in Indonesian community activities over the previous two years, though as we will see, they are uncertain about whether they are members of the same ethnic community.) This interaction is also interesting because it shows how they categorize the semiotic world through the ratification of what houses in Kuningan look like on line 7. Even so, at this stage, the social domain of the meaning of signs of place seems to be limited to Desi and Gun. We need to follow their talk to see whether and to what extent the social domain of place as a sign for understanding other content expands over interactional time.

Following the talk in 7.4.1, participants don't say much until the first advertisement break that occurs nearly ten minutes later. Some of the signs that these participants have access to before their next extended conversation include a taxi, which drives into the driveway of Dewi's newly acquired house, and the exchanges that follow between the taxi driver and the passenger (Susi), Susi and Dewi, and Dewi and the taxi driver (see, e.g., extracts 3.5.5 to 3.5.7). These signs may or may not disambiguate earlier signs about setting. For example, there is the text "Bandung Taxi Company" on the taxi door and the taxi also has a license plate prefixed by the letter "D" (see figure 3.5.1). For those who notice these signs, they may recognize them as pointing to a setting in West Java, in particular, the capital city of Bandung.

As noted in section 3.5, there are also marked contrasts in linguistic signs exchanged in interactions between different participant pairs. For example, in the speech event involving Dewi and Susi, they exchange linguistic forms stereotypically associated with Indonesian. In contrast, in the interaction between Dewi and the taxi driver that immediately follows, participants exchange many forms stereotypically associated with Sundanese, together with embodied ways of speaking not used in the earlier interaction (see section 3.5 for a multimodal analysis of these representations). Shortly thereafter, there are some brief exchanges between Susi and Ucup, Dewi and Ucup, and finally an advertisement before the participants in the viewing session start to talk again (extract 7.4.2).

Extract 7.4.2 From engaged listening to discourses of sameness

Desi (S)
1 apa sih . judulnya . +judulnya apa sih .   So what is the title? So what is the
2 judulnya apa sih+ =   title? So what is the title?

Lina
3   = apa tadi judulnya   What was the title earlier?
4 =

Research Assistant
5 = ci . cipoa =   Ci, Cipoa.

Desi (S)
6   = +judulnya+ =   The title.

Zane
7   = cipoa=   Cipoa.

Research Assistant
8   =
9 cipoa =   Cipoa.

Desi (S)
10 = cipoa itu apa ya (0.7)   What is [the meaning of] Cipoa?

Gun (S)
11   itu (while turning gaze toward Desi   That isn't Sundanese is it?
12   and smiling) bukan bahasa sunda
13   bukan =
Desi (S)
14   = (while moving body forward   Yeah so what does this
                                                  [potentially
15   and turning gaze toward Gun) ya apa   Sundanese] term Cipoa mean?
16   sih (0.6) cipoa itu (0.5)
Slamet
17   nggak tahu =   [I] don't know.
Desi (S)
18   = pak gun =   Mr. Gun?
Gun (S)
19   = nggak tahu   [I] don't know (the meaning?) of
20   (artinya?) cipoa . cipoa =   cipoa, cipoa.
Desi (S)
21   = (laughs)(2.3)   Laughs.

In this interaction, there is the continued use of repetition, which helps participants align with each other on a number of topics while also establishing further common ground (e.g., the title of the serial in lines 1–9 and the meaning of the word *cipoa* from lines 10–20). We also see that Gun's earlier attempt at indexing engaged listening (extract 7.4.1, line 7) is being reciprocated through the emergence of a type of discourse of sameness between Desi and Gun. In particular, we see that while Gun's gaze direction and question left some ambiguity as to whether the question was addressed to the group or someone whom he thought knew Sundanese (lines 11–13), nevertheless, we see that Desi self-selects, suggesting that she was the target of the question. In doing so, she changes her body position so that she can see around Lina and Slamet to look at Gun and ask again about the meaning of this potentially Sundanese term (lines 14–15). In terms of discourses of sameness, what this interactional work appears to be doing is creating common knowledge about participants' ethnolinguistic identities. For example, in asking Desi about provenance (lines 11–13), Gun appears to be saying "you are Sundanese and may know" while also implying "you are of the same ethnolinguistic background as me." Taking a sequential view, it also appears that Desi ratifies this categorization by checking whether Gun (as opposed to Slamet and Lina whom she looks around) can provide a meaning for the term (lines 14–16 and 18).

In terms of the multiple functions of talk, what we also get from the talk in extract 7.4.2 is a tiny glimpse into Gun's expectations about the relationship between words and signs of place (i.e., houses in Kuningan) and how these are used together to evaluate the ethnolinguistic provenance of a new word (line 11). While, the word *cipoa* was initially semantically empty in Vološinov's (1973 [1929]: 88) terms, now and in this context, it starts to gain a potential meaning for two participants, while others are given a lesson or reminder that words in general are associated with particular places. In this case, apart from the earlier mention of place (Kuningan), we are unsure what triggers a potential ethnolinguistic meaning for Gun (line 11) and Desi (lines 15, 16, and 18), but we can suggest that it may also have been the house architecture, the vehicle signage, the agreed-upon potential West Java setting (extract 7.4.1), and/or the Sundanese usage in the interaction between the characters. Whatever the case, they have started to build common ground about ideas of Sundanese-ness.

While the social domain of *cipoa* as having an ethnolinguistic meaning appears to be only as wide as Gun and Desi, this topic will be revisited a number of times and by other participants throughout the viewing session and the interview, thus establishing further common ground among participants. As we will see, repetition also becomes important in other ways, especially as the repetition of others' utterances increases in a way that appears to help build convivial relations. The use of repetition in the talk that follows (extract 7.4.3) also co-occurs with the activity of determining the provenance of the term *cipoa*. This talk follows directly after the talk represented in extract 7.4.2.

Extract 7.4.3 Repetition and the linking of language with place

Zane
22   tukang bohong apa =   Is it con artist?
Research Assistant
23   = tukang bohong =   Con artist.
Zane
24   =
25   tukang bohong kayanya =   Maybe it's like con artist.
Desi (S)
26   =+bahasa   Is it Sundanese?
27   sunda?+ (0.8) E::H? =   REALLY
Zane
28   = kurang tahu   I'm not sure.
29   saya (1.0)
Gun (S)
30   mungkin bandung mungkin ya . daerah   Maybe its Bandung, maybe. A
31   daerah sunda gitu'.   Sundanese area, yeah.

Desi (S)
32 [kayanya <u>nama daerah</u> ya   Yeah, it's like a <u>place name</u>.
Slamet
33 [settingnya <u>bandung</u> itu . settingnya   The setting is <u>Bandung</u>, the setting. It
34 (2.0) bisa <u>nama daerah</u> juga ya =   can be a <u>place name</u> yeah.
Desi (S)
35   = saya   I
36 kira =   think so.
Slamet
37   = <u>cipoa</u> =   <u>Cipoa</u>.
Desi (S)
38   = heeh (0.7)   Yeah.
Slamet
39 (??????) =
Research Assistant
40   = <u>nama daerah</u> itu pak .   It's a <u>place name</u> Mr. Zane.
Zane
41 oh <u>nama daerah</u> . ya .   Oh a <u>place name</u>, yeah.
Desi (S)
42 nggak tau tuh   I don't know.

In the above talk, we can see that repetition continues to function as a way of establishing topic (lines 30–34). Just as important, we also see that although the topic of provenance has been established by Gun and Desi (lines 30–32), Slamet also repeats this information (lines 33–34). This informational redundancy suggests that repetition is doing something else. As with my earlier interpretations of a non-minimal response (extract 7.4.1) and discourses of sameness (extract 7.4.2), this repetition appears to be part of ongoing relationship-building efforts, this time on the part of Slamet, who can be seen to be aligning with both Gun and Desi. In lines 35 and 36, we also see that Desi repeats, via her agreement (*saya kira*), the earlier series of repetitions involving herself, Gun, and Slamet (lines 30–34). This suggests that she is reciprocating Slamet's interpersonal relationship work.

It is also interesting to note that in addition to repetition between utterances, we also now start to see repetition that does not always immediately follow a preceding turn (i.e., it is temporally distant). These instances are indicated by a broken underline. For example, although Desi, who is pursuing a master's degree in Japanese language, uses some Japanese (e.g., the use of "eh" in line 27 that is in bold italic small caps), her whole utterance repeats what Gun said in extract 7.4.2 in lines 11–13. This repetition can also be seen as part of ongoing efforts by Desi and Gun to align with each other's stances toward the meaning of the word *cipoa*. In so doing, their alignment solidifies some common ground between them while adding to their earlier pursuits of social sameness, this time, sameness in their evaluations of provenance.

At the same time, this talk seems to contribute to the building of convivial relations in this setting. Just as important, this repetition also again foregrounds Desi's claims as someone who is entitled or able to evaluate what is Sundanese and what is not. In so doing, she is also further strengthening her ethnolinguistic identity claims made in extract 7.4.2. In this case, something like "I can evaluate this term's provenance because I am Sundanese." In so doing, she continues to engage in the pursuit of social sameness by implying that she is also the same ethnic social type as Gun, namely a Sundanese.

In focusing more squarely on the multiple and often simultaneous functions of talk, we can see that working out provenance is intimately tied to identity work (in this case, claims about native speakership and entitlement to evaluate terms) and relationship work (getting along). For example, after my attempt at assigning a meaning relating to a personal trait (line 22), *cipoa*'s provenance is again questioned. In repeating Gun's uncertainty about *cipoa*'s provenance (extract 7.4.2, lines 11–13), Desi directs the question to me (lines 26 and 27), a question that I am unable to answer. Gun then suggests it is a term found in Bandung or a Sundanese area (lines 30 and 31). In doing so, *cipoa* is not only again linked with a named language, but also with the region that is stereotypically linked with this language. Apart from Lina, one of these links appears to be repeated by all participants from line 31 onward. In this sense, the social domain of one of the meanings attached to *cipoa* appears to widen to include Desi, Slamet, Gun, my research assistant, and myself. In this case, a place name rather than the earlier ethnolinguistic meaning.

After the talk represented in extract 7.4.3, there was no more extended conversation about the word *cipoa* until the end of the serial. Before looking at this talk, I take a look at one of the few extended conversations that occurred among this group before the serial ended. This piece of talk is interesting insofar as it provides examples of the building of common ground and the use of non-minimal responses and teasing to build and reproduce convivial relations among several of the participants. This talk begins with a discussion about the actors' spouses.

Extract 7.4.4 Teasing and conviviality

Gun
1 ini namanya siapa (glancing toward   What's her name?
2 Desi) =
Desi
3   = dian nitami (0.8)   Dian Nitami.
Gun
4 (???) (4.4) suaminya anjasmara nih =   (???) her husband is
                                           Anajsmara, yeah?
Desi
5   =
6 iya . >iya huuh> (0.5) dian nitami (7.6)   Yeah, yes, yes, Dian Nitami.
Gun
7 tapi udah itu kan . udah cerai ini =   But [they] are already, already
                                           divorced, right?
Desi
8   =
9 (looking toward Gun) e:h . ngga::k .   What? No [they] are
10 [masih   still [together].
Slamet
11 [(looking toward Gun) nggak =   No.
Gun
12   = (looks
13 toward Desi) eh masih [(laughs)   Oh still [together].
Desi
14   [awet . awet   Still together, still together.
15 (0.4)
Slamet
16 (after glancing away looks back at
17 Gun) jangan bikin gosip pak =   Don't spread gossip Pak [Gun].
Gun
18   = (looks
19 at Slamet) +hehehe+ [hehe   Laughs.
Slamet
20   [hehehehe   Laughs.

In this interaction, we can see participants showing that they share some common ground and are thus the same at some level. In particular, we see that after Desi mentions the actress's name on line 3 (Dian Nitami), both Gun and Slamet demonstrate that they share some knowledge about this actress and her spouse (lines 4 and 11). As in the previous extract, there are also instances of non-minimal responses. The first instance of a non-minimal response is found in line 6 where Desi answers Gun's question (line 4) with three "yes" responses. The first seems to be a response signaling hearer-ship, while the second "iya huuh," although seemingly redundant, may in fact be signaling engaged listening. Similarly, while both Desi and Slamet answer Gun's question about whether the actress playing Ayu is already divorced in lines 8–10, we also see that in line 14, Desi rephrases her answer. This answer repeats what has already been said ("awet awet," which literally means "to last long," but here it means something like "still together"). In so doing, her talk is again more than required and invites us to interpret this repetition as helping to build convivial relations, this time with Slamet, who has aligned with Desi on the question of whether the actor is divorced or not.

We also see that although Desi aligns with Slamet, Slamet is also quick to try and build convivial relations with Gun by teasingly accusing him of spreading gossip (lines 16 and17). The teasing touches on multiple ideologies about gossip and piousness. For example, Gun arrived a little earlier than the other participants and was finishing his afternoon prayers when other participants arrived. Performing his prayers indexed not only his Islamic identity, but also his piousness. Engaging in gossip, which is categorized as sinful, is thus part of the joke. The other part is that while gossip can often be meant to be heard by the person being gossiped about, in this setting, the people being gossiped about would be very unlikely to hear it. Gun appears to orient to this joke by his loud laughter (indicated by a "+" surrounding the hehe) and his gaze (lines 18 and 19). Again, given that this sequence is not informational, it seems to invite an interpretation of another local strategy for producing convivial relations. After this sequence, participants don't say much until the end of the serial when Dewi's grandmother makes her fourth and final appearance to give Dewi the following warning (extract 7.4.5).

Extract 7.4.5 From the serial: Another warning from grandmother

1 hati hati dewi (0.8) orang suka   Be careful Dewi, those who like
2 cipoa::? . +untuk menutupi   to *cipoa* do so to cover up
3 kekurangan kekurangannya yang   their gross inadequacies.
4 besar'+

At this stage, one of the viewers, Slamet, reiterates that the grandmother is a ghost before then hearing the word *cipoa*. Upon hearing this term, he then initiates the talk represented in extract 7.4.6.

Extract 7.4.6 Negotiating meanings and conviviality

Slamet
1   neneknya hantu (1.8) +oh+ (1.8) oh Her grandmother is a ghost. Oh. Oh it
2   (looks at Desi) cipoa itu bahasa ini deh . looks like cipoa is Sundanese.
3   sunda kayaknya (0.8)

Desi
4   nggak tahu = [I] don't know.

Slamet
5   = cipoa . orang suka cipoa = A person who likes to cipoa.

Desi
6   =
7   tiga puluh tiga tahun jadi orang sunda [I've] been a Sundanese for thirty-three
8   baru denger (laughs) = years and [I've] just heard [this word].

Slamet
9   = cari di ini Look in this,
10 (looks at Desi) . (turns back to look at
11 Slamet) apa kamus bahasa Indonesia what is it the Indonesian dictionary
12 sama anu . kamus . and the um, dictionary.

Lina
13 orang suka cipoa:: katanya . She said "Those who like to cipoa have a
14 [suka bohong apa (1.0) tendency to tell white lies all the time, or something like that."

Slamet > Gun
15 [bahasa indonesia . kamus besar Indonesian, the Large Authoritative
16 bahasa indonesia = Indonesian dictionary.

Desi
17   = bohong = To tell white lies.

Lina
18   = untuk To
19 menutupi kekurangannya = hide their inadequacies.

(continued)

Extract 7.4.6 (Continued)

Desi

20	= <u>menipu</u> .	To deceive,
21	eh =	eh?

Slamet

22	= cipoaé apa ya (1.75)	What does cipoa mean?

Lina

23	suka:: <u>berdusta</u> mungkin .	Maybe [someone] who regularly deceives,
24	ndak tahu itu (1.2) ah omong kosong	[someone who] doesn't know,
25	(0.9)	[or] talks rubbish.

Slamet

26	[bahasa	It's language.

Zane

27	[mudah mudahan tidak begitu	Hopefully this hasn't been too
28	membosankan =	boring.

Desi

29	= nggak . bagus (while	No, it was good,
30	laughing) [lucu	it was funny.

Slamet

31	[bahasa sunda . bahasa	It was Sundanese,
32	sunda kuno (2.7) bahasa sunda kuno	old Sundanese, old Sundanese.

In the above talk, we can see that the provenance of the term *cipoa* again becomes a topic as Slamet suggests *cipoa* is Sundanese (lines 2 and 3). Desi doesn't align fully with Slamet's interpretation through her self-identifying as a Sundanese who has never heard the term (lines 7 and 8). While her comment repeats her uncertainty about provenance, which she shared with Gun (extracts 7.4.2 and 7.4.3), we can see that this talk also represents a point in which explicit social identification occurs through Desi's claims to native speakership. This social identification occurs as part of another sequence where participants assign an ethnic meaning to the word *cipoa*. We also see that Slamet, although not making native-speaker claims, defers to *kamus besar* ("Authorative Dictionary"; lines 9–12 and 15–16) where he notes we may find this term. (*Kamus besar* claims authority by being both written and endorsed by the government-funded language center in Jakarta.)

In other words, he still holds onto the idea that the provenance of the term is Sundanese despite Desi's claims of not knowing it. His position on this does not change as the viewing session is brought to a close, and he notes that it is old, archaic Sundanese in lines 31–32. In short, the social domain of one of the meanings associated with the word *cipoa*—namely its potential Sundaneseness—now seems to have widened from Gun and Desi to include Slamet. In the early part of the interview that follows immediately after this viewing session (extract 7.5.2), however, Desi takes up the theme of archaic-ness in a way that suggests alignment with Slamet on a number of levels.

Lina also offers a meaning for *cipoa* that doesn't relate to provenance, but rather to morality, especially a tendency to tell white lies or not be entirely honest (lines 13 and 14). This interpretation is oriented to by Desi in her repetition of *bohong*, "to tell white lies or not be entirely honest" (line 17), and her upgrade of this term to *menipu*, "to deceive" (line 20), which Lina ratifies through her expansion of the meaning to "someone who doesn't know or talks rubbish" (lines 23 and 24). In short, the social domain of the meaning of *cipoa* as relating to a moral trait also widens from me (extract 7.4.3) to include Desi and Lina. This sequence also appears to be similar to earlier instances of repetition insofar as they function to establish common ground but also as a type of non-minimal response. In other words, the repetition from line 15 onward seems to be doing more than just repeating the meaning of the term as something to do with dishonesty. Instead, this repetition seems to be contributing to the building of convivial relations, this time between Desi and Lina, who to this point have not interacted much.

In addition to showing how the word *cipoa* gains two separate meanings for the pairs Slamet and Desi and Lina and Desi, this talk offers a number of other insights. First, it foregrounds Desi's and Slamet's expectations about the association between linguistic forms and place. In particular, we see that their talk here repeats earlier talk (extracts 7.4.1–7.4.3) that anchored the actors to a particular place in West Java and suggested that the term *cipoa* was Sundanese. Second, it highlights the idea that native speakers are those who can be associated with a particular place (Desi's comment on lines 7 and 8; Slamet's attempt to get a judgment from another "native speaker"; Gun on lines 10–12, 15 and 16).

In summary, during this viewing session, we saw how one group of transnational Indonesians built common ground and ultimately convivial relations through the use of repetition, non-minimal responses, and teasing. I also pointed out the multiple functions of their talk. For example, I showed that this interpersonal relationship work was intimately and often simultaneously tied to working out the meaning of an unfamiliar word and establishing ethnolinguistic identities as a way of adding expertise to judgments about the meaning of the word. As we follow the participants' talk in the interview that was conducted directly after this viewing session, the meaning of *cipoa* solidifies along with participant identities and interpersonal relations.

7.5 Identities, Togetherness, and Meaning Revisited

In the rest of my analysis, I focus on talk that occurred in the interview that immediately followed the viewing session. We see here that as participants move into a different speech situation (e.g., from a viewing session to an interview), they continue to engage in the building of convivial relations using the features of talk discussed thus far. This practice is facilitated by the common ground already established during the viewing session. What is also striking about this talk is that, while thus far, the meaning of *cipoa* has been multiaccentuated, in the interview that followed, the meanings of the word *cipoa* became increasingly shared among participants, especially the meanings that related to a moral trait and provenance. The transcript below represents responses to my fourth question, which I formulated while listening to participants talk during the viewing session.

Extract 7.5.1 Jointly constructing the meaning of *cipoa*

Zane
1 tadi itu . nanya nanya masalah cipoa?   Earlier, there were questions
2 (0.6)   about cipoa.

Desi
3 hm [m =   Yes.

Lina
4   [hmm =   Yes

Zane
5   = itu. memang (0.5)   Indeed,
6 seperti di::: (0.5) saya juga kurang tahu it was like in, I also wasn't sure
7 tadi itu .   earlier.

Desi and Lina
8 [laughter   Laughter.

Zane
9 [kayak? . orang bohong . suka apa .   It was like someone frequently
                                             tells white lies, or likes to,
10 gimana gitu? =   whatever, you know?

Slamet
11   = dijelaskan terakhir itu   It was explained at the end
                                             yeah?
12 ya .

Lina
13 heem. orang cipoa suka apa (0.6)   Yes, person with the character-
                                             istic of cipoa likes to um

Slamet
14 [nutupi   To hide.

Lina

15 [apa ya . yang menutupi   What was it, yeah. [Someone]
                                      who hides
16 kekurangannya =   their inadequacies.

Desi

17   = kekurangan (???) =   Inadequacies (???).

Slamet

18   =   Becomes [someone called]
19 jadi cipoa #mungkin# =   cipoa, maybe.

Desi

20   = berarti (0.6)   Which means . . .

Lina

21 jadi cipoa itu seperti apa ya =   So cipoa is like what, yeah?

The importance of the above talk is threefold. First, although there are no non-minimal responses, the use of repetition here again seems interesting insofar as it is frequently used to show hearer-ship and the establishment of common ground (lines 14–17). Second, we also see how the establishment of common ground widens the social domain of one meaning of the word *cipoa*, in this case, "to lie and cover up personal inadequacies," from three participants (me, Desi, and Lina) to now also include Slamet (lines 14 and 19). Third, and related to the first two points, as in the case of their earlier talk about "place name" and "language name," the meaning of the word *cipoa* has been jointly achieved. Even so, this aspect of *cipoa*'s meaning does not appear to solidify further as participants start to again focus on the term's provenance and commonness. Extract 7.5.2 represents this talk that follows immediately after the previous extract.

Extract 7.5.2 Naming languages, native speakership, and pursuing social sameness

Desi

22	= sebenarnya bukan yang jelas . (starts	Actually, it is not clear.
23	looking at Gun) kayaknya bukan	It appears that it isn't
24	bahasa sunda itu . [<u>kayanya</u> istilah	Sundanese, <u>it appears like a term</u> . . .

Gun

25	[<u>kayaknya</u> (???)	That's what <u>it appears like</u> (???).

Slamet

26	[<u>kayaknya</u> .	It's like, it's like if we opened
27	kayaknya kalau kita buka kamus besar	the authorative dictionary,
28	kayaknya ada itu . cipoa itu (0.5) tapi	it's like the term *cipoa* would
29	bahasa yang jarang dipakai kayaknya .	be there. But it's like lan-
30	tidak [<u>umum</u> #jadi#	guage that is rarely used, so it's not common.

Desi

31	[<u>bahasa karuhun</u> =	Ancestor's language.

Lina

32	= <u>bahasa tidak</u>	Language [which] isn't
33	[<u>umum</u>	common.

Slamet

34	[jangan suka cipoa (1.1) #untuk	Don't *cipoa* to
35	menutupi kekurangannya# (1.8)	cover up inadequacies.

In keeping with her earlier position on the provenance of *cipoa* (e.g., extract 7.4.3 in lines 23 and 24 and extract 7.4.6 in lines 7 and 8), Desi reiterates that the term is probably not Sundanese (lines 23 and 24), a position Gun appears to ratify (line 25). In doing so, she appears to be also identifying Gun as someone with native-speaker expertise like herself. When viewed together with earlier instances of repetition, this pursuit of social sameness seems to also add to the building of convivial relations between these two participants. Slamet, however, does not fully align with this suggestion. Instead, in lines 26–30, he reiterates his earlier position (see extract 7.4.6) about its probable existence in a dictionary and that it is probably an uncommon or archaic form. In doing so, he adds "uncommon" to the term's ever-expanding meanings. The social domain of this meaning also seems to widen to include Desi and Lina, who appear to ratify this meaning on line 31 and lines 32 and 33, respectively.

This time, however, his suggestion of *cipoa* being an uncommon Sundanese form is ratified by Desi on line 31. In this sense, it represents an occasion when Desi and Slamet, who have earlier disagreed on provenance, now achieve some common ground. After again reiterating one of the term's meanings as relating to a negative personal trait (lines 34 and 35), in the talk that follows immediately afterward, Desi repeats her alignment with Slamet and Lina around the "archaicness" or "uncommonness" of the term *cipoa* (extract 7.5.3). This repetition seems to be going beyond conversational alignment by repeating the concept that "we have aligned/agreed on this topic" to do conviviality.

Extract 7.5.3 It's uncommon Sundanese spoken by the elderly

Zane

36	jadi ada? . yang bahasa bahasa lain yang	So is there other language from
37	tadi #juga# . mungkin ndak (1.0) [ndak	earlier that maybe [you] didn't, didn't
38	mengerti gitu .	understand, you know?

Slamet

39	[heem	Yes.

Desi

40	mungkin kan . kalau di <u>bahasa sunda</u> itu	Maybe, right, if it is <u>Sundanese</u>
41	pak Zain' . ah <u>bahasa sunda</u> itu ada istilah	Mr. Zane, ah <u>Sundanese</u> has a term
42	bahasa karuhun ya . >bahasa karuhun	*bahasa karuhan* yeah. *Bahasa*
43	itu> <u>bahasa yang tidak digunakan sehari</u>	*karuhan* means <u>a language that isn't used</u>
44	<u>hari</u>:: . tapi sebenarnya orang orang tua	<u>daily</u>, but actually the elderly
45	di:: . tanah jawa barat itu menggunakan	in West Java use it, you
46	gitu' .	know.

Slamet

47	[heem	Yes.

Desi

48	[mungkin. generasinya saya . pak gun	Maybe my generation [and] Mr. Gun's
49	#gitu# tidak begitu mengena::l . (looks	don't really know the
50	and points open hand at Gun) +eh+	[language or its words]. Oops!
51	><u>orang sunda</u>> bukan .	[You're] <u>Sundanese</u> aren't [you]?

(continued)

Extract 7.5.3 (Continued)

Gun

52   heem =   Yes.

Slamet

53   = orang [sunda tapi tidak pernah di   [He's] Sundanese but rarely lives in

54   sunda #dia# (said while smiling)   Sunda. (a joke pointing to Gun's near decade-long stay in Japan)

Lina

55   [(???????????)   (Unclear utterance. Each three question marks indicated a word.)

Desi

56   [(??????) ya . heeh (1.4)   (??????) yes, yes.

As noted in the introduction to this extract, this talk is interesting because of the continued use of certain features that contribute to the building of convivial relations among participants. In particular, we see Desi again pursuing social sameness by literally asking Gun "are you the same as me" in lines 50 and 51: *eh orang sunda bukan* ("You're Sundanese aren't you"). In lines 53 and 54, Slamet teases Gun, this time about his ambiguous native-speaker credentials, given his near decade-long stay in Japan. This is a further example of how teasing is used to build convivial relations among a group of relative strangers. We also see that Desi is repeating Slamet's earlier suggestion that the word *cipoa* is old or archaic in lines 42–46, 48 and 49. In so doing, she repeats her earlier alignment with Slamet about the archaic-ness of the form, while repeating Lina's earlier contribution about the form's uncommonness. In doing so, the social domain of old and/or archaic Sundanese as one meaning of the word *cipoa* has now widened to include Slamet, Desi, and Lina.

In addition to highlighting a return to the activity of working out the provenance of the term *cipoa*, we also see how ideas about place and native speakership fit into explanations about provenance. For example, Desi tries to gain alignment from Gun (lines 48 and 49) before checking his native-speaker credentials (lines 50 and 51). In doing so, we get to see again the importance that Desi places on native speakership when talking about language. In this instance, it appears that her explanation of the term *cipoa* rests on both the identity that has emerged over interactional time (i.e., her identity as a native speaker of Sundanese) and her wish to have another native speaker (in this case, Gun) align with her ideas about why she does not know this term. We also see that Desi has clear ideas about the links between Sundanese and a specific region, by her reference to elderly Sundanese speakers living in West Java (line 45).

In the next extract, we see that Slamet, who has actually lived and studied for five years in Bandung (stereotypically a heartland of Sundanese speakers), now also appears to be authorized by Desi to explain aspects of Sundanese-ness. In these interactions, we are also provided with some of the signs on which Desi and Slamet base their judgments about provenance. The talk in extract 7.5.4 follows directly after extract 7.5.3.

Extract 7.5.4 The grandmother is just so Sundanese

Desi (S)

57 jadi e:: . >buat generasi saya tida::k>   So er for my generation [I] don't, don't
58 tidak mengenal bahasa #itu# (0.6) tetapi   know that language. But because the
59 karena yang menjadi neneknya inisangat   grandmother is very
60 sunda . [<u>sundanese</u> banget gitu ya' .   Sundanese, very <u>Sundanese</u>, you know.

Slamet

61   [hmmm (while nodding head)   Yeah.

Zane

62 gi. gimana [a apa . apa yang? . misalnya   (False start), why, what, what is it, for example?

Desi (S)

63   [(orang sunda?) (1.0) +dari   ((Sundanese?)) From [the] dialect, from
64 dialek+ . dari dialek . dari mis[al kan   the dialect, from for example, right.

Lina

65   [<u>logat</u> =   Accent.

Desi (S)

66   =
67 <u>logat</u> dari bicara itu (0.5) banyak bahasa   The speaking accent, a lot of Sundanese
68 sunda keluar . dari . dari (0.5)   also came with it. From, from

(continued)

Extract 7.5.4 (Continued)

Slamet

69   psik psikologinya . (looking at Desi)   Psch, their psychology.

Desi (S)

70   [heeh   Yes

Slamet

71   [ah bukan psikologi apa namanya .   Ah not their psychology, what is it, their

72   (looks at Desi) <u>filsafat hidupnya</u>:: =   philosophy of life.

Desi (S)

73   =

74   <u>filsafat hidupnya</u> itu:? . jadi kalau   Their philosophy of life. So if

75   membersihkan halaman rumah? . maka:? .   you clean your yard, then . . .

76   (looks at Slamet and smiles) >apa lagi>   what else Slamet?

In extract 7.5.4, we see the continued use of repetition as a way of showing hearer-ship, establishing reference, and establishing common ground. For example, Lina and Desi align on the topic of accent in lines 65–67, and Desi and Slamet align on the topic of the philosophy of life (lines 72 and 73). When viewed in relation to the prior talk in extract 7.5.3—where "archaic" becomes a ratified meaning of the word *cipoa* between these two—we can say that this talk repeats much of the earlier talk. It also adds to their earlier alignment in a way that builds on the relationship work that has occurred throughout the whole session (viewing and interview). What appears even more striking is that while Desi contested Slamet's knowledge about things Sundanese (extract 7.4.6, lines 7 and 8), here she has made a number of concessions that have helped to build common ground between the two while also building convivial relations between Desi and Slamet.

    In particular, although Desi continues to foreground her expertise and identity as a Sundanese through her positive evaluation of the authenticity of the televised representations of Sundanese-ness that she had just watched (lines 59 and 60), nevertheless, she also ratifies Slamet's comments about things Sundanese. For example, after Slamet seeks approval from Desi in lines 69 and 72, Desi ratifies his contribution through the use of "heeh" (line 70), as well as repetition and expansion (lines 74–76). In particular, Slamet goes on to explain that the reason for classifying *cipoa* as uncommon and archaic relates to the old-fashioned social practices engaged in by the old woman represented in the soap. In this case, it is her philosophy of life, which Slamet discusses at length after being invited to do so by Desi (in line 76). Without providing a transcript of the rest of the talk, Slamet notes that this philosophy relates to something like a clean environment around the home and means that we have a clean spirit and healthy life.

    In summary, in yet another speech situation, we see the continued use of features that seem to be used for the building of convivial relations among this group of Indonesians, including the use of repetition (both temporally close and temporally distant), teasing, and the social pursuit of sameness. These features are intimately tied to the establishment of common ground (personal ethnic backgrounds, provenance, archaic-ness, and traditional philosophies of life), the social identification of participants, and the assigning of meaning to an unfamiliar word.

7.6 Conclusion

This chapter looked at how a group of transnational Indonesians who were studying in Japan did conviviality through talk. I drew upon some of the scholarship on common ground and small talk discussed in section 7.2 to focus on a specific type of talk that occurred in two temporally close speech situations. I showed that repetition was the primary way in which participants went about establishing reference and common ground. While some common ground was emergent, nevertheless, the agreement on referents formed the basis for subsequent convivial talk. In explaining the importance of this type of mundane talk, I suggested that we need to keep in mind the wider context in which these Indonesians find themselves and the research design of this project that brought together transnational Indonesians. Although it was certainly not a type of context one finds in other studies of small talk or doing togetherness in difference, nevertheless, the bringing together of this group created a setting where they needed to build and reproduce interpersonal relationships that would enable them to access the important informal support networks that existed in Nagoya (section 7.3).

In relating my discussion to scholarship on how people from diverse backgrounds do togetherness in difference (e.g., Ang, 2003; Brettell, 2003; Vertovec, 2007; Werbner, 1997; Wise, 2005), I focused on recent work on superdiversity and the idea of conviviality as both an outcome and requirement for this condition (Blommaert, 2013b; Williams & Stroud, 2013). In showing how conviviality is established in face-to-face interaction, I tried to add to earlier studies of conviviality that were primarily concerned with performance (Williams & Stroud, 2013), rather than performance and its reception (as found in face-to-face talk). A concrete example of the outcome of small talk across two temporally close speech situations (a viewing session and an interview) was the convivial relationship that developed between Desi and Slamet. In particular, though he was not a native speaker in the terms defined by Desi, nevertheless by the end of the session, Slamet was authorized by Desi to talk about the Sundanese-ness of a particular character. This practice of commenting upon or evaluating represented ethnic social types was actually quite common among the seventeen Indonesians involved in this study. In the following chapter, I focus on this aspect, which is a part of the practice of knowledging that has been discussed in previous chapters.

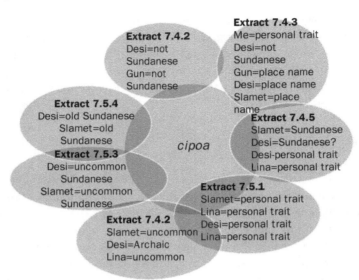

FIGURE 7.6.1 Meaning across time

Finally, in examining these Indonesians' talk, I also touched on my discussion of the multiple functions of talk. For example, in sections 7.4 and 7.5, I pointed out how interpersonal relationship work was intimately tied to working out the meaning of an unfamiliar word (*cipoa*), as well as establishing ethnolinguistic identities. In doing so, I also pointed to the tensions around how this group jointly constructed the meaning of televised signs, while also contributing to the reification of one of the meanings of these signs. In relating this to arguments laid out by Vološinov (1973 [1929]) and Agha (2007a), sections 7.4 and 7.5 provided an example of the circularity involved in the action, structure, and meaning nexus. This was done by following how knowledge of structure (semiotic registers) can inform action to make meaning while contributing to a new structure (the meaning of *cipoa* that relates to deviance). Thus, while multiaccentuality was clearly a feature of participants' talk, we also saw how the social domain of one particular meaning could widen through face-to-face interactions over time, as illustrated in figure 7.6.1.

8

Knowledging, Conviviality, Community, and Togetherness in Difference

8.1 Introduction

In this chapter, I expand on the themes of knowledging and conviviality that were introduced in previous chapters. I continue to use the frame of television viewing discussed in chapter 7. In contrast to that chapter, however, I follow a different group of Indonesians over the course of two weeks: this provides some more insights into how togetherness is reproduced over longer timescales. I suggest that this is important because it helps differentiate conviviality as a fleeting social practice among strangers from conviviality as an outcome of face-to-face interactions over longer periods of time. Borrowing from Ang (2003), I refer to the latter practice as "doing togetherness in difference." I suggest that practicing togetherness in difference is consequential for this group of transnational Indonesians because it ensures access to important resources from within the wider Indonesian community living in Japan. In turn, such access enables these Indonesians to cope with the demands of a transnational lifestyle.

In looking at knowledging and the doing of togetherness in difference, I place my analysis into broader discussions about community and communicative competence (CC). What is especially interesting is that long-term processes of enregisterment of the type discussed in chapters 2 to 6 have enabled this group of Indonesians to interactionally index their participation in a particular Indonesian public that can recognize, evaluate, and use signs associated with ethnic communities of practice (COP) that they do not belong to or identify with. I argue that these practices suggest a need to revisit notions of CC, which have to date presupposed that it is learned locally, often in a geographically isolated space. In contrast, the CC we see here is acquired from multiple dispersed sources, typically institutions that have different concepts of expertise and authority from those found in geographically isolated communities. I discuss ideas around community and CC in section 8.2.

In section 8.3, I focus on how these Indonesians go about engaging in social identification, knowledging, and the doing of conviviality through the identification of represented signs. In doing so, I will show how this relates to simultaneously indexing participation in a number of communities. In section 8.4, I continue this process, but focus on how participants increase their practices of evaluating sign representations. I suggest that these practices are part of a gamut of other forms of talk that help to do togetherness in difference among this group of Indonesians. In concluding, I point out that for sociolinguistics (broadly defined), an ability to delineate communities and practices that enable conviviality, such as knowledging, can provide a more nuanced approach to work on talk in superdiverse settings.

8.2 Community and Communicative Competence

The idea of community and the types of competences one needs to display and enact community have typically been discussed from four different viewpoints. These include emergent communities or identities that are the outcome of situated face-to-face interaction (Antaki & Widdicombe, 1998; Bucholtz & Hall, 2004). A series of interactions across time in a locale produces another type of community that is often referred to as a "community of practice" (COP; Barton & Tusting, 2005; Eckert & McConnell-Ginet, 1999; Holmes & Meyerhoff, 1999; Wenger, 1998). The existence of multiple COPs also enables distinctions among them (Bourdieu, 1984). The practice of making such distinctions helps to sharpen the boundaries between each of them (e.g., Barth, 1969; Bucholtz & Hall, 2004; Irvine, 2001). Publics or audiences represent another type of community. Publics and audiences not only live in the imaginations of media professionals, writers, and bureaucrats (Anderson, 2006 [1991, 1983]; Ang, 1996; Livingstone, 2005), but they are also constituted through acts of media consumption in living rooms and elsewhere, as well as lesson consumption in classrooms, lecture halls, and other teaching venues.

There are a number of overlaps between the terms "publics" and "audiences." For example, in the media and sociological literature (e.g., Dayan, 2005; Kitley, 2000; Livingstone, 2005), publics seem to be differentiated from audiences because of a public's ability to debate the meaning of semiotic representations in the media through interactions among strangers who are typically not spatially or temporally co-present. Yet work in linguistic anthropology and sociolinguistics (e.g., Loven, 2008; Miller, 2004) shows us that audiences too are constituted by spatially and temporally separated strangers who interact with each other when contesting the meaning of certain representations (e.g., letters to the editor and subsequent responses to such letters, posts to fan websites and subsequent comments on these posts). Thus, when I use the term "publics," it also covers "audiences" (i.e., strangers who become connected by responding to representational practices).

Criteria for membership in a public differ somewhat from criteria for membership in COPs and other interactionally constituted communities. In face-to-face interactions, for example, there will be a range of competences that can be involved, and these will be determined by membership in a particular COP. In COPs, sharing ways of speaking and the CC associated with these ways of speaking are primary indicators of membership, and they are typically developed in a specific locale among a stable and often small, isolated population (Hymes, 1972a, 1972b; Ochs, 1988; Schieffelin, 1990; Wenger, 1998). In cases where there are members from multiple COPs, membership in one COP or another is often determined by distinctions made between different ways of speaking (Bourdieu, 1984; Irvine, 2001).

While there are often a limited number of members in a particular COP, publics typically have many more members. This is so because one-to-many participation frameworks help to circulate ways of speaking—albeit with much more fragmented models—to many more people. As linguistic anthropologists and sociolinguists have engaged with each of these notions, they have provided ways of understanding the relationships and overlaps among the communities and the competences involved (Agha, 2007; Cody, 2011; De Fina, 2003; Inoue, 2006; Wortham, 2006). My point of departure is to draw on notions of participation frameworks and enregisterment (Agha, 2007) together with work on semiosis and intertextuality (Agha, 2007; Bakhtin, 1981; Bauman & Briggs, 1990; Silverstein & Urban, 1996; Wortham, 2006). In doing so, I discuss the relationships among these different types of communities together with the different types of CC that are developed by their members, while also relating the ideas of conviviality and knowledging to concepts about publics.

Semiosis can be defined as the appropriation and reuse of a sign or set of signs from one context in another context. Rampton's (1995) account of youths engaging in crossing represents one example of semiosis whereby the words of ethnic others from one COP are appropriated and reused to build another COP among a peer group. We can also see relationships between COPs and publics if we turn to Rampton's (2006) later work and work by Cutler (1999: 433–434). Both show how their subjects appropriate and reuse the voices of different publics to do face-to-face interactional work that helps to constitute emergent COPs.

In turning our focus back to the idea of CC, we can also see that the types of competence in a COP and a public can be quite different. Many of the groundbreaking language socialization studies of the late 1970s and early 1980s (e.g., Ochs, 1988; Schieffelin, 1990) were often conducted in isolated communities. Typically, those studied were a few novices involved in language socialization activities at any given moment (i.e., a one-to-few participation framework). Authority to model ways of speaking for these novices was also limited to older siblings, parents, elders, healers, and missionaries. Communicative competence in these types of COPs were locally determined and reproduced.

While it may have been straightforward for the above-mentioned scholars to define the competences that one needed to be seen as an authentic community member in these settings, an increasingly mobile and connected world has brought into focus distinctions in the ways of speaking of members from different COPs while also inviting scholars to reexamine ideas of CC. A common theme in scholarship that engages with ideas around mobility is the need to understand how histories of mobility figure in a person's ability to understand, differentiate, and use semiotic fragments from whole genres that are indexically associated with ways of speaking in other communities (e.g., Blommaert, Collins, & Slembrouck, 2005a; Blommaert, Collins, & Slembrouck, 2005b; Kramsch & Whiteside, 2008; Warriner, 2010). Even so, a number of these studies were similar in their underlying assumptions about community and CC, namely that mobile persons were originally part of a community that was anchored to a locale, and members became communicatively competent through participation in one-to-one and one-to-few participation frameworks.

These small-scale language socialization settings and the CC developed within them contrast with large-scale language socialization situations where novices can range from a classroom full of students to a television audience. In this sense, large numbers of novices create a quantitatively different participation framework, namely a one-to-many participation framework (Agha, 2007: 74–77). Another difference from earlier studies of CC is that now, message forms and content—part of what made up "act sequence" in Hymes's (1972a: 59–60) SPEAKING model—are multiple, dispersed, and accessed through participation in daily life in urban neighborhoods, government institutions (e.g., schools, correction facilities, hospitals, welfare offices, etc.), when listening to radio, when viewing televisions, computer screens, and so on. The role of institutions is also different. For example, the institutions of family, extended family, clan, and so on that have in the past been primary socialization settings have increasingly been replaced by government institutions, mass media, and so on (e.g., Giddens, 1990).

The increasing role of government institutions and government-sponsored institutions has also meant a change in ideas relating to authority. Now, authority to influence another's life trajectory has increasingly moved from siblings, parents, and elders to those with formal education. Authority is also much more dispersed, with many institutions having the power to model and normalize particular ways of speaking (e.g., family and elders versus schools and media institutions). In terms of how those in positions of authority interact with novices, one-to-many participation frameworks are also increasingly common. Finally, while in small communities, linguistic forms are imbued with cultural value through interactions with siblings, parents, and elders (e.g., honorific forms, terms of address for elders, etc.), in larger urban contexts, government institutions and the mass media do much of this work (e.g., Agha, 2007; Inoue, 2006; Jaffe, 2003). The results of such processes are different centers of normativity, with institutions and their actors typically being at the top of the indexical order created by such processes (Blommaert, 2010; Bourdieu, 1991).

8.3 Social Identification, Conviviality, and Community

In this section, I focus on how participants go about socially identifying themselves and how this relates to conviviality and membership in different types of communities. Although only one participant, Nuraeni, works at producing an interactional identity as someone of Sundanese ethnicity, the rest of the group's talk shows that they have knowledge and an apparent entitlement to comment about things Sundanese. Over the course of the viewing and interview session, this group indexes their membership in an ethnic COP, a locally emergent COP, and a public, as well as the wider community of transnational Indonesians living in Japan. What I present below is talk that was recorded as part of the research project described in chapter 7, although it is talk among a different group of participants. To present a temporal view of how talk figures in the building of convivial social relations in this group, I follow their talk across the first two viewing and interview sessions. During this session, I played an episode titled *Cipoa (Con Artist)*, the same comedic soap discussed in section 3.5. Table 8.3.1 summarizes some self-reported information from these participants.

TABLE 8.3.1
Participant backgrounds

NAME (age)	Place of residence	HISTORY OF MOBILITY		LANGUAGES (reported)
		Start year of residence	Years there	
Endang (34)	Kendal (Central Java)	1976	2	Javanese
	Semarang (Central Java)	1979	5	Indonesian
	Yogyakarta (Central Java)	1983	7	English
	Kendal (Central Java)	1989	3	
	Batam, (island located between Sumatra and Singapore)	1992	3	
	Purwokerto (Central Java)	1995	7	
	Jakarta	2002	6	
	Japan	2008	0.8	
Farid (27)	Padang (West Sumatra)	1982	5	Minang,
	France	1986	5	French
	Padang	1991	17	Indonesian
	Japan	2008	0.8	English
Fatimah (28)	Surabaya (East Java)	1981	27	Javanese,
	Japan	2008	0.8	Banjar
				Indonesian
				Japanese
Nina (25)	Yogyakarta (Central Java)	1984	22.5	Javanese
	Japan	2005	0.5	Indonesian
	Yogyakarta (Central Java)	2006	1	English
	Japan	2007	1	Japanese
Nuraeni (28)	Bandung	1981	3	Sundanese
	France	1984	5	French
	Bandung (West Java)	1989	20	Indonesian
	Japan		0.83	English

These participants were all newcomers to Japan and relative strangers. Indeed, it was the first time that Farid had met Nuraeni and Nina, and only Endang and Nuraeni had occasion to meet more regularly through the weekly involvement of their children in the Saturday school set up by and for the Indonesian community living in Nagoya. It was also the case that as the only Christian in this group, Endang was not involved in monthly Islamic prayer sessions and gatherings. Even so, like other non-Muslims, she and her family did participate in religious festivities tied to the end of the Islamic fasting month that were held by the Indonesian community at Nagoya. It is also important to point out that this group may or may not have known about each other's linguistic and ethnic backgrounds, and only Nuraeni reported having any knowledge of Sundanese.

At the first session, all five participants were present. Diagram 8.3.1 shows where each participant was seated in the classroom that was used during this viewing session. (I have also included Nuraeni's daughter who spent some of the viewing session sitting with Endang.) As pointed out in section 3.5 and in the introduction to extract 7.4.1, in the first two minutes of the soap, there was a short monologue by one character in the national language, Indonesian, that included one accented word, which may or may not have provided participants with a clue about the language setting of the serial. Participants then recognize one of the actors and provide her name. Shortly thereafter, the episode title *Cipoa* appears on the screen, and the talk represented in extract 8.3.1 follows.

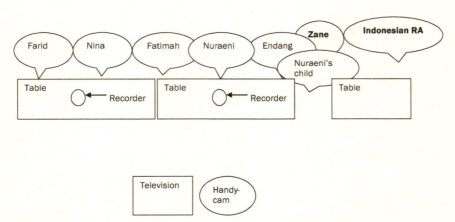

DIAGRAM 8.3.1 Transnational Indonesians watching television and doing community

Knowledging, Conviviality, Community, and Togetherness in Difference   207

Extract 8.3.1 Indexing membership in a public

Endang
1   cipor =   Cipor.
Nuraeni
2   = cipoa =   Cipoa.
Endang
3   = cipor =   Cipor.
Fatimah
4   = cipo (0.5) ah   Cipo, ah,
5   (0.5) eh bukan ya .   eh, no right?
Endang
6   ci . cipor gitu (0.5) sungai por gitu =   Ci, like Cipor, like the river Por.
Nina
7   =
8   cipoa apa ci por . artinya apa .   Is it cipoa or cipor, what's the
                                                          meaning?
Endang
9   ci . por =   Cipor.
Fatimah
10   = ci =   Ci.
Nuraeni
11   = sungai por =   The river Por.
Nina
12   = artinya   Sister [Endang] what does it
                                                          mean?
13 apa mbak =
Fatimah
14   = sungai por gitu =   Like the river Por.
Endang
15   = iya .   Yeah,
16 kali (laughs) (1.0)   a river.
Fatimah
17 kayak cirebon gitu (laughs) cipoa =   Like Cirebon yeah? Cipoa.
Nina
18   =
19 kayak nama tempat =   Like a place name?

In the above transcript, we see that participants are establishing common ground among themselves by trying to assign meaning to an apparently unfamiliar word, *cipoa*. There are two things of interest in this talk. First, we get a little bit of an insight into the extent to which participants who have not identified themselves as Sundanese speakers nevertheless display familiarity with this medium. For example, only Nuraeni has claimed an ability in Sundanese (table 8.3.1), which is a semiotic register where the prefix "ci" is found in place names. Second, we also see that it is actually a participant from a non-Sundanese background (Endang) who tells Nina about the meaning of this prefix (line 6), rather than Nuraeni. Put in terms of knowledging, we are seeing Endang and Fatimah displaying knowledge of linguistic features associated with a particular ethnic community (in lines 9 and 14–17). Put in terms of a public, we are seeing Endang and Fatimah demonstrating their knowledge of what the prefix "ci" means, in this case, "river," which indexes their participation in a community of Indonesians who know these types of things. As the actors' names appear on the screen, Nuraeni notes that one of the actors, Nike Ardila, is from the same neighborhood as she, namely Bandung (the capital city of West Java and the stereotypical Sundanese-speaking heartland), as can be seen in extract 8.3.2.

Extract 8.3.2 Indexing participation in an ethnic community of practice

Nuraeni
1 (looks at Fatimah, smiles and touches chest   Heh, the same, the same neighborhood
2 rapidly) eh satu . satu kampung . satu   [as me], the same neighborhood [as
3 kampung [makanya dikenali .   me], that is why I recognize [her].

Endang
4   [oh ya]   Oh yeah.

Nuraeni
5 bandung . bandung . he he he [he (breaths   Bandung, Bandung ((laughs)).
6 in) .

Endang
7   [ciamis   Ciamis right?
8 bukan =

Nuraeni
9   = cipoa kan he he he   Cipoa right? ((laughs))

The importance of extract 8.3.2 is that in identifying her place of origin as Bandung (lines 2, 3, and 5), Nuraeni also implicitly identifies herself as a Sundanese speaker. It is also worthwhile noting that Nuraeni's embodied language (e.g., her gestures, smiles, and laughter on lines 1–3, 5, and 9) has an affective character. This may be a sign of her positive alignment toward both the actor and the place (Bandung) that she comments upon, although at this stage, this alignment is still ambiguous. By identifying herself as belonging to a particular geographical community, her talk by way of indexical links among region, language, and ethnic social type also presupposes membership in a particular ethnic COP.

In a sense, Nuraeni's talk has differentiated her from the public inhabited by Endang and Fatimah (extract 8.3.1, line 11) by associating herself with the ethnic community being represented. In other words, she is starting to index her membership in an ethnic COP, though without ratification by other co-present participants, this claim is still ambiguous. Nuraeni's self-identification continues in extract 8.3.3 through her recognition and translation of linguistic forms that others do not know. The talk in extract 8.3.3 occurs after a conversation between the main character (Dewi) and the taxi driver (this represented dialogue was analyzed in sections 3.5.5–3.5.7). In this televised conversation, there are many Sundanese forms, although interestingly it is only *sabaraha* ("how much") that gets any attention. When an advertisement break occurs, Nina asks about the meaning of this word, as in extract 8.3.3.

Extract 8.3.3 Solidifying participation in an ethnic community of practice

Nina

1   apa .   What?

Farid

2   **sabaraha** =   How much?

Nina

3   = [**sabaraha** (while turning   How much?
4   toward Nuraeni)

Nuraeni

5   [(turns toward Farid and
6   Nina) **sabaraha** tu . berapa (while still   **Sabaraha** means "how much."
7   looking at Farid and Nina points and   ((laughs)) understand, [you
8   smiles) ha ha ngerti . nggak ngerti ya   both] don't understand do you?
9   [ha ha   ((laughs))

Farid

10 [(shakes head from side to side while   No.
11 smiling)

In extract 8.3.3, Nuraeni not only offers the Indonesian equivalent *berapa* (line 6) of the word in question (*sabaraha*), but then goes on to jokingly pointing to Nina and Farid while saying "you don't understand do you" (lines 8 and 9). These two acts further identify Nuraeni as a speaker of the medium being used in the serial. At the same time, she also positions Farid and Nina as having no competence in this medium. Put in terms of community, here Nuraeni is simultaneously indexing her membership in a particular ethnic COP that is knowledgeable about these linguistic signs while also suggesting that Farid and Nina must not be part of that community. With reference to long-term relationships among linguistic forms, region, and essentialized ethnic identities, we might also suggest that Nuraeni is also inferring that both Nina and Farid have different ethnic identities from the one being represented in the serial.

As this social identification ensues, there is also some interpersonal relationship- building. In particular, Nuraeni's identification of Farid and Nina as not able to understand the medium being represented is framed as teasing by her laughter surrounding the utterance that co-occurs with her waving her finger up and down and smiling at Nina and Farid. Nina aligns by smiling, while Farid appears also to do so by nodding his head while smiling. In a sense, we are starting to see the emergence of a local COP through the pursuit of convivial practices of the type described in chapter 7. While the medium that Farid and Nina supposedly do not understand has not yet been explicitly named by any as Sundanese, some five minutes later, Nuraeni identifies the medium as Sundanese, as in extract 8.3.4. This talk occurs after an elderly woman appears for the third time and again talks with Dewi, this time using many Sundanese forms and a heavy accent (see extract 3.5.1, which examines this bit of represented talk).

Extract 8.3.4 Identifying and evaluating medium usage

Farid
1   (while laughing and looking toward
2   Nuraeni) [+translation please+ (laughs)   Translation please.
Nuraeni
3   [aduh **resep iyeuh** . bahasa   Wow **this** Sundanese **is good**
4   sunda**na** (while pointing to self with   [which is my language].
5   hand laughing and [gazing at Nina)
Nina
6   [(gazing at Nuraeni
7   and Fatimah and laughing) ya aku juga   Yeah, I also don't
8   nggak ngerti (laughs) =   understand.
Endang
9   = (while gazing
10 toward others and smiling) sunda **téa** =   It's Sundanese?
Nuraeni
11   =
12 sunda   Sundanese.

On line 1, we can see that the old woman's monologue has led Farid to loudly ask for a translation while also laughing. (The increase in volume is indicated by "+," and laughter while talking is indicated with a double underline.) Nina aligns with Farid's claim of not understanding by her explicit note of "not understanding also" (lines 7 and 8). In doing so, she is also establishing common ground with Farid by pursuing social sameness about their states of knowledge of things Sundanese. While Nuraeni offers no translation and laughs herself—which appears to ratify the jovialness of Farid's request—she does evaluate the represented signs as "good Sundanese" (lines 3 and 4). These turns achieve three things. First, Farid and Nina continue to build on their emerging identities as not members of Nuraeni's ethnic COP, which has now been named. Second, Farid and Nina are also engaged in building convivial relations between themselves. Third, Nuraeni's evaluation also continues to index and solidify her emerging identity as a speaker of the medium being represented and a member of a Sundanese COP.

The way Nuraeni evaluates this representation is also important in that it simultaneously adds weight to her earlier claims of being Sundanese. For example, while her earlier talk was in Indonesian, she now uses linguistic signs stereotypically associated with Sundanese (*resep, iyeuh*, and the suffix *na*) while pointing to herself. In this case, we are seeing Nuraeni performing Sundanese-ness while simultaneously evaluating other's usage of signs associated with Sundanese-ness, all of which help solidify her emerging identity as a Sundanese speaker and member of an ethnically Sundanese COP.

It is also important to note here that Nuraeni's identity work sits in contrast to Endang's, who builds on her earlier claims (extract 8.3.1) that she is familiar with Sundanese through her performance of one linguistic sign, *téa* (line 10). In terms of publics, we are seeing Endang showing not only membership in a public that recognizes forms associated with a particular ethnic COP, but also membership in an Indonesian public that can use some of these forms. In engaging in crossing, Endang is also doing unity in diversity in a medium that is not solely Indonesian. Endang's performance also appears to be ratified by Nuraeni, who has earlier built up an identity as a native speaker of this medium. This ratified act of crossing can be seen as the linguistic pursuit of sameness with Nuraeni, which may be building and/or reproducing convivial relations between the pair. It also appears to be the case that the earlier teasing of Farid by Nuraeni in regard to his inability to comprehend Sundanese is used as a resource by Farid to joke with Nuraeni. In this case, he uses gaze, smiling, and laughter to frame his utterance "translation please" in line 2 as a joke. This sequence builds on earlier strategies for building convivial relations between these two participants, who before this research session had never met.

Thus far we have seen Nuraeni's identity as a Sundanese and speaker of Sundanese solidify over the course of the viewing session. Nina and Farid, on the other hand, have emerged as not knowledgeable about Sundanese and not the same ethnic social types as Nuraeni. Fatimah appears to be someone who has some knowledge of the signs that index Sundanese and Sundanese-ness. Endang too has emerged as someone who can use some Sundanese, and her crossing practices thus far seem to have been positively received by Nuraeni. In addition to Nuraeni and Endang, convivial relations seem to be emerging among Nuraeni, Farid, and Nina by their teasing and laughing. In the interview that followed, participants' identities solidified further. I will just summarize this interview here so that I can move on to the following week's session with this group of participants.

At the start of the interview, I asked a general question about what they thought of the serial. Nuraeni began by noting that it was very Sundanese and made her feel like she was back home watching in Bandung. After I asked her for examples of what made it very Sundanese, she pointed out a number of the Sundanese tokens used and followed these by translations into Indonesian. These acts of evaluation and translation helped to further index her membership in an ethnically Sundanese COP, as well as her identity as a speaker of Sundanese. However, Nina's earlier identity as someone "not competent in Sundanese" tended to be more fluid. For example, Nina noted that the main character Dewi (Nike Ardila) was very Sundanese. She added that the prefix *Ci* in *Cipoa* also helped her identify the serial as being set in West Java. Thus, here Nina's acts of evaluation and grammatical explanation show that she is at least familiar with some of the signs associated with Sundanese-ness. Here she is aligning with an Indonesian public that can recognize and/or evaluate the authenticity of representations of Sundanese-ness. As in the previous chapter, this ability to engage in this type of knowledging is explainable in terms of her participation in the authorized processes of enregisterment that occurred from the start of the New Order period in 1966 and continued until the time of this recording (e.g., chapters 2–6).

Farid also noted that the actors' accents had helped him identify the medium being represented as Sundanese. In other words, through his talk, Farid also aligned with an Indonesian public that could recognize members from an ethnic COP. These claims initiated a discussion about which characters used Sundanese. The discussion included all participants, and the upshot of this was that it continued to solidify Nina's identity as someone who can recognize linguistic signs associated with Sundanese. Fatimah added that a number of the particles used were ones commonly heard and identified as Sundanese. While the provenance of these terms was then debated, all agreed that the pronunciation identified them as Sundanese. Again, this talk helped to index Farid's, Fatimah's, Endang's, and Nina's participation in an Indonesian public from the New Order period.

Shortly thereafter, I asked whether and to what extent people outside of Sundanese-speaking areas might be able to identify the medium used and understand the story. Farid, Endang, Fatimah, and Nina started by suggesting that they wouldn't, but then went on to say that many were familiar with Sundanese because the national broadcaster, TVRI, had screened many previous films and serials that were very Sundanese, including the television and wide-screen versions of *Si Kabayan*, which I will focus on shortly. Indeed, the non-Sundanese participants' abilities to comprehend signs of Sundanese-ness seem to be evidence of this circulation.

After I asked about the relationship between the taxi driver and Dewi, Nuraeni's identity as a Sundanese speaker continued to solidify as she explained that the co-occurrence of body language, facial expressions, and Sundanese forms all pointed to an intimate relationship. Nina, Endang, and Fatimah compared these features to what happened in interactions between Javanese speakers. In doing so, Nina, Endang, and Fatimah also began to socially identify themselves as knowledgeable about Javanese, an identity that solidified in the rest of the interview as they identified the other characters in the film by comparing social practices and pronoun usage with Javanese usage. The interview ended after all participants further solidified their positions as being "knowledgeable about Sundanese" through their discussion of how Sundanese forms are widely known. Importantly, their continual indexing of their membership in an Indonesian public that recognizes members of other ethnic COPs can also be seen as the social pursuit of sameness where they have created further common ground among themselves based upon knowledge about signs associated with Sundanese and Sundanese-ness. This pursuit of sameness contributes to the construction of an emergent COP through practices of conviviality.

In summary, this section introduced another group of transnational Indonesians who had volunteered to be part of a wider project that initially set out to look at how television representations were understood. In this viewing and interview session, they watched the same comedic soap, *Cipoa*, as the group discussed in chapter 7. Unlike the group we met in chapter 7, however, nearly all were relative strangers. Most had lived in Nagoya for only about six months. Although only one person, Nuraeni, reported being Sundanese, nevertheless, all participants engaged in the recognition of representations of Sundanese. In addition, some started to evaluate these representations. Both this recognition and evaluation indexed their participation in a community of Indonesian citizens (i.e., a public) knowledgeable about things ethnic. I suggested that this knowledge was gained through involvement in the processes of enregisterment described in chapters 2–6. For Nuraeni, her commentaries and later performance of Sundanese pointed to her membership in an ethnically Sundanese COP. One participant, Endang, also used fragments of linguistic forms associated with Sundanese. In so doing, she not only indexed her membership in an Indonesian public that could recognize members of other ethnic groups, but she also engaged in crossing to do unity in diversity, which contrasted with ideologies about Indonesian as the language of doing unity in diversity.

Endang's crossing had multiple meanings, and in this setting, it was part of a broader pattern of convivial talk. I pointed out that, more generally, the way all participants posted and aligned to comments, and the regular occurrence of teasing and laughter suggested that these convivial practices were part of building membership in a locally emergent COP, as well the wider Indonesian community living in Nagoya. As discussed in chapter 7, conviviality was important because of the need to access the support networks that existed for these sojourners in Nagoya (section 7.3). In a real sense, the pursuit of convivial relations in the here and now also indexed participation in this wider community of sojourners, who engaged in togetherness on a much larger scale and in many more social domains. As we will see in the following section, the pursuit of convivial relations among members of this group was an ongoing project, and in the following week's viewing and interview sessions, we see more of this type of conversational work along with some interesting knowledging practices.

8.4 Doing Togetherness in Difference and Knowledging

In the previous section, I focused on commentaries that occurred as participants viewed television and on post-viewing interviews. Conviviality was interactionally achieved by establishing common ground about place and participant background, while social identification was interactionally achieved by the positioning of self and other as competent or incompetent in Sundanese and by explicit self-identification. In comparison, there was only one instance of social identification that was achieved through the evaluation of represented sign usage (extract 8.3.4). This situation contrasts considerably with the talk that I examine in this section. This talk occurred in the second viewing session held the following week when Nuraeni (the person who has built up a Sundanese identity) and the others all comment on the authenticity of represented ethnic social types. In doing so, we are again seeing four of the participants engage in what I refer to as knowledging. As with the previous section and the last chapter, this commentary was also very much tied to the building of convivial relations among this group of Indonesians. In contrast to chapter 7, however, here I argue that what we are seeing is an example of togetherness in difference because participants have come together again in a different time and place. Indeed, unlike other groups were there was often someone who did not attend viewing sessions, on this and following occasions, participants continued to attend viewing sessions. At this session, all five participants were present. Nuraeni had also brought her two young daughters. Diagram 8.4.1 shows where each participant was seated. During this second session, I played an episode from the comedic soap *Si Kabayan*, which

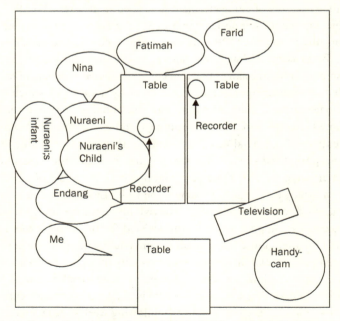

DIAGRAM 8.4.1 Transnational Indonesians watching television and doing togetherness

had been brought up in the previous week's interview (I discussed this episode of *Si Kabayan* in section 3.6). While I was setting up the audio recorders and television, the participants engaged in quite a bit of jovial talk. As the introduction to the serial began, accompanied by shots of the main characters and a number of rural settings, the following conversation ensued (extract 8.4.1).

Extract 8.4.1 Recognizing signs and their associated medium

Endang
1   kabayan (0.9)   It's Kabayan.
Fatimah
2   oh kabayan =   Oh, it's Kabayan.
Farid
3   = heeh (0.8)   Yeah.
Endang
4   ini sunda **téa** (18)   It's Sundanese, **right**?
Nuraeni
5   sctv (0.9)   ((The television station)) SCTV.
Endang
6   sctv (1.1)   SCTV.
Nuraeni
7   ah si kabay [an   Hey, it's Kabayan.
Endang
8   [kabayan (3.2)   It's Kabayan.
Nina
9   sunda lagi sih (4.3)   Gee, it's Sundanese again.
Farid
10 teh melulu . kopi sekali sekali =   ((literally)) Always tea, what about coffee occasionally. ((but better translated as "The same thing again, what about variety."))
Nuraeni
11   = butuh   Do you need
12 translater (said while smiling and pointing   a translator?
13 to Nina and Endang) =
Nina
14   = iya aku nggak   Yeah, I don't
15 ngerti   understand.

At the start of the viewing session and after seeing the title on the screen and hearing the song accompanying it, Endang and Fatimah point out that the serial is *Kabayan* (lines 1 and 2). Endang then goes on to point out that it is Sundanese (line 4). While it is possible that the Sundanese-ness of Kabayan was established in the viewing session in the previous week when Kabayan and his Sundanese-ness happened to be discussed, what seems to be more noteworthy is how Endang performs this recognition, which is done through the use of *téa* (a linguistic form associated with Sundanese). This practice is an example of crossing. In other words, here Endang has shown that she has some knowledge of linguistic signs associated with Sundanese by her performance, despite earlier reporting no competence in Sundanese. Although neither Nuraeni nor anyone else ratifies this usage, Endang's use of *téa* seems to have links with the interpersonal relationship work that occurred between Endang and Nuraeni in the previous week (extract 8.3.4, line 10). In other words, given that the Sundanese-ness of Kabayan was established in the previous viewing session, this sequence seems to continue convivial talk as Endang and Nuraeni repeat known information.

As the main character Kabayan is talking using some Sundanese, Nuraeni smiles and points to Nina and Endang and asks them if they need a translator (lines 11 and 12). Although she does so in jest, this move also achieves three other things. First, it establishes links with the talk in the previous week (see section 8.3), when Nuraeni established her expertise and background as a speaker of Sundanese. Second, it identifies Fatimah and Nina as not competent in Sundanese, despite their obvious recognition of this serial as Sundanese (lines 4 and 9) and their interactional work in the previous week. Even so, Nina aligns with Nuraeni's talk on lines 14 and 15 with her comment: "yeah, I don't understand." In doing so, Nina appears to be modifying the identity she established through her conversational activity in the previous week.

Third, Nuraeni's teasing on lines 11–13 also mirrors the strategies she used to build convivial relations with Farid in the previous week. Indeed, this talk seems to repeat much of the content about translation and translators, as well as Nina's response to the joke (lines 14 and 15), which is nearly an exact copy of her response to this activity in the previous week (see extract 8.3.4, line 4). As in chapter 7, in this interaction, we can also see that repetition—indicated by underline—seems to be important in establishing common ground and convivial relations. Of special interest is how Nina's affective stance toward the television show, in this case one of disappointment (line 9), is repeated on line 10 by Farid. In aligning with this stance and doing it in a poetic way, Farid's response also seems to be doing positive interpersonal relationship work. Importantly, all of this talk also indexes the different senses of community that emerged in the previous week. These include:

1. An Indonesian public: Those who have the ability to recognize signs associated with different ethnic COPs (Endang in line 4, Nina in line 9, and Farid in line 10), as well as use fragments of them (in this case, Endang's talk in line 4), though her usage is not ratified here.
2. A member of an ethnically Sundanese COP: Those who not only can recognize these signs but are acknowledged by others as authentic speakers

Knowledging, Conviviality, Community, and Togetherness in Difference **217**

of the particular community whose signs are being used (in this case, Nuraeni, whose claim to authenticity in lines 11–13 is ratified by Nina in lines 14 and15). This recognition and usage also simultaneously presupposes that others belong to different ethnic COPs.
3. An emergent COP: The emergent COP made up by this particular group of Indonesians who have been building convivial relations in a research setting over a couple of weeks through the use of small talk, repetition, pursuits of sameness, teasing, and joking.
4. The wider community of Indonesians living and studying in Nagoya who need to access support networks.

After this bit of talk, Nuraeni's identity as a speaker of Sundanese further solidifies by her answering of questions about some unfamiliar words and offering their Indonesian equivalents. The setting then moves to a house and yard with three other characters. At this stage, Nina, Nuraeni, and Endang jointly identify the actor playing one of these characters, Iteung, as somebody they don't know. While establishing further common ground among participants, this act of identification also shows their familiarity with the characters, previous versions of the story, and potentially their knowledge about semiotic representations associated with these characters. This is shortly followed by a dialogue between two elderly characters, Abah and Ambu (see extract 3.6.1), and then between Iteung and Abah. After Iteung finishes talking, Nina initiates comments about the authenticity of the actor playing Iteung (extract 8.4.2).

Extract 8.4.2 Iteung isn't very Sundanese

Nina
1 (While turning to look at Nuraeni and
2 touching her on the arm) si iteungnya   Iteung
3 nggak [sunda . nggak [nggak begitu sunda   isn't Sundanese, isn't isn't
4 sih?   very Sundanese, yeah?

Endang
5   [siapa sih (0.8)   Who is she?

Nuraeni
6   [(while shaking
7 head) nggak juga =   No, not at all.

Endang
8   = ngomongnya nggak   Her speech isn't
9 sunda ya =   Sundanese, is it.

Nina
10   = heeh =   Yeah.

Endang
11   = agak kejawaan   It's rather Javanese.

In the above extract, we can see that after seeking agreement from Nuraeni (lines 1 and 2) and getting it in lines 6 and 7, Nina then evaluates one of the characters, Iteung, in a way that questions the ability of the actor playing Iteung to faithfully represent Sundanese-ness (lines 2–4). This is despite Nina's earlier comments that she doesn't understand Sundanese, Nuraeni's earlier positioning of her as "not competent in Sundanese," and Nina's own claims and self-reports about having no competence in Sundanese. In terms of knowledging, Nina's evaluation is demonstrating a familiarity with signs of Sundanese-ness. Nuraeni aligns with Nina's opinion (lines 6 and 7), and this suggests that such evaluations are interactionally appropriate.

The talk in extract 8.4.2 is also telling because it highlights a need to interpret Nina's talk in terms of her membership in an Indonesian public that can recognize and evaluate representations of ethnic others. Indeed, if we only paid attention to Nina's history of participation in one-to-one or one-to-few participation frameworks and her own statements about her lack of competence in Sundanese (i.e., her socialization in a particular place and her lack of mobility within Indonesia), it would be hard to account for her talk here unless we consider her involvement in one-to-many participation frameworks (i.e., her socialization through schooling and consumption of mass-mediated representations of the ethnic other).

In addition to continuing to index her membership in a particular Indonesian public, we also see Nina continue to pursue social sameness with Nuraeni (this time in opinions about authenticity). This practice can be seen as further positive interpersonal relationship work that simultaneously points to membership in an emergent COP and the wider Indonesian community living in Nagoya. We see that this entire interaction is characterized by this type of work. For example, after Nina's comment is ratified by Nuraeni (the person whose identity as a speaker of Sundanese has emerged across a number of speech situations), we see that Endang also notes that Iteung's talk is not Sundanese. She is thus also simultaneously indexing membership in the same communities as Nina.

We also see that although Nina has already pointed out the inauthenticity of the television representations of Sundanese-ness in lines 1–3, nevertheless, she repeats this information by her agreement with Endang's comment in lines 8 and 9. This part of the sequence achieves two things. First, it is evidence of Endang continuing to build convivial relations with Nuraeni by way of agreeing with her evaluation (i.e., building common ground), and by extension agreeing with Nina's original evaluation. At the same time, this talk continues to index Endang's membership in the same three communities as earlier. Second, we can see that Nina also continues to build convivial relations with Endang through her pursuit of sameness in opinion (line 10). As the characters are introduced, these types of evaluations become quite frequent, as we can see extract 8.4.3.

Extract 8.4.3 Were the protests because these two characters weren't Sundanese?

Nuraeni

1	kalau nggak salah kan . awal awalnya	If [I'm] not mistaken, right, at the early stages
2	sempat diprotes (0.4) karena nggak	there were protests because there wasn't
3	ada logat sundanya =	a Sundanese accent.

Endang

3	= oh gitu =	Is that right.

Fatimah

4	= (moving	
5	body and gaze toward Nuraeni) atau ini	Or is it these two who don't have a
6	yang:: karena nggak ada logat sundanya =	Sundanese accent.

Nuraeni

7		=
8	iya kali	Yes, maybe.

In lines 1–3, Nuraeni recalls that maybe it was this episode that attracted protests because Iteung's accent wasn't Sundanese. Although I did not ask about what type of protest, I assume that this was in the form of letters to the station, a common practice in Indonesia, as pointed out by Loven (2008). Note that to this point, the discussion has only been about Iteung, and Nuraeni hasn't evaluated other actors' accents as inauthentic. This is important because while Fatimah's background and self-reports about her linguistic abilities do not suggest any competence in Sundanese, she nevertheless goes on to ask whether the protests might relate to two new characters who have just appeared on the screen and started speaking (lines 4–6). In doing so, she is evaluating these new characters' accents while identifying herself as someone who is familiar with signs of Sundanese-ness. In short, she is engaging in knowledging.

By engaging in knowledging, Fatimah is also demonstrating her membership in the same Indonesian public inhabited by Nina and Endang. At the same time, Fatimah is also pursuing sameness with Nina's, Endang's, and Nuraeni's earlier opinions about authenticity. In short, conviviality is being pursued by indexing her membership in the same locally emergent COP inhabited by all participants, as well as the wider community of Indonesians living in Nagoya. That Nuraeni's talk on lines 7 and 8 seems to ratify Fatimah's claim helps smooth the way for further talk of this type. Shortly thereafter, Endang comments about the speech of one of the characters who was the object of discussion in lines 4 and 5 in extract 8.4.3.

Extract 8.4.4 Wow, these guys have very noticeable accents

Endang
1 lho kok ini medok ngomongnya (0.8)   Wow, gee his speech is really accented.

Farid
2 [tamu   [He is] an <u>outsider</u>.

Nina
3 [pak ini ya =   This one [on the screen now] yeah?

Endang
4 = itu <u>tamu</u> ya? =   He is an <u>outsider</u> is he?

Farid
5 = <u>tamu</u>:: =   Yeah an <u>outsider</u>.

Endang
6 =
7 wong itu petugas desa kok . medok (1.1)   Gee, that person, the village official, [his] speech is very accented.

Nuraeni
8 <u>iya</u> =   <u>Yeah</u>.

Nina
9 = <u>heeh bener</u> (1.5)   <u>Yes, yes</u>.

Farid
10 ya kan pegawai desa kan . kan belum tentu   Yeah, right a village official right, doesn't necessarily have
11 dari desa:: [setempat   to be from the village where they work right.

Nina
12 [oh iya <u>dimutasi</u> [<u>mutasi</u>   Oh yeah, [they] can be <u>transferred, transferred</u>.

Farid
13 [<u>heeh kan</u>   Yes, [they can be] <u>transferred, right!</u>
14 <u>dimutasi</u> =

Endang

15	= bukannya . pega . orang situ	Aren't officials usually from there [the
16	biasanya =	village that they work].

Farid

17	= bersedia ditempatkan di mana	Prepared to move anywhere.
18	saja (laughs) (0.5) pns kan . bisa siapa saja	Civil servants can be anyone [from anywhere], right!

In the talk represented in extract 8.4.4, we can see that the representation of one of the characters, Diran, has resulted in further commentary. Although participants approach the issue of authenticity from different angles, their talk suggests that it is a mismatch between the semiotic anchor of geographic place and other represented signs. In terms of knowledging, we continue to see Farid, Nina, and Endang showing their knowledge about signs associated with other ethnic COPs by engaging in an evaluation of the authenticity of represented sign usage. For example, Endang's comment about the thickness of the character's accent in lines 1, 6, and 7 shows that she has clear ideas about what this character's accent should sound like given the Sundanese setting of the soap. In explaining this mismatch (lines 2, 10, 11, 13, 14, 17, and 18), Farid is also showing that he knows what should be the case and why it isn't on this occasion. For example, he explains that this is a result of the well-known practice of moving civil servants around Indonesia (see chapter 2). Nina aligns with Farid's position that this mismatch is due to the character being an outsider (line 12).

By engaging in these knowledging practices, Endang, Nina, and Farid also index their membership in the particular Indonesian public that they have interactionally inhabited during the course of two viewing sessions. By continuing to pursue sameness in activity type (i.e., questioning the authenticity of representations), they are also pursuing conviviality and thus indexing participation in the other two communities that they have interactionally inhabited over the course of two viewing sessions. More generally, we also see that the achievement of common knowledge and ultimately convivial relations is also done through non-minimal responses in talk between Nuraeni and Nina. For example, in line 9, Nina uses *heeh* (yes) to show hearer-ship or alignment, while her second yes (*bener*) shows engaged listening. Similarly, we see that Farid also uses non-minimal responses in lines 13 and 14 in a way that also suggests a continuation of convivial talk with Nina. In this case, the *heeh* (yes) on line 13 shows hearer-ship, while the use of *kan dimutasi* (lines 13 and 14), which is basically a longer form of saying yes, repeats the *heeh* and thus shows engaged listening.

In the rest of the viewing session, participants continue to engage in these sorts of commentaries in a way that supports their earlier positions relating to the inauthenticity of social type representation. For example, Nina, Endang, and Fatimah point to Iteung's face, which they note is Javanese-looking. In this sense, they continue to index their membership in the same three communities that they have interactionally inhabited to date. Nuraeni also indexes her membership in their locally emergent COP and the wider community of Indonesians living in Nagoya through her reiteration that Iteung's accent is also not Sundanese. In short, her repetition continues to build convivial relations with members of this group by showing that they hold the same opinion as Nuraeni. Nuraeni also continues her practice of providing further translations for Sundanese words and grammatical explanations about the functions of certain Sundanese forms. In doing so, she continues to show her expertise in Sundanese, which continues to index her participation in an ethnically Sundanese COP.

During the interview that followed this viewing session, I delved further into the extent of these participants' familiarity with television and film versions of *Si Kabayan*, finding that all participants had rather in-depth knowledge about the series of actors who had played Iteung and other characters. In addition to comparing the authenticity of portrayals in earlier versions of *Si Kabayan*, participants made comparisons with other actors' portrayals in other ethnic teledramas, which also indexed their membership in the same three communities that they had inhabited during the viewing session. In what follows, I present some examples of these practices.

Extract 8.4.5 Knowledging and pursuing sameness in opinion

Zane
1   itu jugu lumayan (0.7) banyak ketawa   There was actually a fair bit
                                                  of laughter
2   juga =   also.
All
3   = laughter =   Laughter.
Nina
4   = tapi yang ini aktingnya   But there is this, their acting
5   mereka kaku =   is strange.
Zane
6   = kaku =   Strange?
Nina
7   = apa jadi   What is it,
8   maksudnya kadang . ah kita ngerti   what [I] mean is sometimes,
                                                  um we know
9   mereka mau buat   they want to give [us] a
10 kesannya sunda . tapi sundanya kok .   Sundanese experience, but
                                                  gee the Sundanese
11 agak (0.6) [nggak luwes . gitu   is <u>not very</u>
                                                  <u>natural</u>, you know.

Nuraeni

| 12 | [<u>agak dipaksakan</u> = | A bit <u>forced/overdone</u>. |

Zane

| 13 | = oh = | I see. |

Fatimah

| 14 | = | Not especially Sundanese. |
| 15 | <u>bukan sunda banget</u> = | |

Endang

16	= itu yang nggak itu	Which ones weren't,
17	. itu . <u>iteung sama si . armasan itu</u> .	<u>Iteung and Armasan</u>,
18	kalo aku liat [sih	In my opinion.

Nina

| 19 | [<u>si iteung sama si</u> | [Yes], <u>Iteung and</u> |
| 20 | [<u>armasan</u> | <u>Armasan</u>. |

Nuraeni

| 21 | [<u>armasan</u> lumayan ah . | <u>Armasan</u> was alright. |

Farid

| 22 | heem = | Yeah. |

Endang

| 23 | = [tapi . agak ini juga . | But rather [strange] as well. |

In the above extract, we see that Nina discusses how unnatural representations of Sundanese-ness have been in the soap they just watched. In particular, she notes that the actors' attempts at providing a Sundanese experience were not really natural (lines 4, 5, 9, and 11). Her position is ratified by Nuraeni in line 12, and also by Fatimah (in line 15). Endang and Nina then take the lead again in singling out Iteung and another character as especially inauthentic (lines 16–20 and 23). In so doing, these three participants continue to engage in knowledging in a way that demonstrates an ability to recognize and evaluate ethnic social types. In doing so, they index their participation in the Indonesian public that they have interactionally inhabited across two viewing sessions.

As with their previous talk, the responses to these evaluations can be considered as evidence of continued efforts to build and reproduce convivial relations, which also indexes continued membership in their local emergent COP and the wider community of Indonesians living in Nagoya. The pursuit of conviviality can be seen if we examine how a series of repetitions that unfold in this sequence contribute to establishing sameness in participants' opinions and thus further common ground. For example, we see that in line 12, Nuraeni aligns with Nina's opinion of representations not being very natural (line 11). Similarly, Endang aligns with these two opinions through a paraphrase (line 15) that summarizes Nuraeni and Nina's position. We also see Nina (lines 19 and 20) aligning with Endang's opinion on just exactly who was the most unnatural (lines 17 and 18). Farid, who doesn't say much in this sequence, also aligns with Nuraeni's opinion (line 21) about one of the characters, Armasan, as being reasonably authentic (line 22). While in line 21, Nuraeni initially challenges one of the evaluations relating to Armasan (Kabayan's close friend in the serial), shortly afterward, Nuraeni ratifies the evaluation of Iteung's authenticity in lines 27–29 of extract 8.3.6 below. This extract represents the talk that directly follows after extract 8.4.5.

Extract 8.4.6 Alignment repetition

Nina

24   [iteung yang jelas =   It was obvious [with] Iteung.

Endang

25   = iteung tuh   [With] Iteung
26   . jelas jelas =   it is really obvious.

Nuraeni

27   = iteung yang paling kaku .   Iteung is the strangest.
28   ekspresinya juga enga::k .   Her gestures and facial expression also
29   [nggak ini . ya .   aren't, aren't [appropriate] yeah.

Endang

30   [iya kalau ekspresinya juga . mungkin   Yeah, also her gestures and facial
31   masih baru . pendatang baru kali . ya (0.6)   expression, maybe she is a newcomer, maybe, yeah?

Zane

32   Heem . jadi kaku gimana . maksudnya =   I see. So what do you mean by strange?

Endang

33   =
34   nggak seperti orang sunda =   Not like a Sundanese.

Nuraeni and Nina

35   = heem   Right.
36   (while nodding heads) =

Zane

37   = heem (0.6)   I see.
38   [jadi se]   So

Endang

39 [untuk <u>logatnya</u> =   Their <u>accent</u>.

Nuraeni

40   = <u>logatnya</u> juga (0.5)   Also <u>their accent</u>. That
41 itu ah: (retrieves pen dropped by child) .

In the above extract, we see that Nina and Endang point out that the character Iteung is the most obvious example of an inauthentic portrayal of Sundanese-ness (lines 24–26). Nuraeni ratifies this evaluation by pointing out that Iteung's portrayal is *yang paling kaku* "the strangest" (lines 27 and 28). We can also see that Nuraeni goes on to evaluate Iteung's embodied language (i.e., her gestures and facial expressions) as strange (lines 28 and 29). Nuraeni's focus on Iteung's embodied language (*expresi*) in lines 28 and 29 offers an extra dimension to her evaluation (re her use of *juga*, "also") along with her differentiation of *logat* from *expresi* in line 40. In so doing, she seems to front her expertise by being able to make such distinctions. Nuraeni thus continues to foreground her expertise as a Sundanese speaker by her ability to differentiate signs of Sundanese-ness, while continuing to index her membership in an ethnically Sundanese COP. Nina and Endang's contribution, on the other hand, continues to engage in knowledging that demonstrates membership in the Indonesian public that can recognize and evaluate ethnic social types.

That their evaluations are also ratified by Nuraeni—who has consistently indexed her participation in the community of Sundanese being evaluated—suggests a continuation of the positive interpersonal relationship work that has occurred during this session and the previous one. Indeed, if we look at this talk more closely, we find that there is also a continuation of features used to pursue conviviality. These include the use of repetition and the pursuit of sameness in opinions. For example, we see repetition as showing both hearer-ship and agreement about evaluations between the pairs Nina-Endang (lines 24–26), Nuraeni-Endang (lines 28–30), and among Endang-Nuraeni-Nina (lines 34 and 35). What moves this repetition from a type of "showing hearer-ship" to engaged listening, at least for Nina and Endang, is that it repeats much of the content and much of the alignment already established in the talk represented in extract 8.4.5 in lines 16–19. This alignment repetition (which occurred across both temporally close speaker turns and those separated by other talk) displays common ground and indexes their continued membership in their locally emergent COPs and the wider community of Indonesians living in Nagoya.

While evaluations thus far have been critical and have primarily questioned the authenticity of particular actors' performances of the ethnic other, this group of participants showed that knowledging can also involve positive evaluations of ethnic representations. In particular, as the interaction proceeds, the other participants continue to index their membership in the communities they have interactionally inhabited thus far. This is done through the recognition and positive evaluation of ethnic social type representations. As can be seen in the talk that follows directly after extract 8.4.6, Endang and Nina go on to highlight the Sundanese-ness of three of the characters.

Extract 8.4.7 Knowledging as positive evaluation

Zane

39   kalau si abah (0.8)   What about Abah?

Endang

40   abah **mah** . [sunda banget =   Well Abah, [is] very Sundanese.

Nuraeni

41   [(nods head while gazing at   Yes,
42   me) abah sunda =   Abah is Sundanese.

Nina

43   = heeh =   Yes.

Endang

44   = sama . sapa =   as is who [else]?

Nina

45   = Kabayan, Kabayan.
46   kabayan [kabayan

Endang

47   [ambunya itu . kabayan itu   Ambu [and]
48   sunda banget   Kabayan [are] very Sundanese.

After my prompt in line 39, we see that in contrast to previous negative evaluations, now Endang positively evaluates some characters' represented sign usage. For example, Abah is seen as "very Sundanese" ion line 40, as are Ambu and Kabayan (lines 45–47). Interestingly, Endang again appears to engage in crossing by her use of the form *mah* (line 40), which is associated with Sundanese. Nuraeni also appears to ratify this usage and evaluation (line 41). In line 43, Nina also repeats the topic/opinion alignment displayed by Nuraeni and Endang in lines 40 and 41. Similarly, in lines 46 and 47, we see Endang aligning with Nina's opinion in line 45. Again, Nina's and Endang's knowledging practices co-occur with the building of convivial relations through the pursuit of common ground, which in this case is sameness in opinions. In doing so, as with earlier examples, they continue to index their membership in the three communities that they have interactionally inhabited over the course of two viewing sessions.

In the following two weeks, participants continued to engage in this type of sociability, which was characterized by participants' positive and negative evaluations of televised sign representations. For example, when I screened an extremely popular ethnic serial, *Si Doel Anak Sekolahan* (*Doel an Educated Lad*), which was set in a Betawi-speaking area of Jakarta, it was not uncommon for those who had spent no time living in Jakarta (Nina, Nuraeni, Fatimah, and Farid) to make comments relating to the authenticity of represented signs and sign users.

In summary, this section followed the group of participants introduced in section 8.3 in their interactions a week later as they again view an Indonesian comedic soap and are interviewed afterward. What was especially interesting during this week was how those who had not been socially identified as members of an ethnically Sundanese COP in the previous week (in this case, only Nuraeni) nevertheless engaged in evaluating representations of Sundanese social types. In engaging in these types of knowledging practices, they indexed their membership in a particular Indonesian public and two other communities. In doing so, they also exemplify Indonesian citizens who are multicultural and multilingual and who can sometimes index and do unity in a medium other than Indonesian. Nuraeni was different from other members of this group because she made more nuanced evaluations of Sundanese-ness. For example, she identified particular facial expressions and body language as Sundanese. As in the previous section and last chapter, however, all participants' evaluations were also very much tied with the building of convivial relations among this group of transnational Indonesians. This was done through teasing, various forms of conversational alignment that established common ground (e.g., alignment in activity types [evaluation], alignment in opinions, alignment repetition), non-minimal responses, and crossing. This conversational work related to the ongoing construction of a local COP. At the same time, this type of interactional work continues to point to their membership in the wider community of transnational Indonesians living, working, and studying in Nagoya.

8.5 Conclusion

In this chapter, I continued to engage with the themes of knowledging and conviviality by examining interactions among a different group of research participants across a larger timescale. In so doing, I placed my analysis into broader discussions about community and its relationship with CC. Many of these Indonesians (Nina, Farid, Endang, and Fatimah) had competence to comprehend signs associated with ethnic communities of practice that they did not identify with. On many occasions, some of these Indonesians also evaluated representations of the ethnic other or even appropriated and used (i.e., engaged in crossing) some of the linguistic forms associated with ethnic others. In displaying these types of competence, they also displayed membership in a particular type of community, in this case, an Indonesian public that had been socialized during a particular historical period when links among linguistic forms, place, and person had been circulated on a mass scale to form ethnic communities of practice. Put more directly in terms of CC, although the group of Indonesians discussed here came from very different parts of Indonesia and had very different patterns of mobility, they nevertheless displayed similar types of CC, which can only be accounted for with reference to notions of enregisterment.

I suggest that the case at hand has implications for how we think about CC more generally. Indeed, that so much of language socialization involves schooling and the consumption of semiotic forms from television and radio programming, films, the Internet, and other forms of one-to-many participation frameworks invites us to reevaluate our understanding of CC (Goebel, 2013). This is so because studies of CC continue to have the underlying assumption that it is learned locally, often in a geographically isolated space, and that it is then brought into other contexts. In contrast, the CC we have seen here is acquired in multiple dispersed institutional settings.

Interactionally displaying membership in a particular Indonesian public (i.e., engaging in knowledging) also became a resource that was used with a whole range of other conversational features to index membership in two other types of communities. Both were related to the notion of conviviality. The first was the locally emergent COP that was developing among this group of research participants, while the second was the wider community of Indonesians living in Nagoya, Japan. Engaging in knowledging, repetition, non-minimal responses, teasing, pursuits of sameness in opinions, etc. all helped to further build convivial relations among this group of Indonesians. In contrast to the type of conviviality discussed in chapter 7, however, in this chapter, we have seen how convivial relations continue to be built and reproduced over two temporally and spatially distinct speech situations. In chapter 7, I referred to this as togetherness in difference and suggested that it helps extend the ideas around conviviality discussed in Williams and Stroud (2013) and Blommaert (2013a, 2013b). In particular, I suggested that taking this approach differentiates conviviality as a fleeting social practice from conviviality as the outcome of face-to-face interactions across longer timeframes.

I suggested that the practices that made up part of these Indonesians' efforts to build convivial relations related to the need to access important support networks in Nagoya. This need mirrored what we find in other settings, especially those couched in terms of superdiversity, because one feature of such settings is the need to access goods, services, and jobs. In engaging in talk that produced these convivial relations, this group of Indonesians thus also indexed their participation in the broader Indonesian community and associated support networks in Nagoya. For the diverse field that is referred to as sociolinguistics (e.g., Bucholtz & Hall, 2008), I suggest that an ability to delineate different types of communities and the competences and communicative practices associated with them can provide a more nuanced approach to the study of talk in superdiverse settings. In particular, superdiverse contexts are settings where interactional alignment with many communities may be the order of the day. What I have shown here is one approach to identifying such alignments.

That some acts of knowledging resembled crossing requires further attention, especially given that I continue to refer to these practices as knowledging rather than crossing. There are four main reasons for this. First, accounts of crossing typically focus on "performances" of features of other's mediums. Knowledging primarily involves comprehension and evaluation of features of other's mediums rather than a performance using these features. Second, work on crossing often accounts for or implies that competence to engage in crossing was gained via participation in face-to-face interactions (i.e., one-to-few participation frameworks; e.g., Blommaert et al., 2005b; Kramsch & Whiteside, 2008; Rampton, 1995). After looking at participants' backgrounds, it is clear that the ability to engage in crossing was not gained via involvement in one-to-few participation frameworks, but rather through involvement in one-to-many participation frameworks.

Third, while those who engage in knowledging seem to be entitled to evaluate representations of "otherness," this is usually not a performance of otherness through the borrowing of linguistic signs associated with this other. Fourth, the practice of knowledging discussed in this book also differs from crossing because crossing occurs in liminal moments and can be flagged by commentaries, laughter, or pauses, all of which were not part of the interactional practices of this group of Indonesians. For example, the practice of knowledging seemed to be habitual among my group (e.g., they did this in each of the four viewing sessions that they attended), and it was ratified as appropriate.

For those with a keen interest in Indonesia, we can also add that while most of this knowledging was typically done in Indonesian (which among other things is an index of being an Indonesian citizen), these practices also demonstrate that the state ideology of unity in diversity can also be enacted through recognition and evaluation of signs associated with other ethnic communities, rather than just Indonesian. In some ways, an unintended outcome of processes of enregisterment that occurred between 1966 and 2009 (see chapters 2–6) is that Indonesians can now also index their Indonesian-ness by knowing about or even speaking fragments of the ethnic "voices" (Hill, 1995) of other Indonesians (e.g., Cole, 2010).

9

Conclusion

9.1 Introduction

This book has examined how a social category, ethnicity, has been semiotically constructed and recirculated in Indonesia since Dutch colonial times and how signs or emblems from this construct are drawn upon in the talk of transnational Indonesians studying in Japan. While the daily challenges of eking out a livelihood as a student were perhaps not so different in 2008 compared to the early twentieth century, what *was* different was that these students now brought with them a deep knowledge of ethnic stereotypes and the emblems associated with them. These Indonesians used their knowledge of such emblems along with other interactional practices to establish and maintain important convivial relations. The concepts of ethnicity and convivial social relations in transnational spaces are two of the main themes of this book and represent points of engagement with scholarship in the areas of language ideologies and superdiversity. In what follows, I summarize the main arguments put forward in each chapter. In section 9.2, I tie these arguments together while highlighting how this work can contribute to sociolinguistics more generally.

Taking inspiration from scholarship in the broad area of language ideologies, chapter 2 examined how ideas about social types, regions, and linguistic forms have been circulated from colonial times until the early 1990s, forming what can be described as imagined communities of ethnic social types. In building on my earlier work, I aligned with three sets of related ideas. The first related to how tracing histories of sign circulation helps us understand how a particular "language" has become associated with particular types of speakers and particular values over time. The second set of ideas I aligned with revolved around ideas of complexity and superdiversity. The third related set of ideas concerned the relationships between different waves of technology and how they have contributed to the massification and up-scaling of the circulation of ideas and people, while also creating new social domains for contact with and commentary about the "other."

More specifically, in chapter 2, I argued that new waves of technology figured in the construction of regional languages, Indonesian, and their imagined communities of speakers on the one hand, and a nearly infinite number of local languages and their situated communities on the other. Situated in this sense refers to both a community that is sedimented over time through habitual interactions in a particular locale (Bourdieu, 1977; Giddens, 1984; Wenger, 1998), and more fleeting communities found in transient settings (Goebel, 2010b). The groups of sign constellations—referred to as semiotic registers (Agha, 2007)—that became regional languages were typically made up of a formula of region + person + linguistic form = regional ethnic language. Ideas about regional languages were produced by academic elites and media professionals. These ideas became widely known through their consumption in increasingly common one-to-many participation frameworks. These participation frameworks included school classrooms and mediated communication. In the former, the teacher represented the one and the pupils the many, while in the latter (e.g., television, radio, newspapers, novels, magazines), the program, the newspaper article, etc. were the one and the readers and audience the many.

A register of Malay eventually became a register of Indonesian, with the most widely circulating reproductions being found in the social domains of schools and bureaucracies, radio, television, and print media. As literary written models of Malay became part of the spoken repertoire of exemplary Indonesians, over time, Indonesian also became associated with new knowledge, education, development, expertise, citizenship, nationhood, and authority (whether personal, bureaucratic, or political). The idea of a citizen who could do unity was exemplified by the Indonesian-speaking subject.

Where interactional practice was concerned, I painted a picture of increased interaction among strangers in an increasingly diverse and expanding set of domains that led to the creation of new sign constellations (semiotic registers). In concluding chapter 2, I pointed out that where interaction across lines of difference occurred, it usually involved mobile, educated, and affluent city types who typically engaged in such interactions on a regular basis. Often, members of this same group of Indonesians subsequently produced representations of such interactions in travelogues, novels, radio shows, and television programs. With the formation of multiple semiotic registers came the formation of multiple centers of normativity relating to what was good language. The existence of multiple centers each with different social values helped in the creation of what Blommaert (2005, 2008, 2010, 2013) refers to as "orders of indexicality." The orders of indexicality that emerged typically had Indonesian at the top of the hierarchy followed by some ethnic languages (e.g., Javanese), then other ethnic languages, and finally mixed languages. The same processes that enabled the creation of these orders also set up the conditions for their reconfiguration, a point I explored in the following chapters.

Chapter 3 sought to examine how personhood and social relations were represented in Indonesian comedic soap operas in the mid-to-late 1990s. I did this with an eye to identifying continuities between these representations and the circulating ideologies about communities of ethnic social types discussed in chapter 2. Taking inspiration from work on media and television more generally, I pointed out that these comedic representations were the outcomes of particular historical circumstances as they related to the emergence of television and local soaps. In looking at these television representations, I took a multimodal approach that helped to show how the co-occurrence of specific words with signs of place, proxemics, gestures, facial expressions, topics, activity types, and prosody helped to produce dense semiotic models of ethnicity with "demeanors" (Goffman, 1967) and interactional histories. For example, ethnic social types were linked with signs of place, emotional social types, and close social relations in all three soaps, while the register that had "Indonesian" within its constellation of signs typically lacked these signs of rapport and involved interactions among strangers. On the other hand, the register(s) that were associated with diversity, mobility, and the city became associated with social types who could engage in register alternation as part of a more long-term local process of becoming an insider, while also mirroring much of the embodied language found in intra-ethnic interactions. These representations of register alternation also can be considered as part of a reconfiguration of orders of indexicality because they started to be represented as commonplace and not stigmatized in one social domain, television.

In thinking about how these representations helped to associate particular demeanors with social types, I also engaged with work on the relationship between television representations and language change. Following up on Richardson's (2010) observation that media professionals erase or foreground "polite" and "impolite" behavior in television dramatic dialogue, I suggested that this could more generally be couched in terms of semiotic change. More specifically, I argued that the construction of social types' demeanors can be viewed as evidence of semiotic change, especially when compared with the ethnic social types that had been circulating prior to the emergence of televised comedic soaps. In short, in comparison to the imagined communities of ethnic social types who spoke another language and lived in a particular region, these social types now audibly spoke and visually acted in particular ways.

What was very common across all three soaps was alternation between fragments of a named regional language and Indonesian. This alternation resembled what has been described in the codeswitching literature as "alternation as the medium" (Alvarez-Cáccamo, 1998; Franceschini, 1998; Gafaranga & Torras, 2002). I argued that this representation of alternation authorized mixing in settings that do not have a close fit with descriptions of television representations elsewhere in the world. In the literature, instances of alternation are associated with liminality and spectacular performances (e.g., Androutsopoulos, 2007; Jaffe, 2000; Kelly-Holmes & Atkinson, 2007; LeCompte & Schensul, 1999), while in the soaps examined here, instances of alternation were unspectacular, mundane, and habitual.

These representations of alternation also provided models of the doing of unity in diversity that sat in contrast to the state ideology, which linked Indonesian to the doing of unity in diversity. I pointed out that this type of representation had, since the early 1990s, become increasingly common on Indonesian television. In a real sense, these soaps were starting to naturalize the type of diversity found in Indonesia's cities. This increasingly naturalized picture of diversity included the "competence to comprehend" (Agha, 2007) fragments of languages that one did not speak. This competence was an unintended consequence of the increasing circulation and consumption of ideas about ethnicity found in one-to-many participation frameworks (e.g., schooling, television and radio programming, etc.), at least in the imaginations of the television producers who created soaps based in urban areas. I referred to the practice of comprehending fragments of others' regional languages in interaction as "knowledging."

Chapter 4 focused on a period of rapid change when ethnicity increasingly became indexed with negative traits. From 1999 onward, ideologies of ethnicity continued to circulate in similar social domains as in the past. For example, people still circulated in transport hubs, shopping malls, schools, and universities. Universities continued to send their students on field placements to other regions as part of their university education. Representations of ethnic social types continued too, and ideologies linking linguistic form to region were recirculated via schools and government artifacts (e.g., census forms that now included ethnic categories).

In exploring what amounted to the criminalization of certain ethnic social types during this period, I started by looking at state developmentalist policies of the earlier New Order period (1966–1998). These policies directly contributed to massive influxes of outsiders—including economic migrants, transmigrants, administrators, police, and military personnel—over a short period of time to the islands outside of Java. I pointed out that the rapid increases in the visibility of outsiders contributed to the creation of the "right" conditions for the construction of social types with negative characteristics. These tensions were primarily local and sometimes emerged in face-to-face interactions or altercations between locals and outsiders. In this sense, the circulation of negative associations with certain identities was primarily local and on a small scale.

However, from early 1997 onward, the effects of an ongoing currency crisis, rapid political change, decentralization, and the emergence across Indonesia of movements whose focus was on the revival of "local" traditions all helped to recirculate older ideologies that linked region to ethnic social type on a much larger scale. As in other places around the world (Collins, Noble, Poynting, & Tabar, 2000; Poynting, Noble, Tabar, & Collins, 2004), the preexistence of stereotypes coupled with economic and political uncertainty, a highly visible group of outsiders, and media reportage about rights and entitlement assisted in the association of negative traits with ethnic social types in certain areas of Indonesia. One outcome of these interrelated processes was that deviance was increasingly laminated onto people who were migrants, replacing earlier, more neutral readings of ethnicity. The consequences of this were the worst cases of communal violence and population displacement seen in Indonesian since the mid-1960s.

Conflict-based displacement and the involvement of military and other outsiders (e.g., aid agencies) created many new social domains for encounters with difference and for the generation of stories about such encounters. During this time, there was also a large increase in the mediatization of conflicts involving those of different ethnic backgrounds, at both the local and national levels. In a real sense, and as with earlier times, registers associated with ethnic social types were now regaining negative associations. This was not just in the regions, but also in Java where almost daily reports of violence perpetrated by one ethnic group against another could be found in national newspapers. In a number of regions in Indonesia, political and fiscal decentralization brought with it increased emphasis on the teaching of ethnic languages and use of ethnic languages in the media. These practices helped to strengthen existing associations among language, group, and region, and with them ideas relating to language as emblematic of ethnicity, while also contributing to an ongoing reconfiguration of existing orders of indexicality.

In chapter 5, I turned my attention to some of the 400 hours of television that I recorded in 2009. Drawing upon the theoretical orientations laid out in chapters 2 and 3, I focused on the tension between how televised representations helped to naturalize language alternation on the one hand, while continuing to anchor it to locale. While I pointed out that language alternation occurred across a number of genres including soap operas, variety shows, on-the-spot news reports, and commercials, I focused primarily on news reports, children's shows, and soaps. What was striking about this alternation was that it occurred in non-liminal and non-spectacular moments and was represented as habitual across many genres, timeslots, and television stations.

The habitualness of this alternation was also assisted via anchoring mechanisms, which I argued also assisted in the recirculation of older ideas about communities of ethnic social types, their language practices, and their link to place. Anchoring was achieved through explicit commentary by a narrator or newsreader, or by metasemiotic commentaries such as maps, subtitles, communities of speakers using similar mediums in a particular setting, the explicit naming of a language, the use of signs of place (e.g., car license plates), and subtitle-like texts. I pointed out two types of alternation practices found in soaps: the first contained large amounts of a local medium, while the second, which I refer to as "stylized alternation," contained just a couple of fragments from these mediums (often referred to as regional languages). I argued that the increasingly ubiquitous nature of ethnic registers and register alternation on Indonesian television also pointed to a reconfiguration or revaluation of ethnic registers vis-à-vis

Indonesian, especially when compared with representations during the first twenty-five years of Indonesian television when Indonesian was the sole medium.

Chapter 6 continued to focus on television representations that were recorded in 2009. Following up on the theme of diversity introduced in chapter 5, I showed how representations of linguistic diversity and the practices of alternation and knowledging that were emerging on Indonesian television by the late 1990s (chapter 3) were by 2009 ubiquitous across a range of television stations and genres. I pointed out that this authorization of diversity also often sat in contrast to the practices described in chapter 5 where linguistic forms were anchored to ethnic social types and/or region. These representational practices not only denaturalized the language ethnicity links that I described throughout the book and with it imagined communities of ethnic social types, but they also demonstrated that the doing of unity in diversity in Indonesia is no longer an activity that is ideologized as something done solely in Indonesian. The representation of alternation and knowledging thus points to a process of revaluing whereby the make-up of orders of indexicality is changing domain by domain.

More specifically, I focused on understanding representations of language alternation practices that typically involved the use of fragments of Indonesian and fragments of regional languages. In contrast to the televised material covered in chapters 3 and 5—where there were representations of multiple voices usually anchored to different parts of Indonesia—in the talk examined in this chapter, these voices were now represented as spoken in settings associated with the city. In examining how mobility and diversity are represented through the use of fragments associated with the voices of imagined ethnic communities, I provided examples of interactions among those who were represented as sharing similar ethnic voices and interactions across lines of difference. As with the representational practices described in section 3.7, interactions across lines of difference typically had participants understanding each other's talk. In short, they were represented as engaging in knowledging as part of wider conversational efforts to do togetherness. The doing of togetherness or conviviality through knowledging and a range of other conversational practices becomes the central focus of my final two chapters.

Chapter 7 looked at how a group of transnational Indonesians who were studying in Nagoya, Japan, built convivial relations through talk. In engaging with more general literature on the doing of togetherness and conviviality, I focused on a specific type of talk referred to as "small talk." This small talk included features, such as non-minimal responses, teasing, and repetition, and helped to establish common ground among participants. The pursuit of common ground also included the pursuit of social sameness at a number of levels, including opinions about the authenticity of televised representations. In focusing on the building of convivial relations across two temporally close speech situations, I linked this type of mundane talk with a number of other contexts: the wider context in which these Indonesians found themselves and the research design of this project, which brought together these transnational Indonesians. Although this is certainly not a type of context one finds in other studies of small talk (Coupland, 2003, 2000) or ethnographic studies of doing togetherness in difference (Wise, 2005), nevertheless, the bringing together of this group created another setting where these Indonesians needed to (re)produce interpersonal relationships that would enable them to (re)access the important informal support networks that existed in Nagoya.

In looking at these transnational Indonesians' talk, I also engaged with scholarship in two other areas. The first area relates to the multiple functions of talk, such as how talk can contribute to the simultaneous development of identities and epistemologies (Goebel, 2010b; Wortham, 2006). In line with Bakhtin's (1981) and Vološinov's (1973 [1929]) ideas about the multiple meanings inherent in discourse, chapter 7 also added to this literature by teasing out the multiple functions of talk in a particular setting. For example, in addition to building convivial relations, I showed how talk also related to ongoing social identification, the assigning of meaning to an unknown word, and the tensions between meaning as fixed and meaning as negotiated.

Chapter 8 continued to use the frame of television viewing discussed in chapter 7, although my data was drawn from the talk that occurred between another group of Indonesians who were involved in the project described in chapter 7. In contrast to chapter 7, I follow this group across the course of two weeks, which provided some more insights into how conviviality was built and reproduced over longer timescales. In so doing, I placed my analysis into broader discussions about community and its relationship with communicative competence. The Indonesians discussed in chapter 8 all had competence to comprehend signs associated with ethnic communities of practice that they did not identify with, and on many occasions, some of the these Indonesians also evaluated representations of the ethnic other or even appropriated and used some of the linguistic forms associated with ethnic others. In displaying these types of competence, they also displayed membership in an Indonesian public that had been socialized during a particular historical period when links among linguistic forms, place, and person had been circulated on a mass scale to form ethnic communities of practice. Put more directly in terms of communicative competence (CC), although the Indonesians discussed here came from very different parts of Indonesia and had very different patterns of mobility, they nevertheless displayed similar types of CC, which can only be accounted for with reference to notions of enregisterment.

Interactionally displaying membership in a particular Indonesian public (i.e., engaging in knowledging) also became a resource that was used with a whole range of other conversational features to index membership in two other types of communities. Both were related to the notion of conviviality. The first was the locally emergent community of practice (COP) that was developing among this group of research participants, while the second was the wider community of Indonesians living in Nagoya, Japan. Engaging in knowledging, repetition, non-minimal responses, teasing, pursuits of sameness in opinions, etc. all helped to further build convivial relations among this group of Indonesians. In contrast to the type of conviviality discussed in chapter 7, I examined how convivial relations continued to be built and reproduced over two temporally and spatially distinct speech situations. I referred to this as "togetherness in difference." I suggested that the practices that made up part of these Indonesians' efforts to build convivial relations related to the need to access important support networks in Nagoya.

9.2 Ideologies, Communities, Competence, and Superdiversity

A major aim of this book was to contribute to discussions about linguistic superdiversity and language ideologies. I engaged with the interrelated nature of these two areas in a number of ways. First, I extended the argument implicit in Rampton (2011) about the need to take a historical look at the development of linguistic superdiversity. Drawing inspiration from ideas about space-time compression discussed by Harvey (1989) and the relationship of technology to language and social life (Eisenlohr, 2010; Weidman, 2010), I focused on how new waves of technology and the intensification of schooling practices produced large increases in the circulation of people and ideas in Indonesia, which in turn had a number of unintended consequences. One unintended outcome was the construction and reproduction of language ideologies about ethnolinguistic communities across the archipelago over a time span of about 150 years.

Related to the development of language ideologies about ethnicity was the development of knowledge about ethnic others that could be used to establish positive interpersonal relations among strangers in transnational settings. The third outcome was the emergence of an uncountable number of locale-specific languages. In a sense, while I have mapped some of the conditions that have engendered superdiversity in Indonesia, I have also highlighted how this process also "sets up" and "sits in constant tension with" standardizing processes that are the outcomes of schooling, television programming, and other one-to-many participation frameworks.

The fleshing-out of a historical account of how linguistic superdiversity has emerged in Indonesia can add a comparative viewpoint to discussions about the emergence of superdiversity in Europe (e.g., Blommaert, 2010; Blommaert & Rampton, 2011; Rampton, 2011; Vertovec, 2007). For example, one characteristic of linguistic superdiversity in European settings is the settlement of people with a wide range of linguistic repertoires in an area already populated by people with an equally wide but different linguistic repertoire. In Indonesia, we have seen how the consumption of commentaries about the other—typically circulated on a mass scale in newspapers, radio, television, and schools—have over time helped to add "competence to comprehend, evaluate, and perform ethnic otherness" to Indonesians' linguistic repertoires. I referred to competence to comprehend, evaluate, and perform ethnic otherness as "knowledging."

In chapters 3, 5, and 6, I was interested in showing how television programming helped to build, reproduce, and change ideologies about ethnic social types. The work in these chapters contributes to some of the discussions on language ideology formation by furthering the multimodal nature of such studies. More specifically, with a few recent exceptions (Bucholtz, 2011; Bucholtz & Lopez, 2011; Mendoza-Denton, 2011), most studies that look at how social types and social relations are constructed, while being associated with particular signs, typically use and focus upon printed sources (e.g., Agha, 2003, 2011a; Inoue, 2006; Inoue, 2011; Miller, 2004). Yet printed sources can only represent certain modes of communication in comparison to the wider array of signs represented in film formats, which have become a ubiquitous one-to-many participation framework. In addition, the extra modes found in the soap format also offer implicit metasemiotic commentaries that help in the construction of social types as ethnic.

Another contribution of this book to scholarship on linguistic superdiversity relates to how people do togetherness in difference in superdiverse settings (Ang, 2003; Goebel, 2010a, 2010b; Smets, 2005; Vertovec, 2007: 1045; Werbner, 1997; Wise, 2005). While work to date focuses on doing togetherness in difference in local encounters, I have shown how Indonesian television models such encounters. In examining the modeling of these encounters, I made two observations. The first related to how this modeling helped to authorize codemixing, while the second was that the modeling of such encounters also modeled a new type of sociability that was based on knowledging practices.

In carrying out my analysis of constructed dialogues in television representations, I found that language alternation was very common. Despite an increasing interest in the media in sociolinguistics (e.g., Agha, 2011b; Bell & Gibson, 2011; Gershon, 2010; Richardson, 2010) and a mountain of work on language alternation and codeswitching more generally, I could find little work that focused on issues around the classification of representations of language alternation. I thus needed to develop an approach to this type of alternation. In theoretical terms, I built on my earlier work in this area (Goebel, 2010b), work on codeswitching, especially Gafaranga and Torras's (2002), Auer's (1995) ethnomethodological approach to language alternation, and reflections on ethnomethodological approaches more generally (e.g., Francis & Hester, 2004; Liddicoat, 2007; Moerman, 1988; ten Have, 2007). Most of the alternation I examined could be classified as "alternation as the medium" (Gafaranga & Torras, 2002). Alternation as the medium resembled the following pattern (adapted from Auer, 1995): AB1 AB2 AB1 AB2 (uppercase letters represent a particular medium and the numbers indicate speakers 1 and 2).

Alternation as the medium is a different type of language alternation from what is found in accounts of television representations elsewhere in the world (e.g., Androutsopoulos, 2007; Jaffe, 2000; Johnson & Ensslin, 2007; Johnson & Milani, 2010; Kelly-Holmes & Atkinson, 2007; LeCompte & Schensul, 1999), and indeed in accounts of the institutionalization of multilingualism more generally. On the one hand, these institutionally authorized representations contrast with commonly found ideologies of multilingualism where multilingualism is constructed as the ability to monolingually speak two or more languages (e.g., Heller, 2007). On the other hand, accounts of the commoditization of multilingualism in the media elsewhere typically represent language alternation as occurring in liminal or spectacular interactional moments (e.g., Androutsopoulos, 2007; Jaffe, 2000; Johnson & Ensslin, 2007; Johnson & Milani, 2010; Kelly-Holmes & Atkinson, 2007; LeCompte & Schensul, 1999). Yet in the television representations examined here, language alternation was typically unspectacular, mundane, and often habitual. The televised modeling of alternation as the medium and language alternation more generally as habitual also pointed to some other presumptions on the part of media professionals about a type of sociability characterized by knowledging practices. In particular, these representations of alternation and knowledging showed that these interactional practices were already part of television producers' imaginations, as well as part of their expectations about their audiences' competence to comprehend.

The modeling of knowledging practices brings us back to another observation relating to studies of superdiversity, namely that the condition of superdiversity requires new ways of understanding how people from different backgrounds with different semiotic systems go about getting along (Ang, 2003; Goebel, 2010a, 2010b; Smets, 2005; Vertovec, 2007; Werbner, 1997; Wise, 2005). I argued that by understanding the mechanisms that enable people to engage in knowledging, we can come to a more nuanced understanding of people's actual interactional practices that involve knowledging. As we found, knowledging was part of a variety of ways in which a group of transnational Indonesian strangers interactionally did togetherness in difference (Ang, 2003).

In discussing how these Indonesians did togetherness through talk, I focused on recent work on the idea of conviviality and its relationship to superdiversity (Blommaert, 2013; Williams & Stroud, 2013). I suggested that a more nuanced account of positive interpersonal relations could be had if we differentiated conviviality from the doing of togetherness in difference. The reason for adding a further set of terms is that although Williams and Stroud (2013) infer that conviviality relates to face-to-face interaction and longer-term social relations, the data they present is made up of fleeting moments and does not follow up on subsequent interaction. In line with scholarship on the need to follow interactions across time (Ochs, 1988; Wortham, 2006), using the concept of togetherness in difference is a way of terminologically recognizing the differences in the semiotic and temporal make-up of a fleeting moment versus a series of interactions.

The idea of community and the types of competences one needs to display and enact it were major focuses of chapter 8. I suggested that an ability to delineate different types of communities and the competences and communicative practices associated with them can provide a more nuanced approach to the study of talk in superdiverse settings where interactional alignment with many communities is the order of the day. We know that in situated interaction, people can not only display membership in a particular COP by using features indexically associated with that community (Antaki & Widdicombe, 1998), but the ongoing talk can also create a locally emergent COP (Goebel, 2010b; Wortham, 2006). In this book, I have also shown how publics (as another type of community) are inhabited and invoked in locally emergent COPs.

Criteria for membership in a public differ somewhat from criteria for membership in a COP and other interactionally constituted communities. In face-to-face interaction, for example, there will be a range of competences that can be involved, and these will be determined by membership in a particular COP. In a COP, sharing ways of speaking and the CC associated with them are primary indicators of membership, and they are typically developed in a specific locale among a stable and often small, isolated population. While there are often a limited number of members in a particular COP, publics typically have many more members. This is so because one-to-many participation frameworks help to circulate ways of speaking—albeit much more fragmented models—to many more people.

That so much of a person's language socialization involves schooling and the consumption of semiotic forms from television and radio programming, films, the Internet, and other forms of one-to-many participation frameworks invites us to reevaluate our understanding of CC (Goebel, 2013). Indeed, what is common for those thinking about CC is that these studies are typically carried out in small, geographically isolated communities. Many of the groundbreaking language socialization studies of the late 1970s and early 1980s (e.g., Ochs, 1988; Schieffelin, 1990) were often conducted in isolated communities and involved studying just a few novices involved in language socialization activities at any given moment (i.e., one-to-one or one-to-few participation frameworks). Those with the authority to model ways of speaking for these novices were also limited to older siblings, parents, elders, healers, and missionaries.

Although it may have been straightforward for the above-mentioned scholars to define a community, its members, and the competences that one needed to be seen as an authentic community member in these settings, an increasingly mobile and connected world has invited scholars to reexamine ideas of CC along with related ideas about community. A common theme in scholarship that engages with these ideas is the need to understand how histories of mobility figure in a person's ability to understand and use semiotic fragments of whole genres that are indexically associated with particular languages (e.g., Blommaert, Collins, & Slembrouck, 2005a; Blommaert, Collins, & Slembrouck, 2005b; Kramsch &

Whiteside, 2008; Warriner, 2010). While much of this work continued to focus on CC developed through participation in one-to-one or one-to-few participation frameworks, some work on "crossing" or "styling the other" pointed to how involvement in one-to-many participation frameworks could feed into performing ways of speaking typically associated with others (e.g., Cutler, 1999; Rampton, 1995; Rampton, 2006). For example, Rampton (2006) and Cutler (1999: 433–434) partly interpret their subjects' abilities to style the other with reference to their consumption of music and television. One point of departure in this book has been to highlight how some of the abilities associated with performances of crossing and styling the other might be incorporated into a definition of CC given the pervasiveness of one-to-many participation frameworks in social life.

For an Indonesianist audience, this book has been a story of continued change in the semiotic make-up of ethnicity and how emblems from these semiotic configurations are mobilized during everyday social practices. The idea of ethnicity and its links with semiotic forms has shown an ability to endure in the imagination and everyday activities of Indonesians. In chapters 2 and 4, I highlighted many gaps in what we know about multiple local instances of language evolution in Indonesia and thus provide areas for future research. At the same time, I pointed out that in some settings and under certain conditions, the idea of ethnicity can become associated with extreme difference and conflict, resulting in massive occurrences of population displacement and death in Indonesia. Even so, I hope that chapters 7 and 8 have shown that another unintended consequence of the circulation of ideas of ethnicity is the doing of togetherness or unity in diversity through knowledging.

While the study of togetherness talk is a hitherto road less traveled in studies of communal relations in Indonesia, nevertheless, what I offer here and elsewhere (Goebel, 2009, 2010a, 2010b) suggests some additional tools for the study of communal relations. For example, understanding how doing unity in diversity is represented in areas that have experienced extended and repeated occurrences of conflict (e.g., South Sulawesi, Maluku, Aceh, Central and West Kalimantan, and Papua) may provide further insights into social relations. Similarly, looking at whether, to what extent, and how members of communities in these post-conflict zones do togetherness through talk may provide insights into communal relations more generally, especially if viewed in relation to ideologies of ethnicity and interaction with the ethnic other.

Finally, while sociolinguistics has long been used to study politics elsewhere in the world, little of this type of work has been done in Indonesia (some notable exceptions being Errington, 1985, 1998a, 1998b, 2000, 2001; Kuipers, 1998). I thus wonder whether looking at the relationships between emblems of identity and orders of indexicality, and how these orders have been reconfigured in Indonesia might provide productive points of engagement with Indonesianists who are seeking new ways to understand political change in contemporary Indonesia (e.g., Aspinall, 2013; Ford & Pepinsky, 2013).

GLOSSARY

Adequation: The habitual pursuit of semiotic sameness in face-to-face interaction.

Centers of normativity: Participant constellations that form and reproduce rules for social interaction including language use. While these centers are emergent, their relationship and involvement with one-to-many participation frameworks (e.g., schools, media) determine whether and to what extent a center becomes more enduring.

Common ground: Knowledge about referents in interaction that is jointly established as either shared or not among a participant constellation.

Communicative competence: The ability to interactionally negotiate appropriate ways of interacting according to participant relations, topic, participant goals, emotional states, and so on.

Conviviality: The use of semiotic forms to establish and build positive social relations in encounters among strangers with different trajectories of socialization. Often this involves the cooperative seeking of common ground that is ultimately tied to the need to survive in a new environment.

Crossing: The practice of using linguistic forms or formulaic utterances typically not associated with the person using them. Crossing usually occurs as part of artful performances of identity or parodies of others during liminal moments, and it regularly attracts commentaries by ratified participants in the communicative event that involves crossing.

Enregisterment: The historical association of cultural value with particular semiotic features or social types.

Knowledging: The practice of recognizing and evaluating emblems of identity relating to the "other," whether ethnic, classed, gendered, etc. The ability to engage in knowledging is gained through participation in schooling, the consumption of media, and other one-to-many participation frameworks.

Massification: Increases in the circulation of knowledge about semiotic features in one-to-many participation frameworks that have some type of institutional authority.

Metasemiotic commentary: Commentaries about a range of multimodal signs rather than just linguistic ones.

New Order: The period between 1966 and 1998 when President Soeharto and his regime were in control of Indonesia.

Old Order: The period between 1945 and 1965 when President Soekarno and his regime were in control of Indonesia.

One-to-few participation framework: A constellation of people where there is one expert or model social type and a few novices or students.

One-to-many participation framework: A constellation of people where there is one expert or model social type and many novices.

Orders of indexicality: Hierarchical relationships between different semiotic registers with different emergent centers of normativity.

Polycentricity: Multiple centers of normativity.

Semiotic register: A group of semiotic features that have become tightly associated with each other over time to the extent that the occurrence of one feature can invoke other features. This term covers what is commonly referred to as "language" and "dialect," but also includes the indexical relationships that linguistic signs have with speakers, social practices, ideas about morality and epistemology, and so on.

Superdiversity: The condition that can be found throughout the world where multiple strangers from multiple backgrounds come into contact to pursue economic, spiritual, and social objectives. Because these strangers do not share trajectories of socialization and do not share the semiotic resources that are often referred to as a language, they use fragments of semiotic resources to pursue their goals. In doing so, they also develop new semiotic registers that are linked to new identities and norms, which contribute further to the diverse nature of a setting and enable further social distinction between those who are old-timers and those who are newcomers.

Transmigration: An Indonesian government-sponsored program whereby people from the islands of Java and Bali are relocated and settled in other areas of Indonesia.

Up-scaling: Increases in people and idea movement that are facilitated by the introduction of new communication or transportation technologies.

REFERENCES

À Campo, J. N. F. M. (2002). *Engines of empire: Steamshipping and state formation in colonial Indonesia.* Hilversum: Verloren.

Abas, H. (1987). *Indonesian as a unifying language of wider communication: A historical and sociolinguistic perspective.* Canberra: Pacific Linguistics.

Acciaioli, G. (2007). From customary law to indigenous sovereignty: Reconceptualizing *masyarakat adat* in contemporary Indonesia. In J. Davidson & D. Henley (Eds.), *The revival of tradition in Indonesian politics: The deployment of adat from colonialism to indigenism* (pp. 295–318). London: Routledge.

Adams, K. (1984). Come to Tana Toraja, "land of the heavenly kings": Travel agents as brokers in ethnicity. *Annals of Tourism Research, 11,* 469–485.

Agha, A. (2003). The social life of cultural value. *Language & Communication, 23*(3–4), 231–273.

Agha, A. (2007a). *Language and social relations.* Cambridge: Cambridge University Press.

Agha, A. (2007b). The object called "language" and the subject of linguistics. *Journal of English Linguistics, 35*(3), 217–235. doi: 10.1177/0075424207304240

Agha, A. (2011a). Commodity registers. *Journal of Linguistic Anthropology, 21*(1), 22–53.

Agha, A. (2011b). Meet mediatization. *Language & Communication, 31*(3), 163–170. doi: 10.1016/j.langcom.2011.03.006

Aitchison, J. (1996). *The language web: The power and problem of words.* Cambridge: Cambridge University Press.

Alesich, S. (2008). Dukun and bidan: The work of traditional and government midwives in Southeast Sulawesi. In M. Ford & L. Parker (Eds.), *Women and work in Indonesia* (pp. 61–81). London: Routledge.

Alisjahbana, S. T. (1975 [1961]). *Indonesia: social and cultural revolution.* Melbourne: Oxford University Press.

Alisjahbana, S. T. (1976). *Language planning for modernization: The case of Indonesian and Malaysian.* The Hague: Mouton and Co.

Alvarez-Cáccamo, C. (1998). From 'switching code' to code-switching. In P. Auer (Ed.), *Code-switching in conversation: Language, interaction and identity* (pp. 29–48). New York: Routledge.

Aman. (1971[1932]). *Si Doel anak djakarta* (8th ed.). Jakarta: Balai pustaka.

Anderson, B. (2006 [1991, 1983]). *Imagined communities: reflections on the origin and spread of nationalism* (revised ed.). London: Verso.

Androutsopoulos, J. (2007). Bilingualism in the mass media and on the internet. In M. Heller (Ed.), *Bilingualism: A social approach* (pp. 207–230). Basingstoke: Palgrave Macmillan.

Ang, I. (1996). *Living room wars: Rethinking media audiences for a postmodern world* London: Routledge.

Ang, I. (2003). Together-in-difference: Beyond diaspora into hybridity. *Asian Studies Review, 27,* 141–154.

Antaki, C., & Widdicombe, S. (Eds.). (1998). *Identities in talk*. London: Sage.

Antlov, H. (2003). Not enough politics! Power, participation and the new democratic polity in Indonesia. In E. Aspinall & G. Fealy (Eds.), *Local power and politics in Indonesia: Decentralisation and democratisation* (pp. 72–86). Singapore: Institute of Southeast Asian Studies.

Anwar, K. (1980). *Indonesian: The development and use of a national language*. Yogyakarta: Gadjah Mada University Press.

Appadurai, A. (1996). *Modernity at large: Cultural dimensions of globalization*. Minneapolis: University of Minnesota Press.

Aragon, L. (2008). Reconsidering displacement and internally displaced persons from Poso. In E.-L. Hedman (Ed.), *Conflict, violence, and displacement in Indonesia* (pp. 173–205). Ithaca: Cornell University Press.

Arnaut, K., & Spotti, M. (2014). Superdiversity discourse. Working Papers in Urban Language and Literacies. Paper 22 (Universiteit Gent, University at Albany, Tilburg University, King's College London).

Arps, B. (2010). Terwujudnya Bahasa Osing di Banyuwangi dan peranan media elektronik di dalamnya (selayang padang, 1970–2009). In M. Moriyama & M. Budiman (Eds.), *Geliat bahasa selaras zaman: Perubahan bahasa–bahasa di Indonesia pasca–Orde Baru* (pp. 225–248). Tokyo: Research Institute for Languages and Cultures of Asia and Africa, Tokyo University of Foreign Studies.

Aspinall, E. (2005). Politics: Elections and the end of the political transition. In B. Resosudarmo (Ed.), *The politics and economics of Indonesia's natural resources* (pp. 13–30). Singapore: ISEAS.

Aspinall, E. (2008). Place and displacement in the Aceh conflict. In E.-L. Hedman (Ed.), *Conflict, violence, and displacement in Indonesia* (pp. 119–146). Ithaca: Cornell University Press.

Aspinall, E. (2011). Democratization and ethnic politics in Indonesia: Nine theses. *Journal of East Asian Studies, 11*, 289–319.

Aspinall, E. (2013). A nation in fragments: Patronage and neoliberalism in contemporary Indonesia. *Critical Asian Studies, 45*(1), 27–54.

Aspinall, E., & Fealy, G. (2003). Introduction: Local power and politics in Indonesia: Decentralisation and democratisation. In E. Aspinall & G. Fealy (Eds.), *Local power and politics in Indonesia: Decentralisation and democratisation* (pp. 1–11). Singapore: Institute of Southeast Asian Studies.

Auer, P. (1995). The pragmatics of code-switching: A sequential approach. In L. Milroy & P. Muysken (Eds.), *One speaker, two languages: Cross-disciplinary perspectives on code-switching* (pp. 115–135). Cambridge: Cambridge University Press.

Auer, P. (Ed.). (2008). *Style and social identities*. Berlin: Mouton de Gruyter.

Bakhtin, M. (1981). *The dialogic imagination: Four essays* (C. Emerson & M. Holquist, Trans.). Austin: University of Texas Press.

Barker, J. (2008). Playing with publics: Technology, talk and sociability in Indonesia. *Language & Communication, 28*, 127–142.

Barkin, G. (2008). The foreignizing gaze: Producers, audiences, and symbols of the 'traditional.' In M. Hobart & R. Fox (Eds.), *Entertainment media in Indonesia* (pp. 1–19). London: Routledge.

Barth, F. (Ed.). (1969). *Ethnic groups and boundaries: The social organization of cultural difference*. Bergen: Universitets Forlaget.

Barton, D., & Tusting, K. (Eds.). (2005). *Beyond communities of practice: Language, power and social context*. Cambridge: Cambridge University Press.
Bauman, R., & Briggs, C. (1990). Poetics and performance as critical perspectives on language and social life. *Annual Review of Anthropology, 19*, 59–88.
Bauman, Z. (2001). *Community: Seeking safety in an insecure world*. Cambridge: Polity.
Bell, A., & Gibson, A. (2011). Staging language: An introduction to the sociolinguistics of performance. *Journal of Sociolinguistics, 15*(5), 555–572. doi: 10.1111/j.1467-9841.2011.00517.x
Berman, L. (1998). *Speaking through the silence: Narratives, social conventions, and power in Java*. New York: Oxford University Press.
Bertrand, J. (2003). Language policy in Indonesia: The promotion of a national language amidst ethnic diversity. In M. E. Brown & S. Ganguly (Eds.), *Fighting words: Language policy and ethnic relations in Asia* (pp. 263–290). Cambridge: MIT Press.
Biezeveld, R. (2007). The many roles of adat in West Sumatra. In J. Davidson & D. Henley (Eds.), *The revival of tradition in Indonesian politics: The deployment of adat from colonialism to indigenism* (pp. 203–223). London: Routledge.
Bjork-Willen, P. (2007). Participation in multilingual preschool play: Shadowing and crossing as interactional resources. *Journal of Pragmatics, 39*(12), 2133–2158.
Bjork, C. (2005). *Indonesian education: Teachers, schools, and central bureaucracy*. New York: Routledge.
Black, P., & Goebel, Z. (2002). Multiliteracies and the teaching of Indonesian. *Babel, 37*(1), 22–26, 38.
Black, P., & Goebel, Z. (2004). Nobody's a native speaker of everything: Teaching dialectal variety and code choice. *Kajian Sastra: Jurnal Bidang Kebahasaan, Kesusastraan dan Kebudayaan, 28*(1), 1–12.
Blommaert, J. (2005). *Discourse*. Cambridge: Cambridge University Press.
Blommaert, J. (2007). Sociolinguistics and discourse analysis: Orders of indexicality and polycentricity. *Journal of Multicultural Discourses, 2*(2), 115–130.
Blommaert, J. (2008). *Grassroots literacy: Writing, identity and voice in Central Africa*. Abingdon, Oxon: Routledge.
Blommaert, J. (2010). *The sociolinguistics of globalization*. Cambridge: Cambridge University Press.
Blommaert, J. (2012). Complexity, accent and conviviality: Concluding comments. *Tilburg Papers in Culture Studies, 26*, 1–14.
Blommaert, J. (2013a). Complexity, accent and conviviality: Concluding comments. *Applied Linguistics, 34*(6), 613–622.
Blommaert, J. (2013b). *Ethnography, superdiversity and linguistic landscapes: Chronicles of complexity*. Bristol: Multilingual Matters.
Blommaert, J., & Backus, A. (2011). Repertoires revisited: 'Knowing language' in superdiversity. *Working Papers in Urban Language and Literacies, 67*, 1–26.
Blommaert, J., Collins, J., & Slembrouck, S. (2005a). Polycentricity and interactional regimes in 'global neighborhoods.' *Ethnography, 6*(2), 205–235.
Blommaert, J., Collins, J., & Slembrouck, S. (2005b). Spaces of multilingualism. *Language & Communication, 25*(3), 197–216.
Blommaert, J., & Rampton, B. (2011). Language and superdiversity. *Diversities, 13*(2), 1–21.
Blommaert, J., & Varis, P. (2011). Enough is enough: The heuristics of authenticity in superdiversity. Working Papers in Urban Language and Literacies 76 (London, Albany, Gent, Tilburg) [Tilburg Papers in Culture Studies 2, Tilburg University].

Booth, A. (2000). The impact of the Indonesian crisis on welfare: What do we know two years on? In C. Manning & P. Van Diermen (Eds.), *Indonesia in transition: Social aspects of reformasi and crisis* (pp. 145–162). London: Zed Books.
Booth, A., & McCawley, P. (1981). The Indonesian economy since the mid-sixties. In A. Booth & P. McCawley (Eds.), *The Indonesian economy during the Soeharto era* (pp. 1–22). New York: Oxford University Press.
Bourchier, D. (2000). Habibie's interregnum: *Reformasi*, elections, regionalism and the struggle for power. In C. Manning & P. Van Diermen (Eds.), *Indonesia in transition: Social aspects of reformasi and crisis* (pp. 15–38). London: Zed Books.
Bourchier, D. (2007). The romance of adat in the Indonesian political imagination and the current revival. In J. Davidson & D. Henley (Eds.), *The revival of tradition in Indonesian politics: The deployment of adat from colonialism to indigenism* (pp. 113–129). London: Routledge.
Bourdieu, P. (1977). *Outline of a theory of practice*. Cambridge: Cambridge University Press.
Bourdieu, P. (1984). *Distinction: A social critique of the judgement of taste*. Cambridge: Harvard University Press.
Bourdieu, P. (1991). *Language and symbolic power*. Cambridge: Polity Press in association with Basil Blackwell.
Bouvier, H., & Smith, G. (2008). Spontaneity, conspiracy, and rumor: The politics of framing violence in Central Kalimantan. In E.-L. Hedman (Ed.), *Conflict, violence, and displacement in Indonesia* (pp. 231–248). Ithaca: Cornell University Press.
Boyd, R., & Richerson, P. (2006). Culture and the evolution of the human social instincts. In N. Enfield & S. Levinson (Eds.), *Roots of human sociality: Culture, cognition and interaction* (pp. 453–477). Oxford: Berg.
Brettell, C. (2003). *Anthropology and migration: Essays on transnationalism, ethnicity, and identity* Walnut Creek: Altamira Press.
Briggs, C. (2005). Communicability, racial discourse, and disease. *Annual Review of Anthropology, 34*(1), 269–291.
Bruner, E. (1959). The Toba Batak village. In W. Skinner (Ed.), *Local, ethnic, and national loyalties in village Indonesia: A symposium* (pp. 52–64). New Haven: Yale University Press.
Bruner, E. (1974). The expression of ethnicity in Indonesia. In A. Cohen (Ed.), *Urban ethnicity* (pp. 251–280). London: Tavistock.
Bucholtz, M. (2011). Race and the re-embodied voice in Hollywood film. *Language & Communication, 31*(3), 255–265.
Bucholtz, M., & Hall, K. (2004a). Language and identity. In A. Duranti (Ed.), *A companion to linguistic anthropology* (pp. 369–394). Oxford: Blackwell.
Bucholtz, M., & Hall, K. (2004b). Theorizing identity in language and sexuality research. *Language in Society, 33*(4), 469–515.
Bucholtz, M., & Hall, K. (2008). All of the above: New coalitions in sociocultural linguistics. *Journal of Sociolinguistics, 12*(4), 401–431.
Bucholtz, M., & Lopez, Q. (2011). Performing blackness, forming whiteness: Linguistic minstrelsy in Hollywood film. *Journal of Sociolinguistics, 15*(5), 680–706.
Bunnell, T., Yea, S., Peake, L., Skelton, T., & Smith, M. (2012). Geographies of friendships. *Progress in Human Geography, 36*(4), 490–507.
Bünte, M. (2009). Indonesia's protracted decentralization: Contested reforms and their unintended consequences. In M. Bunte & A. Ufen (Eds.), *Democratization in post-Suharto Indonesia* (pp. 102–123). London: Routledge.

Burns, P. (2004). *The Leiden legacy: Concepts of law in Indonesia*. Leiden: KITLV Press.
Bush, R. (2008). Regional sharia regulations in Indonesia: Anomaly or symptom? In G. Fealy & S. White (Eds.), *Expressing Islam: Religious life and politics in Indonesia* (pp. 174–191). Singapore: Institute of Southeast Asian Studies.
Carnegie, P. (2010). *The road from authoritarianism to democratization in Indonesia*. New York: Palgrave Macmillan.
Castells, M. (1996). *The rise of the network society*. Cambridge: Blackwell.
Chambers, J. (1998). TV makes people sound the same. In L. Bauer & P. Trudgill (Eds.), *Language myths* (pp. 123–131). London: Penguin.
Chauvel, R. (2001). The changing dynamics of regional resistance in Indonesia. In G. Lloyd & S. Smith (Eds.), *Indonesia today: Challenges of history* (pp. 146–160). Singapore: Institute of Southeast Asian Studies.
Chauvel, R. (2008). Refuge, displacement, and dispossession: Responses to Indonesian rule and conflict in Papua. In E.-L. Hedman (Ed.), *Conflict, violence, and displacement in Indonesia* (pp. 147–172). Ithaca: Cornell University Press.
Clarke, S., & Hiscock, P. (2009). Hip-hop in a post-insular community: Hybridity, local language, and authenticity in an online Newfoundland rap group. *Journal of English Linguistics, 37*(3), 241–261.
Cody, F. (2011). Echoes of the teashop in a Tamil newspaper. *Language & Communication, 31*(3), 243–254.
Cohen, M. (2006). *The Komedie Stamboel: Popular theater in colonial Indonesia, 1891–1903*. Athens: Ohio University Press.
Cole, D. (2010). Enregistering diversity: Adequation in Indonesian poetry performance. *Journal of Linguistic Anthropology, 20*(1), 1–21.
Collins, J., Noble, G., Poynting, S., & Tabar, P. (2000). *Kebabs, kids, cops and crime: Youth, ethnicity and crime*. Sydney: Pluto Press.
Colombijn, F. (1996). The development of the transport network in West Sumatra from pre-colonial times to the present. In J. Lindblad (Ed.), *Historical foundations of a national economy in Indonesia, 1890s–1990s* (pp. 385–400). Amsterdam: Koninklijke Nederlandse Akademie van Wetenschappen Verhandelingen.
Coppel, C. (1983). *Indonesian Chinese in crisis*. Oxford: Oxford University Press.
Coupland, J. (2003). Small talk: Social functions. *Research on Language & Social Interaction, 36*(1), 1–6.
Coupland, J. (Ed.). (2000). *Small talk*. London: Longman.
Creese, A., & Blackledge, A. (2011). Separate and flexible bilingualism in complementary schools: Multiple language practices in interrelationship. *Journal of Pragmatics, 43*(5), 1196–1208.
Cribb, R. (1990). Introduction: Problems in the historiography of the killings in Indonesia. In R. Cribb (Ed.), *The Indonesian killings of 1965–1966: Studies from Java and Bali* (pp. 1–43). Clayton, Victoria: Centre of Southeast Asian Studies, Monash University.
Cribb, R., & Ford, M. (2009a). Indonesia as an archipelago: Managing islands, managing the seas. In R. Cribb & M. Ford (Eds.), *Indonesia beyond the water's edge: Managing and archipelagic state* (pp. 1–27). Singapore: Institute of Southeast Asian Studies.
Cribb, R., & Ford, M. (Eds.). (2009b). *Indonesia beyond the water's edge: Managing and archipelagic state*. Singapore: Institute of Southeast Asian Studies.
Crouch, H. (1988). *The army and politics in Indonesia* (revised ed.). Ithaca: Cornell University Press.

Crouch, H. (2003). Political update 2002: Megawati's holding operation. In E. Aspinall & G. Fealy (Eds.), *Local power and politics in Indonesia: Decentralisation and democratisation* (pp. 15–34). Singapore: Institute of Southeast Asian Studies.

Cutler, C. (1999). Yorkville crossing: White teens, hip hop and African American English. *Journal of Sociolinguistics, 3*(4), 428–442. doi: 10.1111/1467-9481.00089

Dardjowidjojo, S. (1998). Strategies for a successful national language policy: The Indonesian case. *International Journal of the Sociology of Language, 130*, 35–47.

Davidson, J. (2008). Violence and displacement in West Kalimantan. In E.-L. Hedman (Ed.), *Conflict, violence, and displacement in Indonesia* (pp. 61–85). Ithaca: Cornell University Press.

Davidson, J., & Henley, D. (Eds.). (2007). *The revival of tradition in Indonesian politics: The deployment of adat from colonialism to indigenism*. London: Routledge.

Dawson, G. (1992). *Development planning for women in the Indonesian transmigration program*. Clayton: Monash Development Studies Centre, Monash University.

Dawson, G. (2008). Keeping rice in the pot: Women and work in a transmigration settlement. In M. Ford & L. Parker (Eds.), *Women and work in Indonesia* (pp. 41–60). London: Routledge.

Dayan, D. (2005). Mothers, midwives and abortionists: Genealogy, obstetrics, audiences and publics. In S. Livingstone (Ed.), *Audiences and publics: When cultural engagement matters for the public sphere* (pp. 43–76). Bristol: Intellect.

De Fina, A. (2003). *Identity in narrative: A study of immigrant discourse*. Amsterdam: John Benjamins.

de Jong, E. (2009). Reshaping Tana Toraja: A century of decentralization and power politics in the highlands of South Sulawesi. In C. Holtzappel & M. Ramstedt (Eds.), *Decentralization and regional autonomy in Indonesia: Implementation and challenges* (pp. 256–292). Singapore and Leiden: Institute of Southeast Asian Studies and International Institute for Asian Studies.

Departemen Pendidikan dan Kebudayaan. (1993). *Tata bahasa baku bahasa Indonesia [Standard Indonesian grammar]*. Jakarta: Balai Pustaka.

Dick, H. (1996). The emergence of a national economy, 1808–1990s. In J. Lindblad (Ed.), *Historical foundations of a national economy in Indonesia, 1890s–1990s* (pp. 21–51). Amsterdam: Koninklijke Nederlandse Akademie van Wetenschappen Verhandelingen.

Dick, H. (2002). Formation of the nation-state: 1930s–1966. In H. Dick (Ed.), *The emergence of a national economy: An economic history of Indonesia, 1800–2000* (pp. 153–193). Crows Nest: Allen & Unwin.

Direktorat Jenderal Pendidikan Tinngi. (2010a). Latar Belakang Beasiswa BPPS, SU.

Direktorat Jenderal Pendidikan Tinngi. (2010b). TOR Beasiswa LN. http://www.dikti.go.id/index.php?option=com_content&view=article&id=782

Eckert, P., & McConnell-Ginet, S. (1999). New generalizations and explanations in language and gender research. *Language in Society, 28*(2), 185–201.

Eisenlohr, P. (2009). Technologies of the spirit: Devotional Islam, sound reproduction and the dialectics of mediation and immediacy in Mauritius. *Anthropological Theory, 9*(3), 273–296.

Eisenlohr, P. (2010). Materialities of entextualization: The domestication of sound reproduction in Mauritian Muslim devotional practices. *Journal of Linguistic Anthropology, 20*(2), 314–333.

Ellis, A. (2002). The Indonesian constitutional transition: Conservatism or fundamental change? *Singapore Journal of International & Comparative Law*, 6, 1–37.
Elson, R. (2008). *The idea of Indonesia: A history.* Cambridge: Cambridge University Press.
Enfield, N. (2006). Social consequences of common ground. In N. Enfield & S. Levinson (Eds.), *Roots of human sociality: Culture, cognition and interaction* (pp. 399–430). Oxford: Berg.
Enfield, N. (2009). Relationship thinking and human pragmatics. *Journal of Pragmatics*, 41(1), 60–78.
Erb, M. (2007). Adat revivalism in Western Flores. In J. Davidson & D. Henley (Eds.), *The revival of tradition in Indonesian politics: The deployment of adat from colonialism to indigenism* (pp. 247–274). London: Routledge.
Errington, J. (1985). *Language and social change in Java: Linguistic reflexes of modernization in a traditional royal polity.* Athens: Ohio University Press.
Errington, J. (1998a). Indonesian('s) development: On the state of a language of state. In B. B. Schieffelin, K. A. Woolard & P. V. Kroskrity (Eds.), *Language ideologies: Practice and theory* (pp. 271–284). New York: Oxford University Press.
Errington, J. (1998b). *Shifting languages: Interaction and identity in Javanese Indonesia.* Cambridge: Cambridge University Press.
Errington, J. (2000). Indonesian('s) authority. In P. V. Kroskrity (Ed.), *Regimes of language: Ideologies, polities, and identities (advanced seminar series)* (pp. 205–227). Santa Fe: School of American Research.
Errington, J. (2001a). Colonial linguistics. *Annual Review of Anthropology*, 30, 19–39.
Errington, J. (2001b). State speech for peripheral publics in Java. In S. Gal & K. Woolard (Eds.), *Languages and publics: The making of authority* (pp. 103–118). Manchester: St. Jerome.
Fairclough, N. (1995). *Media discourse.* London: Arnold.
Fasseur, C. (1994). Cornerstone and stumbling block: Racial classification and the late colonial state in Indonesia. In R. Cribb (Ed.), *The late colonial state in Indonesia: Political and economic foundations of the Netherlands Indies 1880–1942* (pp. 31–56). Leiden: KITLV Press.
Feith, H. (1962). *The decline of constitutional democracy in Indonesia.* New York: Cornell University Press.
Florey, M. (1990). Language shift: Changing patterns of language allegiance in Western Seram, Ph.D. diss., University of Hawaii.
Ford, M. (2003). Who are the *Orang Riau*? Negotiating identity across geographic and ethnic divides. In E. Aspinall & G. Fealy (Eds.), *Local power and politics in Indonesia: Decentralisation and democratisation* (pp. 132–147). Singapore: Institute of Southeast Asian Studies.
Ford, M. (2004). A challenge for business? Developments in Indonesian trade unionism after Soeharto. In M. C. Basri & P. van der Eng (Eds.), *Business in Indonesia: New challenges, old problems* (pp. 221–233). Singapore: Institute of Southeast Asian Studies.
Ford, M. (2008). Indonesia: Separate organizing within unions. In K. Broadbent & M. Ford (Eds.), *Women and labour organizing in Asia: Diversity, autonomy and activism* (pp. 15–33). London: Routledge.
Ford, M., & Pepinsky, T. (2013). Beyond oligarchy? Critical exchanges on political power and material inequality in Indonesia. *Indonesia*, 96, 1–9.

Foucault, M. (1978). *The history of sexuality (Volume 1: An introduction)* (R. Hurley, Trans.). New York: Pantheon Books.

Foulcher, K. (1986). *Social commitment in literature and the arts: The Indonesian "Institute of People's Culture"1950–1965*. Melbourne: Centre of Southeast Asian Studies, Monash University.

Foulcher, K. (2000). Sumpah Pemuda: The making and meaning of a symbol of Indonesian nationhood. *Asian Studies Review, 24*(3), 377–410.

Fox, J., Adhuri, D., & Resosudarmo, I. A. P. (2005). Unfinished deifice or pandora's box? Decentralization and resource management in Indonesia. In B. Resosudarmo (Ed.), *The politics and economics of Indonesia's natural resources* (pp. 92–108). Singapore: ISEAS.

Franceschini, R. (1998). Code-switching and the notion of code in linguistics: Proposals for a dual focus model. In P. Auer (Ed.), *Code-switching in conversation: Language, interaction and identity* (pp. 51–72). New York: Routledge.

Francis, D., & Hester, S. (2004). *An invitation to ethnomethodology: Language, society and interaction*. London: Sage.

Gafaranga, J., & Torras, M.-C. (2002). Interactional otherness: Towards a redefinition of codeswitching. *The International Journal of Bilingualism, 6*(1), 1–22.

Garrett, P., & Bell, A. (1998). Media and discourse: A critical overview. In A. Bell & P. Garrett (Eds.), *Approaches to media discourse* (pp. 1–20). Oxford: Blackwell.

Geertz, C. (1959). The Javanese village. In W. Skinner (Ed.), *Local, ethnic, and national loyalties in village Indonesia: A symposium* (pp. 34–41). New Haven: Yale University Press.

Geertz, C. (1960). *The religion of Java*. Chicago: University of Chicago Press.

Geertz, H. (1959). The Balinese village. In W. Skinner (Ed.), *Local, ethnic, and national loyalties in village Indonesia: A symposium* (pp. 24–33). New Haven: Yale University Press.

Georgakopoulou, A. (2007). *Small stories, interaction and identities*. Amsterdam: John Benjamins.

Gershon, I. (2010). Media ideologies: An introduction. *Journal of Linguistic Anthropology, 20*(2), 283–293.

Giddens, A. (1984). *The constitution of society: Outline of the theory of structuration*. Berkeley: University of California Press.

Giddens, A. (1990). *The consequences of modernity*. Cambridge: Polity and Blackwell.

Ginsburg, F., Abu-Lughod, L., & Larkin, B. (2002). Introduction. In F. D. Ginsburg, L. Abu-Lughod & B. Larkin (Eds.), *Media worlds: Anthropology on new terrain* (pp. 1–36). Berkeley: University of California Press.

Goebel, Z. (2000). Communicative competence in Indonesian: Language choice in inter-ethnic interactions in Semarang, Ph.D. diss., Northern Territory University, Darwin.

Goebel, Z. (2002). When do Indonesians speak Indonesian? Some evidence from inter-ethnic and foreigner-Indonesian interactions and its pedagogic implications. *Journal of Multilingual and Multicultural Development, 23*(6), 479–489.

Goebel, Z. (2008). Enregistering, authorizing and denaturalizing identity in Indonesia. *Journal of Linguistic Anthropology, 18*(1), 46–61.

Goebel, Z. (2009a). Semiosis, interaction and ethnicity in urban Java. *Journal of Sociolinguistics, 13*(4), 499–523.

Goebel, Z. (2009b). Semiotic registers, televised signs and reflexivity: Ethnic personhood in Indonesia. Paper presented at the the American Anthropological Association's 108th Annual Meeting: The End/s of Anthropology, Philadelphia.

Goebel, Z. (2010a). Identity and social conduct in a transient multilingual setting. *Language in Society, 39*(2), 203–240.
Goebel, Z. (2010b). *Language, migration and identity: Neighborhood talk in Indonesia.* Cambridge: Cambridge University Press.
Goebel, Z. (2011a). Competence and communities: Investigating competence to comprehend using television. Paper presented at the Japanese Society for Language Sciences, Kansai University, Osaka.
Goebel, Z. (2011b). Enregistering identity in Indonesian television serials: A multimodal analysis. In K. O'Halloran & B. Smith (Eds.), *Multimodal studies: Exploring issues and domains* (pp. 95–114). London: Routledge.
Goebel, Z. (2011c). Talking about mediated representations: Exploring ideologies and meanings. *Text & Talk—An Interdisciplinary Journal of Language, Discourse & Communication Studies, 31*(3), 293–314.
Goebel, Z. (2012a). Enregisterment, communities, and authenticity: Watching Indonesian teledramas. *Journal of Linguistic Anthropology, 22*(2), 1–20.
Goebel, Z. (2012b). Indonesians doing togetherness in Japan. Paper presented at the American Association for Applied Linguistics Conference, Boston.
Goebel, Z. (2013). Competence to comprehend and knowledging. *Language & Communication. 33*(4), 366–375.
Goethals, P. (1959). The Sumbawan village. In W. Skinner (Ed.), *Local, ethnic, and national loyalties in village Indonesia: A symposium* (pp. 12–23). New Haven: Yale University Press.
Goffman, E. (1967). *Interaction ritual: Essays on face-to-face behavior.* New York: Anchor.
Goffman, E. (1971). *Relations in public: Microstudies of the public order.* New York: Basic Books.
Goffman, E. (1983). The interaction order. *American Sociological Review, 48*, 1–17.
Goodwin, C. (2006). Human sociality as mutual orientation in a rich interactive environment: Multimodal utterances and pointing in aphasia. In N. Enfield & S. Levinson (Eds.), *Roots of human sociality* (pp. 96–125). London: Berg.
Gumperz, J. (1982). *Discourse strategies.* Cambridge: Cambridge University Press.
Hall, S. (2006 [1980]). Encoding/decoding. In M. Durham & D. Kellner (Eds.), *Media and cultural studies: Key words* (pp. 163–173). Oxford: Blackwell.
Hanan, D. (1993). Nji Ronggeng: Another paradigm for erotic spectacle in the cinema. In V. Hooker (Ed.), *Culture and society in New Order Indonesia.* New York: Oxford University Press.
Hanks, W. (2006). Joint commitment and common ground in a ritual event. In N. Enfield & S. Levinson (Eds.), *Roots of human sociality: Culture, cognition and interaction* (pp. 299–328). Oxford: Berg.
Hardjono, J. M. (1977). *Transmigration in Indonesia.* Kuala Lumpur and London: Oxford University Press.
Harvey, D. (1989). *The condition of postmodernity: An enquiry into the origins of cultural change.* Oxford: Blackwell.
Haviland, J. B. (2004). Gesture. In A. Duranti (Ed.), *A companion to linguistic anthropology* (pp. 197–221). Oxford: Blackwell.
Hedman, E.-L. (2008a). Back to the barracks: *Relokasi pengungsi* in post-tsunami Aceh. In E.-L. Hedman (Ed.), *Conflict, violence, and displacement in Indonesia* (pp. 249–273). Ithaca: Cornell University Press.

Hedman, E.-L. (2008b). Introduction: Dynamics of displacement in Indonesia. In E.-L. Hedman (Ed.), *Conflict, violence, and displacement in Indonesia* (pp. 3–28). Ithaca: Cornell University Press.

Hefner, R. W. (2001). Introduction: Multiculturalism and citizenship in Malaysia, Singapore, and Indonesia. In R. W. Hefner (Ed.), *The politics of multiculturalism: Pluralism and citizenship in Malaysia, Singapore, and Indonesia* (pp. 1–58). Honolulu: University of Hawaii Press.

Heller, M. (2007). Bilingualism as ideology and practice. In M. Heller (Ed.), *Bilingualism: A social approach* (pp. 1–22). Basingstoke: Palgrave Macmillan.

Heller, M. (2011). *Paths to post-nationalism: A critical ethnogaphy of language and identity*. New York: Oxford University Press.

Henley, D., & Davidson, J. (2007). Introduction: Radical conservatism—the protean politics of adat. In J. Davidson & D. Henley (Eds.), *The revival of tradition in Indonesian politics: The deployment of adat from colonialism to indigenism* (pp. 1–49). London: Routledge.

Herriman, N. (2010). The great rumor mill: Gossip, mass media, and the ninja fear. *Journal of Asian Studies, 69*(3), 723–748.

Heryanto, A. (2007). Then there were languages: Bahasa Indonesia was one among many. In S. Makoni & A. Pennycook (Eds.), *Disinventing and reconstituting languages* (pp. 42–61). Clevedon: Multilingual Matters.

Heryanto, A. (2008). Pop culture and competing identities. In A. Heryanto (Ed.), *Popular culture in Indonesia: Fluid identities in post-authoritarian politics* (pp. 1–36). London: Routledge.

Hill, D., & Sen, K. (2005). *The Internet in Indonesia's new democracy*. London: Routledge.

Hill, J. (1995). The voices of Don Gabriel: Responsibility and self in a modern Mexicano narrative. In D. Tedlock & B. Mannheim (Eds.), *The dialogic emergence of culture* (pp. 97–147). Urbana: University of Illinois Press.

Hoey, B. A. (2003). Nationalism in Indonesia: Building imagined and intentional communities through transmigration. *Ethnology, 42*(2), 109–126.

Holmes, J., & Meyerhoff, M. (1999). The community of practice: Theories and methodologies in language and gender research. *Language in Society, 28*(2), 173–183.

Holt, E., & Clift, R. (2007). *Reported talk: Reporting speech in interaction*. Cambridge: Cambridge University Press.

Hooker, V. (Ed.). (1993). *Culture and society in New Order Indonesia*. Kuala Lumpur: Oxford University Press.

Hoon, C.-y. (2006). Assimilation, multiculturalism, hybridity: The dilemmas of the ethnic Chinese in post-Suharto Indonesia. *Asian Ethnicity, 7*(2), 149–166.

Hoshour, C. A. (1997). Resettlement and the politicization of ethnicity in Indonesia. *Bijdragen tot de Taal, Land-en Volkenkund, 153*(4), 557–576.

Hymes, D. (1972a). Models of the interaction of language and social life. In J. Gumperz & D. Hymes (Eds.), *Directions in sociolinguistics: The ethnography of communication* (pp. 35–71). New York: Holt, Rinehart, & Winston.

Hymes, D. (1972b). On communicative competence. In J. B. Pride & J. Holmes (Eds.), *Sociolinguistics: Selected readings* (pp. 269–293). Harmondsworth: Penguin Books.

Hymes, D. (1974). *Foundations in sociolinguistics: An ethnographic approach*. Philadelphia: University of Pennsylvania Press.

Hymes, D. (1996). *Ethnography, linguistics, narrative inequality: Toward an understanding of voice*. Washington, DC: Taylor & Francis.
Ikhsan, M. (2003). Economic update 2002: Struggling to maintain momentum. In E. Aspinall & G. Fealy (Eds.), *Local power and politics in Indonesia: Decentralisation and democratisation* (pp. 35–62). Singapore: Institute of Southeast Asian Studies.
Inoue, M. (2006). *Vicarious language: Gender and linguistic modernity in Japan*. Berkeley: University of California Press.
Inoue, M. (2011). Stenography and ventriloquism in late nineteenth century Japan. *Language & Communication, 31*(3), 181–190.
Inoue, T. (1986). Rural mobilization in East Sumatra. In A. Reid, O. Akira, J. Brewster & J. Carruthers (Eds.), *The Japanese experience in Indonesia: Selected memoirs of 1942–1945* (pp. 191–216). Athens: Ohio University Center for International Studies, Center for Southeast Asian Studies.
Irvine, J. (2001). "Style" as distinctiveness: The culture and ideology of linguistic differentiation. In P. Eckert & J. Rickford (Eds.), *Style and sociolinguistic variation* (pp. 21–43). Cambridge: Cambridge University Press.
Irvine, J. (2005). Knots and tears in the interdiscursive fabric. *Journal of Linguistic Anthropology, 15*(1), 72–80.
Jaffe, A. (2000). Comic performance and the articulation of hybrid identity. *Pragmatics, 10*(1), 39–59.
Jaffe, A. (2003). "Imagined competence": Classroom evaluation, collective identity, and linguistic identity in a Corsican bilingual classroom. In S. Wortham & B. Rymes (Eds.), *Linguistic anthropology of education* (pp. 151–184). Westport: Praeger.
Jaworski, A., Coupland, N., & Galasiński, D. (Eds.). (2004). *Metalanguage: Social and ideological perspectives*. Berlin: Mouton, Walter de Gruyter.
Jaworski, A., Thurlow, C., Lawson, S., & Yälnne-McEwen, V. (2003). The uses and representations of local languages in tourist destinations: A view from British TV holiday programs. *Language Awareness, 12*(1), 5–29.
Johnson, S., & Ensslin, A. (2007a). Language in the media: Theory and practice. In S. Johnson & A. Ensslin (Eds.), *Language in the media* (pp. 3–22). London: Continuum.
Johnson, S., & Ensslin, A. (Eds.). (2007b). *Language in the media*. London: Continuum.
Johnson, S., & Milani, T. (Eds.). (2010). *Language ideologies and media discourse: Texts, practices, politics*. New York: Continuum.
Johnstone, B. (2011). Dialect enregisterment in performance. *Journal of Sociolinguistics, 15*(5), 657–679.
Johnstone, B., Andrus, J., & Danielson, A. (2006). Mobility, indexicality, and the enregisterment of "Pittsburghese." *Journal of English Linguistics, 34*(2), 77–104.
Jones, G., & Hull, T. (1997). Introduction. In G. Jones & T. Hull (Eds.), *Indonesia assessment: Population and human resources* (pp. 1–15). Singapore and Canberra: Institute of Southeast Asian Studies, NUS; and Research School of Pacific and Asian Studies, ANU.
Jones, S. (2004). Political update 2003: Terrorism, nationalism and disillusionment with reform. In M. C. Basri & P. van der Eng (Eds.), *Business in Indonesia: New challenges, old problems* (pp. 23–38). Singapore: Institute of Southeast Asian Studies.
Jørgensen, J. N., Karrebæk, M. S., Madsen, L. M., & Møller, J. S. (2011). Polylanguaging in superdiversity. *Diversities, 13*(2), 22–37.
Jukes, A. (2010). Someone else's job: Externalizing responsibility for language maintenance. Paper presented at the fourteenth foundation for endangered language

conference: Reversing language shift: How to re-awaken a language tradition, September 13–15, Carmathan, Wales.
Kahin, G. (1970 [1952]). *Nationalism and revolution in Indonesia*. Ithaca: Cornell University Press.
Karno, R. (1998). *Si Doel anak sekolah*. Jakarta: Karnog Film.
Katoppo, A. (2000). The role of community groups in the environment movement. In C. Manning & P. Van Diermen (Eds.), *Indonesia in transition: Social aspects of reformasi and crisis* (pp. 213–219). London: Zed Books.
Kelly-Holmes, H., & Atkinson, D. (2007). 'When Hector met Tom Cruise': Attitudes to Irish in a radio satire. In S. Johnson & A. Ensslin (Eds.), *Language in the media* (pp. 173–187). London: Continuum.
Kendon, A. (1985). Some uses of gesture. In D. Tannen & M. Saville-Troike (Eds.), *Perspectives on silence* (pp. 215–314). New York: Ablex.
King, R., & Wicks, J. (2009). "Aren't we proud of our language?": Authenticity, commodification, and the Nissan Bonavista television commercial. *Journal of English Linguistics, 37*(3), 262–283.
Kitley, P. (2000). *Television, nation, and culture in Indonesia*. Athens: Ohio University Press.
Kitley, P. (2001). After the bans: Modelling Indonesian communications for the future. In G. Lloyd & S. Smith (Eds.), *Indonesia today: Challenges of history* (pp. 256–269). Singapore: Institute of Southeast Asian Studies.
Kramsch, C. (2006). From communicative competence to symbolic competence. *Modern Language Journal, 90*(2), 249–252.
Kramsch, C., & Whiteside, A. (2008). Language ecology in multilingual settings: Towards a theory of symbolic competence. *Applied Linguistics, 29*(4), 645–671. doi: 10.1093/applin/amn022
Kress, G., & Van Leeuwen, T. (2001). *Multimodal discourse: The modes and media of contemporary communication* London: Hodder Education.
Kuipers, J. (1998). *Language, identity and marginality in Indonesia: The changing nature of ritual speech on the island of Sumba*. Cambridge: Cambridge University Press.
Kulick, D., & Willson, M. (2004 [1994]). Rambo's wife saves the day: Subjugating the gaze and subverting the narrative in a Papua New Guinea swamp. In K. Askew & R. Wilk (Eds.), *The anthropology of the media: A reader* (pp. 270–285). Oxford: Blackwell.
Kurniasih, Y. K. (2007). Local content curriculum 1994: The teaching of Javanese in Yogyakarta schools. Paper presented at the First International Symposium on the Languages of Java (ISLOJ), August 15–16, Graha Santika Hotel, Semarang.
Kusumaatmadja, S. (2000). Through the crisis and beyond: The evolution of the environment movement. In C. Manning & P. Van Diermen (Eds.), *Indonesia in transition: Social aspects of reformasi and crisis* (pp. 205–212). London: Zed Books.
Labov, W. (1972). *Sociolinguistic patterns*. Oxford: Basil Blackwell.
Labov, W. (2001). *Principles of linguistic change, vol. 2: Social factors*. Oxford: Blackwell.
Lambert, W. E. (1986 [1967]). A social psychology of bilingualism. In J. Holmes (Ed.), *Sociolinguistics: Selected readings* (pp. 336–349). Harmondsworth: Penguin Books.
Le Compte, M., & Schensul, J. (1999). *Designing and conducting ethnographic research*. New York: Altamira Press.
Legge, J. (1961). *Central authority and regional autonomy in Indonesia: A study in local administration, 1950–1960*. Ithaca: Cornell University Press.

Lenhart, L. (1997). *Orang Suku Laut* ethnicity and acculturation. *Bijdragen tot de Taal, Land-en Volkenkund, 153*(4), 577–604.

Le Page, R. B., & Tabouret-Keller, A. (1985). *Acts of identity: Creole-based approaches to language and ethnicity*. Cambridge: Cambridge University Press.

Levinson, S. (2006). On the human "interaction engine." In N. Enfield & S. Levinson (Eds.), *Roots of human sociality: Culture, cognition and interaction* (pp. 39–69). Oxford: Berg.

Li, T. (2007). Adat in Central Sulawesi: Contemporary deployments. In J. Davidson & D. Henley (Eds.), *The revival of tradition in Indonesian politics: The deployment of adat from colonialism to indigenism* (pp. 337–370). London: Routledge.

Liddicoat, A. (2007). *An introduction to conversation analysis*. London: Continuum.

Liddle, R. W. (1972). Ethnicity and political organization: Three East Sumatran cases. In C. Holt (Ed.), *Culture and politics in Indonesia* (pp. 126–178). Ithaca: Cornell University Press.

Liebes, T., & Katz, E. (1990). *The export of meaning: Cross-cultural readings of Dallas*. New York: Oxford University Press.

Lindsey, T. (2001). The criminal state: *Premanisme* and the new Indonesia. In G. Lloyd & S. Smith (Eds.), *Indonesia today: Challenges of history* (pp. 283–297). Singapore: Institute of Southeast Asian Studies.

Liszkowski, U. (2006). Infant pointing at 12 months: Communicative goals, motives, and social-cognitive abilities. In N. Enfield & S. Levinson (Eds.), *Roots of human sociality: Culture, cognition and interaction* (pp. 153–178). Oxford: Berg.

Livingstone, S. (2005). On the relation between audiences and publics. In S. Livingstone (Ed.), *Audiences and publics: When cultural engagement matters for the public sphere* (pp. 17–41). Bristol: Intellect.

Loven, K. (2008). *Watching Si Doel: Television, language, and cultural identity in contemporary Indonesia*. Leiden: KITLV Press.

Lowenberg, P. (1990). Language and identity in the Asian state: The case of Indonesia. *Georgetown Journal of Languages and Linguistics, 1*(1), 109–120.

Lowenberg, P. (1992). Language policy and language identity in Indonesia. *Journal of Asian Pacific Communication, 3*(1), 59–77.

Malinowski, B. (1996 [1922]). The essentials of the Kula. In R. J. McGee & R. L. Warms (Eds.), *Anthropological theory: An introductory history* (pp. 157–172). Mountain View: Mayfield.

Malley, M. (2003). New rules, old structures and the limits of democratic decentralisation. In E. Aspinall & G. Fealy (Eds.), *Local power and politics in Indonesia: Decentralisation and democratisation* (pp. 102–118). Singapore: Institute of Southeast Asian Studies.

Mauss, M. (1966 [1925]). *The gift: Forms and functions of exchange in archaic societies* (I. Cunnison, Trans.). London: Cohen and West Ltd.

McCarthy, M. (2003). Talking back: "Small" interactional response tokens in everyday conversation. *Research on Language & Social Interaction, 36*(1), 33–63.

McCawley, P. (1981). The growth of the industrial sector. In A. Booth & P. McCawley (Eds.), *The Indonesian economy during the Soeharto era* (pp. 62–101). New York: Oxford University Press.

McGibbon, R. (2003). Between rights and repression: The politics of special autonomy in papua. In E. Aspinall & G. Fealy (Eds.), *Local power and politics in*

Indonesia: Decentralisation and democratisation (pp. 194–216). Singapore: Institute of Southeast Asian Studies.

Meek, B. A. (2006). And the Injun goes "How!": Representations of American Indian English in white public space. *Language in Society, 35*(1), 93–128.

Mendoza-Denton, N. (2011). The semiotic hitchhiker's guide to creaky voice: Circulation and gendered hardcore in a Chicana/o gang persona. *Journal of Linguistic Anthropology, 21*(2), 261–280.

Mietzner, M. (1999). From Soeharto to Habibie: The Indonesian armed forces and political Islam during the transition. In G. Forrester (Ed.), *Post-Soeharto Indonesia: Renewal or chaos?* (pp. 65–104). Bathurst: Crawford House.

Mietzner, M. (2001). Abdurrahman's Indonesia: Political conflict and institutional crisis. In G. Lloyd & S. Smith (Eds.), *Indonesia today: Challenges of history* (pp. 29–44). Singapore: Institute of Southeast Asian Studies.

Mietzner, M. (2009). Indonesia and the pitfalls of low-quality democracy: A case study of the gubernatorial elections in North Sulawesi. In M. Bunte & A. Ufen (Eds.), *Democratization in post-Suharto Indonesia* (pp. 124–149). London: Routledge.

Miles, D. (1976). *Cutlass and crescent moon: A case study of social and political change in outer Indonesia*. Sydney: Centre for Asian Studies, University of Sydney.

Miller, L. (2004). Those naughty teenage girls: Japanese kogals, slang, and media assessments. *Journal of Linguistic Anthropology, 14*(2), 225–247.

Min, S. S. (2006). 'Eventing' the May 1998 affair: Problematic representations of violence in contemporary indonesia. In C. Coppel (Ed.), *Violent conflicts in Indonesia: Analysis, representation, resolution* (pp. 39–57). Abingdon, Oxon: Routledge.

Moeliono, A. M. (1986). *Language development and cultivation: Alternative approaches in language planning*. Canberra: Pacific Linguistics.

Moerman, M. (1988). *Talking culture: Ethnography and conversation analysis*. Philadelphia: University of Pennsylvania Press.

Moriyama, M. (2005a). Language change and regional literature after Soeharto. Paper presented at the Indonesia Culture Workshop: Arts culture and political and social change since Soeharto, School of Asian Languages and Studies, University of Tasmania, Launceston.

Moriyama, M. (2005b). *Sundanese print culture and modernity in nineteenth-century West Java*. Singapore: National University of Singapore Press.

Moriyama, M. (2012). Regional languages and decentralization in post-New Order Indonesia: The case of Sundanese. In K. Foulcher, M. Moriyama & M. Budiman (Eds.), *Words in motion: Language and discourse in post-New Order Indonesia* (pp. 82–100). Tokyo: Research Institute for Languages and Cultures of Asia and Africa, Tokyo University of Foreign Studies.

Morley, D. (1986). *Family television: Cultural power and domestic leisure*. London: Comedia/Routledge.

Moyer, M. (2011). What multilingualism? Agency and unintended consequences of multilingual practices in a Barcelona health clinic. *Journal of Pragmatics, 43*(5), 1209–1221. doi: 10.1016/j.pragma.2010.08.024

Mrázek, R. (2002). *Engineers of happy land: Technology and nationalism in a colony*. Princeton: Princeton University Press.

Muhidin, S. (2002). *The population of Indonesia: Regional demographic scenarios using a multiregional method and multiple data sources*. Amsterdam: Rozenberg Publishers.

Nababan, P. W. J. (1985). Bilingualism in Indonesia: Ethnic language maintenance and the spread of the national language. *Southeast Asian Journal of Social Science, 13*(1), 1–18.

Nababan, P. W. J. (1991). Language in education: The case of Indonesia. *International Review of Education, 37*(1), 113–131.

Norris, S. (2004). *Analyzing multimodal interaction: A methodological framework.* London: Routledge.

Ochs, E. (1988). *Culture and language development: Language acquisition and language socialization in a Samoan village.* Cambridge: Cambridge University Press.

Ochs, E. (2006 [1979]). Transcription as theory. In A. Jaworski & N. Coupland (Eds.), *The discourse reader.* London: Routledge.

Okada, F. (1986). Dotō no naka no koshū. In A. Reid, O. Akira, J. Brewster & J. Carruthers (Eds.), *The Japanese experience in Indonesia: Selected memoirs of 1942–1945* (pp. 129–158). Athens: Ohio University Center for International Studies, Center for Southeast Asian Studies.

Otsuka, T. (1986). Sumatora jōkyū gakkō no kotodomo. In A. Reid, O. Akira, J. Brewster & J. Carruthers (Eds.), *The Japanese experience in Indonesia: selected memoirs of 1942–1945* (pp. 1–5). Athens: Ohio University Center for International Studies, Center for Southeast Asian Studies.

Palmer, A. (1959). The Sundanese village. In W. Skinner (Ed.), *Local, ethnic, and national loyalties in village Indonesia: A symposium* (pp. 42–51). New Haven: Yale University Press.

Parker, L. (2002). The subjectification of citizenship: Student interpretations of school teachings in Bali. *Asian Studies Review, 26*(1), 3–37.

Petet, H. D. (1996). *Si Kabayan.* Jakarta: SCTV television studio.

Philips, S. U. (1983). *The invisible culture: Communication in classroom and community on the Warm Springs Indian reservation.* New York: Longman.

Poedjosoedarmo, S. (1982). *Javanese influence on Indonesian.* Canberra: Pacific Linguistics.

Poynting, S., Noble, G., Tabar, P., & Collins, J. (2004). *Bin Laden in the suburbs: Criminalising the Arab other.* Sydney: Institute of Criminology.

Prastowo, J., & Suyono, E. A. (Eds.). (2007). *Kuliah kerja nyata: Pembelajaran pemberdyaan masyarakat (KKN PPM) perguruan tinggi di Indonesia.* Jakarta: Direktorat jenderal pendidikan tinggi departemen pendidikan nasional.

Purdey, J. (2006). *Anti-Chinese violence in Indonesia, 1996–1999* Singapore: National University of Singapore Press.

Putnam, R. D. (2000). *Bowling alone.* New York: Simon and Schuster.

Quinn, G. (1992). *The novel in Javanese.* Leiden: KITLV Press.

Quinn, G. (2003). Coming apart and staying together at the centre: Debates over provincial status in Java and Madura. In E. Aspinall & G. Fealy (Eds.), *Local power and politics in Indonesia: Decentralisation and democratisation* (pp. 164–178). Singapore: Institute of Southeast Asian Studies.

Quinn, G. (2012). Emerging from dire straits: Post-New Order developments in Javanese language and literature. In K. Foulcher, M. Moriyama & M. Budiman (Eds.), *Words in motion: Language and discourse in post-New Order Indonesia* (pp. 65–81). Tokyo: Research Institute for Languages and Cultures of Asia and Africa, Tokyo University of Foreign Studies.

Rachmah, I. (2006). Watching Indonesian sinetron: Imagining communities around the television, Ph.D. diss., Curtain University, Perth.
Rachmah, I. (2008). Consuming Taiwanese boys culture: Watching *Meteor Garden* with urban *Kampung* women in Indonesia. In A. Heryanto (Ed.), *Popular Culture in Indonesia: Fluid Identities in post-authoritarian politics* (pp. 93–110). London: Routledge.
Rampton, B. (1995). *Crossing: Language and ethnicity among adolescents*. London: Longman.
Rampton, B. (1999). Styling the other: Introduction. *Journal of Sociolinguistics, 3*(4), 421–427.
Rampton, B. (2006). *Language in late modernity: Interaction in an urban school*. Cambridge: Cambridge University Press.
Rampton, B. (2011). From 'multi-ethnic adolescent heteroglossia' to 'contemporary urban vernaculars.' *Language & Communication, 31*(4), 276–294.
Ramstedt, M. (2009). Regional autonomy and its discontents: The case of post-New Order Bali. In C. Holtzappel & M. Ramstedt (Eds.), *Decentralization and regional autonomy in Indonesia: Implementation and challenges* (pp. 329–379). Singapore and Leiden: Institute of Southeast Asian Studies and International Institute for Asian Studies.
Reid, A. (1988). *Southeast Asia in the age of commerce, 1450–1680*. New Haven: Yale University Press.
Reid, A., & Akira, O. (1986). Introduction. In A. Reid, O. Akira, J. Brewster & J. Carruthers (Eds.), *The Japanese experience in Indonesia: Selected memoirs of 1942–1945* (pp. 1–5). Athens: Ohio University Press.
Resosudarmo, B. (2005). Introduction. In B. Resosudarmo (Ed.), *The politics and economics of Indonesia's natural resources* (pp. 1–9). Singapore: ISEAS.
Richardson, K. (1998). Signs and wonders: Interpreting the economy through television. In A. Bell & P. Garrett (Eds.), *Approaches to media discourse* (pp. 220–250). Oxford: Blackwell.
Richardson, K. (2010). *Television dramatic dialogue: A sociolinguistic study*. New York: Oxford University Press.
Ricklefs, M. C. (1981). *A history of modern Indonesia since c.1300*. Basingstoke: Macmillan.
Rinakit, S. (2005). *The Indonesian military after the New Order/Sukardi Rinakit*. Copenhagen and Singapore: NIAS and ISEAS.
Robinson, G. (2008). People power: A comparative history of forced displacement in East Timor. In E.-L. Hedman (Ed.), *Conflict, violence, and displacement in Indonesia* (pp. 87–118). Ithaca: Cornell University Press.
Roesli, M. (1965 [1922]). *Sitti Nurbaja: Kasih tak sampai* (11th ed.). Jakarta: Balai Pustaka.
Ryoo, H.-K. (2005). Achieving friendly interactions: A study of service encounters between Korean shopkeepers and African-American customers. *Discourse and Society, 16*(1), 79–105.
Sakai, M. (2003). The privatisation of Padang Cement: Regional identity and economic hegemony in the new era of decentralisation. In E. Aspinall & G. Fealy (Eds.), *Local power and politics in Indonesia: Decentralisation and democratisation* (pp. 148–163). Singapore: Institute of Southeast Asian Studies.

Sangkoyo, H. (1999). Limits to order: The internal logic of instability in the post-Soeharto era. In G. Forrester (Ed.), *Post-Soeharto Indonesia: Renewal or chaos?* (pp. 170–180). Bathurst: Crawford House.
Schefold, R. (1998). The domestication of culture: Nation-building and ethnic diversity in Indonesia. *Bijdragen tot de Taal, Land-en Volkenkund, 154*(2), 259–280.
Schegloff, E. A. (1991). Reflections on talk and social structure. In D. Boden & D. Zimmerman (Eds.), *Talk and social structure: Studies in ethnomethodology and conversation analysis* (pp. 44–70). Cambridge: Polity.
Schieffelin, B. (1990). *The give and take of everyday life: Language socialization of Kaluli children*. Cambridge: Cambridge University Press.
Scollon, R., & Scollon, S. W. (2003). *Discourses in place: Language in the material world*. London: Routledge.
Sen, K., & Hill, D. T. (2000). *Media, culture and politics in Indonesia*. Oxford: Oxford University Press.
Shibata, Y. (1986). Shibata shirei chōkan no shuki. In A. Reid, O. Akira, J. Brewster & J. Carruthers (Eds.), *The Japanese experience in Indonesia: Selected memoirs of 1942–1945* (pp. 278–287). Athens: Ohio University Press.
Shigetada, N. (1986). Shōgen: Indoneshia dokuritsu kakumei—aru kakumeika no hanshō. In A. Reid, O. Akira, J. Brewster & J. Carruthers (Eds.), *The Japanese experience in Indonesia: Selected memoirs of 1942–1945* (pp. 254–275). Athens: Ohio University Press.
Shizuo, M. (1986). Jawa Shūsen Shoriki. In A. Reid, O. Akira, J. Brewster & J. Carruthers (Eds.), *The Japanese experience in Indonesia: Selected memoirs of 1942–1945* (pp. 219–250). Athens: Ohio University Press.
Shunkichiro, M. (1986). Jawa senryō gunsei kaikoroku. In A. Reid, O. Akira, J. Brewster & J. Carruthers (Eds.), *The Japanese experience in Indonesia: Selected memoirs of 1942–1945* (pp. 114–125). Athens: Ohio University Press.
Sidel, J. (2008). The manifold meanings of displacement: Explaining inter-religious violence, 1999–2001. In E.-L. Hedman (Ed.), *Conflict, violence, and displacement in Indonesia* (pp. 29–59). Ithaca: Cornell University Press.
Silverstein, M. (2003). Indexical order and the dialectics of sociolinguistic life. *Language & Communication, 23*, 193–229.
Silverstein, M., & Urban, G. (Eds.). (1996). *Natural histories of discourse*. Chicago: University of Chicago Press.
Silvey, R. (2004). Gender, socio-spatial networks, and rural non-farm work among migrants in West Java. In T. Leinbach (Ed.), *The Indonesian rural economy: Mobility, work and enterprise* (pp. 134–151). Singapore: Institute of Southeast Asian Studies.
Skinner, W. (1959). The nature of loyalties in rural Indonesia. In W. Skinner (Ed.), *Local, ethnic, and national loyalties in village Indonesia: A symposium* (pp. 1–11). New Haven: Yale University Press.
Smets, P. (2005). Living apart or together?: Multiculturalism at a neighbourhood level. *Community Development Journal, 41*(3), 293–306.
Sneddon, J. (2003). *The Indonesian language: Its history and role in modern society*. Sydney: University of New South Wales Press.
Soedijarto, Moleong, L., Suryadi, A., Machmud, D., Pangemanan, F., Tangyong, A., & Thomas, R. M. (1980). Indonesia. In T. N. Postlethwaite & R. M. Thomas (Eds.),

Schooling in the ASEAN region: Primary and secondary education in Indonesia, Malaysia, the Philippines, Singapore and Thailand (pp. 48–96). Oxford: Pergamon.

Spitulnik, D. (1996). The social circulation of media discourse and the mediation of communities. *Journal of Linguistic Anthropology, 6*(2), 161–187.

Stevens, R., & Hall, R. (1998). Disciplined perception: Learning to see in technoscience. In M. Lampert & M. Blunk (Eds.), *Talking mathematics in school: Studies of teaching and learning* (pp. 107–149). Cambridge: Cambridge University Press.

Stoler, A. L. (1995a). *Capitalism and confrontation in Sumatra's plantation belt, 1870–1979* (2nd ed., with a new preface). Ann Arbor: University of Michigan Press.

Stoler, A. L. (1995b). *Race and the education of desire: Foucult's history of sexuality and the colonial order of things* (2nd ed., with a new preface). Durham: Duke University Press.

Strachle, C. (1993). "Samuel?" "Yes, Dear?": Teasing and conversational rapport. In D. Tannen (Ed.), *Framing in discourse* (pp. 210–230). New York: Oxford University Press.

Stuart-Smith, J. (2006). The influence of media on language. In C. Llamas, P. Stockwell & L. Mullany (Eds.), *Routledge companion to sociolinguistics* (pp. 140–148). London: Routledge.

Stuart-Smith, J., Timmins, C., Pryce, G., & Gunter, B. (n.d.). Accent change: Is television a contributory factor in accent change in adolescents? *Report: Economic and social research council award R000239757*. Retrieved June 30, 2011.

Sudarkam, M. (2014). The decentralization of schooling in Palu, Central Sulawesi, Indonesia, Ph.D. diss., Department of Asian Studies, La Trobe University, Melbourne.

Suharsono, & Speare, A. (1981). Migration trends. In A. Booth & P. McCawley (Eds.), *The Indonesian economy during the Soeharto era* (pp. 289–314). New York: Oxford University Press.

Suryadi,. (2006). The 'talking machine' comes to the Dutch East Indies: The arrival of Western media technology in Southeast Asia. *Bijdragen tot de Taal, Land-en Volkenkund, 162*(2/3), 269–305.

Suryadinata, L. (Ed.). (2004a). *Chinese Indonesians: State policy, monoculture and multiculture*. Singapore: Eastern Universities Press.

Suryadinata, L. (Ed.). (2004b). *Culture of the Chinese Minority in Indonesia*. Singapore: Marshall Cavendish.

Suryadinata, L., Arifin, E., & Ananta, A. (2003). *Indonesia's population: Ethnicity and religion in a changing political landscape*. Singapore: Institute of Southeast Asian Studies.

Suzuki, S. (1986). Toishi no uta–aru kyōikujin no aruita michi. In A. Reid, O. Akira, J. Brewster & J. Carruthers (Eds.), *The Japanese experience in Indonesia: Selected memoirs of 1942–1945* (pp. 161–171). Athens: Ohio University Center for International Studies, Center for Southeast Asian Studies.

Swigart, L. (1992). Two codes or one? The insiders' view and the description of codeswitching in Dakar. In C. Eastman (Ed.), *Codeswitching* (pp. 83–102). Clevedon, Avon: Multilingual Matters.

Tabloid Jelita/Dv/Idh. (n.d.). *Rano Karno: Si Doel adalah konsep pembangunan Jakarta*. Retrieved from http://news.indosiar.com/news_read.htm?id=60553 on June 8, 2007.

Tadmor, U. (2009). Voices from the past: Betawi dialects in Firman Muntaco's Gambang Djakarté. Paper presented at the the Thirteenth International Symposium on Malay/Indonesian Linguistics (ISMIL 13), June 6–7, Senggigi, Lombok.
Tannen, D. (1984). *Conversational style: Analyzing talk among friends*. Norwood: Ablex.
Tannen, D. (1989). *Talking voices: Repetition, dialogue, and imagery in conversational discourse*. Cambridge: Cambridge University Press.
Tannen, D. (1993). What's in a frame?: Surface evidence for underlying expectations. In D. Tannen (Ed.), *Framing in discourse* (pp. 14–56). New York: Oxford University Press.
Teeuw, A. (1972). The impact of Balai Pustaka on modern Indonesian literature. *Bulletin of the School of Oriental and African Studies, 35*(1), 111–127.
Teeuw, A. (1994). *Modern Indonesian literature I*. Leiden: KITLV Press.
Teeuw, A. (1996). *Modern Indonesian literature II* (2nd ed.). Leiden: KITLV Press.
ten Have, P. (2007). *Doing conversation analysis: A practical guide* (2nd ed.). London: Sage.
Thee Kian Wie. (2001). Reflections on the New Order 'miracle.' In G. Lloyd & S. Smith (Eds.), *Indonesia today: Challenges of history* (pp. 163–180). Singapore: Institute of Southeast Asian Studies.
Thee Kian Wie. (2002). The Soeharto era and after: Stability, development and crisis, 1966–2000. In H. Dick (Ed.), *The emergence of a national economy: An economic history of Indonesia, 1800–2000* (pp. 194–243). Crows Nest: Allen & Unwin.
Tomasello, M. (2006). Why don't apes point? In N. Enfield & S. Levinson (Eds.), *Roots of human sociality: Culture, cognition and interaction* (pp. 506–524). Oxford: Berg.
Tyson, A. D. (2010). *Decentralization and adat revivalism in Indonesia: The politics of becoming indigenous*. Hoboken: Taylor & Francis.
van Klinken, G. (2007a). *Communal violence and democratization in Indonesia: Small town wars*. London: Routledge.
van Klinken, G. (2007b). Return of the sultans: The communitarian turn in local politics. In J. Davidson & D. Henley (Eds.), *The revival of tradition in Indonesian politics: The deployment of adat from colonialism to indigenism* (pp. 149–169). London: Routledge.
Vertovec, S. (2007). Super-diversity and its implications. *Ethnic and Racial Studies, 30*(6), 1024–1053.
Vickers, A. (2002). Bali merdeka? Internal migration, tourism and Hindu revivalism. In M. Sakai (Ed.), *Beyond Jakarta: Regional autonomy and local society in Indonesia* (pp. 80–101). Adelaide: Crawford House.
Vickers, A. (2005). *A history of modern Indonesia*. Cambridge: Cambridge University Press.
Vološinov, V. N. (1973 [1929]). *Marxism and the philosophy of language* (L. Matejka & I. R. Titunik, Trans.). New York: Seminar Press.
von Benda-Beckmann, F., & von Benda-Beckmann, K. (2009). Rentralization and decentralization in West Sumatra. In C. Holtzappel & M. Ramstedt (Eds.), *Decentralization and regional autonomy in Indonesia: Implementation and challenges* (pp. 293–328). Singapore and Leiden: Institute of Southeast Asian Studies and International Institute for Asian Studies.
Warren, C. (2007). Adat in Balinese discourse and practice: Locating citizenship and the commonweal. In J. Davidson & D. Henley (Eds.), *The revival of tradition in Indonesian politics: The deployment of adat from colonialism to indigenism* (pp. 170–202). London: Routledge.

Warriner, D. (2010). Communicative competence revisited: An ethnopoetic analysis of narrative performances of identity. In F. Hult (Ed.), *Directions and prospects for educational linguistics* (pp. 63–77). New York: Dordrecht and Springer.

Weidman, A. (2010). Sound and the city: Mimicry and media in South India. *Journal of Linguistic Anthropology, 20*(2), 294–313.

Wenger, E. (1998). *Communities of practice*. Cambridge: Cambridge University Press.

Werbner, P. (1997). Introduction: The dialectics of cultural hybridity. In P. Werbner & T. Modood (Eds.), *Debating cultural hybridity. Multi-cultural identities and the politics of anti-racism*. (pp. 1–28). London: Zed Books.

Wikipedia. (2011). Pekan Olahraga Nasional. http://en.wikipedia.org/wiki/Pekan_Olahraga_Nasional. Accessed on May 26, 2011.

Williams, Q., & Stroud, C. (2013). Multilingualism in transformative spaces: Contact and conviviality. *Language Policy, 12*(4), 289–311.

Wise, A. (2005). Hope and belonging in a multicultural suburb. *Journal of Intercultural Studies, 26*(1–2), 171–186.

Wise, A. (2009). Everyday multiculturalism: Transversal crossings and working class cosmopolitans. In A. Wise & S. Velayutham (Eds.), *Everyday multiculturalism* (pp. 21–45). New York: Palgrave MacMillan.

Wolff, J., & Poedjosoedarmo, S. (1982). *Communicative codes in Central Java*. New York: Cornell University Press.

Wortham, S. (2006). *Learning identity: The joint emergence of social identification and academic learning*. Cambridge: Cambridge University Press.

Yuyun W. I. Surya. (2006). The construction of cultural identity in local television stations' programs in Indonesia. Paper presented at Media: Policies, cultures and futures in the Asia Pacific region, November 27–29, Curtain University, Perth.

Zohra A. Baso, & Nurul Ilmi Idrus. (2002). Women's activism against violence in South Sulawesi. In K. Robinson & S. Bessell (Eds.), *Women in Indonesia: Gender, equity and development* (pp. 198–208). Singapore: Institute of Southeast Asian Studies.

INDEX

À Campo, Joseph 21–22
Abas, Hasan 13, 27, 48
Acciaioli, Greg 112
Adams, Kathleen 47
Adequation
  definition 55, 243
  mediated representations of 85–86, 92–94, 100–103, 144–145, 153–154, 161, 169–171, 175
Alesich, Simone 45, 119
Agha, Asif 3–5, 13–17, 51–55, 61, 101–102, 126, 141, 200, 203–204, 231, 233, 238
Alisjahbana, Sutan Takdir 13, 27, 33
Alvarez-Cáccamo, Celso 68, 175, 232
Aman 28–29
Anderson, Ben 2, 15, 21, 202
Androutsopoulos, Jannis 7, 54, 101, 125, 232, 239
Ang, Iem 2, 10, 56, 144, 172–174, 199, 202, 238–239
Antaki, Charles 2, 15, 55, 60, 176, 202, 240
Antlov, Hans 110
Anwar, Khaidir 27
Appadurai, Arjun 14–15
Aragon, Lorraine 113
Arps, Ben 48, 111, 117, 122
Arnaut, Karel 8
Aspinall, Ed 12, 106, 109, 112–116, 241
Auer, Peter 7, 67–68, 131, 176, 238

Bakhtin, Mikhail 11, 174, 203, 236
Barker, Joshua 17
Barkin, Gareth 118
Barth, Fredrik 2, 202
Barton, David 2, 202
Bauman, Richard 12, 15, 203
Bauman, Zygmunt 15
Bell, Allan 6, 56
Berman, Laine 176
Bertrand, Jacques 1
Biezeveld, Renske 30, 112–113
Bjork, Christopher 40, 48
Bjork-Willen, Polly 175
Blommaert, Jan 3, 7–11, 14, 16, 102, 117, 144, 171, 173, 176, 199, 204, 237, 239–240
Booth, Anne 45, 108

Bourchier, David 33, 47, 109, 112, 115
Bourdieu, Pierre 2–5, 11, 14–18, 20, 202–204, 231
Bouvier, Hélène 113–114
Brettell, Caroline 173–174, 199
Briggs, Charles 4, 12, 15–16, 203
Bruner, Edward 38, 40, 46
Bucholtz, Mary 2, 6, 18, 55, 85, 94, 101, 142, 175, 202, 228, 238
Bunnell, Tim 176
Bünte, Marco 109, 112
Burns, Peter 20
Bush, Robin 118

Carnegie, Paul 113
Castells, Manuel 5
Centers of normativity 16–17, 21–22, 25, 27, 31, 42–43, 50, 101, 105, 116, 123, 125, 204, 231
Chambers, Jack 57
Chauvel, Richard 106, 109, 116
Clarke, Sandra 56
Codeswitching (*see also* language alternation) 54, 68, 131–132, 232, 238
Cody, Francis 203
Cohen, Matthew 21–23
Cole, Debbie 229
Collins, Jock 107, 114, 233
Colonial linguistics 13
Common ground
  and conviviality 10, 173, 176, 181, 191, 198, 216, 218, 226
  definition of 57, 176
  interactional pursuit of 8, 180–188, 191–193, 195, 198–199, 208, 211, 213–214, 216–218, 223, 225–227, 235
  and non-minimal responses 181, 186, 191
  and positive interpersonal relations 92
  and repetition 180–181, 183–184, 191, 193, 225, 227, 235
  and semioitic density 53–54, 101
  televised representations of 69, 78, 79
Communicative competence (CC)
  and communities of practice 2–3, 201–204, 240
  and community 2–3, 11, 201–204, 236, 227–228, 236, 240

265

Communicative competence (CC) (*Cont.*)
  and crossing 228
  definition of 10, 102, 201, 204, 240–241, 243
  development of 204, 240–241
  and publics 2–4
  and symbolic competence 102
Community
  adat 112
  and authenticity 112
  and competence to comprehend 227–228
  denaturalization of 156
  definitions of 2–3, 11, 15, 204, 231
  and enregisterment 11, 209–213, 218
  ethnic 62, 89, 122, 156, 208–209, 236
  imagined 21, 62
  and indexicality 218–219, 225, 227, 240
  interactional construction of 210, 213, 216–217, 223
  and language 28, 62, 208–209
  and mobility 3, 240
  and subtitling practices 126, 128, 137
  and territory 19, 89, 112, 141, 209
Community of practice (COP)
  and communicative competence 2–3, 201–204, 240
  definition of 2–3
  and distinction 2–3, 202–203
  emergent 217–218, 222–223, 225, 228
  ethnic 205, 208–213, 216–217, 221, 225, 227
  and identity 94
  interactional production of 205, 208–209, 213, 217, 236
  and language alternation 68,
  and publics 3, 240
Competence to comprehend 33, 102, 144
  and communities of practice 227, 236
  definition of 3, 5, 9
  and knowledging 102, 238–239
  and publics 3
  and superdiversity 167–168, 233
Conviviality
  and common ground 173–174
  and communicative competence 173, 236
  and communities of practice 213, 219, 228, 236
  and crossing 175, 211
  definition of 10
  and doing togetherness in difference 10, 173–175, 201, 228, 235, 237
  interactional achievement of 195, 214, 221, 223, 225, 235
  and knowledging 201–203, 236
  and repetition 195, 223, 225
  and small talk 174, 235
  and superdiversity 173, 176, 199, 239

Coppel, Charles 107, 165
Coupland, Justine 236
Creese, Angela 7, 126
Cribb, Robert 1, 42, 45
Crouch, Harold 36, 112–113, 115
Crossing
  and adequation 153, 175
  and language alternation 7, 54, 68, 101, 153, 175
  and communicative competence 228, 241
  and communities of practice 203, 228
  and conviviality 175, 211, 213, 227, 228
  definition of 7, 54, 85, 101, 153, 229
  and knowledging 9, 102, 216, 226, 228–229
  and styling the other 241
  and televised representations of 101, 150, 153
  unity in diversity 213

Dardjowidjojo, Soenjono 13, 27, 40–41, 48–49
Davidson, Jamie 19, 38–39, 43, 106–108, 112–114
Dawson, Gaynor 44,
Dayan, Daniel 202
Decentralization
  and *adat* 113, 117, 223
  of education 117, 234
  and ethnic languages 11, 111, 114, 116–117, 123–124, 234
  and ethnicity 11, 111, 114, 117, 123–124, 234
  and ethnopolitics 113
  and communities of practice 110, 113
  and ideas about community 110, 113
  and infrastructures of superdiversity 119
  legislation 109
  and mobility 119
  political and fiscal 105, 108, 234
  and televised representations of ethnicity 123
  and territory 11, 111, 114, 116–117, 123–124
De Fina, Anna 203
de Jong, Edwin 20, 31, 47
Dick, Howard 21–22, 31–32, 34–38, 45

Eckert, Penelope 2, 202
Eisenlohr, Patrick 17, 237
Ellis, Andrew 34
Elson, Robert 25–27, 30, 32–34, 36–39, 42, 44, 46, 109
Enregisterment
  and communicative competence 4, 171, 228, 236
  and communities of practice 4, 201
  definition of 4
  and demeanor 7, 56
  and distinction 20

and emblems of identity 56
and ethnic languages 19–20
and ethnicity 19–20, 104
and indexicality 4, 11, 229
and infrastructures of 5, 31, 55
and interaction 11, 54
and knowledging 154, 171, 212
and language alternation 145
and language ideology 20
and Malay 20
and participation frameworks 4, 203, 212
and sociability 154
and stereotypes 6–7, 19
and television representations 154
and up-scaling 170
and unintended consequences 143, 229
Enfield, Nicholas 53, 55, 57, 176
Erb, Maribeth 47
Errington, J. Joseph 1, 13, 18–19, 21, 24, 47–49, 61, 241
Ethnicity
  and adat 47, 113, 117
  and centers of normativity 22, 43, 105, 123
  changing configurations of 6–7, 11, 123–124, 143, 170, 176, 230, 234, 241
  commodification of 47, 51, 118
  and communities of practice 44–45
  and conflict 106, 234, 241
  construction of 2, 13, 22, 34, 51, 132, 230
  and demeanor 232
  and distinction 22, 25, 85, 112
  emblems of 11–12, 19, 39, 51, 84–85, 110, 121, 128, 234, 241
  enregisterment of 18, 25, 30, 33, 39, 45, 51, 104, 170
  ideas about 6, 11, 25, 33–34, 39, 45, 111–112
  and ideology 1, 7, 104–105, 111–112
  and indexicality 2, 76, 79, 85, 105
  and infrastructure 5, 108, 110–111, 116, 233
  and interaction 11–12, 176, 241
  and intimacy 76
  and language 1, 7, 19, 23, 40, 45, 64, 84, 94, 105, 110, 116, 128
  and language documentation 117
  and the management of diversity 19
  and the mass media 47, 60, 112–113, 118
  and orders of indexicality 22, 43, 85, 100, 105, 234
  and politics 35–36, 39, 105–106, 111
  and regionalism 39, 111, 116
  and registers of 11, 23, 44
  and semiotic density 85, 232
  and schooling 13, 117
  and social value 6–7, 11–12, 34, 39, 42–45, 104, 106, 114, 123–124, 176, 233

  television representations of 7, 60, 76, 118, 132, 177
  and territory 1, 7, 19, 23, 25, 26, 39–40, 64, 110, 116
  and unity in diversity 2, 46, 48, 60, 94, 110, 112–113, 235, 241
  and up-scaling 110, 116

Fairclough, Norman 56
Fasseur, Cornelis 20
Feith, Herbert 39
Florey, Margaret 49
Ford, Michele 1, 31, 45, 50, 110, 112
Foucault, Michel 16
Foulcher, Keith 27, 40, 50
Fox, James 113
Franceschini, Rita 68, 232
Francis, David 54–55, 238

Gafaranga, Joseph 7, 54, 61–62, 67–68, 131, 175, 232, 238
Garrett, Peter 6, 56
Geertz, Clifford 36, 38
Geertz, Hildred 40
Georgakopoulou, Alexandra 176
Gershon, Ilana 14, 17, 54, 238
Giddens, Anthony 3, 11, 15, 204, 231
Goebel, Zane 1–2, 8–11, 13, 16–17, 45–46, 49, 54–55, 59–60, 68, 85, 144, 153–154, 165, 172, 174–175, 177, 228, 231, 236, 238–241
Goffman, Erving 6, 15, 29, 53, 57, 101, 175, 232
Goodwin, Charles 55, 60
Gumperz, John 15, 60–61, 174

Hall, Stuart 56
Hanan, David 67
Hanks, William 53, 55, 57, 176
Harvey, David 5, 14, 17, 237
Haviland, John 60
Hedman, Eva-Lotta 38, 42–43, 114–115
Hefner, Robert 18
Heller, Monica 1, 7, 126, 239
Henley, David 19, 106–108, 112–113
Herriman, Nicholas 42,
Heryanto, Ariel 13, 118
Hill, David 41, 47, 50, 59, 86, 116, 119
Hill, Jane 139, 229
Hoey, Brian 44
Holmes, Janet 202
Holt, Elizabeth 129
Hooker, Virginia 47
Hoon, Chang-yau 47, 165
Hoshour, Cathy 44
Hymes, Dell 2, 4, 9, 15, 18, 55, 60–61, 203–204

Identity
  emblems of 57, 241
  ethnic 36–37, 43, 46, 50–51, 56–57, 111, 142, 186, 205, 211–213, 216–217
  and governmentality 19
  and knowledge 212
  theories of 8, 15, 176
  ideologies of 107, 111
  interactional emergence of 54, 65–70, 94, 176, 186–188, 196–198, 205, 211–213, 216–217
Indexical relations 2, 6–7, 17, 27, 64, 74, 79, 81, 105–106, 164–165, 233, 240
  and anchoring 28
  and Chineseness 165
  and community 212–227, 237, 240
  and conviviality 131, 183, 213–229
  and demeanor 74, 101
  and enregisterment 6–7, 17, 27–28, 52, 70, 79, 85, 105–106, 233
  and ethnicity 19, 22, 28, 31, 35, 47–48, 51, 55, 64, 76, 79, 85, 102, 105–106, 111, 142
  and focus 76, 79, 81, 84
  and Indonesian 27, 48, 118, 227
  and interaction 11, 175, 188, 205, 209, 211–229, 237
  and knowledge 55, 201, 204, 208, 211
  and language alternation 68, 131
  and linguistic forms 19, 22, 28, 31, 47, 51, 63–64, 79, 111, 141
  and semiotic density 85, 101
  and territory 19, 22, 27–28, 35, 47–48, 51, 64, 79, 111, 141
  and unity in diversity 118, 227
Infrastructure
  and changes in 18, 34
  and circulation of ideas 5, 17, 22, 58
  and circulation of people 5, 17, 22, 24, 31, 35, 45–46
  and community 18
  and enregisterment 18, 31, 34, 58
  and social interaction 17, 22, 24, 31, 35, 46
  and time-space compression 5, 17, 22
  and up-scaling 17, 43–48
Inoue, Miyako 1, 4, 6, 13, 16–17, 53, 101, 107, 117, 203–204, 238
Inoue, Tetsuro 32
Irvine, Judith 3, 18, 125, 202–203

Jaffe, Alexandra 4, 7, 54, 101, 125, 204, 232, 239
Jaworski, Adam 126, 153
Johnson, Sally 6, 54, 56, 125–126, 239
Johnstone, Barbara 16, 126
Jones, Gavin 46
Jones, Sidney 112
Jørgensen, J. Normann 7, 9, 102, 104
Jukes, Anthony 49

Kahin, George 35–36
Katoppo, Aristides 45, 107, 112
Kelly-Holmes, Helen 54, 101, 125, 232, 239
Kendon, Adam 60
King, Ruth 5, 16, 56
Kitley, Philip 41, 50–51, 58–59, 62, 67, 109, 116, 128, 202
Knowledge
  definition of 5, 9–10, 55, 102, 229
  and communicative competence 9, 55, 102, 203
  and conviviality 10–11, 201–203, 226, 228, 237
  and crossing 9, 102, 229
  and enregisterment 10, 92, 94, 100, 102, 138–139, 144, 150, 160–164, 170–171, 212
  infrastructures of 144, 170–171
  in interaction 11, 144, 208, 218–223, 238
  and language alternation 150, 154, 160–164
  and polylanguaging 9, 102
  and superdiversity 10, 144, 154, 239
  and symbolic competence 102
  televised representations of 10, 92, 94, 100, 102, 138–139, 144, 150, 160–164, 235
  and togetherness in difference 10–11, 97, 201, 227, 235, 241
  and unity in diversity 86, 92, 97, 102, 227, 239, 241
Kramsch, Claire 3, 9, 102, 174, 202, 229, 240
Kress, Gunther 55–56
Kuipers, Joel 49, 241
Kulick, Don 56
Kurniasih, Yacinta 48
Kusumaatmadja, Sarwono 45, 107, 112

Labov, William 15, 18, 57
Lambert, Wallace 177
Language alternation (*see also* codeswitching)
  and adequation 55
  approach to 54–55, 238
  authorization of models of 74, 153
  classification of 54–55
  and codeswithing 54
  and ethnomethodology 54
  habitual 55, 126, 239
  and medium 7, 67, 175, 239
  naturalization of 125, 234
  representations of 53–54, 74, 234–235, 238
Language ideology
  formation processes 6, 13, 54, 100–101, 142, 238
  methods for investigating 141, 238

Legge, John 36–37, 39
Lenhart, Lioba 44
Le Page, Robert 176
Levinson, Stephen 176
Li, Tania 112
Liddicoat, Anthony 54, 130, 238
Liddle, R. William 39
Liebes, Tamar 56
Lindsey, Tim 109
Livingstone, Sonia 2, 202
Loven, Klarijn 5–6, 16, 28, 56–59, 62, 74, 85–86, 89, 101, 117, 136, 202, 219
Lowenberg, Peter 48–49

Malinowski, Bronislaw 175
Malley, Michael 107
Massification
  definition of 4
  and enregisterment 50
  of schooling 40, 48, 50
  and superdiverstiy 124
Mauss, Marcel 175
McCarthy, Michael 175
McCawley, Peter 45
McGibbon, Rodd 109, 119
Meek, Barbara 56
Mendoza-Denton, Norma 6, 101, 142, 238
Mietzner, Marcus 108–109, 119
Metasemiotic commentary 6, 14, 27, 48, 51, 73, 86, 121–122, 126, 132, 135, 141–142, 148, 153, 214, 221, 230, 234, 243
Miles, Douglas 38
Miller, Laura 5–6, 16, 52, 101, 202, 238
Min, Sai Siew 42
Moeliono, Anton 13
Moerman, Michael 54, 238
Moriyama, Mikihiro 19–21, 29, 117–118
Morley, David 56
Moyer, Melissa 7, 14, 126
Mrázek, Rudolf 21, 23–24, 27
Muhidin, Salahudin 45
Multiaccentuatuality 19, 176–177, 200

Nababan, P. 13, 48–49
Norris, Sigrid 55, 61

Ochs, Elinor 2–3, 60–61, 102, 203, 239–240
Okada, Fumihide 33
one-to-few participation frameworks
  and communicative competence 3, 102, 203, 228–229, 240–241
  and cultural value 4
  definition of 4–5
  and registers 4
  and role of institutions 3–5

  and socialization 3
  and superdiversity 171
one-to-many participation frameworks
  and authority 4, 17
  commonness of 52, 59, 101, 204, 231, 238, 241
  and communicative competence 3, 4, 9, 102, 164, 203–204, 218, 228–229, 240–241
  and cultural value 4
  definition of 4–5, 16
  and diversity 9
  and infrastructure 18, 50–52
  and knowledging 8
  and registers 4
  and role of institutions 3–5, 124
  and standardization 52, 237
  and superdiversity 144–145, 153, 171
Orders of indexicality
  during colonial period 22, 30
  definition of 5, 11, 18
  modelling of 74, 85, 90, 94, 101, 154
  during New Order period 51, 74, 85, 90, 94, 101
  during post New Order period 105, 111, 116, 123–124, 154, 161
  during Soekarno period 34, 36–37
  reconfiguration of 11, 14, 105, 111, 116–117, 123–124, 154, 161, 171, 232, 234–235, 241
  regimentation of 90, 103, 231
Otsuka, Tadashi 33

Palmer, Andrea 36, 38, 40
Parker, Lyn 47–48
Philips, Susan 18, 60
Poedjosoedarmo, Soepomo 61, 165
Polycentricity 3, 16, 36, 52
Polylanguaging 9, 102
Poynting, Scott 114, 233
Prastowo, Joko 49
Purdey, Jemma 165
Putnam, Robert 15

Quinn, George 20–21, 40, 50, 111, 117

Rachmah, Ida 51, 53, 59, 62, 67, 74, 101, 118
Rampton, Ben 7, 9, 54, 67, 85, 102, 144, 150, 171, 174, 177, 203, 229, 237, 241
Ramstedt, Martin 112–113, 117
Recontextualization 12
Reid, Anthony 22, 32
Resosudarmo, Ida 106–107, 113
Richardson, Kay 54, 56–57, 103, 135, 232, 238
Ricklefs, Merle 18, 32–44
Rinakit, Sukardi 36

Robinson, Geoffrey 43, 115
Roesli, Marah 26–27
Ryoo, Hye-Kyung 175

Sakai, Minako 112
Sangkoyo, Hendro 45, 106
Sen, Krishna 41, 47, 50, 59, 86, 116, 119
Schefold, Reimar 43–44
Schegloff, Emanuel 15
Schieffelin, Bambi 2–3, 102, 203, 240
Scollon, Ron 55, 61
Semiotic density
  definition of 57
  and television 76, 85, 89
Semiotic register
  and centers of normativity 5, 31, 231
  and communicative competence 16–18
  definition of 4, 14–15, 20
  and demeanor 74
  and distinction 18, 74, 132
  and diversity management 18
  emergent 9, 24–25, 31–32, 35–37, 40, 42, 45–46, 48–49, 175
  and enregisterment 4, 20, 22, 47–48, 231
  fragments of 14, 169, 171
  and language 14–15, 126, 141
  and norms for social conduct 44
  and participation frameworks 18
  reconfiguration of 53, 74, 86, 125
  and social types 15, 17, 21, 23
  and social value 17, 20, 47, 169
  and stereotypes 6, 47, 85, 142
  and superdiversity 9, 142–144
Shibata, Yaichiro 32
Shigetada, Nishijima 32
Shizuo, Miyamoto 32
Shunkichiro, Miyoshi 32–33
Sidel, John 42, 44, 107, 113, 115
Silverstein, Michael 15, 17, 203
Skinner, William 37–38
Smets, Peer 10, 144, 172, 238–239
Sneddon, James 1, 20–22, 30, 33, 41
Soedijarto 40, 48
Spitulnik, Debra 56
Stoler, Ann 19, 21, 24
Strachle, Carolyn 175
Stuart-Smith, Jane 56–57
Sudarkam, Mertono 117
Suharsono 46
Superdiversity
  and adequation 171
  authorization of 145, 153–154, 168
  and common ground 8
  and communicative competence 9, 11, 144, 154, 167
  and community 11, 228
  and competence to comprehend 9, 144, 154, 167, 238
  and complexity 8, 143
  and conviviality 8, 10, 144, 173–175, 199, 228, 239
  definition of 8, 144
  and displacement 124
  and diversity management 52
  and economic migrants 124
  and enregisterment 154, 237–238
  and infrastructures of 8, 124
  and interactional practice 10, 144, 167
  and knowledging 9, 102, 144, 154, 171, 173–174, 237–238
  and language ideologies 8, 237
  and linguistic repertoire 14, 144, 165–169, 173–174, 237
  mass mediated representations of 9, 102, 144, 153–154, 161–162, 168–170, 239
  and metasemiotic commentaries 6, 9, 14, 237–238
  and naturalization of 153–154, 168, 170
  and one-to-many participation frameworks 144–145, 171
  and refugees 124
  and theory 171–172
  and time-space compression 14, 237
  and togetherness in difference 10, 172–175, 199, 238–239
  and truncated competence 14, 144, 165–169, 173–174
  understanding the emergence of 52, 124, 230, 237
  and up-scaling 6, 9, 14, 119, 124, 230, 237
Suryadi 23
Suryadinata, Leo 1, 30, 44–45, 122, 165
Suzuki, Seihei 33
Swigart, Leigh 68

Tadmor, Uri 39
Tannen, Deborah 15, 18, 60, 72, 129, 174–175, 177
Teeuw, Andries 21, 26, 30–31, 33, 39–41, 50
ten Have, Paul 54, 238
Thee Kian Wie 45, 48, 108
Time-space compression 5, 14, 17, 237
Togetherness in difference (*see also* unity in diversity)
  approaches to the study of 174
  and communicative competence 201, 228
  and community 201
  and conviviality 10, 173–175, 201, 228, 235, 237
  definition of 10, 173, 201, 228

and enregisterment 201
and interactional practice 199
and knowledging 10–11, 97, 201, 227, 235, 241
and linguistic repertoires 202
and superdiversity 10, 172–175, 199, 238–239
television representations of 10, 238
understanding the emergence of 199, 201, 214, 236–237, 239

Transmigration
and conflict 105–106
definition of 32, 244
during colonial period 24–25
during Japanese occupation 32
during New Order 43–45, 104
resistance to 107
during Soekarno period 37

Unity in diversity
and interactional practice 11, 211, 213, 229
and knowledging 102, 241
and Indonesian 2, 48, 51, 54, 94, 97, 100, 102, 155, 158, 161–162, 170–171, 213
and language of 2, 9, 48, 51–52, 55, 86, 94, 97, 100, 143
and language alternation 7, 55, 86, 97, 100, 143, 145, 150, 158, 162, 171, 213, 229, 233
marketed models of 47
and state ideology 2, 42, 46, 55, 86, 100, 102, 116, 213, 229, 233, 235
televised models of 7, 9, 55, 60, 86, 94, 97, 100, 145, 150, 161, 172, 233, 235

Up-scaling
definition of 5, 244

and enregisterment 6, 170
and ethnicity 110, 116
and infrastructure 17, 43–48, 50, 230
and meta-semiotic commentary 6, 230
and one-to-many participation frameworks 170
and superdiversity 6, 9, 14, 119, 124, 230, 237
and time-space compression 14

van Klinken, Gerry 112–114
Vertovec, Steven 6, 8, 10, 14, 52, 143–144, 171–174, 199, 237–239
Vickers, Adrian 1, 32, 34, 36, 38, 41–42, 44, 46–47, 59, 107–108
Vološinov, Valentin 11, 19, 56, 174, 176, 184, 200, 236
von Benda-Beckmann, Franz 113

Warren, Carol 107, 113–114
Warriner, Doris 3, 204, 241
Weidman, Amanda 17, 23, 237
Wenger, Etienne 2, 15–16, 94, 202–203, 231
Werbner, Pnina 10, 144, 172–174, 199, 238–239
Williams, Quentin 6, 10, 173–175, 199, 228, 239
Wise, Amanda 10, 144, 172–174, 176, 199, 236, 238–239
Wolff, John 165
Wortham, Stanton 11, 17, 60, 174, 176, 203, 236, 239–240

Yuyun W. I. Surya 118

Zohra A. Baso 111

Uwe Fuhrmann
**Frauen in der Geschichte der Mitbestimmung –
Pionierinnen in Betriebsräten, Gewerkschaften und Politik**